The Literature of Shetland

The Literature of Shetland

Mark Ryan Smith

To Michael, with thanks for publishing several essays which eventually ended up in this book.

6 June 2014

Mark Smith

The Shetland Times Ltd.
Lerwick
2014

The Literature of Shetland.

First published by The Shetland Times Ltd., 2014.

© Mark Ryan Smith.

All rights reserved.
No part of this publication may be reproduced, stored in a retrieval system, or transmitted, in any form, by any means, electronic, mechanical, photocopying, recording or otherwise, without the prior written permission of the publishers.

A catalogue record for this book is available from the British Library.

ISBN 978-1-904746-88-1

Printed and published by
The Shetland Times Ltd.,
Gremista, Lerwick,
Shetland ZE1 0PX.

CONTENTS

		Page
Acknowledgements		vi
List of Illustrations		viii
Map		ix
Introduction		1
1	Beginnings	13
2	Flourishing	41
3	J.J. Haldane Burgess	72
4	Sons of Rasmie	92
5	Hugh MacDiarmid	113
6	The *New Shetlander*	142
7	William J. Tait	187
8	Contemporary Writers	207
Conclusion		244
Bibliography		248
Index		260

ACKNOWLEDGEMENTS

I would firstly like to thank my employer, Shetland Amenity Trust, for generously funding this PhD thesis that gave rise to this book. I would also like to thank my friends and colleagues at the Shetland Museum and Archives for sharing their expertise and knowledge of the isles. My colleagues Craig Gauld, Jenny Murray, and especially Brian Smith all read portions of this work and provided valuable comments and observations. I am also grateful to my colleague John Hunter for producing the map. Many non-work friends gave up their own time to read and discuss parts of this study, and I thank Penny Fielding, Mary Blance, Christine De Luca, Laureen Johnson, John Cumming, Brydon Leslie, Jim Mainland, and particularly my wife Lexy for doing so. I also want to thank Kirsten Matthews for our discussions of MacDiarmid, Michael Schmidt for publishing several of my essays on Shetland's literature in *PN Review*, Lucy Gibbon of the Orkney Archives for sending material on George Mackay Brown, Marie Anderson and Wendy Gear of Yell for sharing a number of poems by their ancestors (which, unfortunately, I have not had space to include), Alan Riach and Gerry Carruthers for being able and encouraging PhD supervisors, Stella Sutherland for her friendship, interest, wisdom and encouragement, and my fellow *New Shetlander* editorial committee members for being receptive to the essays I have submitted to the magazine during the writing of this work. Finally, I would like to pay a heartfelt and admiring tribute to John and Lollie Graham, both of whom passed away during the writing of this book. Although I only met John Graham once, and never met Lollie, I have learned a great deal about Shetland's literature from them. The two men did more than anybody else to encourage new local writing, to discuss and celebrate Shetland's writers, and to keep older work in print. Their work is crucial for any Shetlander who wants to think about writing done by other islanders and, for this reason, the Graham brothers are two of the archipelago's most important cultural figures. *The Literature of Shetland* is dedicated to their memory.

Poems reproduced in their entirety by kind permission of the copyright holder.

Hugh MacDiarmid material © Carcanet Press
William J. Tait material © Brian Tait
Vagaland – 'Kwarna Farna?' © Shetland Archives
Stella Sutherland – 'A Celebration' © Stella Sutherland
Robert Alan Jamieson – 'Avunavara' © Robert Alan Jamieson
Jim Mainland – 'Prestidigitator' © Jim Mainland

ILLUSTRATIONS

	Page
Thomas Irvine's Notebook	30-31
Illustration from *The Pirate*	34
George Stewart	43
James Stout Angus	47
Jessie Saxby (young)	55
Jessie Saxby	60
Basil Ramsay Anderson	65
J. J. Haldane Burgess	75
J. J. Haldane Burgess	85
John Peterson	99
Hugh Macdiarmid and family	116
Hugh Macdiarmid	125
New Shetlander (No.1)	143
Peter Jamieson	145
T. A. Robertson during University days	148
T. A. Robertson and Martha	154
Rhoda Bulter	157
Lollie Graham	164
John Graham	171
Stella Sutherland	177
Billy Tait (young)	193
Billy Tait	199
Christine De Luca	208
Robert Alan Jamieson	221
Jen Hadfield	229
Paolo Dante Ritch	234
Jim Mainland	238

SHETLAND ISLANDS

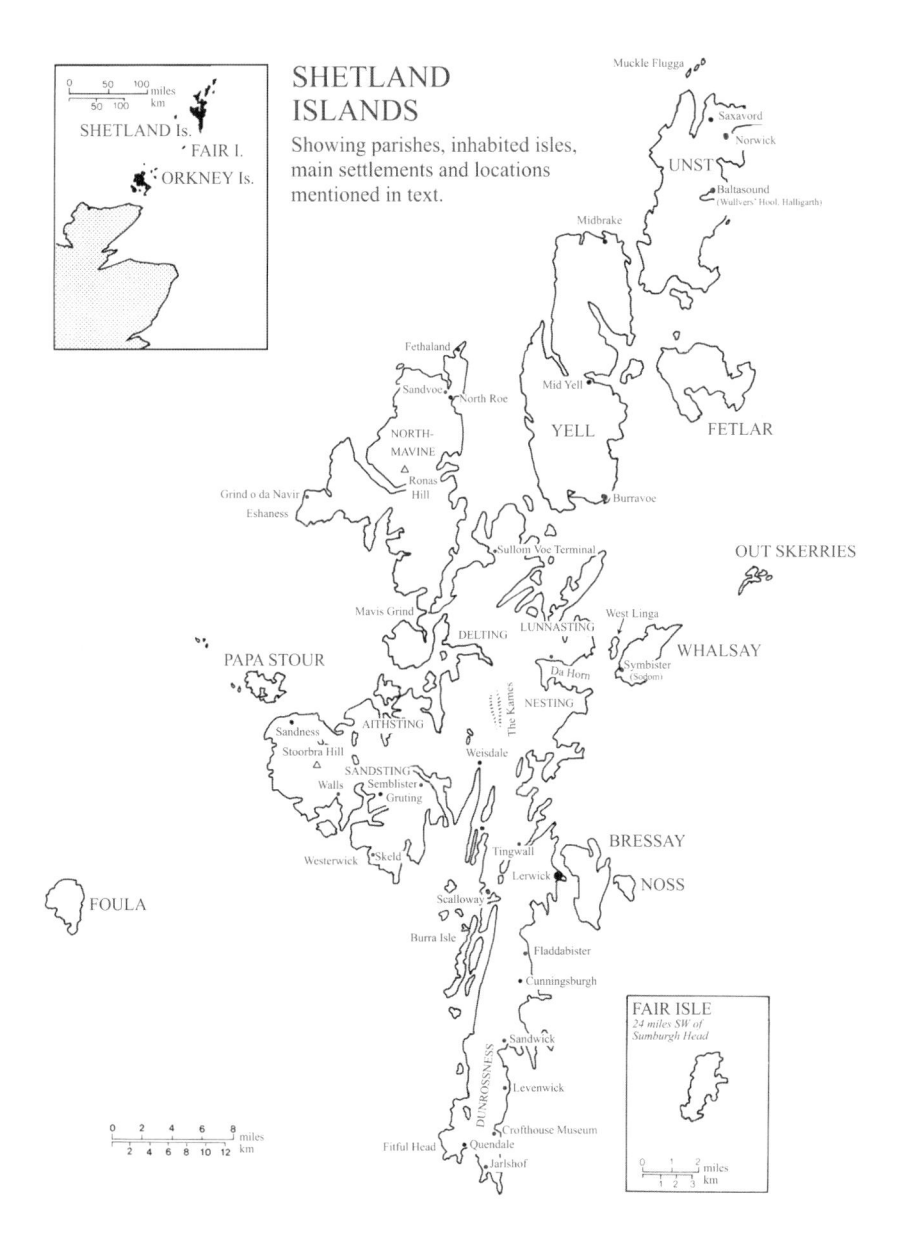

Showing parishes, inhabited isles, main settlements and locations mentioned in text.

FAIR ISLE
24 miles SW of Sumburgh Head

INTRODUCTION

Halfway through Neil Gunn's 1941 novel *The Silver Darlings*, the *Seafoam*, a little fishing boat on which Gunn's hero, Finn, is a crew member, sets off on an unprecedented voyage:

> There was a crowd on the beach seeing them off, for this was the first time a Dunster boat was to venture beyond the Moray Firth. They were bound for Stornoway, and it was a brilliant morning, with an air of wind off the land.[1]

As the vessel skirts the north coast of the Scottish mainland, the nation reveals itself to Finn and his comrades. They pass Clyth Head at the north end of their native parish. They sail around Duncansby Head and west through the Pentland Firth, where 'looming gigantic out of the haze' (p.282), they see Orkney. And, as they round Dunnet Head, Finn reflects on what he has experienced since leaving home:

> how splendid it was to be adventuring in this wild world of islands and rocks and headlands and dangerous seas. The Orkneys were like a fabulous tale he had heard of in some remote time. (p.284)

Orkney is at the limit of Finn's knowledge but, after sailing past the archipelago, it is a place he can incorporate into his world. Finn's journey makes a semi-mythical place into a real one.

But, the next day, when the *Seafoam* leaves its anchorage in Loch Eriboll, the voyage becomes rather more fraught. The crew plan to pass Cape Wrath and then, by adjusting their course south, to strike the Butt of Lewis. But, with no compass, chart, or knowledge of the seas they are in, and having been forced off-course by the weather, they get lost. Things look bleak and the crew fear ending up far out into the Atlantic. To their relief, a ship appears. As the vessel approaches, they realise she is a cod smack from Lerwick in Shetland. The Shetlanders tell them that Lewis is forty miles to the east and, as the larger boat leaves for Rockall, Finn and the crew discuss its native port:

> 'Good for the Shetlanders!' cried Roddie. 'They're brave seamen.'

> 'They have a great trade in dried cod,' said Henry. 'They export it all over the world.'

> 'We must go up and see them one of these seasons!' (p.304)

Finn's voyage has made some of the most remote parts of the nation palpable, but Shetland is still a distant place. The crew sees Orkney, but Scotland's northernmost archipelago remains outside the physical bounds of their narrative. And, just as Shetland does not become part of Finn's experience of the country, Shetland's literature does not feature in many readers' experience of Scottish writing. Other than Walter Scott's 1822 novel *The Pirate*, and Hugh MacDiarmid's sojourn in the archipelago in the 1930s, Shetland is not a presence in any account of Scottish literature. For Finn, Orkney becomes tangible, and most readers of Scottish literature know something about the stories and poems which have their roots in those islands, but writing from Shetland remains, to borrow the title of a Tom Leonard book, outside the narrative.[2] *The Literature of Shetland* addresses this absence. In the following eight chapters, we will, metaphorically speaking, make the voyage north that Finn and his crew one day hope to experience.

This book contains the first comprehensive analysis of the archipelago's poetry and fiction (there is no body of dramatic writing). Other than Penny Fielding's book *Scotland and the Fictions of Geography* (2008), and several essays by her (all of which we will draw on in our first chapter), scholars and critics have had little to say about Shetland's literature. The essays 'The Development of Literature in Shetland', by archivist and historian Brian Smith,[3] and 'Shetland Literature and the Idea of Community' by poet, critic, and former editor of the *New Shetlander* magazine, Laurence (Lollie) Graham, provide brief but valuable surveys of some of the writing covered in this study.[4] Julian Meldon D'Arcy, in his 1996 book *Scottish Skalds and Sagamen* discusses a few references to old northern themes by Shetland authors,[5] and Danish linguist Laurits Rendboe's short survey *The Shetland Literary Tradition* (1985) also provides an introduction to some of the writers we are about to discuss.[6] Rendboe's views about the islands' ancient language, Norn, however, lead him into a number of eccentric readings of modern poetry from Shetland, and his work is of somewhat limited value.

Although none of these works aims to cover Shetland's literary output in detail, they all omit several authors that are important presences in this book, MacDiarmid being the most well known. His Shetland period is the subject of the 1992 volume *MacDiarmid in Shetland* but, in the few short surveys that have been written, and in the anthologies *Shetland Verse* (1953), *Nordern Lichts* (1964), *A Shetland Anthology* (1998), and *Bright Pebbles* (2010), neither MacDiarmid, nor the writers discussed in our opening chapter, appear. This book, by including the work of these authors, adopts a more inclusive view of the literature than has been taken previously. If *The Literature of Shetland* represents a geographical stretching of Scotland's literature, it also broadens the story that has been told of Shetland's.

The date of our earliest text, however, Dorothea Campbell's *Poems* of 1811, may not suggest a particularly broad canvas. But, from before the nineteenth century, virtually no literary work – printed or oral – survives, and we know hardly anything about what Shetlanders were singing and reciting in ancient times. Both Arthur Edmondston, in his *A View of the Ancient and Present State of the Zetland Islands* (1809), and Samuel Hibbert in his 1822 book *A Description of the Shetland Islands*, suggest that there was a native poetic tradition, and that some Shetland poets even came to the attention of St Rognvald, but whatever body of verse may once have existed in Shetland is not available to modern readers.[7] What we have from before the nineteenth century are fragments of what, perhaps, was enjoyed around fires and at communal gatherings in the isles in previous centuries. Other than the few scraps that have survived, the most important of which we will discuss below, Shetlanders today cannot read the literary work of their ancient forebears.[8]

This paucity of early literary work can, in part, be explained by Shetland's unusual linguistic history. From the Norse colonisation in the ninth century, to sometime in the eighteenth, there was a Scandinavian tongue, Norn, spoken in the northern isles. In 1469, however, Shetland was pledged to James III of Scotland as part of a wedding dowry and, over the next few centuries, Shetland, ecclesiastically, legally (the Scandinavian laws ceased to apply in 1611), economically, politically and linguistically, became firmly part of Scotland. Scots and English became the most important languages in the isles and, by the last quarter of the eighteenth century, Norn, which had been gradually falling out of use, ceased to exist as a living language.[9] And, when a language is no longer used, any poetry composed in that language is unlikely to enjoy widespread survival.

Most of what we know about Norn is based on the work of Jakob Jakobsen, a Faroese philologist who did extensive fieldwork in Shetland from 1893 to 1895.[10] While he was in the islands, Jakobsen, in a remarkable piece of scholarship, recorded around 10,000 words that he would later use to compile his *Etymologisk ordbog over det norrøne sprog på Shetland* (1908-1921). This monumental work was translated into English as *Etymological Dictionary of the Norn Language in Shetland* (1928-1932) and, as we shall see, became a valuable source for several Shetland writers, including MacDiarmid and Robert Alan Jamieson. What Jakobsen encountered in Shetland, however, was not a language in everyday use. He found thousands of Norn words, and the small number of phrases that are included in the introduction to his dictionary, but he did not encounter people who routinely spoke the language. A researcher going to Lewis in the 1890s would have heard Gaelic spoken wherever he went, but, when Jakobsen was in Shetland, Norn was no longer a usable means of communication or expression. Although people (mostly older ones) could remember Norn words, they did not know how to speak to each other in Norn, and whatever oral literary tradition once existed in the language was dead by the time Jakobsen arrived in the isles.[11]

Although Jakobsen, as he was able to do in Faroe, could not salvage a large corpus of native songs and stories, we do have one lengthy Norn artefact, 'The Hildina Ballad'.[12] The ballad was recorded by George Low, a minister in Orkney, who heard William Henry of Foula recite it in 1774.[13] The ballad which, in thirty five four-line stanzas, tells of conflict between the Earl of Orkney and the King of Norway on account of the King's daughter's marriage to the Earl, is the most substantial Norn text we have, but we will never know the extent of the literature it was part of.[14] It is, however, a remarkable example of literary survival and gives us a tantalising glimpse of what Shetland's cultural life might once have looked like.

Not all of the pre-literature remnants we have are in Norn. There are also a few scraps of verse and song in the language that replaced it, the Shetland dialect, a variant of Scots that retains a substratum of words from the older tongue.[15] There is, for example, a fragmentary dialect version of the Orpheus story,[16] and there is also part of a poem which now has the title 'The Unst Lay':

> Nine days he hang pa da rötless tree,
> For ill was da fök an göd was he;
> A blöddy mett was in his side,
> Made wi a lance at widna hide;
> Nine lang nichts i da nippin rime
> Hang he dere wi his naked limb,
> Some dey leuch
> Bit idders grett.[17]

This striking fragment was recorded by George Sinclair, a Shetlander, who heard it from an old woman (who he names as Russlin) in the village of Norwick, Unst, in 1865. It was then passed to Arthur Laurenson, a Lerwick antiquary and scholar, who sent it to the German folklorist Karl Blind. In 1879 Blind wrote a long essay on the fragment titled 'Odinic Songs in Shetland', in which he quotes part of a letter that Laurenson, who was well-read in Scandinavian literature, sent him:

> It is evidently a Christianised version of the Rune Rime of Odin from the *Háva-mál*, and is curious for the way in which the Rootless Tree of the Northern mythology is confounded with the Cross. The second line is quite Christian, the fifth purely Pagan. The old woman who recited this was quite aware that the verses could not strictly apply to Christ. She knew in what points they differed from the Gospel, but she repeated them as she had learned them. [...] I am afraid this fragment is all we can now recover of 'The Unst Lay'. No doubt there was more, which, by time's attrition, has been rubbed away.[18]

As Blind shows by comparing the Unst fragment with other examples of Odinic poetry, 'The Unst Lay' has ancient roots. But, if it was known in Shetland in antiquity (when the islands were linguistically Scandinavian), when did it become a Shetland dialect poem? Brian Smith argues, convincingly, that Scots was widely understood in the isles in the sixteenth century, so is it the case that a Shetlander, at this time, rendered the kinds of ancient poems Blind and Laurenson discuss into the local variant of the language?[19] Or is it the case that the translation was done at a much later date? We are unlikely to ever know but, again, the fragment gives an indication of the poetry that may once have circulated in the isles. Unlike 'The Hildina Ballad', however, 'The Unst Lay' is in the language that almost every writer in this book has concerned themselves with.

For centuries, Shetlanders no doubt sang songs and told stories but, as so little of this material survives, it is not easy to make much of what we do have. The extant material provides an intriguing link with the cultural past of the islands, but, ultimately, that link is a broken one. We simply do not know enough about the pre-literature literature of Shetland to form a coherent picture of it. In this study, then, we are concerned with the printed poetry and prose that has been written by Shetlanders, and about Shetland by non-native writers, from the early nineteenth century to the present day.

That our material is all from the last two centuries makes this study rather different from literary analyses of other British regions. Alan M. Kent in his *The Literature of Cornwall*, for example, is able to begin in the year 1000,[20] any account of literature from the Hebrides can look back over a venerable Gaelic tradition, and, in the study which, geographically, is most closely related to this one, Simon Hall's *The History of Orkney Literature*, we find the following passage:

> The great medieval Icelandic prose work *Orkneyinga Saga*, written *circa* 1200, is the bedrock underlying all subsequent literature in the Orkney islands. Lumbering out of the Dark Ages and bristling with the myths of Orcadian origin and the exploits of pagan, Viking earls, its first full translation appeared in 1873. As well as providing Orkney with a vivid and mostly historical account of its early medieval past, the saga has proven itself to be a deeply compelling and identity-shaping narrative. For many nineteenth and twentieth-century readers and writers, *Orkneyinga Saga* would come to be regarded as a 'national' epic.[21]

It would be impossible to begin this book with a similar statement. Shetland does appear in the sagas, but none of the material is centred on the isles in the way that *Orkneyinga Saga* is on Orkney. But, even if we did have a comparable Shetland work, would the use of it as a foundational text be apposite? Would it be sensible to suggest that it somehow provides a foundation for 'all subsequent literature'?

Hall's approach seems rather reductive. It is certainly useful to discuss the influence of *Orkneyinga Saga* on the work of George Mackay Brown, but to attempt to place Edwin Muir in a similar context does not get us very far. Although *The Literature of Shetland* is also about the writing of a Scottish archipelago, it is emphatically not an attempt to make later work conform to a literary or theoretical paradigm. Creative work by dozens of writers over two centuries is inherently heterogeneous, and this study is an attempt to reflect that diversity and respect the individuality of each author's voice. To begin, as Hall does, with this kind of generality, is to pre-empt and limit discussion unnecessarily. As Vladimir Nabokov, in his *Lectures on Literature*, puts it:

> In reading, one should notice and fondle details. There is nothing wrong about the moonshine of generalization when it comes *after* the sunny trifles of the book have been lovingly collected. If one begins with a ready-made generalization, one begins at the wrong end and travels away from the book before one has started to understand it.[22]

The work of Shetland's writers will be at the centre of our discussion. What did they write? What are their technical accomplishments? What are their ideas and themes? What did they have to say? By, as Nabokov puts it, fondling the details of their work, I will try to answer these questions and provide readers with an inclusive, hopefully entertaining, picture of the multiplicity of writing that both Shetlanders and visitors to the isles have produced.

What this book shares with the work of Hall and Kent, however, is a belief that studying writing from a particular region is a worthwhile thing to do. Orkney, the Hebrides, Cornwall and Shetland are all very far from metropolitan cultural centres, but consideration of writing which engages with these environments extends our knowledge and enjoyment of literature. Stories and poems which are concerned with these places allow readers a glimpse into distinctive locales, and this study upholds the principle that reading and thinking about these works leads to greater literary and cultural heterogeneity. Looking at writing in this regional way allows us to see Scotland's literature, or Britain's for that matter, as increasingly pluralistic and varied.

When we use the term 'region', however, what exactly do we mean? What kinds of writers do we designate as regional, and is it useful to do so? Because it is a remote island it is easy to see Shetland as a region, but what about Scotland as a whole? Is it a nation, or is it region of the UK? Is its literature an example of regional writing? Are Hardy and Lawrence regional novelists, or are they English novelists writing about particular places? Proust and Joyce wrote about relatively limited geographical spaces, but no critic would call either of them a regional writer. Is Scott a national novelist for Scottish people and a regional one for English readers? In a speech delivered at the 2012 Edinburgh International Book Festival, Irvine Welsh deals sharply with these kinds of questions:

> We can spend all day debating what is national and regional literature to the point where it becomes meaningless. In an American context, look at *Wikipedia*, and you'll find writers as diverse as Steven King, John Steinbeck, Mark Twain, William Faulkner and Raymond Chandler all described as regional. The criterion for being a national writer often seems to be as trite as living close enough to Manhattan to be able to attend the occasional *New Yorker* cocktail party.[23]

Welsh suggests that classifying writers as regional or national is a rather pointless exercise. The terms are mutable. They mean different things to different people. As Alison Lumsden, in an essay on writing from the north-east of Scotland, puts it:

> The definition of 'regional' is itself problematic, for it to some extent depends upon perspective. To many readers Scotland itself may be seen as a region, while from within Scotland the distinct identity of the north-east (or indeed other areas of the country) sets it apart from the rest of Scotland.[24]

What is a region to some is a nation to others, and vice versa. The categories are fluid, moveable, difficult to demarcate. We see this problem of definition in an essay by K.D.M. Snell, editor of the collection *The Regional Novel in Britain and Ireland* (1998). Snell begins his essay by saying, straightforwardly, what he understands regional fiction to be:

> By 'regional novel' I mean fiction that is set in a recognisable region, and which describes features distinguishing the life, social relations, customs, language, dialect, or other aspects of the culture of that area and its people.[25]

When Snell introduces the term 'national', however, we see the same sort of difficulty arise that Lumsden identifies in her essay. He writes

> 'Regional' thus conceived is not the same as national, but it does not exclude that: the term includes regional writing within the four countries of the British Isles. A 'nationalist' novel, say of Wales, lacking clear regional specificity within Wales would not be included here; but a Welsh regional novel might in some cases be open to interpretation as a 'national' novel.[26]

Some regional novels can be national novels, and, if it has a flavour of local life, Snell seems to suggest that a national novel can also be thought of as regional novel. Again, we see a certain instability between the two terms and, to return to Lumsden's point, categorising pieces of writing as regional or national depends ultimately on the reader's point of view. Some readers, for example, as Cairns Craig points out in his essay 'Scotland and the Regional Novel', would see any Scottish novel, because of the country's status in the Kingdom, as an inherently regional piece of writing.[27]

What is often going on, of course, when terms like 'regional' and 'national' are used, is a judgement of value. When we call somebody a regional writer it seems all too easy to say '*only* a regional writer'. As Lumsden points out: 'the regional is, almost by definition, constantly haunted by the tendency towards parochialism.'[28]

Using these sorts of classifications creates an implicit hierarchy, with regional writers being seen as somehow inferior to writers with supposedly wider national concerns. There is no reason, though, to denigrate writers who choose to engage deeply with a specific locale and, in his speech, Welsh advocates the value of writing which some might term regional. Citing authors such as James Kelman and Alan Warner, he writes:

> Global mass culture is now largely governed by an increasingly image-dominant, rather than linguistic-dominant, means of cultural production. Therefore, it's more difficult for it to be limited by national boundaries. In such an environment, the main question for storytellers who see themselves as working outside the global cultural highway of London, New York and LA is, what kind of room for manoeuvre do we have, in a global literary marketplace, to express national or regional culture? Moreover, can writing still be undertaken – and indeed, writers be formed – within a "national" culture?
>
> The Scottish experience says a resounding 'yes' to this.[29]

Whether Kelman is a Scottish regional, Scottish national, or British regional novelist, Welsh suggests that, because his work is distinctively Scottish, it resists the homogenising force of an increasingly globalised culture. Kelman's writing, like most of the writers in this study, is engaged with a particular community – with its class structures, its language, its social life – and Welsh sees this as something which makes literature more diverse and multifarious. In other words, writing which is concerned with a definable environment – a regional piece of writing, if you like – is a way of combating uniformity. The more we know about different places, the more cosmopolitan our literary outlooks will be.

Welsh sees Scotland as a fruitful locus of resistance vis-à-vis a mass globalised culture but, even within Scotland, there are many distinctive regions. The term 'Scotland' itself, we might argue, could even be thought of as a homogenising concept, bringing to mind icons and symbols such as tartan, bagpipes, and Bannockburn. But, for Shetland, as we shall see, these things find little or no place in its tradition of cultural expression. Just as the global culture Welsh is concerned about tends to eradicate difference, simplistic ideas about Scotland can be seen as doing the same. MacDiarmid, in his poem 'Direadh?', writes about 'our multiform, our infinite Scotland', and this study is a contribution to that idea of the country.[30] We can only see Scotland as multiform if we think in a detailed way about all its component parts and, in opening up Shetland's literature for consideration, and by showing how it intersects with other literatures, this book adds another element to our picture of the country's creative work.

The Literature of Shetland, for the reasons I have mentioned, sees the study of 'regional' literature as valuable, but our primary focus will always be on the words writers have written. This may seem, to some readers, to allow insufficient space for contextual material. While recognising that writers do not work in a vacuum (local publishing opportunities are especially important, for example), this book does not attempt to make many connections between the lives of authors and their work. For most readers, however, the writers we are about to study will be completely obscure, so a certain amount of biographical information is desirable. A primary aim of this study is to introduce Shetland's literature to readers who may know very little about the subject, and it seems appropriate and useful to give some sense of who the writers in question are.

Because we are concerned with the work of particular authors, many of whom, as we shall see, came to prominence in two significant periods of literary growth, the material has been arranged in eight chronological chapters. This use of chronology gives us a neat and convenient means of ordering a large body of writing, but our central concern is not with how social change through time may impact on the production of literature, but with what Martin Amis calls 'the thing itself, the art itself'.[31] Relevant social contexts will be mentioned, but they are not our main avenue into the writing. My approach will be more akin to what Ezra Pound advocates in his *ABC of Reading*:

> The proper method for studying poetry and good letters is the method of contemporary biologists, that is careful first-hand examination of the matter, and continual comparison of one 'slide' or specimen with another.[32]

General themes and ideas do emerge, but the fundamental concern of this study is with the individuality of each writer's work. Teasing out the particularities of each individual aesthetic seems, to me, the best way of bringing their work into the light.

The words on the page are the most important things but, in looking at the writing of a particular place, certain questions do suggest themselves. All writers are different, but the ones we are concerned with here are brought together because Shetland is a presence in their work. Not all the writing we will look at is about the isles, but the question of how writers have engaged with the archipelago is a pertinent one. How have writers seen Shetland? How does Shetland inhabit or colour their writing? Are there differences in the way natives and incomers have written about the place?

Central to most local writers' engagement with the isles is language. Almost every author we are about to discuss has produced a large amount of work in Shetland dialect, but what have they done with it? How have they developed the language as an expressive medium?

These questions will be posed throughout this book, but the question of who Shetland's writers are and, more importantly, the question of what they have written, is at the heart of what we are trying to address. Very few people know anything about these writers so, by the end of this study, I hope that readers will be left with a clear and enriching view of the literature of Shetland.

Notes

1. Neil M. Gunn, *The Silver Darlings* (London: Faber and Faber, 1969), p.271. To avoid large numbers of unnecessary endnotes, when quoting from a primary source I will initially give a full reference, and will provide subsequent page numbers within the text. Where this may be confusing – for example, when a number of quotations from several books by the same author are used in close proximity – I will give the name of the volume, sometimes in an abbreviated form, alongside the page number.
2. Tom Leonard, *Outside the Narrative: Poems 1965-2009* (Buckfastleigh: Etruscan Books, 2009).
3. Brian Smith, 'The Development of Literature in Shetland', *New Shetlander*, 174 (Yule 1990), 29-31 and 175 (Voar 1991), 18-19.
4. Laurence Graham, 'Shetland Literature and the Idea of Community', in *Shetland's Northern Links: Language and History*, ed. by Doreen J. Waugh (Edinburgh: Scottish Society for Northern Studies, 1996), pp.52-65. Graham recycles much of this essay in his introduction to *A Shetland Anthology* (1998), which he co-edited with his brother John.
5. Julian Meldon D'Arcy, *Scottish Skalds and Sagamen: Old Norse Influence on Modern Scottish Literature* (East Linton: Tuckwell Press, 1996), pp.187-193.
6. Laurits Rendboe, *The Shetland Literary Tradition: An Introduction* (Odense: Odense University, 1985). For a severe, but in my view judicious, critique of Rendboe's work, see Brian Smith's essay 'The Development of the Spoken and Written Shetland Dialect: A Historian's View', in *Shetland's Northern Links*, ed. by Waugh, pp.30-43.
7. Arthur Edmondston, *A View of the Ancient and Present State of the Zetland Islands* vol.1 (Edinburgh: James Ballantyne and Co., 1809), pp.144-145. Samuel Hibbert, *A Description of the Shetland Islands* (Edinburgh: Archibald Constable and Co., 1822), pp.560-561. Both authors seemingly base their remarks on a sentence in Jonas Jonæus' pioneering facing-page Latin translation of *Orkneyinga Saga*, published in Copenhagen in 1780, which says that Rognvald encountered two native poets, Oddi Glumson the Little and Armodr, in Shetland in 1151 (pp.266-267). This would have been the only version available to Hibbert and Edmondston, but modern translations state that the poets were in fact from Iceland.
8. For this early material See *A Shetland Anthology: Poetry from the Earliest Times to the Present Day*, ed. by Laurence L. Graham and John J. Graham (Lerwick: Shetland Publishing Company, 1998), pp.1-16.
9. See Michael P. Barnes, *The Norn Language of Orkney and Shetland* (Lerwick: Shetland Times, 1998).

10. See *Jakob Jakobsen in Shetland and the Faroes*, ed. by Turið Sigurðardóttir and Brian Smith (Lerwick / Tórshavn: Shetland Amenity Trust / University of the Faroe Islands, 2010).
11. For a discussion of Jakobsen's work see Michael P. Barnes, 'Jakob Jakobsen and the Norn Language of Shetland', in *Shetland's Northern Links*, ed. by Waugh, pp.1-15.
12. For an outline of Jakobsen's work on Faroese folklore see Barnes, 'Jakobsen', p.1.
13. Low gives an account of this in his book *A Tour Through the Islands of Orkney and Schetland* (Kirkwall: William Peace & Son, 1879), p.107. Low could not understand what was being sung – it is not clear if Henry could either – so made a phonetic transcription. The volume also contains a Norn version of the Lord's prayer (p.105).
14. For a guide to scholarly work done on the ballad, see Michael P. Barnes, 'The Study of Norn', *Northern Lights, Northern Words. Selected Papers from the FRLSU Conference, Kirkwall 2009*, ed. by Robert Millar (Aberdeen: Forum for Research on the Languages of Scotland and Ireland, 2010) <http://www.abdn.ac.uk/~wag020/uploads/files/Barnes,%20The%20Study%20of%20Norn.pdf> [Accessed 17 April 2012].
15. Throughout the book I will use the terms dialect, language, vernacular, tongue, and Shetlandic interchangeably. Dialect is the most common way of referring to what is spoken in the isles but, to me, this term seems to have connotations of inferiority. It is easy to think of a dialect as a debased form of a language. Linguists may baulk at the phrase Shetland Language, and Shetlanders generally dislike the coinage Shetlandic, but by utilising all the available terms, any distinctions or hierarchies which may be seen to exist between them break down. We are interested here in the literary use of language, not in technical differentiation. As Tom Leonard puts it 'all livin language is sacred' (Tom Leonard, *Intimate Voices: Selected Work 1965-1983* (Buckfastleigh: Etruscan Books, 2003), p.134) and, whatever we decide to call the speech of Shetlanders, this is a principle I uphold.
16. See Adam Grydehøj, 'The Orpheus of the North', *New Shetlander*, 240 (Simmer 2007), 23-27.
17. *A Shetland Anthology*, p.11.
18. Karl Blind, 'Discovery of Odinic Songs in Shetland', *Nineteenth Century*, vol.5 (1879), 1091-1113 (p.1092). The circumstances of how the fragment was recorded are included the essay.
19. Smith, 'Historian's View', pp.31-33.
20. Alan M. Kent, *The Literature of Cornwall: Continuity, Identity, Difference* (Bristol: Redcliffe Press, 2000).
21. Simon W. Hall, *The History of Orkney Literature* (Edinburgh: John Donald, 2010), p.9.
22. Vladimir Nabokov, *Lectures on Literature*, ed. by Fredson Bowers (New York: Harcourt, 1982), p.1.
23. Irvine Welsh, 'Is There Such a Thing as a National Literature?', *Guardian*, 19 August 2012. <http://www.guardian.co.uk/books/2012/aug/19/irvine-welsh-a-national-literature> [Accessed 21 November 2012].
24. Alison Lumsden, '"To Get to Live": Negotiating Regional Identity in the Literature of North-East Scotland', in *The Edinburgh History of Scottish Literature*, vol.3, ed. by Ian Brown (Edinburgh: Edinburgh University Press, 2007), pp.95-105 (p.100).

25. K.D.M. Snell, 'The Regional Novel: Themes for Interdisciplinary Research', in *The Regional Novel in Britain and Ireland, 1800-1990*, ed. by K.D.M. Snell (Cambridge: Cambridge University Press, 1998), pp.1-53 (p.1).
26. Snell, 'Themes', p.2.
27. Cairns Craig, 'Scotland and the Regional Novel', in *The Regional Novel in Britain and Ireland, 1800-1990*, ed. by Snell, pp.221-256 (p.221).
28. Lumsden, 'Negotiating Regional Identity', p.97.
29. Welsh, 'National Literature'.
30. Hugh MacDiarmid, *Complete Poems*, vol.2, ed. by Michael Grieve and W.R. Aitken (Harmondsworth: Penguin, 1985), p.1170.
31. Martin Amis, *The War Against Cliché: Essays and Reviews 1971-2000* (London: Vintage, 2002), p.251.
32. Ezra Pound, *ABC of Reading* (London: Faber and Faber, 1961), p.17.

Chapter One

BEGINNINGS

Introduction

In the first three decades of the nineteenth century, four books by two Lerwick women, and a notebook of poems by a man from Yell, inaugurated the literature of Shetland. Margaret Chalmers, Dorothea Primrose Campbell, and Thomas Irvine, despite not featuring in any anthology of Shetland writing, were the first local people to publish fiction and poetry. In recent years, as we shall see, some scholarly attention has been paid to Campbell and Chalmers, but all three writers remain obscure. Their work has never been reprinted and their books are rare. Even within Shetland, their names are hardly known at all.

In contrast to their invisibility stands Walter Scott, whose 1822 novel *The Pirate*, set in the northern isles, was a roaring commercial success. As Andrew Wawn, in the foreword to his 1996 edition, shows, *The Pirate* was astonishingly popular in the nineteenth century, inspiring stage versions, travellers' accounts of Orkney and Shetland, and reflections on the story by figures such as George Bernard Shaw and George Eliot's Maggie Tulliver.[1] But Scott's novel, as I will explore, engages with Shetland in a different way than the work of Chalmers, Campbell or Irvine. The fact that Shetland had not enjoyed much literary attention, however, is important in a discussion of both Scott and his lesser-known northern contemporaries.

These writers were looking at a place that was not inscribed in any literary discourse, but, in the early nineteenth century, Shetland presented several less abstract problems for anybody who wanted to write. The islands were poor, with most of the population living in very basic housing and subsisting on what income they could get from fishing or knitting.[2] As Hugh MacDiarmid, in his key Shetland poem 'On a Raised Beach', puts it: 'A culture demands leisure and leisure presupposes / A self-determined rhythm of life'.[3] Chalmers, although she had financial difficulties, did not scrape together a meagre living on a croft but, in the Shetland of her time, many people did. As we shall see in Chapter Two, a widespread readership for local writing developed later in the century but, for Chalmers and Campbell, this did not exist. The cultural experience of most Shetlanders was one of storytelling, myth and music, and, although Chalmers' *Poems* (1813) includes a traditional song, 'The Shaalds of Foula', and although Campbell's verse occasionally draws on local superstition, Shetland's folk culture is not a significant presence in their work.[4] Their books, none of which were published in Shetland, were not written for the general population of the archipelago, but for the market that existed in Britain for women's poetry.[5] Local crofters were not settling down at their firesides with the books we are about to discuss and, in a society where arduous work and inadequate housing were the norm, it is easy to see why not many writers emerged. Writing needs time and space, and most Shetlanders of the period had little of either.

Also hampering the emergence of literature in Shetland were the rudimentary levels of education and literacy,[6] and the lack of any local media or printing industry. Shetland's first newspaper, the *Orkney and Zetland Chronicle*, appeared from 1824 to 1826, but was printed in London and shipped north. The first locally printed paper, the *Shetland Advertiser*, was not published until 1862 (it lasted a year), and it is only from 1872 onwards, with the appearance of the *Shetland Times*, that the media, print and publishing industries truly became part of Shetland society. The writers in this chapter could not publish locally, and the islands had to wait until 1885 before the first book rolled off a local press, J.J. Haldane Burgess' little volume *A Nicht in Tammy Scolla's But End*.

But this book is not concerned with the absence of literature, or with the social and economic conditions that may have led to that absence. What interests us here is the literature that does exist. What is the nature of the work these writers did? How did they engage with their archipelago? How did people from a place with no literature find ways of writing about that place?

Margaret Chalmers (1758-1827) [7]

In her poem 'The Author's Address to the Critics', Margaret Chalmers makes a striking claim for herself as a literary pioneer:

> Since Scandinavia rul'd our Isles,
> We ne'er have woo'd the muses' smiles;
>   Yet own their power
> Oft wheels away, in rapid course,
>   The wint'ry hour.
>
> *Now* in the pure Castalian rill
> Dips the first British Thulian quill
>   To fame addrest;
> In slumber lull'd, the poet's art
>   Long lay supprest.[8]

Coming two years after Dorothea Primrose Campbell's debut book of verse, Chalmers' positioning of herself as 'the first British Thulian quill' is not quite accurate. But, as Penny Fielding, in her book *Scotland and the Fictions of*

Geography, shows, the question of where Chalmers places herself, and her native islands, is central to her work.[9] Chalmers' poetry investigates Shetland's position in the wider world, especially in terms of the nation, but she is also concerned with the problem of how to be a poet in a place with no living literary tradition. In the above stanzas she suggests that the muses came north during Shetland's Scandinavian period but, empathically, she asserts the novelty of her enterprise. Chalmers was writing without the influence of any recent local precedent, and about a landscape which did not conform to conventional ideas of beauty but, as we shall discuss, she finds ways of overcoming the problems she faced.

Chalmers' primary motivation for publishing her only book, however, was not to contribute something new to Shetland's culture. She certainly did this but, rather more mundanely, the book was an attempt to make money. The eldest of seven children, she was born in Lerwick to William Chalmers and Catherine Irvine. Her father, a customs officer, was dead by 1772, and her only surviving brother, also William, died at Trafalgar, leaving Margaret, her mother, and four sisters (a younger brother died in infancy) without a source of income.[10] In 1813, in an attempt to alleviate the family's debts, she published her book by subscription. In the preface, she writes of herself and her subscribers:

> Impelled, as she was, by circumstances of severe domestic affliction, to obtrude her claims upon their notice, it is with emotions of the most lively and lasting gratitude she has to acknowledge, that her appeal has not been made in vain, and that she has experienced the encouragement and support which she took the liberty of soliciting. (p.v)

This is politely put, but the difficult financial circumstances the family faced were very real indeed, things not being helped by the poor health of Chalmers' mother and sister. In 1816, however, with Thomas Irvine as her sponsor, she was awarded £10 by the Royal Literary Fund.[11] And, in 1823, she appealed to Arthur Nicolson, the laird of Fetlar, for financial aid, accompanying her letter with a printed sheet detailing the family's finances.[12] As the sheet makes clear, the money from Chalmers' book made a dent in their debts, but could not turn their fortunes around. For an unmarried woman in Shetland at this time, with a deceased father and an ailing family, the economic options would have been limited. Writing and publishing was one of the few things to which she could turn.

But, grim as her circumstances were, it is the writing they drove her to do which interests us here. In subsequent chapters we shall see how Shetland's language becomes the most prominent feature in the work of local authors. But, at the beginning of the nineteenth century, with no local literary models to either draw on or react against, Chalmers is vitally engaged, not with the vernacular, but with the place itself and with finding ways of seeing and writing about it. What did Shetland mean to Chalmers? How did she see her native isles? How does her verse engage with the archipelago?

Fielding, in *Scotland and the Fictions of Geography*, writes that 'Chalmers is eager to situate Shetland as part of the nation – not a distant or peripheral part, but as British as anywhere else.'[13] Living in an isolated place, far from metropolitan cultural and political centres, Chalmers does not see herself as outside the bounds of the United Kingdom. With her 'British Thulian' moniker, and in the three patriotic poems which open her book, Chalmers combines a sense of herself as a Shetlander with a clear assertion of her Britishness. Years later, in his poem 'In the Shetland Islands', MacDiarmid would write: 'I am no further from the "centre of things" / In the Shetlands here than in London, New York, or Tokio' (*CP1*, p.574). He would have had little time for Chalmers' British patriotism or liking for royalty but, in both poets, there is a sense of their connectedness with things outside the literal bounds of their coastline.

Shetland, however, is isolated, and, with poorer transport and communication links, would have been much more so in Chalmers' day than in our own. Fielding shows how Chalmers draws Shetland into a national and imperial orbit, but also how she retains a sense of the archipelago's peripherality and distinctiveness. She writes: 'Chalmers is fond of depicting Shetland as at once distant and extreme, the mythic *Ultima Thule*, and absolutely central to the geography of modern Britain.'[14] Fielding then goes on to quote from an unpublished poem of Chalmers', 'Address to the Ward Hill in the Island of Bressay', in which we see the rather MacDiarmidian image of a solitary figure on a stony beach in Unst. Chalmers tells us how her traveller: 'Picks up a pebble from the farthest beach, / And shows it, as a token he has been / As far to North, as Britain gave him ground.' MacDiarmid's Shetland work, as we will explore in Chapter Five, encompasses both the lonely figure in a stony, barren place, and the need to be connected to the world's multifariousness. Chalmers is concerned with the place of Shetland in the nation and the Empire, whereas MacDiarmid, especially in the later epic verse he wrote in Whalsay, attempts to rove through global intellectual vistas. Although I do not want to push a comparison between two very different writers any further, in the work of both poets we find an engagement with a harsh, austere, not conventionally poetic landscape, and we see how they attempt to negotiate the fact of their isolation and place themselves in wider contexts. Neither MacDiarmid nor Chalmers accept that physical isolation equates with intellectual, political or cultural isolation and, in their different ways, they assert the validity of an outward-looking poetic which is partially built on the unusual landscapes in which they lived.

As I will explore below, Chalmers retains a strong sense of locality through her use of landscape. She is a patriotic poet but she does not allow her native islands to be obscured by that patriotism. She sees Shetland as firmly part of the nation, but, in terms of its own past, how does she see the place? A passage from Chalmers' contemporary, historian Arthur Edmondston, gives us a useful corollary. In his 1809 book *A View of the Ancient and Present State of the Zetland Islands*, he writes:

The character of the Zetlanders, like that of all rude countries, was long marked by ignorance and ferocity; and they appear to have subsisted chiefly by fishing and plunder. The insecurity attending the possession of landed property, under the feudal system, made them view agriculture as a matter of secondary consideration, and the ground long remained in an uncultivatedstate. United by no general principle of public good, and uncontrolled by the operation of equal laws, each individual joined the standard of the most successful leader, and aggrandised himself as accident gave him an opportunity, withoutregarding former relations or future punishment. Such seems to have been the state of society in Zetland, during the whole period that it was under the sovereignty of Norway.[15]

Edmondston shows little enthusiasm for Shetland's Scandinavian heritage and, in the poem quoted at the beginning of this section, we see Chalmers display a similar lack of nostalgia. For them, Shetland's Scandinavian period was, happily, long in the past. In Chapters Two and Three we shall see how Scandinavia came to be celebrated by local writers, but the later utilisation of Norse themes, and the continuing celebration of them in the annual Up Helly Aa fire festival, stand in polar contrast to the views of Chalmers and Edmondston.[16] Victorian writers looked back to Viking Shetland as a place of liberty, but this is not something we find in the work of their literary predecessors.

As later chapters will show, in the late twentieth and early twenty-first centuries, Shetland's history has become an increasingly popular theme, especially for novelists. But history, as Fielding points out, is not a major concern for Chalmers.[17] The Shetland landscape, and the ways in which she sees that landscape, are of much greater importance in a discussion of her work. This landscape, because nobody had written about it, was invested with no poetic meaning. Chalmers could not read a poem or look at a painting of Shetland and, without any artistic associations, the landscape – treeless, a barren coastline, miles of dark, unvariegated moors – may have seemed a rather bleak and uninspiring prospect. In 'Verses in Humble Imitation of Burns', for example, she tells us that 'The Lyre will greet' (p.48) if it ever ventures to Shetland, then shows us why: 'For, whan it comes amang your damps, / And a' your plashy, miry swamps, / 'Twill spoil the strings' (p.49). Chalmers suggests that Shetland does not provide the conventional raw material of poetry so, instead of invoking the nine muses, she goes on to propose Neptune, Aeolus and Boreas, gods of wind and water, as suitable figures for Shetland poets to call on. The landscape may be inhospitable to the artist but, if that artist can invoke the appropriate gods and learn to cope with the hostile conditions, then there may actually be poetic virtues to be found locally.

So, if Chalmers had to deal with a lack of a local literature, and with a landscape that may not have seemed particularly beautiful or poetic, how does she find suitable sources for her poetry? In 'A Fire-Side Vocal Concert', the assembled company decide to pass the evening by singing to one another:

> Tay, Tweed, and Yarrow's celebrated streams,
> Where the pleas'd muses whisper sylvan themes,
> Glide thro' the pastoral vale and flowery mead,
> Thro' which the passive fancy pleas'd they lead;
> And, in their tranquil murmurings, is drown'd
> The wild, the wintry roar of Bressa [sic] Sound. (p.68)

The 'wintry roar' does not obliterate the delicate images, and the songs provide an escape from the harsh conditions outside the window. Beauty is to be found elsewhere. In 'Lines on the Drawing Room of an Intimate Friend of the Author's' we see ('doubly' because it is reflected in a mirror) a sunlit picture of the friend's garden:

> It must be own'd that in our Northern clime
> Summer is rather chary of his time,
> His tardy visit transient and sweet,
> Slow in advance, but in retreating fleet;
> What can we more to counteract his haste
> Than doubly view his beauties while they last. (p.91)

Beauty is fleeting, but it is there. The world outside the window can be a source for poetry, but the things she wants to draw on are ephemeral and must be grasped while they are available. The poem then moves away from the window as tea is brought in:

> And now arrives the hour which brings the board
> With China's fragrant leaf and porcelain stor'd,
> Where British cups with China's porcelain vie,
> (What cannot British industry supply?)
> The spotless white and golden circles gay,
> Simplicity with splendour join'd display,
> And rival that which every tint doth show,
> Which gaily paints the bright ethereal bow.
> And see the native produce of our ground,
> The crimson jelly 'in its crystal bound,'
> Does honour to Lerwegian clime and soil,
> And well rewards the active gardener's toil [...]. (pp.91-92)

Fielding reads this use of tea as 'the signifier that links the Lerwick drawing room to the mobility of global trade', but, alongside this, in the way the speaker lingers over the foreign things, we see their exotic nature brought sensually to the fore.[18] There is no hierarchy of beauty created, but the local 'crimson jelly' (jam) is not celebrated in quite the same way as the cups. The cups give the speaker pleasure because they are artistic objects. The jam, although it is not disgraced by being seen next to the other objects is, in a rather more mundane and homely way, a thing of the soil. The tea and cups, as Fielding suggests, represent trade and Empire, but the cups also serve as things which give aesthetic pleasure. As our first quote from the poem shows, Chalmers is more optimistic here about Shetland as a source of beauty than in some of her other compositions, but, with the introduction of the exotic things, she ultimately suggests that art and beauty are easier to find in things that come from outside the isles.

In these poems, even though the settings are domestic, the world outside is always kept in view. In several other poems, however, Chalmers widens and heightens her perspective and gives the reader some striking views of the world outside the drawing rooms and parlours of early-nineteenth century Lerwick. In one of her finest poems, 'The Rose of the Rock', accompanied by a group of friends she 'exchange[s] / Lerwegian scenes for rural, calm delights' (p.21) and, from the top of the precipitous cliffs at Noss (Chalmers uses the Dutch name Hangcliff), a small island on Shetland's east side, she gives us a panoramic view of the whole archipelago:

> Hope's vivid promise well nigh realiz'd,
> We Hangcliff's steep and lofty summit gain,
> Which o'er the deep in awful form projects;
> And, in one wide and heart-dilating view,
> Give's Thulè's utmost boundaries to the eye.
>
> Eastward, beyond where keenest sight can pierce,
> The German Ocean rolls his frequent wave
> To Berga's coast remote. Far in the north,
> Rise Vaalifield's high ridge and Saxaford;
> In yonder space, that points to Faro's Isles
> And Iceland's lasting snows, towers Rona's Hill,
> Majestic 'midst his tributary mountains.
> Turning thence the obedient eye to where
> The setting sun gleams on Orcadian shores,
> See cloud-girt Foula fam'd in classic lore;
> Then circling still the penetrating gaze,
> Lo! Fitful lifts on high his aged head;
> While, far beyond the south extreme, appears
> (Seen as an azure cloud) the lone Fair Isle. (pp.21-22)

From her elevated point of view the speaker can see from the north of Unst to the most southerly part of Shetland, Fair Isle. Her view ranges from one end of her native isles to the other, as if she is surveying the territory on which her poetry is going to be built. In other poems, as we have seen, she points towards the difficulties that territory creates but, here, by letting her gaze rove over the islands, instead of seeing Shetland's 'plashy, miry swamps', she can see the place as 'exhibiting / Nature's stupendous grandeur' (p.22). The landscape inspires awe and, by presenting it in this way, she offers a view filled with artistic possibility.

But, surprisingly, the poem does not find its ultimate source of literary potential in this grand vista. As the group stands on Noss, the speaker, peering over the cliff, notices something she does not expect to see in such a place:

> Half way adown the bleak and rugged steep,
> Secur'd from the most intrepid schoolboy's reach,
> Nature, amid a scene whose wild sublime
> Might chill the blood and even to horror rouse,
> Had dropt a lovely solitary flower,
> As remembrancer of another style
> Of beauty, by full contrast heighten'd seen. (p.23)

As with the cups in the drawing room, the flower provides an exotic contrast and the speaker (imaginatively) seizes it. It is precious because of where it is, but it is also beautiful because it reminds her of 'another style'. The flower stands out against the black, dangerous coastline, but the speaker also mediates the view of that flower through art. It is fundamentally a native thing but, seen through the speaker's artistically inclined consciousness, it draws on aesthetic ideas she has garnered from writing and painting which have nothing to do with Shetland. The flower may call these ideas into her mind, but we also see how she is able to find a source of beauty and pleasure in something growing in such an unlikely place. Because of where it is found – a beautiful thing in a landscape which is not supposed to contain beautiful things – the flower takes on a great importance. As the speaker looks at it, she remembers that another member of the party, 'whose childish, rash, impetuous years, / Less listen'd to the strict restraint of care, / Than curiosity's supreme impulse' (p.24), might stray perilously close to the edge in order to better see the flower. So, until they return to safer ground, she tells no one about it. When she does, however, the friend is disappointed and says '"O why conceal / From me a sight so beauteous and rare?"' (p.24). The speaker then tries to persuade the friend that they cannot return to the cliffs but, so uncommon is the flower, the friend ends the poem by saying '"I care not, I would travel Zetland o'er, / To see the Rose that grows amid the Rock"' (p.25). For the speaker and her friends, the rose is invested with an aesthetic importance that it would not be able to carry were it seen in a different kind of landscape. It immediately reminds the speaker of other beautiful things, but it is also a thing which has grown in Shetland's soil. In Shetland, beauty is scanty, but, if one knows how to look, it is there to be found.

In these poems, whether set in a drawing room or on a precipice, Chalmers is concerned with the ways her poetry can engage with her environment. It is as if she is feeling around, testing, trying to ask if the islands she wants to write about *can* be written about. She is looking for things that can be utilised in her verse. Sometimes she fastens onto imported objects which can offer her aesthetic pleasure and, sometimes, as she does in 'The Rose of the Rock', she finds something local which, to her surprise, can provide her with something like the beautiful things she wants. With absolutely no local literary precedent on which to draw, Chalmers is trying to find ways of writing poetry about her native isles.

In her poem 'Description of Sound, Near Lerwick', Chalmers finds the answer to the aesthetic problems we have traced. The poem opens with a view of Sound (a hamlet which has now been subsumed into Lerwick), which the speaker sees from the same kind of lofty viewpoint she adopts in 'The Rose of the Rock':

> 'Heavens! what a goodly prospect spreads around,'
> From the steep eminence whereon I stand;
> Summer meridian beauty widely pours
> On the delighted eye [...]. (p.102)

She then asserts, emphatically, that she can see a landscape fit for art:

> Here might the poet, or the painter find
> Field for the pencil or descriptive art.
> O! would some Muse the pleasing theme attempt,
> Who should with candour, fearless of the charge
> Which to a partial native might belong,
> To truth and poesy give all the reins;
> Yet who, lov'd Thulè, should thy daughter dread
> To sing her natal scenes, while justly sung;
> Come, Muse, we'll to the task, let who will frown. (p.102)

The place she is looking at *is* beautiful. It does not repel the artist but is entirely suitable for somebody to paint, draw or write about. And, as a native, despite the fact that there are no Shetland poets, she claims the authority to do so. Her gaze then wanders across the scene, testing out, aesthetically, what she sees. She looks at a hill on Bressay, the island opposite Lerwick and, remarking on the lack of trees, does confess that 'Pines and elms / Would with superior beauty grace these shores' (p.103). This leads her to imagine the islands when they were covered in trees, but the vision ends abruptly when she says 'But now I ween such censure I incur, / As they who of departed beauty boast' (p.103). She suggests that, yes, the islands may have been more conventionally beautiful when enhanced with trees, but that what she needs to do is find the possibilities those islands offer now. She rejects 'another style / Of beauty' and says that she will locate her poetry in what is in front of her, that she will find her aesthetic sources in what her view provides. Even the seemingly artless parts of the landscape will be part of her tableaux: 'Nor shall yon wild, bleak hill remain unsung; / For what were painting, but for stroke of shade, / Of beauty's heighten'd lustre, but from foil? (p.104). The contrasts offered by the 'wild, bleak hill' are not the sharp, polarised juxtapositions of the unexpected rose or the beautiful porcelain cups, but are created by a 'stroke of shade'. The landscape she views – a moor perhaps – is not unvariegated and uniform but, when the viewer really tries to see, it offers subtle gradations of colour and tone which are ripe for exploration in art.[19]

In the next two lines, however, Chalmers shifts her gaze and announces the true setting of her poem: 'But chiefly through thy beauteous limits, *Sound*, / Fain would I wander, and attempt to sing' (p.104). The rest of the poem traces her journey through Sound and, as her attention focuses closely on what she finds – the flora and fauna, the dwellings, a pre-Reformation chapel, the streams – she asserts, with more confidence than anywhere else in her work, that this landscape can sustain art. The absence of literature in Shetland, she suggests, is not due to a paucity of raw natural material but can be explained in a different way: 'And who can tell but this sequester'd spot / Might guiltless Cromwells, and mute Miltons boast, / Had culture rear'd the seeds by nature sown' (p.105). Shetland *can* be fruitful poetic territory, but it is a territory which has never been seen in cultural terms. A poetic culture can be founded on the places she sees and moves through, and it is up to people to discover the beautiful things and places Shetland has to offer:

> Thou traveller, led by design or chance
> To Lerwick's harbour, often visited,
> Form not thy notion of the Zetland soil
> From the bleak scene that mounts behind the town.
> From it no just idea mayst thou draw.
> We blazon not our best appearance first;
> No! we reserve it to reward the search
> Of active visitant. (p.112)

It is the 'active visitant' that will be aesthetically rewarded. As her other poems suggest, not everything in the landscape is beautiful but, for those who can find the right way to see, there are beautiful things to be found.

When we consider Chalmers' verse as coming at the very beginning of the literary tradition this book will work through, we can see her trying to reconcile her environment with her calling as a poet. As Fielding points out, in Chalmers' work we find references to poets such as Ramsay, Pope, Thomson, Gray, Akenside, and Scott and, although she is clearly influenced by these poets, unlike her contemporary Dorothea Primrose Campbell, she is not a derivative writer.[20] In the poems we have looked at here, we see Chalmers trying to define and develop a kind of poetry which takes account of her influences, but which also retains a strong and positive sense of what Shetland has to offer. Her work did not inaugurate a revolution or movement in local letters, but the single book of poems Chalmers produced offers us a probing, intelligent voice which eventually succeeds in finding ways of seeing the harsh and peculiar landscapes of her native isles.

Dorothea Primrose Campbell (1792-1863)

For Chalmers, Shetland was both part of the nation and was able to offer something worth writing about. Despite lacking a local literary tradition, she affirms that a Shetland poetry is realisable. In the work of Dorothea Primrose Campbell, however, we find a less hopeful, much more ambiguous, attitude to the isles. In her poem 'Address to the Evening Star', for example, she writes:

> Still must these barren plains and hills,
> These rugged rocks and scanty rills,
>   My narrow prospects bound?
> Must I, where Nature's bounteous hand
> Doth every rural charm command,
>   Say, must I ne'er be found?
>
> [...]
>
> Still must this ocean's liquid round
> My dreary prospects ever bound,
>   On Fancy's wings while borne
> My weary soul delights to roam
> To other lands, another home,
>   Nor wishes to return? [21]

What 'prospects' are these? Does she mean her economic and social opportunities are limited in Shetland? Or is she saying that, as an artist, the view Shetland offers is uninspiring? Either way, the poem is not hopeful about the archipelago. She is trapped, oppressed, and her imagination provides the only means of escape.

That Campbell had mixed feelings about her native isles is not surprising, for her years there were marked by struggle and adversity.[22] She was born in Lerwick on 4 May 1792 to Duncan, a military surgeon, and Elizabeth Scott, daughter of landowner Walter Scott of Scottshall, Scalloway. The family was debt-ridden and financial difficulties were to plague Campbell for the rest of her life. Her father died when she was sixteen and her mother became addicted to opium. Like Chalmers, Campbell was left with major responsibilities and few economic options. She ran a small school, but also tried to make money by writing. Her first book of poems was published, by subscription, in 1811, the publication being arranged by James Young of Inverness, who Campbell was working for at the time. She returned to Shetland in around 1815 and her second volume of poems, published by Baldwin, Cradock and Joy of London, appeared a year later. Her final book, the novel *Harley Radington*, was published in 1821. She corresponded with Sir Walter Scott (who she met in Shetland in 1814) and Francis Jeffrey (who, in 1844, wrote a reference for her successful application to the Royal Literary Fund – she was awarded £30). As historian Linda Riddell argues, Campbell's letters were often written to try and elicit money from wealthy men.[23] In 1841 she did what she advocates in 'Address to the Evening Star' and left Shetland, moving to London, where she was employed as a governess by Mary Smith, daughter of Adam Clarke, a Methodist missionary who had visited the isles. She never returned to Shetland, and died, on 6 January 1863, in an asylum for aged governesses in Kentish Town.

Campbell ended up far from Shetland and, in her writing, unlike Chalmers, she gives us a view of the archipelago which emphasises its distance, and difference, from the rest of Britain. Chalmers is careful to maintain a balance between local particularity and Shetland's place in the nation, but Campbell, especially in her novel, suggests that drawing Shetland from the periphery to the centre is problematic.

The novel tells the story of a young man from London, Harley Radington, who is spoiled terribly by his mother while growing up in high society. After the death of his father, and his mother's subsequent relationship with the Irish bigamist Mr Lawler, Harley runs off to sea. He is wrecked on Shetland and wakes to find himself in an alien and disorientating place:

> I lay in a state of utter helplessness for many days. When I began to observe what was going on about me, I found myself in a miserable cabin. Heaven forgive me, for the idea which has so often recurred! but a very wicked man, on recovering, in the situation in which I was, might well have imagined himself in the infernal regions. I lay in a horrible hole, enclosed with wood, resembling a press, which was so short, narrow, and low, that I could neither turn myself, stretch out my limbs, nor sit upright, without knocking my head on the roof. The air I breathed was loaded with every odour which thick smoke, excessive filthiness, and total want of fresh air, could create. My bedclothes were – but, reader, spare me the relation! Enough to say, that your imagination can scarcely exaggerate their wretchedness.[24]

Harley is in a box-bed in a crofter-fisherman's cottage. Everything is strange and foreign and the passage goes on, at some length, to describe the room – its unusual furniture, its smallness, and especially its profusion of dirt. Harley's view of the inhabitants extends the idea of his sudden immersion in a savage and alien environment:

> Uncouth figures flitted through the smoke in strange dresses, talking what I first supposed to be a language entirely foreign, but which I afterwards discovered was English, or rather Scotch, mixed with words and phrases of which I knew not the meaning. (vol.1, p.136)

Harley has moved from, in his conception of things, a civilised, modern place, to a place where barbarous people live in filthy houses. The language they speak, which Campbell supplies a lengthy glossary for, connects them to the country of Harley's birth, but its bastardised nature also marks their distance from the linguistic mainstream.

But, in the first of a series of plot twists, Harley discovers that the house is, in fact, that of his aunt and uncle. His mother is unmasked as a Shetlander, making him kin to the savages he encounters. We are then introduced to more of Harley's new family, the more civilised Irvingsons, and, when he finds his way into the more elevated social stratum they represent, he meets and falls in love with Ellen Edenborg. Then, after another shipwreck, Harley ends up on a whaling voyage to Greenland. His ship is destroyed in the ice but, on the vessel which picks him up, there are a number of Shetlanders and, eventually, he makes it back to the isles where he hopes to marry Ellen. His second landing in the archipelago contrasts sharply with his first:

> How changed was the appearance of the country! It appeared to me a perfect paradise. Even the russet colour of the high hills, and the uncultivated morasses, delighted my eyes, which had for so many months gazed on the ocean, and tractless deserts of frost and snow. (vol.2, p.149)

Shetland has become a 'perfect paradise' because he has fallen in love with one of the natives, and, after being in an even more alien environment, his eye has become attuned to the Shetland landscape. As happens in Chalmers' poems, Harley has learned how to get something from the islands. Shetland is no longer a place of filth and barbarity but, at this point of the novel, is a place which gives him pleasure and in which we can imagine him coming to live.

When he goes to see Ellen, however, he finds that she has died. Bereft, he goes back to London:

> I now again found myself one of the most lonely and isolated beings in existence. In one of the most populous cities in the world, I wandered about without meeting with a human creature that knew me, or that took an interest in my fate. (vol.2, p.170)

Despite his initial horror, Harley finds kin and community in Shetland. With Ellen gone, however, he cannot settle in the isles. Towards the end of the novel, after a successful naval career, a knighthood, and a good marriage, he returns briefly, but most of the people he knows have died. On leaving Ellen's (fictional) home isle of Mora, he writes:

> I quitted Mora next day, and never visited Zetland again. I was a husband and a father; a place where recollections and regrets, like the above, were cherished and awakened, was not for me to remain at. (vol.2, p.225)

Harley has become partially reconciled to Shetland but, in the wake of his social elevation, the idea of him becoming a part of its society is never entertained. The rapturous engagement with the landscape he experienced on returning from Greenland is an isolated incident and, now that he has wealth, status, and a family of his own, he can leave the isles behind, both psychologically and literally. The novel allows Harley's story a happy resolution, but it is a resolution in which Shetland is not included.

Penny Fielding, in a discussion of *Harley Radington* in terms of the National Tale genre, suggests that trying to incorporate Shetland in the novel's resolution is difficult:

> The transmutation of "wild" Scottish Highlanders living outside British political structures into a disciplined military force asserting British national identity in her imperial wars surfaces in works from Smollett's *Expedition of Humphry Clinker* (1771) to Christian Isobel Johnson's *Clan-Albin: A National Tale* (1815). But Campbell faced a demographic problem in introducing her novel into this tradition – Shetland was not Ireland or the Highlands of Scotland and did not obviously fit into the model of the Celtic other, simultaneously romanticized and rendered primitive, that marks the novel of the period.[25]

Shetland, Fielding argues, cannot be easily incorporated into the nation and, therefore, cannot provide the reconciliation that the National Tale requires. She goes on to say:

> Scotland's Northern Isles were not inscribed in a recognisable novelistic discourse. Shetland does not establish historical markers in the mind of the reader as Irish and other Scottish regional novels would.[26]

In 1821, a novel about Shetland may have been an unusual proposition for readers, but, for somebody to sit down and try writing a novel about the isles at this time, how to portray Shetland must have presented a conundrum. Campbell could not draw on a fictional model in which Shetland was used. Scott, as we shall see, constructs the archipelago (in contrast to the local authors) as culturally Scandinavian, and the idea of a partially Norse Shetland is an idea which is still with us today. Later Shetland writers would draw from this spring which Scott uncovered but, for Campbell, the only fiction she could take direction from did not mention the place she was writing about. Chalmers finds an affirmative way of seeing Shetland while drawing on models from the literary mainstream, but Campbell, who is clearly less fond of the isles than her contemporary, does not really try to do this. She uses Shetland as a strange and unsettling place to drop her hero, but is not concerned, as Chalmers is, with thinking about an aesthetic which could, in some sense, be described as indigenous. In Campbell's novel, and this, one suspects, may have been true for Campbell herself, Shetland is ultimately a place to leave behind.

Thomas Irvine (1790-1877)

Our third poet, Thomas Irvine, also spent a number of years in London.[27] Unlike Campbell, however, he did make the return trip north. He was the son of a merchant and landlord from the Midbrake estate at the north end of the island of Yell. At the age of nineteen he went to London to teach in the Deaf and Dumb Asylum in Kent Road, where he stayed until 1820. He then returned to Shetland and took up his inheritance. In addition to running the estate, he spent a great deal of time travelling all over the islands, working as a land surveyor, and his surveying notebooks contain a wealth of information about local folklore, language, antiquities and Shetland's culture generally.[28] In London he was secretary and treasurer of an organisation called the Zetland Patriotic Society and,[29] back in Shetland in 1822, he had an idea for a local journal which does not seem to have come to anything.[30] He may also have been involved in an organisation called the Literary Society of North Yell in 1863, although not, apparently, as a founding member.[31]

A few years before he left for London, Irvine started to write poetry. His work, which has never appeared in book form, is contained in a notebook of twenty-one poems which was found in the Shetland Archives during the course of this research.[32] Two poems in the notebook refer to events in 1807, and Irvine notes that he had poems published in the *European Magazine* in September 1811 and June 1812.[33] Although his record of publication was sparse, being able to get his work into a journal would have been much easier in the capital than it would have been in Yell.

Even though he lived outside Shetland for over a decade, many of Irvine's poems take the isles for their subject. In 'For Zetland: on leaving it for the first time', for example, he looks yearningly north:

> On Anfra-mire's weld, and by Gasa's broad water
> In Rules-gill's deep glade and on Scola's broad lea
> Tho' far I may roam o'er the scorching equator
> Often shall fancy restore you to me.
> E'en mid the gay city's rich pageant pedantic,
> Where luxury's minions soft pleasures adore
> I'll sigh for the cliffs that are wild and romantic
> The grand ocean caves and the white sandy shore.

Irvine never made it as far as the 'scorching equator', but his fondness for Shetland, if conventionally expressed, is clear. In his poem 'The Native Harp', he shows that he was aware, and enthusiastic, about some of the literary developments we have been tracing in this chapter:

To Miss D.P. Campbell – on reading her poems at Edinburgh in June 1813

> Behold! 'Mid Zetland's heath clad isles,
>   The northern harp awakes again!
> The pitying muse benignant smiles
>   And bids it sound a native strain.
>
> Long in some dark sequester'd cell
>   Unstrung it moulder'd to decay
> No more it wak'd to mirth the dale
>   Tun'd to the Bard's spontaneous lay.
>
> Till thou o maid of genius bright
>   (As days first twinkling radiance sprung)
> Dispel'd the long, dark, barren night
>   That o'er the Thulian regions hung
>
> With joy I hail the dawn of song
>   As on my native hills it gleams
> May future bards the ray prolong
>   Till high as noon-tide sun it beams.

Irvine must have sent Campbell this poem because, in her 1816 volume, she includes the poem 'To the Northern Islander' (the name Irvine used when publishing his poems in the *European Magazine*) as a reply. Like Campbell, Irvine does not have the range or intelligence of Chalmers, but, in these stanzas, we see him, as Chalmers does, say that writing poetry is a new thing for Shetlanders to be doing. What he praises in Campbell's work, however, is that, as well as it being an example of something new, it is also an example of a 'northern harp', a poetry native to Shetland.

But what would writing native to Shetland look like? As this book will demonstrate, a primary reason for the distinctiveness of Shetland's literature is that, aside from the writers we have looked at so far, almost every local author has produced a large percentage of their work in the vernacular. But, in this early period, almost all the writing which appeared was in English. Campbell's use of dialect in *Harley Radington* (and the accompanying glossary) serves to make the locals look stupid, backward and alien. In Irvine's notebook, we see him working in the Shetland dialect too:

Fragment – Shetland Dialect

> O simmer is blooming and bonie
>   And spring is lightsome and green
> But hearst I like better than onie
>   O' a' the four season's it's queen.

> For then wi the lang yellow corn
> The gay laughing rigs are sae braw
> They wave to the breeses o' morn
> While the due [sic] frae the dripping rips fa'.

This is the earliest Shetland dialect poem extant. Like his homeward-looking poems, this is sentimental and derivative, but it also shows that, decades before the widespread literary use of the vernacular, there was a writer using the language. The next poem in the notebook, by Irvine's brother Alexander, is identified as being in 'Scottish Dialect', which suggests that the Shetland language is seen as distinct from what is spoken further south. A second poem by Irvine also experiments with the Shetland tongue:

> Twa breeder in a unco' land
> Met on a new Yull day
> The time the place – they thought and sighed
> It made their hearts fu wae.
>
> It wasna like da Yulls day'd [sic] seen
> When dey were boys at hame
> Dey strangers were – the folk were strange
> Nane kindly speer'd at dem.

The use of the pronouns 'dey' and 'dem', and the use of the definite article 'da' mark this poem as more distinctively Shetlandic than the previous one. For the first time, we see a Shetland writer suggesting that a native poetry can be written in the language spoken in the isles. And, although it would not be wise to make too much of these two little poems, it should be noted that Irvine's experiments with the Shetland language presage the much more significant vernacular works local authors would produce later in the century. The use of dialect in Shetland's literature only really gets going with the Victorian writers, none of whom show any evidence of having read any of the work we have looked at so far. Irvine, however, deserves recognition for producing the earliest examples we have of poetry in the Shetland tongue.[34]

The final poem in Irvine's notebook, like the one to Campbell, enthuses about the writing of poetry in Shetland:

> Awake o harp of former days
> That oft has sung to Hetlands [sic] praise
> O shades of Minstrels past away
> Awake! revive the dormant lay.

In this poem, unlike Chalmers' 'The Author's Address to the Critics', Irvine sees the (hypothetical) poetry of old as being something which could be revived. The poem goes on:

Extempore – On being called to for a Toast by the Chairman of a convivial meeting of friends

My leal light heart with bounding glee
  Doth answer to thy call
Like to a billow of the sea
  So doth it swell and fall
    With its own spring of joys
  As "Bumpers" loud you bawl –
  A "Friend and Glass" my hearty boys
I pledge you one and all –

"Mirvan Hiestë or
Hialtland De"

Fragment Shetland Dialect

O Simmer is blooming and bonie
  And Spring is lightsome and green
But Hearst I like better than onie
  O' a' the four seasons its Queen

For then we the "lang yellow corn"
  The gay laughing Rigs are sae braw
They wave to the breezes o' morn
  While the dew frae the dripping rips fa'

Notebook of Thomas Irvine.   *Courtesy of Shetland Museum and Archives*

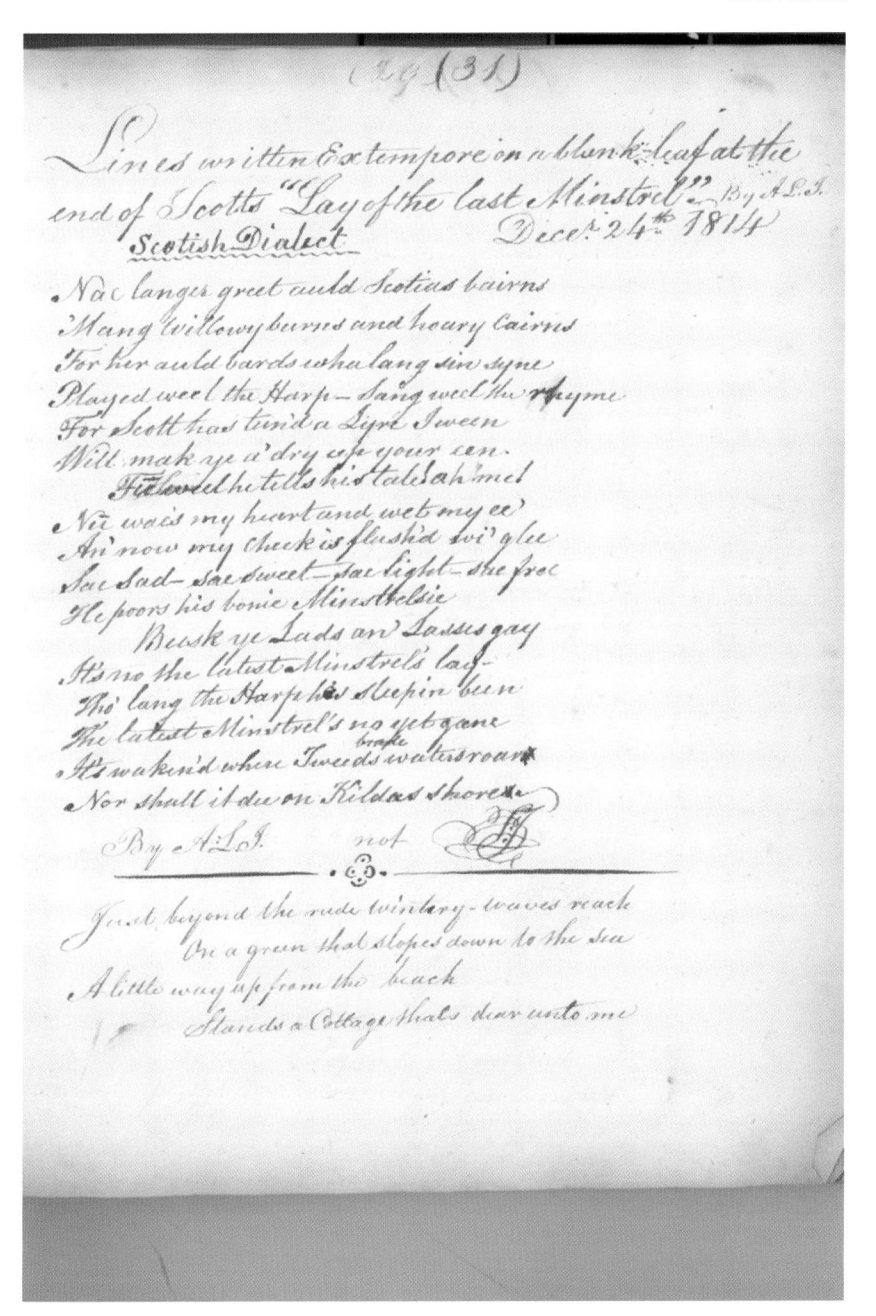

Lines written Extempore on a blank-leaf at the end of Scott's "Lay of the last Minstrel" By A.L.I.
Scotish Dialect   Dec.r 24.th 1814

• Nae langer greet auld Scotias bairns
'Mang Willowy burns and hoary Cairns
For her auld bards wha lang sin syne
Played weel the Harp — Sang weel the rhyme
For Scott has tun'd a Lyre I ween
Will mak ye a' dry up your een.
Fu~~ loud~~ he tells his tales ah me!
• Nae wae is my heart and wet my ee'
An' now my cheek is flush'd wi' glee
Sae Sad — Sae Sweet — Sae light she free
He poors his bonie Minstrelsie
    Busk ye Lads an' Lasses gay
It's no the latest Minstrel's lay
Tho' lang the Harp has sleepin been
The latest Minstrel's no yet gane
• It's waken'd where Tweed's waters roar
• Nor shall it die on Kildas shore

    By A.L.I.   not

—⁂—

Just beyond the rude wintery-waves reach
    On a green that slopes down to the sea
• A little way up from the beach
    Stands a Cottage that's dear unto me

> Raise on the breeze the measures bold
> The martial strain – the deeds of old
> Tell to the years of time to come
> What worthies call'd this land their home
> When Harald led Norwegias host
> From Bergan's shore to Zetland's coast
> And Merca's chief stout Ronald came
> Of dauntless soul and giant frame
> What warriors throng'd grim Hela's strand
> Journeying to Gimle's azure land
> Valhala's high celestial gates
> Wide for the hero's spirit waits.

In his invocation of Shetland's Scandinavian past, Irvine suggests that these kinds of themes may be of use to the native poet. Although he only wrote a very small number of poems, most of which were unpublished, and most of which are fairly amateur, in his use of dialect, and in his utilisation of Norse themes, Irvine is trying to mark out new directions for local literature. The use of Scandinavian motifs becomes common in the work of later writers such as Haldane Burgess and Jessie Saxby, not that either of them would have known about Irvine's literary efforts. They would, however, have known about *The Pirate*. Irvine's poem is undated, but one wonders if he wrote it after the appearance of Scott's Zetlandic blockbuster.

Walter Scott (1771-1832)

When Walter Scott came to Shetland in 1814, and when he published *The Pirate* in 1822, the archipelago was drawn into the orbit of a literary superstar. Chalmers, Campbell and Irvine were (and remain) almost completely unknown local authors, and Scott was one of the most famous writers in the world. But Scott contrasts with the local writers in a more revealing and important way than in terms of their relative popularity. Chalmers and Arthur Edmondston, as we have seen, disassociate early-nineteenth century Shetland from its Scandinavian past. Apart from the single poem by Irvine, the writers discussed so far had little enthusiasm for anything Norse. Scott, on the other hand, fills his vision of Shetland with Scandinavian images and motifs. His subject is Shetland in the late seventeenth century, more than two centuries after the northern isles became part of Scotland, but Scott's construction of the archipelago owes more to medieval Scandinavia than to Shetland during the time in which the action takes place.[35]

Is Scott's dubious grasp of Shetland and Orkney history important, though? Historian Brian Smith, in a review of the novel, writes that 'Of course, he got the history completely wrong'[36] and, much more censoriously, Simon Hall compares the novel with *Waverley* as follows:

> While a good deal of *Waverley* can be described as historical, *The Pirate* lacks its predecessor's historical backdrop. [ ] *The Pirate* suffers from the absence of the convincing, confident and encyclopaedic historical understanding that is the foundation of its predecessor. Scott goes beyond the limits of his knowledge.[37]

Although Smith's review does go on to praise the 'freshness and excitement' of the novel, both critics see the historical inaccuracy as a problem. But is it not more worthwhile to ask how Shetland and Orkney exercised Scott's imagination, than to attack the novel for its shaky historical foundations? How did Scott engage with the archipelagos in his fiction? How did Scott see Shetland and Orkney?

I will argue below that the differences in how Scott utilises the two archipelagos are of central importance to the novel but, first, I want to look at how the northern isles, Shetland especially, allowed Scott to construct a story which incorporated his interest in Scandinavian literature.

Marinell Ash writes of Scott's trip north: 'It was the only time in his life that Scott would see archaeological sites which he could connect with events in saga literature and his wide knowledge of Scandinavian history.'[38] As Andrew Wawn and Peter Mortensen have shown, Scott is a major figure in the development of old-northern-inflected British literature.[39] His library contained several rare Scandinavian texts and, in 1814, he published a précis of *Eyrbyggja Saga* which, as Mortensen points out, 'has since been praised as a breakthrough in Old Norse academic scholarship.'[40] Scott was knowledgeable about Scandinavian literature and, after exploring some of the Norse remains in Shetland, he had a setting which allowed him to use this knowledge. Wawn writes: 'In the novel Scott took the two centuries of old northern scholarship that had been "gathered into the barns of the learned", and found a way of animating it within a British context.'[41] He then goes on to say that *The Pirate* was 'the first extended treatment of any aspect of the old north in the English language'.[42] Scott's novel was historically spurious, certainly, but it was also a key text in the introduction and popularisation of Norse themes in British writing, setting off a stream of influence that would eventually feed into novels such as H. Rider Haggard's *Eric Brighteyes* (1891), J. Storer Clouston's *Vandrad the Viking* (1898), and J.J. Haldane Burgess' *The Viking Path* (1894).

As we have seen, Chalmers and her peers all had to deal with the lack of a native literature. Scott did own copies of Chalmers' and Campbell's books (whether he read them or not is unclear) but, when he came to write *The Pirate*, he had for his setting a place with hardly any contemporary literary baggage or associations. As we will discuss, to satisfy the thematic development of his story, Scott had to construct his picture of Shetland in a certain way, and a writer as well known as him was unlikely to take for his foundation a few obscure books by two unknown female authors from the northern isles. In terms of literature, especially fiction, Shetland was undeveloped territory. He called the journal of his 1814 trip *A Voyage in the Lighthouse Yacht to Nova Zembla and the*

Scene from The Pirate. *Courtesy of Shetland Museum and Archives*

Lord Knows Where[43] and, in this title, we see Shetland presented as distant and illusive – as 'wild, misty, almost legendary Zembla', as Vladimir Nabokov's demented annotator Charles Kinbote says, in *Pale Fire*, of his fantastical northern kingdom.[44] For Scott, despite Campbell and Chalmers' efforts, Shetland was a pristine canvas, a *tabula rasa*, onto which he could project his Scandinavian-flavoured tale. Scott's Shetland, his Nova Zembla, was a place which provided him with dramatic scenery, unusual local customs and words, wild weather and stormy seas. It was also a place nobody had written a best-selling novel about. His view of Shetland may have been inaccurate but, as we shall see, his construction of the isles as Norse was thematically strategic. His Norse Shetland is a place of myth, magic and romance but, when the action moves to Orkney, we see these things begin to unravel and, by the end of the novel, to break down entirely.

As we have seen, much of the recent work on *The Pirate* concentrates on its Norse themes. Some general comments on Scott, however, give us a different way into the novel. Douglas Mack and Suzanne Gilbert write:

> Scotland's ancient (but deposed and exiled) Stuart royal family had a romantic appeal that made strong claims on Scott's sense of history and on his sense of patriotic loyalty. Nevertheless, he was sufficiently

a product of the Scottish Enlightenment to believe that progress and modernity lay with commercial, postunion, Hanoverian Britain.[45]

And, in *The Literature of Scotland*, Roderick Watson says something similar:

> His young heroes, whose inheritance is progress and the United Kingdom, learn to accept what Scott calls 'the prose of real life', but it seems colourless by comparison with the old ways and the 'poetry' of a lost Scotland.[46]

The thematic movement both quotations describe is one in which romance and adventure fade away, to be replaced by rationality and acceptance of reality. In *The Pirate*, this maps onto Scotland's two northern archipelagos.

For Scott, Shetland and Orkney offered very different propositions, as we see in his journal entry for 13 August 1814: 'The soil of Orkney is better, and its air more genial, than Shetland; but it is far less interesting and possesses none of the wild and peculiar character of the more northerly archipelago.'[47] Scott was clearly more taken with Shetland than he was with Orkney. He sees Orkney in practical terms – its soil is more suitable for cultivation – but Shetland is the place which will really get his imagination working. In *The Pirate*, he uses the contrast between the places to move his story through what David Daiches calls 'the inevitability of a drab but necessary progress'.[48]

Chapter Three of the third volume ends with Magnus Troil, his daughters Minna and Brenda, the poet Claude Halcro and the hapless agricultural improver Triptolemus Yellowley, in a small fisherman's hut. The Troils have been to visit the 'pythoness', Norna of the Fitful Head, and she has turned them, inhospitably, from her cliff-top tower, obliging them to spend the night in the only basic accommodation they can find. Brenda and Minna are unaccustomed to such surroundings, but Halcro encourages them and the rest of the party to make the best of it:

> 'There is an inner crib here, where the fishers slept, – somewhat fragrant with the smell of their fish, but that is wholesome. They [Minna and Brenda] shall bestow themselves there, with help of what cloaks you have [...].' [49]

The next chapter opens with a lengthy description of St Magnus Cathedral and the Earl's Palace in Kirkwall. The difference between the hut in Shetland and the much grander, more sophisticated, buildings in Orkney is marked. The largest buildings we see in Shetland are the 'rude building of rough stone' (p.6) which Basil Mertoun rents at Jarlshof, and the Troil residence at Burgh Westra, which Scott describes as being 'of various dates, with large and ill-contrived additions, hastily adapted to the original buildings, as the increasing estate, or enlarged family, of successive proprietors, appeared to each to demand' (p.109). Magnus is one of the chief citizens of Shetland, but his house is haphazard and eccentric. The buildings in Shetland, all of which are solitary and isolated, contrast with the grandeur of the buildings in Orkney. The picture Scott creates of Shetland is of an overwhelmingly rural place (Lerwick is never visited) in which one occasionally comes across a somewhat outlandish structure. The cathedral, although it is old, is used as a symbol of civilisation and rationality. It sits in a town, which has things like streets and a council chamber – things which are not part of the Shetland sections of the novel. Also, in Kirkwall, we encounter a number of local officials – the town clerk, the magistrates, the provost – and, again, there are no counterparts in Shetland. Magnus Troil is referred to as 'Udaller' and 'Fowde', and, after Cleveland's ship is wrecked, it falls to the Ranzleman to ensure that whatever is salvaged gets divided equally among the locals. As is the case with the buildings, the use of these medieval Scandinavian titles, especially when read against the much more modern, recognisable titles given to Orcadian public officials, makes Shetland seem alien and strange.

Shetland, constructed in this way – as stranger, older, more *outré* than Orkney – allows Scott to develop the supernatural and romantic themes of the novel. It is easier to set strange events in a place which is made to seem strange, and nothing in the novel is stranger than Norna of the Fitful head. She is the Reim-kennar, versed in ancient lore, garbed in mystical runic symbols and in league with supernatural forces. When we see Norna in Shetland, she seemingly has the power to control the weather, to predict the future, to cure maladies and to appear and disappear at will. She, more than any other character, draws on the worlds of myth and magic we find in saga and edda. But, in Orkney, her abilities are shown to be no more than clever tricks (albeit ones she herself believes in). She is ingenious, rather than eldritch or uncanny. By moving his characters to the more civilised, but, in Watson's terms, more prosaic, setting of Orkney, Scott can pull back the curtain and show his audience how Norna's illusions are performed.

Similarly, Minna Troil, although she does not pretend to have magical powers, also looks back to Scandinavian times. She sees in Cleveland something of the spirit of the Vikings she so admires, and it is her construction of him as a modern-day saga hero that makes her fall in love. But, again, when the action shifts to Orkney, her fantasy melts away. When they meet in St Magnus Cathedral she says to him:

> 'We must indeed say farewell,' said Minna; 'for fate and your guilt have divided us for ever. – Cleveland, I have seen your associates – need I tell you more - need I say that I know NOW what a pirate is?' (p.349)

After seeing the kind of men Cleveland has spent his life with, Minna is no longer under any illusion about the nobility of pirate life. Wawn writes of Norna that 'her eventual ineffectiveness serves only to confirm the folly of projecting old northern dreams onto post-medieval realities', and Minna suffers from the same shattering of fantasy.[50] At the end of the novel, Scott links the two characters explicitly:

> Like Norna, but under a more regulated judgement, she [Minna] learned to exchange the visions of wild enthusiasm which had excited and misled her imagination, for a truer and purer connection with the world beyond us, than could be learned from the sagas of the heathen bards, or the visions of later rhymers. (pp.390-391)

Minna and Norna are the most altered characters in the book. Norna, after her bizarre house is knocked down and she has reverted to her own name of Ulla Troil, ends up as a bible-reading, benevolent, slightly dotty old woman. Minna, despite the narrator's assertion of her happiness (p.390), is given a rather plaintive tint in the novel's final paragraph. She is reduced from 'the high and imaginative Minna' (p.390) to a woman who spends the rest of her life in resigned service to others. It is Brenda, her plainer, more rational, more practical, less romantically inclined sister who marries the hero. Minna and Norna draw closer to ancient ideas, myths and themes than any other characters in the novel and, when these things cannot be sustained, they suffer the damaging consequences.

Scott's construction of Shetland may have been historically inaccurate, but, as a thematic and structural device, it allows him to use Orkney as a more rational and modern counterpoint. Orkney is relatively civilised and urban, and it is in the more southerly archipelago that the world of myth, ancient custom, magic and romance he creates in Shetland begins to come apart. Scott's Shetland, his Nova Zembla, may be fantastical, but he is no Charles Kinbote. His fantasy does not run madly away and he remains in control of what he is doing. In Orkney, reason is established, and the older, stranger, more colourful world of Scott's Shetland is left behind.

Conclusion

Scott, Campbell, Irvine, and Chalmers all had to find ways of writing about Shetland. The ways in which they could see the place could not be mediated through the eyes of artists who had tried to see the place before them. And Shetland – its landscape, its weather, its customs, its language – was an unusual proposition. Campbell emphasises the backwardness of the place and suggests that it is somewhere to escape from, if one can. Irvine, however, is more positive about the poetic possibilities Shetland could offer. The next chapter will discuss the explosion of Shetland dialect writing from 1877 onwards, but Irvine was the first writer to realise that poems could be made from the local language. Scott's novel also augurs some of the developments we will look at next. Chalmers discounts Shetland's Scandinavian period as something worth writing about, but Scott seizes on this era with alacrity and, for tens of thousands of nineteenth-century readers, this was the only picture of Shetland they had. It is in Chalmers' work, however, that we find the most thoughtful exploration of what Shetland could give to the artist. Shetland may have been without a literature, and it may not have conformed to ideas of beauty Chalmers would have found in contemporary verse, but she finds ways of seeing the islands that assert their validity as a foundation for art. No writer, however, would work on the ground she cleared and, at the end of the nineteenth century, we see local writing move in directions that continue to influence writers today.

NOTES

1. Andrew Wawn, Foreword, in *The Pirate*, by Walter Scott, ed. by Andrew Wawn (Lerwick: Shetland Times, 1996), pp.i-xix.
2. See Hance D. Smith, *Shetland Life and Trade, 1550-1914* (Edinburgh: John Donald, 1984).
3. Hugh MacDiarmid, *Complete Poems*, vol.1, ed. by Michael Grieve and W.R. Aitken (Manchester: Carcanet, 1993), p.431. Subsequent page numbers given in text as *CP1*.
4. For a contemporary view of Shetland's folk culture see Samuel Hibbert *A Description of the Shetland Islands* (Edinburgh: Archibald Constable and Co., 1822). And, for a modern discussion of Shetland's musical tradition, see Peter Cooke, *The Fiddle Tradition of the Shetland Isles* (Cambridge: Cambridge University Press, 1986).
5. See Stephen C. Behrendt, *British Women Poets and the Romantic Writing Community* (Baltimore: John Hopkins University Press, 2008).
6. John J. Graham, *A Vehement Thirst After Knowledge: Four Centuries of Education in Shetland* (Lerwick: Shetland Times, 1998).
7. Isobel Grundy, 'Chalmers, Margaret (b. 1758)', in *Oxford Dictionary of National Biography* <http://www.oxforddnb.com/view/article/45839> [Accessed 2 November 2011]. The ODNB entry does not give the date of Chalmers' death, but the Old Parochial Register for Lerwick records it as the 10 March 1827. See SA, SA1/2/5.
8. Margaret Chalmers, *Poems* (Newcastle: S. Hodgson, 1813), p.12.
9. Penny Fielding, *Scotland and the Fictions of Geography: North Britain, 1760-1830* (Cambridge: Cambridge University Press, 2008).
10. I am indebted to Blair Bruce, my colleague at the Shetland Archives, for his knowledge of William Chalmers and his family.
11. Penny Fielding, '"A Lady of the Isles": Margaret Chalmers' Letters to Walter Scott and Two New Poems', *Scottish Literary Review*, vol.2, no.2 (Autumn/Winter 2010), 23-44 (p.24).
12. Shetland Archives (SA), D24/12/42, Letter from Margaret Chalmers to Arthur Nicolson, 14 November 1823.
13. Fielding, *Fictions*, p.142.
14. Fielding, 'A Lady', p.35.
15. Arthur Edmondston, *A View of the Ancient and Present State of the Zetland Islands* vol.1 (Edinburgh: James Ballantyne and Co., 1809), p.110.
16. For a discussion of the festival's Norse themes see Brydon Leslie, *Borgar Jarl: J.J. Haldane Burgess and Up Helly Aa* (Lerwick: Shetland Amenity Trust, 2012).
17. Fielding, *Fictions*, pp.142-143.

18. Fielding, *Fictions*, p.145.
19. For a discussion of the aesthetic possibilities of the Shetland landscape see Mark Ryan Smith, 'The Artist and the Wilderness', *PN Review* 193 (May-June 2010), pp.8-10.
20. Fielding, 'A Lady', p.25.
21. D.P. Campbell, *Poems* (Inverness: J. Young, 1811), pp.53-54.
22. Isobel Grundy, 'Campbell, Dorothea Primrose (1792-1863)', in *Oxford Dictionary of National Biography* <http://oxforddnb.com/view/article/45837> [Accessed 2 November 2011]. Isobel Grundy, 'Dorothea Primrose Campbell', in *Scottish Women of the Romantic Period* <http://www.alexanderstreet2.com/SWRPLive/bios/S7030-D001.html> [Accessed 20 August 2008].
23. Linda Riddell 'Sir Walter Scott's Piano: The Life and Times of Dorothea Campbell' (unpublished paper given at the conference Shetland: A Women's Island, Shetland Museum and Archives, 2007).
24. D.P. Campbell, *Harley Radington: A Tale in Two Volumes* (London: A.K. Newman and Co., 1821), vol.1, pp.134-135.
25. Penny Fielding, 'Genre, Geography and the Question of the National Tale: D.P. Campbell's *Harley Radington*', forthcoming in *European Romantic Review*.
26. Fielding, 'Genre'.
27. Jane Mack, Thomas Irvine of Midbrakc', parts 1-3, *Shetland Life* 91 (May 1988), 24-25; 92 (June 1988), 37-38; 93 (July 1988), 40-41.
28. SA, D/16, Papers of Thomas Irvine.
29. SA, D16/388/75-78, Papers concerning Zetland Patriotic Society of London, 1815-1816.
30. SA, D16/387/48, Letter from Gilbert Spence to Thomas Irvine, 5 January 1822.
31. SA, D16/388/51, Constitution of the Literary Society of North Yell, 13 April 1863. SA, D16/388/54/1, Letter from P.M. Sandison, secretary, Literary Society of North Yell, to Thomas Irvine, undated.
32. SA, D15/136, Manuscript notebook of Thomas Irvine. For a critical survey of the notebook's contents see Mark Ryan Smith, '"Minstrel of the Mossy Isle": The Poetry of Thomas Irvine of Midbrake', *New Shetlander*, 244 (Simmer 2008), 29-34.
33. For a guide to the *European Magazine* see Emily Lorraine de Montluzin, 'Attributions of Authorship in the *European Magazine*, 1782-1826' <http://etext.firginia.edu/bsuva/euromag/> [Accessed 18 January 2012].
34. For another early example of dialect writing, see the satirical letter of 1817 by Archibald Barclay (1786-1855), the son of an Unst minister, to John Sands of Liverpool, which is in Irvine's commonplace book, SA, D16/394/3. Twelve copies of the letter were printed, by Irvine, at the school in London and circulated in Shetland. For a discussion of this letter see Brian Smith, 'The Development of the Spoken and Written Shetland Dialect: A Historian's View', in *Shetland's Northern Links: Language and History*, ed. by Doreen J. Waugh (Edinburgh: Scottish Society for Northern Studies, 1996), pp.30-51.
35. Alison Lumsden and Mark Weinstein argue, persuasively, that the novel is set in 1689. See Mark Weinstein and Alison Lumsden, Historical Note, in *The Pirate*, by Walter Scott, ed. by Alison Lumsden and Mark Weinstein (Edinburgh: Edinburgh University Press, 2001), pp.485-497 (p.487).

36. Brian Smith, Review of *The Pirate*, by Walter Scott, *New Shetlander*, 199 (Voar 1997), 46.
37. Simon W. Hall, *The History of Orkney Literature* (Edinburgh: John Donald, 2010), p.43.
38. Marinell Ash, '"So much that was new to us": Scott and Shetland', in *Essays in Shetland History*, ed. by Barbara E. Crawford (Lerwick: Shetland Times, 1984), pp.193-207 (p.193).
39. Andrew Wawn, *The Vikings and the Victorians: Inventing the Old North in Nineteenth-Century Britain* (Cambridge: D.S. Brewer, 2000). Peter Mortensen, '"The Descent of Odin": Wordsworth, Scott and Southey Among the Norsemen', *Romanticism*, vol.6 (July 2000), 211-233.
40. Morternsen, 'Descent', p.220.
41. Wawn, *Vikings*, p.61.
42. Wawn, *Vikings*, p.80.
43. Walter Scott, *Northern Lights: or, A Voyage in the Lighthouse Yacht to Nova Zembla and the Lord Knows Where* (Hawick: Byway Books, 1982). The reference in the title is to Alexander Pope's *An Essay on Man*, Epistle II, ll.208-212, in *The Poems of Alexander Pope*, ed. by John Butt (London: Methuen, 1968). P.523. For a discussion of Scott's use of Pope's lines see Fielding, *Fictions*, p.135.
44. Vladimir Nabokov, *Pale Fire* (London: Penguin, 2000), p.201.
45. Douglas Mack and Suzanne Gilbert, 'Scottish History in the Waverley Novels', in *Approaches to Teaching Scott's Waverley Novels*, ed. by Evan Gottlieb and Ian Duncan (New York: Modern Language Association of America, 2009), pp.26-37 (p.29).
46. Roderick Watson, *The Literature of Scotland*, vol.1 (Basingstoke / New York: Palgrave Macmillan, 2007), p.264.
47. Scott, *Northern Lights*, p.61.
48. David Daiches, *A Critical History of English Literature*, vol.2 (London: Mandarin, 1994), p.136.
49. Walter Scott, *The Pirate*, ed. by Mark Weinstein and Alison Lumsden (Edinburgh: Edinburgh University Press, 2001), p.285.
50. Wawn, *Vikings*, p.72.

Chapter Two

FLOURISHING

Introduction

By the end of the nineteenth century, Shetland was a better place for writers and their work. Campbell and Chalmers could not publish their writing in the isles but, by 1900, there were several local publishing firms, two weekly newspapers, the *Shetland Times* and the *Shetland News*, and the annual *Manson's Shetland Almanac and Directory*, which included a large section of poetry and short stories. With this new media, and with the greater levels of literacy that came with the 1872 Education Act, a readership for local writing emerged.

Shetlanders had never enjoyed a local media, but the emergence of one was not unique to the isles. As William Donaldson, in his important study *Popular Literature in Victorian Scotland* shows, in the nineteenth century, newspapers were appearing all over Scotland, and, in the work they contained, regional dialects were prominent:

> One of the most striking things about the popular press in Victorian Scotland was its readiness to use the language of the people – vernacular Scots. This took place on an extensive scale and in some respects was pioneering, indeed revolutionary, in its implications. A whole new vernacular prose came into being with a range and diversity unknown for centuries.[1]

In Chapter One, we saw some experimentation with Shetland dialect but, in the work we are about to discuss, the language was used much more extensively. Thomas Irvine could not place his work in a local paper, but, in 1877, when James Stout Angus' poem 'Eels' was published in the *Shetland Times*, and when George Stewart's book *Shetland Fireside Tales* (parts of which had been in the same paper) and Jessie M.E. Saxby's novel *Rock Bound* appeared, literature was part of Shetland society in a way it was not for the writers in Chapter One. The writers in this chapter still had no local precedent (none of them seem to have known anything about Chalmers and her peers), but, as William Findlay in his essay 'Reclaiming Local Literature', and Tom Leonard in his anthology *Radical Renfrew* (1990), show, regional literatures were emerging across the country.[2] With the exception of James Stout Angus, all the writers we are about to look at lived in Edinburgh, but, by drawing on the culture and language of their native archipelago, their work represents another strand of the contemporary regionalism that Donaldson, Findlay and Leonard identify. The most useful context in which to place the writers discussed below is not that of a local literary tradition, but one in which other little-known Scottish writers were producing work, often in dialect, about their locales. Coming from Scotland's most remote archipelago gave Shetland's writers a repository of unique raw material to do the same.

The press and better education fostered the development of literature in Shetland but, in the last decades of the century, what kinds of work were Shetland's writers doing? The most prolific author was Jessie M.E. Saxby. She was the first professional writer to come from Shetland and, in her work, especially in *Rock Bound*, we see her working some of the ground cleared by Scott. But, in the period covered by this chapter, it is the emergence of dialect literature which is most striking, and which has proved most influential. Saxby did not use the vernacular much but, in the work of those who did, we see the emergence of a Shetland-language literature that writers in our own day continue to draw on. In the writing we are about to discuss, we see the language used in increasingly ambitious and sophisticated ways. What did writers do with their native language? How did they make it into a valid medium for art?

George Stewart (1825-1911)

George Stewart's book *Shetland Fireside Tales, or, The Hermit of Trosswickness*, is an important inaugural marker in the development of Shetland's vernacular literature. Despite Campbell and Irvine's dabbling with the tongue, it is only with Stewart and, as we shall see, James Stout Angus that Shetland dialect literature really gets underway.[3]

Stewart was born in Levenwick in the south of Shetland. By the age of fifteen, he was employed at the local school, tutoring pupils close to his own age and fishermen who were landbound until the summer fishing begun. He left Shetland aged nineteen to work in a shipping company in Leith and, apart from a brief spell in the late 1840s when he taught at a school in Dunrossness, he never lived in the isles again. He emigrated to Canada in 1892, where some of his sons had founded a city called Stewart, and died in Saanich, Victoria, in 1911.[4] But, despite only living in Shetland as a young man, Stewart remained deeply connected to his homeland. He was a regular contributor to the Shetland newspapers and attended meetings of the expatriate societies that had been established in the capital. Thousands of people left Shetland in the late nineteenth century, and organisations such as the Orkney and Shetland Literary Association and the Leith Thule Club, gave islanders the opportunity to socialise, and to reminisce, often nostalgically, about their native archipelagos.[5] They also gave writers the chance to read their poems and stories aloud.[6] There was a burgeoning readership in

George Stewart. *Courtesy of Shetland Museum and Archives*

the Shetland for what Stewart and his peers were doing, but much of their work was written, and performed, in Edinburgh. Exile, as many Victorian Shetlanders found out, cast the isles in a new light and, in the writing we are about to discuss, we find an affirmative, sometimes idealised, view of Shetland, in which local culture and language are central. Like Dorothea Campbell, Stewart ended up far from Shetland, but, for him, the language, folklore and traditions of the islands were rich and valuable things.

Fireside Tales, written and published when Stewart was in his early 50s, was successful and popular, reaching in its third edition in 1923. It is not really a novel (although a melodramatic short novel does form part of it), but is better thought of as a kind of Shetland clamjamfry, incorporating ethnological notes, folk stories and poems. It is also the first book to contain long sections of Shetland dialect prose. Stewart poured what he knew about Shetland into the book. Although it is set in the mid-eighteenth century, the book draws heavily on the kinds of folk tales that were no doubt circulating in Levenwick when Stewart was a boy, and takes for its settings the kinds of houses that so appalled Harley Radington.

The book opens with a meeting between the hermit of the title and the old crofter-fisherman Yacob Yunson. When meeting the hermit on a narrow cliff-top path, Yacob falls over the edge. The hermit rescues him, the two men go to the hermit's cottage, and Yacob hears the story of how he loved, lost, and regained his sweetheart, Lelah Halcro. The way the characters speak is important, with the hermit telling his story in English and Yacob commenting in the Shetland language:

> 'The tender passion in early youth comes forth like a mountain stream, sparkling in joyous murmurs, and reflecting heaven in its transparent beauty. As such God made it, and as such He intended it to flow through all time, gladdening and blessing mankind; but, alas! how soon, and how often, does the stream grow muddy, as in its onward progress it stirs the impurities which lie hidden in the dark channels of the human heart; or, bounding away like a mountain torrent, it dashes on its whirling eddies of uncontrolled passion, carrying its victims into the awful maelstrom of inevitable and irretrievable ruin.'

> 'Eh! Mr Ollison, what a gift ye hae,' exclaimed old Yacob, lifting both his hands and looking up to the roof; 'in place o' livin' in a bit hovel here by yoursell, an' makin' your ain bit meat like a boddie that gengs wi' der staff an' der cashie, ye sud a been waggin' your pow in a poopit, wi' a muckle stipend, a grand manse, servants an' sairin men to wait ipa you; wi' a' glebe o' guid infield land, fat chuckies ta your dinner, an' ance in da ouk to luik ower a lock o' auld sermons, an' wale ane o' dem fir da Sunday; an' dis pits in my mind to say dat I never cud see da meanin' o' feeding da minister sae weel, fir a' my

days I aye fan dat a fat man wis a lazy man. Dere wis Willie Bigiltie dat rowed ta da sea wi' me ae simmer. He never wis düne eatin' liver muggies till, Lord bless me, as he turned as fat as a tiestie, and as round as a pellick, and yet, for a' dat, he wis o' nae mair üse in da boat nor a ballish stane. An' sae I'm just tinkin' it's wi' da ministers – da mair dey hae o' da flesh, the less de'll hae o' da Speeret; an' whin onything o' dat kind is gaen, I'm tinkin' it comes mair fae da whiskey keg den fae da Lord.'[7]

Yacob may be impressed by what he perceives as the hermit's eloquence, but the use of different languages does not establish a hierarchy. In *Harley Radington*, Campbell used the local language to symbolise backwardness but, in *Fireside Tales*, Stewart sees the Shetland dialect as a viable way to write, in an affirmative way, about the archipelago. Yacob is uneducated, but he is not stupid. A look around the hermit's modest home opens into a reflection on the greed of parish ministers, which he illustrates with a simile drawn from his knowledge of fishing. The hermit's narrative is portentous and overblown, whereas Yacob's comments are digressive, spontaneous and metaphorical. His discourse is rooted in the workaday world of the crofter-fisherman and the hermit's lofty tone is that of a book-learned man. The hermit speaks like a character in a novel, but Yacob represents the vigour and dynamism of an oral culture. Speaking to an educated man, however, makes Yacob aware of the erratic, unschooled nature of his conversation:

'Ye wir no laek ta ken dat I wis gaen ta tak up da half o' da time wi' my ain clash an' havers; bit dey auld stories an' bits o' sangs o' my young days comes jimpin in ta my mind whin ye'r spakin' o' da sam subjeck, dat I canna haud my tongue.'

'And there is no reason you should,' rejoined the hermit; 'for it is really my opinion, that if what we have both said were written down, your stories would be considered more interesting than mine.' (p.37)

The hermit is right. The Shetlandic sections have an energy, a way of moving into memory, into stories, into half-remembered songs and tales, that the hermit's narrative lacks. Stewart gives the Shetland language the authority of print. Yacob's voice is that of a community which, despite not having a long-standing literary tradition, does have a rich and fertile spoken one.

Coming right at the start of a corpus of Shetlandic writing, Stewart's book uses the language in a culturally legitimising way. He places sections of Shetland dialect alongside passages of English, but he does so in a way that does not demean the vernacular speakers. When Campbell was writing *Harley Radington*, there was no local readership, and her Shetlandic prose was not going to be read by many dialect speakers. Her use of the language contributes to a picture of the isles addressed to readers who had never been to the archipelago. But, for Stewart, and the others writers in this chapter, what they wrote was going to be widely read in Shetland. It is easy to make dialect speakers seem dim-witted when few of them are going to read what you write, but Stewart, as a man who, looking north from Edinburgh, was proud and enthusiastic about his island heritage, could not use dialect in this way. *Fireside Tales* was addressed to people who knew the life and language of the archipelago well. Unlike Campbell, Stewart did have a Shetland readership, and, had he made his characters speak like savages, he would have insulted hundreds of his fellow islanders. The emergence of a local readership meant that a confident and affirmative use of their language was the most appropriate choice to make.

James Stout Angus (1830-1923)

Stewart is interested in the local language in a broad way. He uses it to stand for the value of an oral culture but, in James Stout Angus' work, we see, for the first time, a writer who focuses closely on the language and sees it as a linguistic resource for its own sake. Angus is more of a craftsman than Stewart but, alongside *Fireside Tales*, Angus' poem 'Eels' is generally seen as a seminal Shetland dialect text.[8]

James Stout Angus was born in Nesting on 20 September 1830, to Hercules Angus, a merchant, and Janet Stout.[9] He was educated at home and school, and was then apprenticed as a joiner in Lerwick. After learning his trade, like hundreds of his contemporaries he went to sea, later returning to Lerwick where he established himself as a housewright. His verse, which had been appearing in the local press since the late 1870s, often under the pseudonym Junda, was collected in 1898 in the volume *Echoes from Kilngrahool* (although 'Eels' wasn't included until the second edition in 1920). The book must have been popular because, by 1954, it had gone through four editions. Angus, as well as writing dialect poetry, was a scholar of the language, publishing *Glossary of Shetland Place-Names* (1910) and *A Glossary of the Shetland Dialect* (1914). The linguistic knowledge evident in these volumes, as we shall see, was put to good use in his poetry.

Although Angus' only book of verse is subtitled *Poems: Mostly in the Shetland* Dialect, from a total of 31 poems, only 14 are in the vernacular. His English verse, which critic Lollie Graham calls 'pretty undistinguished stuff',[10] often shows us the kind of inhospitable landscape we saw in Chalmers' work:

> The solid hills, the everlasting rocks,
>   The caverns desolate and drear,
>   The foamy waters, their wild career
> Shaking the mountains like an earthquake's shocks.
> These were my poetry and music. These
> Had voices heard like distant sounding seas.[11]

James Stout Angus. *Courtesy of Shetland Museum and Archives*

In Chalmers' poetry there is a questioning of the Shetland landscape. She eventually finds ways of seeing and reading it, of appreciating it as an artistic resource, but that is something she has to work towards. Angus does not ask these kind of questions. The grand nature of the place – its cliffs, stacks, and seascapes – are all he needs to write a verse like this. But the true value of Angus' poetry is not to be found in the affirmation of these awesome vistas. This stanza, although it asserts the validity of Shetland as a poetic resource, is perhaps somewhat forgettable. Angus is a rather better poet when, like Chalmers' speaker in 'The Rose of the Rock', he narrows his gaze and focuses on the small, the specific, the particular. He does this in 'The Kokkilurie':

> Dey wir a peerie white kokkilurie 'at grew
>   At da side o da lodberry waa;
> Hit wid open hits lips ta da moarneen dew,
> An close dem at nicht whin da caald wind blew,
> An rowe up hits frills in a peerie roond clew
>   As white as da flukkra snaw. (p.9)

The English verse aims to lay out an awe-inspiring prospect in a high-flown diction but, here, we see Angus work in much more microscopic and exact way. His etymological knowledge enhances the specificity. The flower is not just as white as snow but 'As white as da flukkra snaw', which Angus glosses as 'snow falling in large drops.' It is not simply snow, but a particular kind of snow. His knowledge of local words allows him to achieve a particularity we do not find in his English verse. As Graham writes:

> Angus obviously had a keen ear for these [local] subtleties of syntax and meaning, and had a real love for them, for their intimacy, for their expressiveness and for the poetry hid in the heart of them. It is that love which makes James Stout Angus one of our finest Shetland poets.[12]

Angus' Shetlandic verse represents a creative encounter with a language he studied all his life. And, as we shall discuss below, 'Eels' is his most fertile and adventurous linguistic experiment.

Although it is also in dialect, Angus' poem 'Da Lad 'at Wis Ta'en in Voar', displays less of the lexical exactitude we see in some of his other compositions. That close attention to language is most often in evidence when Angus is writing about the rural environment – its wildlife, the weather – but, in this poem, his subject is something which appears frequently in Shetland's folk history – the taking of men by the Press Gang.[13] Angus writes the poem in the voice of a young woman whose 'bonny young laad' (p.14) has been captured. That the poem is from a female point of view is unusual in Shetland verse of the time which, with the exception of Jessie Saxby, was an overwhelmingly male field. Critic Karen Eunson writes:

Shetland women were largely absent from early Shetland poetry (including Angus') except for their stock roles as "flytin wifes" of abstract love objects but, in 'Da Lad 'at Wis Ta'en in Voar', Angus creates a living, breathing woman whose thoughts and reactions speak to us as well in the 1990s as they would have in the 1890s.[14]

The women in Stewart's book are examples of the types Eunson identifies, but Angus avoids portraying his speaker as either:

> Hit wis i da first o da voar
> Wi da towe o da hidmist snaa;
> Whin a ship cam sailin in ta wir shore
> Frae some place far awa;
> I sat at da window dat day,
> An I stüd i da open door,
> An I heard da rinkle o her iron shain,
> Shü anchored dat near da shore. (p.14)

There are no histrionics. No fainting or tearing of hair. Instead, there is a dignified, somewhat detached and objective description of events. The feelings of the woman are repressed and, because the reader knows what she lives with, the buried emotions are all the stronger in our minds. What is unsaid, because it is unsaid, is the most powerful part of the poem. The last lines, addressed to other sailors who might happen to see the impressed man, bring home the speaker's strength of feeling:

> If ever ye happen ta see
> Or meet wi, ta spaek till, my boanie young laad,
> Will ye tell him dis wird frae me,
> At I'm livin, an lippenin, an still hae a hoop
> At I'll see him afore I dee. (p.15)

At the end of the poem we realise we are listening to an old woman. This is a woman, like Catrine in *The Silver Darlings*, who has endured a long, terrible absence. She has learned to keep her feelings under control, but they are still there. The irregularity of the metre in the second line, where the words seem to overflow the ballad form, reads like a slight quiver in her voice. For a moment it seems as if her emotions might come to the surface, but the regular metre returns and we are left with an ending which she says is hopeful, but which we know is not.

'Eels'

The circumstances in which Angus' best-known poem came to be written are very odd indeed. In 1877 there was a controversy in the *Shetland Times* about whether live eels could be generated by placing horses' or pigs' hairs in a burn.[15]

Angus wrote 'Eels' as a humorous contribution to this debate. Here is how he describes the carcass of a pig which is lying in a watery 'gref' (the pit made when peats are dug):

> He pokit it ower wi' da point o' his staff,
>   An', O, what a whirl an' a giel!
> He said he could hardly believe his e'en,
>   For every hair was a eel.[16]

The image, which is usually omitted in collections of Shetland poetry, is unusual and surreal. The poem then moves to a section more congenial to anthologists:

> Da Lammas spates, laek flugit aets
>   Abün a flacky lauvin',
> Fell frae da lift, wi' a heavy drift,
>   Da sam' as it hed been cauvin'.
>
> Da burns a' raise abün da braes,
>   For stanks and stripes were tümed in;
> Till every lyoag, whaur an eel could oag,
>   A neesick might a swümed in.

We see in the first of these stanzas the specificity of Angus' vernacular verse discussed above. It is not simply rain we are seeing, but heavy showers of rain at a certain time of year. And to use the winnowing of grain as a simile for that rain hitting the ground is unconventional. He then draws back and creates a picture of a land flooded so severely that porpoises can swim across it. The poem continues exuberantly when the peat bank bursts and a seaward deluge ensues:

> An' a' da eels cam' head-owre-heels,
>   Oot wi' da force o' da watter;
> A foon fan' hads among da clods,
>   An brugs, an' moory gutter.
>
> An' doon, doon, doon – grey, green, an' broon,
>   Dey wirmed an' dey wumbled:
> Some sma' an' lang laek a stilke o' tang,
>   An' some laek a baa gaein' heady craw,
>   Till i' da sea dey tumbled.

From the onomatopoeic notes in 'wirmed' and 'wumbled', to the quickening rattle of monosyllables at the start of stanza two, Angus revels in this language. The extra line in the second stanza makes the poem overspill itself, and this, alongside the imperfect rhyme scheme, emphasises the anarchical nature of the eels. The additional line also means the image of eels and gushing water is retained for just a little longer, thus making the dénouement in the sea all the more effective. This high-spiritedness shifts to a different mood in the poem's third section:

> Da surge at da mooth o' da Yalkin gyoes
>   Moans dolefully a' da night;
> Da heaving shorebod comes and goes,
>   Da sautbrak glimmers white.
>
> Da slimy waarblades rise an' fall
>   Wi' a slow an' solemn lauve,
> An' to an' fro gray particks crawl
>   Feedin among da grauve.

This is a contrast and a step back from the tangle of eels. Angus widens his field of vision and gives us a quiet and lyrical picture of the Shetland coastline.

The poem ends when the eels are caught by the crofter who first found the rancid pig:

> D'ir eel-tows hev been set a' night
>   At da rüt o' da waurry baa;
> An' noo dey're come ta tack dem up
>   Afore it comes on ta blaw
> It's an ill sign when da lünabrak
>   Flees ta da girse laek snaw.

The eels, which are now part of the normal life of a Shetland crofter-fisherman, end up being eaten. The poem has moved from its surrealist opening, through a lyrical rendering of the natural environment, to a simple scene in a crofthouse where two people sit down and share a meal.

'Eels' is a poem of different moods and modes, oscillating between lyricism and surrealism. It is carefully controlled and displays Angus' hallmarks of close observation and etymological nimbleness. George Stewart utilises the Shetland language for what it represents, but Angus is interested in what the language can be made to do. For him, the local dialect is a resource in which he could find words unavailable in English. His work in English, as we have seen, aims at grandeur but is, I think it fair to say, somewhat clichéd. In his vernacular work, however, he is the first Shetland poet to really engage creatively with the tongue and try to find, as MacDiarmid puts it, 'names for nameless things.'[17]

Laurence James Nicolson (1844-1901)

Although he was known by the rather grand appellation The Bard of Thule, L.J. Nicolson was not primarily a dialect poet. As W. Fordyce Clark puts it in Nicolson's obituary 'He was never at his best when he essayed the dialect'.[18] His title identifies him closely with the archipelago but, as we shall see, the views he gives us of Shetland are perhaps the least stimulating parts of his oeuvre.

Nicolson was born in Lerwick in 1844, but moved to Edinburgh aged 11, living there until his death.[19] As well as reading his poems at the expatriate societies we have already mentioned, Nicolson contributed to periodicals such as the *Peoples Friend* and *Manson's Shetland Almanac and Directory*, and had his poems set to music and sold as songsheets.[20] In 1894 his verse was collected and published as *Songs of Thule*, and this proved to be his only book.

Although Nicolson lived in the Scottish mainland for most of his life, his poems often look yearningly north. In 'Thule, My Fatherland', for example, he writes:

> Oh sing me a song of the far northern sea,
> Where Thule arises in lone majesty;
> The hills, and the glens, and the wave sounding shore,
> Come back, oh come back, with the memories of yore.[21]

This quatrain, like all of Nicolson's verse, is formally conventional and rather derivative. In the rather pathetic, hopeless note in the first five words of the final line, we see Shetland as a lost idyll, forever fixed in the psyche of a boy uprooted from all he has known. We see the same thing in 'The Bard of Thule':

> He roamed, a boy, the heather hills,
> He wandered by the shore,
> And then awoke in joyous thrills
> The love his young heart bore. (p.10)

For Nicolson, Shetland is an ideal, a longed-for homeland. This view of the isles is accentuated when they are seen against an urban tableau:

> One eve, on city, spire, and dome,
> Light fell he could not see;
> At last! at last! 'mid scenes of home
> In fevered dream was he. (p.11)

The city is evoked through a simple list, but the tone becomes rhapsodic when the imagination produces a view of Shetland. These are poems written by somebody who felt themselves to be in exile.

But, as I say, not all Nicolson's poems are about Shetland and, in my opinion, he is a better poet when not gazing mistily north. His poems about Shetland are all structured around an idealised place but other poems use historical figures and situations as their starting points. Nicolson's non-Shetland poems, which often have a radical, polemical tone, display a concern with the human capacity for cruelty and oppression. These are things he often lays at the door of the Christian faith. For example, in his poem 'Giordano Bruno' which has the explanatory subtitle 'burnt for asserting a plurality of worlds, by order of the Church, Feb. 1600' Nicolson writes:

> 'With greater fear you now pronounce my doom
> Than I unyielding take it from your hands.'
> He stood before them in the council-room
> Erect and free, despite their iron bands. (p.137)

In the face of torture and death, Bruno remains an independent and dignified figure. Even on the pyre he does not look towards any greater power:

> Some had supernal joys before their sight,
> And felt a Saviour's hand within their own;
> He had not this, but fought the final fight,
> And went into the darkness all alone. (p.138)

The object of Nicolson's anger is, in this case, the Catholic church, but it is not only Catholicism he rails against. 'Michael Servetus' (p.150) is a tirade against Calvin and his 'cruel creed' and, in 'Christ in Bonds', it is Christianity in general that Nicolson attacks:

> Behold! ten thousand temples reared on high
>   To Christ of Nazareth,
> And there, the heirs of Freedom, creed-bound lie
>   In living death.
>
> Oh, Satire! greater never saw the light,
>   A people still in chains
> Who cry from out the darkness of their night:
>   'Christ Jesus reigns!' (p.184)

And, even more directly, in 'Blasphemy':

> Fearless Science daring to be free,
> Fire and sword fulfilled the church decree.
> Thought now leaves her to her own dark laws,
> Truth has robbed her of her teeth and claws,
>   No more agony of blood,
>   Shall she give for love of God,
> Learning from her victims if she can,
> Higher, nobler faith, the Love of Man. (p.226)

Nicolson is scathing about the destruction he sees as being caused by Christianity. In the last poem quoted, in contrast to the nostalgic reverie of his Shetland poems, Nicolson celebrates the liberatory potential of modern science. He has no time for God and sees hope in discarding religious ideas. There is an anger and a vigour in these anti-religious poems which makes them stand out. These relatively extreme views, however, were seen less than favourably in Nicolson's day:

The well-known views on religion held by the poet did not commend themselves to the majority, and the inclusion of some poems in his book in which the views expressed were not quite of the orthodox pattern, robbed it of its value in the eyes of some. These, however, are the days of freedom of thought, and there is no need to dwell too much on the debatable portions of the poet's productions.[22]

But it is their lack of orthodoxy which makes these poems worth reading. The radical outlook and iconoclasm which Nicolson sometimes displays is also, as we shall see in the next chapter, a powerful tool in the hands of a slightly younger Shetland poet, J.J. Haldane Burgess.

Jessie M.E. Saxby (1842-1940)

Stewart and Angus both represent important steps in the development of vernacular writing in Shetland. Jessie Margaret Edmondston Saxby, although contemporary with them, stands outside this tradition and is also located at a distance from the canon of Shetland writing established by later critics. She is not mentioned in Lollie Graham's essay 'Shetland Literature and the Idea of Community',[23] nor in his introduction to *A Shetland Anthology* and, in the entire run of the *New Shetlander* magazine (1947-present) there is only a single three page profile of her.[24] But she is, without any doubt, the most prolific and commercially successful Shetland writer. She wrote almost forty books, some of which were reprinted up to eight times, and published hundreds of articles and stories in the popular press, both in Shetland and the British mainland.[25] But, with the exception of her book on local folk traditions, *Shetland Traditional Lore* (1932), she is little read today. Brian Smith, present co-editor of the *New Shetlander*, did write an *Oxford Dictionary of National Biography* entry for her, but this extremely popular and prolific author, who came from the landowning class, and who did not produce much work in dialect, has been completely ignored by the left-leaning Shetland critical establishment.[26] Despite this, in her own day, Saxby, alongside Scott, was the most widely read literary exporter of her native archipelago.

She was born on 30 June 1842 into the wealthy and talented Edmondston family of Unst.[27] She was the ninth of eleven children and there was literary and intellectual precedent in her family. Her uncle Arthur wrote the history *A View of the Ancient and Present State of the Zetland Islands* (1809) that we briefly discussed in Chapter One; her father, Laurence, a doctor, contributed to scientific and ornithological journals; her mother, Eliza, wrote a book of folk stories and general descriptions of Shetland called *Sketches and Tales of the Shetland Islands* (1856); and her brother Thomas wrote *Flora of Shetland* (1845) when just twenty years old. The Edmondston home at Halligarth, Baltasound, was visited by naturalists, linguists, scholars and intellectuals,

George Webbe Dasent, translator of *Njal's Saga*, being a prominent example. Most Shetlanders in the latter half of the century lived in very basic and often overcrowded houses,[28] but Saxby was brought up in a relatively wealthy, cultured and privileged environment.[29] In 1859 she married Henry Linckmyer Saxby, a doctor who had been visiting Unst for several years, with whom she was to have six children, a daughter who died, and five sons. In the early 1870s, the couple took their family and moved to Inverary in Argyll, where Henry was to die in 1873. But Saxby, instead of going back to Unst, chose to go to Edinburgh, where she set about making her living as a writer. As a single mother, far from home, this was a brave thing to do and, despite her privileged background, her early days in the capital cannot have been easy. Soon, however, she was involved in literary circles and was making a success of her chosen career. One of the most important contacts she made was the surgeon (and Doyle's model for Holmes) Joseph Bell. Saxby, as we shall see, became a kind of parental figure for the poet

Jessie M. E. Saxby.   *Courtesy of Shetland Museum and Archives*

Basil Anderson, and Bell, who read her manuscripts and introduced her into Edinburgh literary life, was a similar figure for her.[30] The path towards being a professional writer was smoothed by making the right contacts. Saxby was brave to choose to support her large family in the way she did, but she was also lucky to meet people, like Bell and publishers William and Robert Chambers (who had visited the family in Unst), who were willing to give her support.

Having said this, however, we should not underestimate Saxby herself. She, like her peers Annie S. Swan and R.M. Ballantyne, was a writer who knew her way around the literary world and could write books which sold in large numbers. Saxby collaborated with Swan and Robina R. Hardy on a novel called *Vita Vinctis* (1889) and, in her autobiography *My Life*, Swan wrote of her friend from Shetland:

> There were two women writers in Edinburgh then whom I knew intimately. Mrs Jessie Saxby, who had made a reputation by her songs and stories of the Shetland isles, of which she was a native. She lived in a dear, quaint little house on a slope facing Samson's Ribs, in the Queens Park. She had a unique and striking personality, very clever and charming. There was true Scandinavian fire in her eyes when denouncing wrongs or injustices. She afterwards returned to Shetland, and is alive still. She must be nearly a centenarian by now. I got in touch with her again, after a lapse of half a century, through a casual paragraph in a newspaper.[31]

Saxby and Swan were smart, well-connected, independent Victorian women who knew how to operate in the literary marketplace. They knew their readership and could satisfy the demand for their work. They were both hugely prolific and, even if some of their work might not have stood the test of time, we should admire them as the strong and self-sufficient women they were. Other Shetland writers of the time may have published their work in the *Shetland Times* or read their poems at the expatriate societies in the capital, but Saxby was the first professional author to come from the isles.

Saxby came back to Shetland in the late 1890s. She was granted a piece of land on the family estate and built the cottage Wullvers' Hool, where she died on 27 December 1940. When back in Shetland, her writing became more scholarly, with folklore being one of her favourite subjects. What interests us here, though, is the fiction she produced in the earlier part of her career. I will discuss her novel *Rock Bound* which, in my opinion, should be thought of as one of the best Shetland novels. But it is also an untypical Saxby book. During her years in Edinburgh it was writing adventure stories for boys that paid the bills and fed her family.

Boys' Fiction and Vikings

Saxby's adventure stories are typically set in a remote Shetland island, obviously based on Unst, and relate the scrapes, japes and escapades of groups of teenage boys. The boys are always the sons of ministers and doctors, prone to scaling perilous cliffs to catch seabirds, shooting seals (although they are usually amateur naturalists too), and having many a caper in boats, the handling of which they are always expert in. Also, and this is important for the way Shetland was seen by Saxby's readers, her characters are very enthusiastic about their Norse heritage. Her novel *Viking Boys* opens with an invocation of the Norse past by Yaspsard Adiesen:

> 'How I wish I had lived hundreds of years ago, when the Vikings lived; it must have been prime!'
>
> He was a Shetland boy of fifteen who so spoke, and he was addressing his young sister of eleven.[32]

Yaspsard spends the rest of the novel recreating Viking adventures and raids, enthusiastically abetted by his friends. Although there is often danger for the boys in Saxby's stories – they are liable to get stuck in a cave or stranded on a rock ledge – the fun is carefree and innocent. Yaspsard's Viking escapades are no different. In his boat he makes forays into the neighbouring isle, takes prisoners, pillages and attacks. All of this is done in high-spirited fun but, behind the sport, Saxby develops and broadens her Norse theme. Here we see Yaspsard in discussion with his younger sister Signy:

> He was not unreasonable, and admitted the comfort of the cup which cheers and a weekly mail-bag. He even allowed that the sloop which looked after her Majesty's dues was a tidy little craft, and that a kirk and Sunday service were advantages of no ordinary kind. 'But,' having admitted so much, he said, 'why couldn't we have all that, and still be Vikings? Why not live like heroes? Why not roam the seas, and fight and discover and bring home spoil and wear picturesque garments, as well as go to church and drink tea?'
>
> 'Well, people *do*,' answered Signy. 'There is always somebody exploring and getting into the most terrible scrapes. And don't you often say that the British people are true sons of the Norsemen, and prove it by the way they are always sending out more and more ships, and bringing home more and more riches. As for fighting – oh dear! There was Waterloo not so very long ago; and the papers say, you know, that we are going to fight the Russians very soon. There's always plenty of fighting – if that's what makes a Viking.' (p.3)

We saw in Chapter One how Chalmers incorporates Shetland into nation and Empire, but disassociates her native islands from their Scandinavian past. Saxby, however, combines her theme of ancient Vikingism with contemporary British imperial life. This is the Shetland she was exporting in her many novels: a place which was Scandinavian *and* British (and therefore part of Empire). What Saxby saw as the values of Empire – manliness, valour, heroism, indomitability, a doughty willingness to explore and conquer – were values she saw as being shared by the Norsemen who colonised Shetland from the ninth century, and the British people who were busy colonising half of the globe in the nineteenth. We see this idea expressed even more bombastically in a speech she gave to the Edinburgh Orkney and Shetland Literary Association:

> When the savages of Africa waxed insolent; when England found herself in difficulty with her turbulent folk of the East, did not the old spirit of our race show itself? From Australia, from Canada, from the far west islands of the sea, did not our brothers come to stand shoulder to shoulder with us in defence of the right? Did they not prove themselves true sons of the Norsemen? The traits which our race received from other sources have been almost entirely absorbed and lost in that Scandinavian element; and the Britons of to-day are wonderfully like the sea kings who came and conquered our islands centuries ago.[33]

The racial undertone is distasteful, but the link between British imperialism and Shetland's Norse past is explicitly made. Saxby's Scandinavianism was a way of incorporating Shetland into what she saw as a 'golden age' of progress and imperial adventure.[34]

The desire to write Shetland into Empire through an invocation of the Norse past is somewhat complicated when Scotland is brought into the mix. In her novel *Rock Bound*, which we will discuss in more detail below, a group of young gentry from throughout Scotland gather in Shetland for a holiday. A programme of amusements is arranged, including the following debate:

> They had gone to pic-nic at the ruins of an old castle, and had promised themselves some rare fun in a mock war (of words) about Scottish interlopers and native Scandinavians.[35]

Although the idea is used light-heartedly, Saxby is engaging with a contemporary discourse which asserted that Scotsmen were rapacious incomers who, since Shetland was mortgaged to Scotland in 1469, had oppressed the native Norse population.[36] She sees no paradox in using Shetland's Scandinavian past to mark difference from Scotland but, at the same time, using the idea to incorporate Shetland into the British imperialist project. In the same speech quoted above she says:

> Perhaps before saying more I ought to point out that "national" at this moment means pertaining to Orkney and Shetland *alone*. I always think of our islands as a nation by itself. Why not? Nations are not made by number of inhabitants, or extent of country. Compare Great Britain with other countries in size, or in population, and how insignificant it appears! Yet nations ten times larger fear to meet the power of Britain. To return then, we are here together because we

are of one nationality; because the same sea-breeze made our blood alike; the same influences were at work to mould our characters after a certain uniformity. The same ancestry belongs to all, the same patriotic instinct moves each one of us. (*Heim-Laund*, pp.71-72)

Again and again in her writing, Saxby expresses patriotic fervour for Shetland, espouses the greatness of Empire, and finds in Shetland's Scandinavian heritage the mortar to hold the edifice together. In her conception, like Magnus and Minna Troil's, Shetland had an ancient Norse culture and was only loosely, and reluctantly, tied to Scotland. But, because of the values Saxby sees as being embodied by the Vikings, Shetland was also part of the great contemporary Empire. This is the vision of Shetland that Saxby was exporting to readers across the Empire she was so enthusiastic about.

Rock Bound

Although it is not typical of her oeuvre, Saxby's novel *Rock Bound* is a major Shetland work. It displays a complexity of technique and series of ideas unparalleled, in terms of Shetland writing, during the period in which she was working.

The book differs from her adventure fiction in that it is for adults, and is written in the voice of a woman. We have already commented how women are virtually invisible in the writing of the time but, like Angus' Press Gang poem, *Rock Bound* is an exception. It tells the story of a young, upper-class woman, Inga Henderson, who narrates the tale of her unusual, traumatic and difficult life to a female companion. At the outset Inga signals her narrative intention:

> You have asked for the history of my life, and, with your passionate eyes bent upon my face, I cannot refuse to tell the story, even if I wished to do so. But I want you to know it all, – every portion of the past, which was so often so painful, at all times stirred by the fever-heat of youth, and which is now but a solemn memory. 'Not the *outer* life only,' say your firmly-set, persuasive lips; and at their wilful bidding I open all the doors of my heart. (p.1)

'Not the *outer* life only' strikes rather a modern note. We are to be given access to things deep in Inga's mind, memory and history. To do this Saxby uses the first person throughout and produces an internalised narrative which contrasts strikingly with the rest of her work. Already, by allowing us a view of the inner turmoil and subjective history of a character, especially a female character, Saxby is doing something very different to what other Shetland writers were doing at the time and, I would suggest, different to almost anything a Shetland author has done since.

Inga lives in the small, fictional isle of Vaalafiel with her unloving mother, called the Lady (always with a capital L), and her cousin, the orphaned Laurence

Jessie M. E. Saxby. *Courtesy of Shetland Museum and Archives*

Tarquair, to whom the Lady is much more motherly and warm than she is to her own daughter. Inga's father, so she is led to believe, is dead, both he and Laurence's father having died long ago in mysterious circumstances. Inga, aided and abetted by Aytoun Weir (a Free Kirk minister's son and student doctor from the neighbouring isle), spends most of the novel trying to uncover the secret of her father, which her mother knows but refuses to relinquish. There is some terrible trauma involved in the secret for, whenever she mentions her father, Laurence is sent into a fit of apoplexy, awakening later with no memory of what has happened. Eventually, after some exciting detective work in which Aytoun (with whom Inga is in love) and Inga discover a hidden passage under her house which is connected to the fate of her parent, she agrees, in exchange for more information about the mystery, to satisfy the Lady's dearest wish and marry Laurence. In the meantime, Aytoun discovers that Inga's father is alive and has been imprisoned in a European asylum by the Lady (he is led to the place via drawings done by Laurence inspired by unconscious memories) in order to cover up that he, in a disagreement over Laurence's father's smuggling activities (for which the hidden passage was used), killed Laurence's father, with whom the Lady was secretly in love. Inga's father, after being visited by Aytoun, escapes his prison and comes back to see his daughter. He dies during the visit, alongside his wife, in the heroic act of rescuing Aytoun and Laurence from a shipwreck. Inga and Laurence then become the lairds of the isle. However, the marriage, as the reader knows, is a compromise and it is Aytoun that Inga really wants.

Despite the imperfect nature of her marriage, Inga, during the course of these events, gains a female companion – a young girl who was a kind of surrogate daughter to her father during his confinement. It is to this girl that Inga tells her story. As we shall see, Inga has been made to feel the pressure of a socially defined gender role, but it is only with a female relationship that the gates of self-expression are opened and repressed feelings and emotions can be brought to the surface. Inga says of the girl:

> My sweet, strange sister to whom I have been rehearsing this story and life – who has come into that heart and life like the severed link between the past and the future, uniting the broken chain once more. (p.182)

This girl, who has grown up with Inga's father, allows Inga to find a way towards the missing parent. She is the symbolic daughter that Inga was not allowed to be. But, more importantly, she allows Inga to tell her story. She is the person who allows Inga to speak, to find catharsis in the flow of her words.

If a female relationship is the most positive one in the novel, however, the fact of Inga's gender is, on the whole, oppressive. Saxby investigates gender in this novel in a striking way, and this investigation is connected with what it means to write a novel about Shetland at this time.

Rock Bound is the first novel about Shetland since *The Pirate*. As we discussed in Chapter One, Scott's novel works towards a conclusion in which Minna, who has tried to find her way into an older and more exciting milieu, ends up having to reconcile herself to the world she lives in. Inga has to do the same thing and is something of a kinswoman to Minna. Saxby constantly reminds us of Inga's wild ways and adventurous proclivities. Unsupervised and unloved by her mother, she spends her childhood engaged in rock-climbing and other thrilling pursuits – activities usually enjoyed by boys in Saxby's other books. She is robust, often insensitive to the feelings of others, and goes about life with a vigour and energy most unbecoming for a young lady of her rank and position. Laurence, on the other hand, is weak (both of body and will) and sickly, more fond of tending his flower garden than of anything more manly. In other words, Inga is a naturally masculine character and Laurence is a feminised man. The fact of her gender, however, despite the reversal of traditional roles in the early parts of the novel, becomes too strong for her to resist. She is persistently told by the Lady, and even sometimes by Aytoun, that she must leave behind her wild inclinations and act more like the upper-class lady she is. We see how far her natural propensities have atrophied when she goes for a cliff-top walk with Laurence and Aytoun:

> He [Aytoun] said that he had discovered that the restless spirit of a Viking haunted those cliffs, and drew me by unhallowed spells to listen to its maunderings over a mis-spent existence; and whenever I seemed more than unusually grave, he declared I was meditating a tryst with the ghost. Laurence took up the story, which was merely a burlesque upon my morbidly, high-strung notions, and the two used to follow me when I went for a solitary wander, and with their jokes and mock-solemnity very soon extinguished the sentimentalism, into which a great deal of my romance had degenerated. (p.64)

As she gets older, Inga is forced, like Minna Troil, against her instincts and her own self, to witness her romantic nature wane and fade away, to be replaced by a more conventional female way of being. As the novel progresses she becomes more feminised under the yoke of an imposed and pre-determined gender role. The final nail in the repression of her romantic or masculine self is hammered home on her wedding day:

> I fancied just then that I felt my real, wilful, childish self slip into the "chapelle," steal along the vault, reach its "floating retreat," and glide over the sea slowly – slowly and silently – to a far land. And if *that* was the foolish Inga of old (as I hope it must have been) then someone thoroughly acquainted with the conventionalities took her bouquet from Madge, and disposed fan and gloves with due propriety. Someone whose heart had learned the regulation beat laid a quiet hand on Aytoun's arm and composedly entered the drawing-room.

Someone who intended to proceed in the way a woman should go, and knew exactly what she was expected to do, walked calmly to the side of Laurence, and "before all these witnesses" pledged herself to be his faithful wife. (p.135)

Inga's marriage is a straightforward business decision. She marries Laurence as a bargain with her mother to learn more about her father. There is no romance or passion in what she does. She is not able to resist the position she has been corralled into and, indeed, accepts that role in a calculated way. The subtle switch to the third person works splendidly here and, to use the title of an R.D. Laing book, Inga becomes a divided self.[37] At the moment of her marriage, Inga leaves behind her desire for a more adventurous life and accepts her role as wife or, to be more specific, as the good Victorian wife of a landed gentleman. She leaves behind the world of romance, the world that she, and Minna Troil, have hankered towards, and accepts (uneasily) a new, less exciting and more constrained, kind of existence.

In this novel Saxby asks what kind of story can be set in the islands. Inga must, by necessity, leave behind the world of romance, but this is not entirely a negative step because, by doing this, Saxby enters into a discussion of what it means to be an upper-class woman in Shetland in the late nineteenth century. By giving us access to the mind of Inga, Saxby does this in a way that no other Shetland writer of the time was doing. At this point of her career, she is asking (for we must remember that she went on to produce a vast oeuvre of very different kinds of books), if Shetland should be imagined as a place of romance and adventure, or should her novel be concerned with aspects of modern life, with the problems faced by some of the people who lived there? Inga may be, as Minna was, reduced by this movement but, by considering the problems, desires, wishes, pressures and disappointments of a female character, Saxby makes a significant leap in the development of the novel in Shetland. In *Rock Bound* she does not move towards the social and economic problems Shetlanders were encountering in the 1870s, but rather towards the plight of a young woman of her own social class. Her focus in the book is more psychological than sociological. She looks at the difficulties women like Inga faced in finding means of self-definition and of self-expression – difficulties that had never been discussed by a Shetland author. Inga does not escape the oppressive forces which come to bear on her but, by working in this area and clearing this ground, Saxby produces a proto-feminist novel which is a psychologically astute, original and penetrating exploration of the life of a Shetland woman.

Saxby is one of the only Shetlanders to have made a living as a writer. But, despite her success, she has been largely ignored by local critics. Stewart and Angus and, as we shall see, Basil Ramsay Anderson, all use the local speech extensively, and all write about rural crofting life. These characteristics, as subsequent chapters will show, are prevalent in the work of writers who come after them. Saxby did produce some scholarly work on the vernacular, but she was not working in the same areas as her contemporaries.[38] This should not, however, stop us including her in a study such as this one.

Basil Ramsay Anderson (1861-1888)

Saxby was also important in the short literary career of Basil Ramsay Anderson. Dying of tuberculosis at the age of 26, Anderson is the tragic figure of Shetland's literature. His single book, *Broken Lights* (1888), was edited posthumously by Saxby who, during his life, served as something as a literary mother-figure.[39] In a 1949 article about Anderson, poet and critic William J. Tait writes of *Broken Lights*:

> To say that it is an unequal collection would be a considerable understatement. Most of the poems in English are mere juvenilia and technical exercises in versification which it is hard to believe would have seen the light of day in book form if Basil Anderson had lived a little longer.[40]

In the same article, however, Tait identifies Anderson's 'Auld Maunsie's Crü' as 'the finest poem yet written in the Shetland dialect', and it is with a discussion of this work that we will end this chapter.

Anderson, one of six children, was born into a fisherman's family in Unst.[41] Despite being raised within a few miles of Jessie Saxby's childhood home, the Andersons were at the other end of the social spectrum from the Edmondstons. When Anderson was five, his father was lost at the fishing, leaving five children and a pregnant widow. This must have made life extremely difficult but, according to Saxby, Anderson's mother, Elizabeth, did everything she could to allow her children an education.[42] Her efforts paid off, and Anderson did well at the Baltasound Parochial school, eventually becoming pupil teacher. In 1875 the family moved to Leith, where Anderson attended the same expatriate groups as Stewart and Saxby. The move to Edinburgh may have opened new social and cultural avenues to Anderson, but was ultimately tragic. Elizabeth Anderson had to endure the deaths of four of her children, all from tuberculosis. In a letter to *New Shetlander* editor John Graham, Basil Anderson's niece, Willa Muir,[43] wrote: 'The cutting short of all their lives by T.B. has always seemed to me a frightful waste – what Edwin calls "a waste of inherited virtue."'[44] Contemporary reviews of *Broken Lights*, written in the wake of this waste, understandably praise all of Anderson's work. An anonymous reviewer in the *Shetland Times*, however, commented:

> It is no small service he has done to philology – had he written nothing else – to have produced 'Auld Maunsie's Crü,' which we take leave to consider the best Shetland dialectal verses yet published.[45]

Basil Ramsay Anderson. *Courtesy of Shetland Museum and Archives*

We have already seen this opinion echoed in Tait's article more than sixty years later and it is to the poem itself we now turn.

'Auld Maunsie's Crü' is a sophisticated example of poetic construction. Divided in two parts, Anderson starts small and gradually widens his poetic gaze to include ever larger themes and periods of time. The poem opens with an event which would have occurred all over Shetland in the nineteenth century: 'Auld Maunsie biggit him a crü / Ta growe him kail for mutton brü' (p.78). Maunsie, very prosaically and practically, builds himself a stone enclosure to keep the weather and the rabbits away from his kail plants. As we shall see, however, the poem broadens its theme and its level of abstraction, but this very down to earth (literally down on the earth) element is retained throughout.

Part One then moves through the span of a single day in a Shetland crofting community. The sun rises, moves across the sky, then sets and the section ends with a night-time prayer. Fishermen and crofters use Maunsie's structure as a landmark and as a means of telling the time. 'Auld Elder Rasmie' turns it into a religious symbol when he uses its rabbit-repelling purpose as a metaphor for the protection offered by God against 'dat black kyunnen ca'd da Deil' (p.81). After Maunsie has 'set the steead an honest O' (p.78), or, to put it another way, after he has written the crü on the landscape, it becomes a communal generator of meaning for the people around it. It is the metaphoric centre of the community, a solid object on which shared narratives can be built. As happens in Wallace Stevens' poem 'The Anecdote of the Jar', an empty landscape is marked by a man-made object.[46] What was uniform and unadorned – 'a weel-kent hill', a 'slovenly wilderness' (1.3) – becomes demarcated by the crü and the jar and these things become nodal points in their respective landscapes. An everyday object goes some way towards taming or civilising the brute, primal wildernesses of Tennessee and Shetland. Anderson, though, does what Stevens does not and places people in his poem, people who can read the newly placed symbol. These readings are not ones intended by Maunsie – all he wants to do is grow kail to boil with his mutton – but, as is the way with symbols, the more people read them, the more meanings they accumulate. In Part One the crü is the symbolic locus around which we see a community rotate.

In Part Two, Maunsie and his crü are ageing. Part One gives an account of a single day but, in Part Two, the sweep of time expands. We see seasons, then years, then generations go past, and the cyclical movement of these things – of the agricultural year, of death and rebirth – reflects the circularity of what Maunsie has built. The environment the crü sits in also changes. In Part One, we meet several characters and are told how they use or interpret the central object, but in Part Two we see a much more desolate, lonely landscape. The land and the crü are now the province of animals – 'raikin' dugs', 'cruggin' sheep', 'mares, an' foals, an' pellat rüls' (p.82) – and the reader does not, at this point, see the community which appears earlier in the poem. The crü itself is different too. It is no longer the newly built, meaning generating object of Part One. Here we are given a poignant view of the structure and its creator:

> At last, despite baith sheep an' kail,
> Maunsie an' his crü began ta fail.
> Time booed his rigg, an' shüre his tap,
> An' laid his crü in mony a slap,
> Snug-shorded by his ain hert-stane
> He lost his senses ene by ene,
> Till lyin' helpless, laek a paet,
> Nor kail, nor mutton he could aet;
> So dee'd, as what we a' maun dü,
> Hae we, or hae we no', a crü. (pp.82-83)

The crü and Maunsie are inextricably joined. As a younger man (although he is always *Auld* Maunsie) he was able to build a crü which could act as a source of meaning for people. As he ages, so does his crü. As he becomes less able physically, the crü becomes of less symbolic use and then:

> An', strange ta tell, da nicht he dee'd
> His crü, in raabin' ta da steead
> Laid stiff and stark his yearald rül,
> A' mangled in a bluidy bül (p.83)

The crü, on Maunsie's passing, falls down, killing his pony as it does. A supernatural note is introduced here when a corbie and a crow hover over Maunsie's broken walls and the speaker tells us that 'A sowl wis flit fae aert dat day' (p.83). Despite this unearthliness, the very practical theme which is present throughout the poem is retained, when the birds do what they do naturally and eat from the horse's carcass. The negotiation between levels of abstraction is skilfully handled. We shift between images of death, the ebbing away of the crü's symbolic ability, the passing of a human soul, to the brutal but commonplace images of an agricultural community.

After Maunsie has gone there is no sentimentality and, again, the inevitable, cyclical movement of the seasons is captured:

> But years gaed by as aye de'r geen, –
> Da winter white, da simmer green, –
> Da voars aye sawn, da hairsts aye shorn,
> Aye some ane dead, aye some ane born [...]. (p.83)

Time passes. People die. Crops are planted. Winter brings snow. Children are born. There is a simplicity and, again, a practicality in these end-stopped lines that emphasises the fortitude or, perhaps, the fatalism of a crofting community living not far above the subsistence level. In the face of adversity and death, there is nothing to do but get on with things. Nothing will be gained by complaining. Again, however, we see the human desire toward symbolic abstraction:

> So after bein' named by a'
> 'Da crü o' him 'at's noo awa''
> (Lord rest his sowl!) it cam ta geng
> By da füle name o' "Ferry-ring." (p.84)

The crü has now passed into the world of folklore and myth. Despite the prosaic reasons for its construction, it is still used as a symbolic object. The speaker distances himself from this reading, but the crü, and the reader, have come a long way from the simple stone circle introduced in line 3.

The poem ends as the crü deteriorates into nothing but a few stones 'whaur hill-baess could claw' (p.84). The land was unadorned before the crü appeared and, by the end of the poem, it has returned to almost the same state. Human structures, like humans themselves, are born and, as time washes over them, they pass. The land reclaims whatever man imposes on it. The poem has come full circle but does not end on a bleak note. The community we saw revolving around the crü in Part One may have forgotten the structure, but the practical ethos of the crofting community provides consolation when we are told that 'later folk had mair ta dü / Dan mind Auld Maunsie or his crü' (p.84). Despite the temporality of life, solace is found in the work which must always be done.

In 'Auld Maunsie's Crü' Basil Anderson produces a kailyard poem which is anything but Kailyard in its execution. Negotiating skilfully between abstract images and ideas, and a very rooted, practical, down-to-earthness, Anderson's poem is the one of the most complex and intelligently crafted Shetland poems. It is a significant reference point for what can be done in the local language and represents a coming of age and an evolutionary leap in Shetland's literature.

Conclusion

In the work of Margaret Chalmers, landscape provides the primary term of engagement with Shetland. In the writers discussed in this chapter, however, the local language becomes the most prominent characteristic and, in a few decades at the end of the century, we see that language develop as a valid literary idiom. In Chapter One we looked at the two little dialect poems of Thomas Irvine but, in the work of Stewart, Angus and Anderson, we see writers put the language to significant use for the first time. Stewart is confident and affirmative in his use of the vernacular, but it is in the work of Angus and Anderson that we begin to see the language used in complex and challenging ways. But the work these writers did, important though it was, adds up to only a few books and poems. Of all the writers discussed in this chapter, Saxby was the only one to produce a large oeuvre and maintain a literary career. Her work hardly engages with the language at all (not that this is a reason to criticise her), and her vision of Shetland, like Scott's, construes the place as having a unique and venerable Scandinavian character. In the work of J.J. Haldane Burgess, the subject of our next chapter, we find many of the ingredients that characterise the work of the writers discussed above. He has the linguistic inventiveness of Angus, the iconoclasm of Nicolson, the ambition of Anderson and, like Saxby, he was enthusiastic about Shetland's Norse past. Although he did not write as much as she did, his work introduces a new level of intellectualism and sophistication into the literature we have seen emerge.

NOTES

1. William Donaldson, *Popular Literature in Victorian Scotland: Language, Fiction and the Press* (Aberdeen: Aberdeen University Press, 1986), p.35.
2. William Findlay, 'Reclaiming Local Literature: William Thom and Janet Hamilton', in *The History of Scottish Literature*, vol.3, ed. by Douglas Gifford (Aberdeen: Aberdeen University Press, 1989), pp.353-375.
3. As this book goes to press, a long story containing significant sections of dialect prose has emerged. 'The Elopement at Grevavoe' was published in the *New Monthly Magazine* in 1862, predating much of the material discussed in this chapter. The authorship of the piece is unclear, but Brian Smith's article 'Goings on at Grevavoe' in Unkans 41 (December 2013) discusses some of the possibilities. Further research into this intriguing work is required.
4. SA, D9/240-243, Material concerning George Stewart, 1889-1952.
5. See material about these societies in scrapbook of Shetland antiquary and historian Gilbert Goudie. SA, D6/292/24. Similar associations existed in Glasgow, Chicago, and Wellington. There was also an organisation based in Edinburgh called the Orkney and Zetland Association, which gave financial support to scholars from the northern isles.
6. See, for example, letter from L.J. Nicolson to J.J. Haldane Burgess, 5 November 1891. Nicolson describes a meeting of the Leith Thule Club, at which he occupied the chair. George Stewart was there and several of Nicolson's poems were recited by the attendees. SA, D2/2/7.
7. G.S.L. [George Stewart], *Shetland Fireside Tales; or, The Hermit of Trosswickness* (Edinburgh / London: Edinburgh Publishing Company / Simpkin, Marshall & Co., 1877), pp.26-27.
8. Brian Smith, 'Eels: Strange Masterpiece', *New Shetlander*, 230 (Yule 2004), 29-30.
9. [Anon.], Obituary of James Stout Angus, *Shetland Times*, 29 December 1923, p.4. [Anon.], Account of James Stout Angus tribute night, *Shetland Times*, 5 April 1957, p.7.
10. Laurence Graham, 'James Stout Angus', *New Shetlander*, 15 (March-April 1949), 24-25.
11. James Stout Angus, *Echoes from Klingrahool: Poems: Mostly in the Shetland Dialect*, 3rd edn (Lerwick: T. & J. Manson, 1926), p.69.
12. Graham, 'James Stout Angus', 24.
13. See J.D.M. Robertson, *The Press Gang in Orkney and Shetland* (Kirkwall: Orcadian, 2011).
14. Karen Eunson, 'James Stout Angus – Our First Dialect Poet', *New Shetlander*, 203 (Voar 1998), 21.

15. Smith, 'Strange Masterpiece', 29.
16. [James Stout Angus], 'Eels', *Shetland Times*, 22 December 1877, p.3.
17. Hugh MacDiarmid, 'Gairmscoile', in *Complete Poems*, vol.1, ed. by Michael Grieve and W.R. Aitken (Manchester: Carcanet, 1993), pp.72-75 (p.74).
18. SA D1/135/p.305, W. Fordyce Clark, obituary of L.J. Nicolson, no provenance, 30 June 1901.
19. For Nicolson's biography see SA D1/135/p.303, [Anon.], 'Minor Scottish Poets – Laurence J. Nicolson', *Glasgow Weekly Mail*, undated.
20. See, for example, L.J. Nicolson and Thomas Manson, *Da Last Noost: A Shetland Folk Song* (Lerwick: T. & J. Manson, 1891). L.J. Nicolson and William Yorston, *A Shetland Lullaby* (Lerwick: T. & J. Manson, 1896). George Stewart and Jessie Saxby also produced sheet-music versions of some of their poems.
21. Laurence James Nicolson, *Songs of Thule* (Paisley / London: Alexander Gardner, 1894), p.12.
22. [Anon.], Obituary of L.J. Nicolson, Shetland News, 6 July 1901, p.5.
23. Laurence Graham, 'Shetland Literature and the Idea of Community', in *Shetland's Northern Links: Language and History*, ed. by Doreen J. Waugh (Edinburgh: Scottish Society for Northern Studies, 1996), pp.52-65.
24. L.S., 'Profiles from the past xxiv – Jessie M.E. Saxby', *New Shetlander*, 70 (Hairst 1964), 12-14.
25. For Saxby's bibliography see J. Laughton Johnston, *Victorians 60° North: The Story of the Edmondstons and Saxbys of Shetland* (Lerwick: Shetland Times, 2007), pp.316-328.
26. Brian Smith, 'Saxby, Jessie Margaret Edmondston (1842-1940)', in *Oxford Dictionary of National Biography* <http://www.oxforddnb.com/view/article/55498> [Accessed 27 Nov 2008].
27. Johnston, *Victorians*, pp.252-284.
28. See Ian Tait, *Shetland Vernacular Buildings 1600-1900* (Lerwick: Shetland Times, 2012).
29. See Biot Edmondston and Jessie M.E. Saxby, *The Home of a Naturalist* (London: James Nisbet & Co., 1888), pp.7-8.
30. [Jessie M.E. Saxby] *Joseph Bell: An Appreciation by an Old Friend* (Edinburgh / London: Oliphant, Anderson & Farrier, 1913).
31. Annie S. Swan, *My Life: An Autobiography* (London: James, Clarke and Co., 1947), p.32-33.
32. Jessie M.E. Saxby, *Viking Boys* (London: James Nesbit & Co., 1892), p.1.
33. Jessie M.E. Saxby, *Heim-Laund and Heim-Folk* (Edinburgh: R. & R. Clark, 1892), p.69.
34. Jessie M.E. Saxby, *Daala-Mist; or, Stories of Shetland* (Edinburgh: Andrew Eliot, 1876), p.303.
35. Jessie M.E. Saxby, *Rock-Bound: A Story of the Shetland Isles* (Edinburgh: Thomas Gray and Co., 1877), p.121.
36. See Brian Smith, 'Udal Law: Salvation or Romantic Fiction?', *Shetland Times*, 3 October 2003, pp.18-19.
37. R.D. Laing, *The Divided Self: An Existential Study in Sanity and Madness* (London: Penguin, 1990).
38. See Jessie M.E. Saxby, 'Notes on the Shetland Dialect', *Saga-Book of the Viking Club*, vol.4, pt.2 (1906-1910), 65.

39. Basil Ramsay Anderson, *Broken Lights: Poems and Reminiscences of the Late Basil Ramsay Anderson*, ed. Jessie M.E. Saxby (Edinburgh / Lerwick: R. & R. Clark / C. & A. Sandison, 1888). In her introduction, Saxby discusses her relationship with Anderson.
40. William J. Tait, 'Basil R. Anderson and Auld Maunsie's Crü', *New Shetlander*, 16 (May-June 1949), 26-33.
41. John J. Graham, 'Basil Ramsay Anderson', *New Shetlander*, 57 (Summer 1961), 10-12.
42. Saxby, Introduction to *Broken Lights*, p.xiii.
43. Willa Muir was the daughter of Basil Anderson's younger brother Peter. See Mark Ryan Smith, 'From Kafka to Maunsie's Crü: Willa Muir and Basil Ramsay Anderson', *Coontin Kin*, 79 (Simmer 2011), 13-15.
44. SA, D1/152/1/1, Letter from Willa Muir to John Graham, 12 March 1955.
45. [Anon.], Review of *Broken Lights*, by Basil Ramsay Anderson, *Shetland Times*, 14 July 1888, p.3.
46. Wallace Stevens, 'Anecdote of the Jar', in *The Norton Anthology of American Literature* vol.D, 6th edn, ed. by Nina Baym and others (New York / London: W.W. Norton & Company, 2003), p.1241.

CHAPTER THREE

J.J. HALDANE BURGESS (1862-1927)

Introduction

James John Haldane Burgess is one of Shetland's most revered people. On his death in 1927 he was given a public funeral and, today, there is a street in Lerwick named after him. For later writers, Burgess and his work became touchstones in Shetland's literature. Lollie Graham considered him to be 'Shetland's only major poet'.[1] Brydon Leslie, in a discussion of how Burgess influenced Shetland's Up Helly Aa fire festival, writes that 'his legacy has been borne by the children of Lerwick, and its glory has indeed rolled down the ages.'[2] And, for John Peterson, picking up on the blindness which afflicted Burgess, he was 'the blind man who saw in the dark; who could not see across the road but saw across centuries'.[3]

Burgess, the son of a tailor, was born in Lerwick and, apart from his university years in Edinburgh, lived in the town all his life.[4] He was educated at a private school, then at the Anderson Educational Institute, where he rose to become pupil-teacher. In 1881 he entered Glasgow University's bursary competition and came first – there were 607 candidates from across Scotland and Burgess finished 47 marks ahead of the student in second place.[5] By the time he went to Edinburgh University in 1886 he was already the author of several books published in Shetland, including, as we saw in Chapter One, the first book ever printed in the isles. He must have had high hopes of a successful academic or literary career but, during his time in the capital, he went blind, an event which Lollie Graham, Burgess' most dedicated critic, called 'the great calamity of his life'.[6] Burgess nevertheless graduated M.A. in 1889 after completing his exams orally. He then embarked on a divinity degree, but did not finish the course.[7] Back in Lerwick, he earned his living as an author and private teacher, schooling pupils in mathematics and classics. His great scholarly interest, however, was languages. He was fluent in all the Scandinavian tongues, many European ones, and had knowledge of several Asian languages. He was also a champion of Esperanto, producing a complete translation into that language of his most important book, *Rasmie's Büddie*.[8]

His contact with young men in Lerwick was political as well as scholarly. Brian Smith writes:

In the 1890s, under the influence of Robert Blatchford's popularizing work, and of young Shetlanders who had sampled the propaganda of the Social Democratic Federation in Edinburgh, he became a Marxist.[9]

In the years following Burgess' return to Shetland, younger people interested in left-wing politics visited his house to talk, debate and learn. George Stewart and Basil Anderson may have found the cosy expatriate meetings in Edinburgh culturally stimulating but, for Burgess, there was a much more radical atmosphere of intellectual ferment to be found at home. As Smith says, Burgess was politically influenced by younger men and, for the rest of his life, he was a paternal and sagely presence for left-leaning Lerwegians.

He was also a prolific writer. In addition to the books we are about to discuss, his papers include dozens of short stories (all typed by Burgess, despite his blindness), and a substantial number of journals in which he was published.[10] Burgess did utilise some of the themes we identified in the last chapter – concentration on the rural environment, Shetland's Norse past – but his writing represents a fresh, exciting and influential development in Shetland's literature. Burgess, in his own time, for later writers, and for this study, is a key figure.

Rasmie's Büddie

Rasmie's Büddie, first published in 1891, a year after Burgess' return from Edinburgh, is one of the most important collections of Shetland dialect writing. It is the first book published entirely in the vernacular and it substantially extends the poetic range and ambition of the Shetland tongue. L.G. Scott, who knew Burgess well, wrote of the book:

> I asked him why he wrote the poems in the dialect. He said he was thinking of issuing a book of poems, when he heard some fellows from the south saying that great thought or feeling could not be expressed in a dialect.[11]

The poems, written in the voice of the old crofter Rasmie, are a response to this notion. In Rasmie, Burgess gives us a character who speaks with intelligence and eloquence, but in a voice which is rooted in everyday things. As Anderson does in 'Auld Maunsie's Crü', *Rasmie's Büddie* shows that the local speech can be used in complex, abstract and challenging ways. Burgess' great achievement in *Rasmie's Büddie*, however, is to sustain the demotic voice over an entire volume, and to extend the thematic and intellectual reach of Shetland dialect poetry. But what kind of voice do we hear in the book? And what kind of things does it speak about?

Although Burgess never entered the ministry, religion remained a central concern. Several poems – 'Tangle Bells'[12] and 'See Ye' (p.37) for instance – are straightforward poems of religious praise, as is 'Nazarene':

> An I hear in music fallin
> Ower da dunder o Life's sea,
> Frae da heichts Dy sweet voice callin
> Ta da true hert, – 'Follow Me!' (p.14)

The language is speechlike, quotidian even – addressing God with the familiar form Dy, instead of the more formal You, for instance – but there is a quiet, assured spirituality in these lines.

In 'Da Restit Fire' he speaks of religion in domestic terms:

> Yiss, heth! inta da louwin sun
>   Da whirlin starns 'ill buch,
> T'o we're no dere ta see da fun,
>   I kno dey'll be a steuch.
>
> Da Pooer 'at sun an starns hurls –
>   Da haand 'at canna tire –
> In aess o hael-an-hadden worls
>   'Ill rest Aald Nater's fire. (p.54)

The motif of resting or covering the fire during the night, which is repeated throughout the poem, always generating subtly different meanings and resonances, is used as a metaphor for the end of the world. God, as Lollie Graham nicely puts it, is seen 'as a kind of cosmic crofter'.[13] Rasmie's images, although they range spiritually and philosophically far, are drawn from the commonplace objects and routines of the croft.

The most challenging religious poem in the book is 'Da Blyde-Maet'. It opens with these lines:

> Whin Aedie üt da blyde-maet for himsell
> An her, pür lass, 'at dan belanged ta him,
> Whin nicht in Aeden wis a simmer dim
> Afore he wis dreeld oot ta hok an dell,
> Hed he a knolidge o da trüth o things,
> Afore da knolidge koft wi what's caa'd sin? (p.100)

Rasmie speculates about the implications of the fall for Adam at the moment of his transgression. He wonders if Adam was permitted a glimpse of 'trüth', if he was allowed to listen to 'da music 'at da starrins sings' (p.100). He asks if, at the instant of his sin, whether Adam was allowed to experience the divine before being exiled from Eden. Again, 'hok an dell' are words which come straight from the croft, and Burgess' achievement in this poem is to use this colloquial language in a theologically probing way.

The second half of the poem broadens out from Eden into a discussion of the relationship between the temporality of man and the eternity which only God knows. For those who care to look, 'Time is spraechin, laek a fraeskit

J. J. Haldane Burgess

J. J. Haldane Burgess. *Courtesy of Shetland Museum and Archives*

bairn, / Ipo da bosim o Eternity' (p.101). Time, which, along with sin and the necessity of physical labour on the land, came into existence after da blydemaet was taken, is nothing but a nettlesome child when seen in relief against the everlasting being of God. The poem is ultimately hopeful, however, that humanity can find 'mony anidder, deeper, graander life' (p.101), and that the temporal and the eternal can achieve some kind of concordance when Rasmie tells us, in a startling and original image, that 'Time sall learn trou aa dis weary strife / Ta sook da fu breests o Eternity' (p.101).

These poems show Rasmie as a man who thinks deeply about spiritual things. They are all quiet, introspective pieces and, in them, we see Burgess take on the denigrating ideas he overheard about the potential of the local tongue. His use of Christian theme takes a different tack in what has become one of Shetland's best-known and most-loved poems, 'Scranna'. Unlike the poems we have looked at so far, 'Scranna' is dramatic, exuberant and rumbustious. It tells the story of the devil coming to Rasmie's croft at Scranna in an attempt to claim the old crofter's soul. It opens with a narrator:

> Da Deil he cam doon ta da hill-daek o Scranna,
> Bit grinnd, or sma openeen, or slap dere he saa na;
> An sae, wi a glumse, an a deevil's ain glower,
> He spat on his lüfs, an clamb tentily ower. (p.1)

Rasmie then takes over the telling of the tale and, initially, retains the contemplative mood of other poems in the volume:

> I wis sittin mi laen bi da sheek o da fire,
> Wi mi een on da spunks as dey aye loupit higher,
> Dan slokkit an fell – I tinkin, 'Aless!
> Sae man an his glory, jüst aess, aye ta aess' [...]. (p.1)

As he does in 'Da Restit Fire', Rasmie looks at the flames and speculates about human mortality. When the unwelcome visitor appears, however, this solitary, meditative tone is left behind. Soon after admitting 'A jantleman, braa-laek and weel cled afore' (p.3), Rasmie cannily figures out who his guest really is. He doesn't let on right away, though, and he and Satan, as they sit on either side of the fire, engage in some verbal jousting. The devil, although he tries not to, keeps letting slip his real identity. He feels cold, despite the fire. His clothes shift and long nails or a cloven hoof are glimpsed. He tries to tempt the teetotal Rasmie with a flask of drink. There is good dramatic tension built up in this section and, as the characters speak, there is an important point is to be found in their respective use of language. When the devil knocks on the door, Rasmie tells us that the voice he hears is in 'da Engleeis tongue' (p.2), and this is the language the devil uses as they sit beside the fire. Rasmie uses the vernacular, and the English speech (the only English in the whole book) becomes the language of dissembling. The devil is educated and eloquent but, to his core, is a liar. His dishonesty reaches its terrible extent when he reveals he is a minister of the church:

> An his een lookit at me as sharp laek as preens:
> Dan he says, 'Look at me, I've been years in the Kirk, –
> I admit you may think I got in by a quirk –
> I dispense the Communion, I preach, I baptise,
> You can manage it all (with a few handy lies,
> As some people call them in vulgar parlance,
> Reservations *we* term them, we men who advance).' (pp.5-6)

The devil has progressed in the church by clever use of the wicked rhetoric he employs while parleying with Rasmie. In the poems looked at above, Burgess expresses what he sees as true reverence for God in the words of a Shetland crofter. Here he associates false piety and nefarious social progress with English, and honesty with the vernacular. And placing the devil as a clergyman also shows an iconoclasm which may have shocked more pious readers in the early 1890s.

As Satan tempts and taunts Rasmie, the crofter becomes angrier and angrier until he explodes: '"Ye scoondril!" says I, an I raise ta mi fit, / "Oot o dis wi dee! Hent disell!! *Heckle noo*! FLITT!"' (pp.8-9). The series of interjections increase the tempo of the line and mark a turn from verbal to physical conflict. Rasmie sets his dog Seemun on the devil, then enters the fray himself. In a somewhat slapstick moment they exchange blows, the devil falls in the fire, and his tail emerges from his clothes. Quarter of an hour later, Rasmie gets the better of his enemy and dumps him unceremoniously outside, trapping the devil's tail in the door as he slams it shut. The devil 'sprikkles laek sin, and he plüts wi a wail, / "Ah! Look oot, min, Rasmie, ye're brukkin mi tail!"' (p.12). Satan now speaks in dialect. His wheedling approach of the fireside gives way to a more straightforward form of speech. He is even more direct in his parting shot to Rasmie: '"Nee! Rass-moos! I'll get dee! Doo's sure ta be damned!"' (p.13). The devil is still the devil, but now his intentions are explicit. In this poem, Burgess associates the English tongue with artifice, and uses the Shetland language to represent honesty, even if that honesty is fiendish. The devil threatening to damn Rasmie is dreadful but, in his ire, he is a less menacing and malign creature than he was when trying to goad with his fine words. The English language is what Rasmie's hellish interlocutor employs for wicked and disingenuous means, whereas the Shetland tongue is what bubbles to the surface when empty rhetoric fails.

'Scranna' is an unusual poem in Burgess' oeuvre, and in the Shetland poetic corpus generally. It moves away from the quiet thoughtfulness and lyricism of some of his other poems, and is much more extrovert and dramatic. It is also very different to what had been written previously by Shetland poets (although, in its ebullience, some comparison may perhaps be made with 'Eels'). Burgess' use of the Shetland language in this poem shows all the verve, confidence and willingness to experiment which characterises his early work.

If 'Scranna' displays a dislike of artifice, and a suspicion of the use of English by a dialect speaker, several other poems in the book show a discontentedness with contemporary society. 'Da Wy O It' (p.18), 'Da Plaesir Yacht' (p.49), and 'Da Picter' (p.107), for example, show a distaste for what their speaker perceives as contemporary decadence and licentiousness. Burgess' poems never celebrate the world he lives in. That world is also considered in 'Da Oobin Wind', but in a less didactic way:

> Aa around I hear da oobin
> O a wind o Discontent,
> Troo aa-thing 'at man is biggit
> I' da glory o his strent [ ]. (p.57)

There are no certainties in the modern world, but some consolation is possible:

> Ev'ry sowl his cross is bearin,
> Aa da Eart's a Calvary,
> Why sood ony type or symbol
> Hoid reality frae me?
> Rodd ta paece trou fields o fancy?
> Trüth himsell 'ill steek da grinnd [...]. (pp.57-58)

Truth is accessible to every human being, provided they do not allow their journey towards it to be obstructed. Rasmie goes on:

> He's a fūl 'at maks a biggin,
> Be it hoose, or law, or creed,
> Tinkin it can staand for ever,
> Ticht anyoch for human need. (p.59)

Rasmie's conception of religious truth is an individualistic one. He gives no credence to the symbolic structures humans have created to take them closer to God. For him, 'Faith is mair din poopits wat o' (p.59). Knowledge and Truth are matters for the autonomous thinker and, in the character of the self-reliant, intelligent crofter, the ideal Truth-seeker is found. The crofter, living independently, in alignment with his environment, is able to deal with the world on his own terms. Rasmie is assured in his use of language, and is also secure within the literal and metaphoric world of the croft. Unlike Anderson's Maunsie, Rasmie is not resistant to symbolism. Maunsie builds his crü and it becomes, irrespective of his intentions, a symbolic generator for the people who engage with it. Rasmie, as we have seen, always couches metaphor or symbol in terms of his immediate surroundings and the world he knows. In Burgess' poetry, it is not symbolism per se which is dangerous, but the wrong kind of symbolism which is to be treated with suspicion. In his novel *The Treasure of Don Andres*, as I will discuss, we see an explicit anti-Catholic agenda at work and, in his verse, one can see a Presbyterian misgiving about recondite systemisation. For Rasmie, metaphors and symbols come from the practical and straightforward microcosm of the croft, not from elaborate creed or esoteric doctrine.

Rasmie has little time for organised religion, and Burgess himself may have given up on entering the ministry but, as we have observed, from the 1890s until the end of his life, he became a fervent supporter of another kind of creed. Much has been made of his leftist politics and, for some twentieth-century writers, Burgess' Marxism has contributed greatly towards his veneration. Lollie Graham, for example, writes:

> Burgess' socialism is never far below the surface in his poetry. It was probably one of the chief reasons why he chose the dialect as his medium. A keen philologist, he loved the old despised language for the linguistic riches it held for him, for the poetry, the warmth, the humour it contained. But he also loved the ordinary working folk whose tongue it was. They too were neglected and looked down upon. For him, they too had a tremendous potential. These twin inspirations combined in *Rasmie's Büddie* to give us some of the finest verse yet written in our island tongue.[14]

For Graham, who was firmly on the left, the attention Burgess gives to the life, language and environment of the crofter all stem from his commitment to socialist principles. By Burgess' own token:

> I belong to the working class and my entire sympathy has always been with the working class – the only class that justifies its own existence. I think every person ought to do a fair share of socially necessary labour. At the time when I wrote *R.B* I was an Ultra-Radical rapidly evolving into a Socialist.[15]

As we have seen, the poems in *Rasmie's Büddie* focus on the plebeian world of the Shetland croft. This letter, however, was written in 1907, sixteen years after the volume was first published. The book was published for the third time in 1913, and this edition includes two new poems which have a more overtly politically didactic tone than those looked at so far. In 'Da Trid Ootset' for instance, Burgess writes:

> Da new time cries ta you, wirkers:
>   'Lie nae langer laek da bass;
> Waaken, rise, an mak da nation
>   Wan great noble wirkin-class.'[16]

The second additional poem, 'Suffrage', also engages with a contemporary political issue, speaking emphatically in favour of female enfranchisement.

These two poems, and several other works from late in Burgess' career – the posthumous *Young Rasmie's Kit* (1928), which combines socialism and Norse myth, and the poem 'Onward: Labour Lines', for example – show the extent to which socialist doctrine came to influence his work.[17] With discussions of Marx taking place in his house, the ideas Burgess exchanged with the young men who came to visit him made their way into his verse. But this image of Burgess as an elder statesman and father of the political left in Lerwick is an image from some time after the publication of *Rasmie's Büddie*. In the first edition of the book, however, an angry and critical tone is sometimes evident, and an interest in left-wing thought can be detected:

> Bit Laabir, feth! 'ill conquer yet
> In spite o aa, I view –
> Dis aristocracies is bit
> Da dokkin on da skroo. (p.80)

His parody of Tennyson's 'Jubilee Ode' is also sharply critical of inequality:

> An weel I mind da hoops I hed o dee,
> O aa da grit an nobble things du'd dü,
> Whin du cam up ta be a wife; hoo du'd no bear
> Ta view da poor wi his aald rivlin girnin at da tae […]. (p.34)

In the poems studied above, we have seen how Burgess utilises the images and objects of the croft to create a contemplative and thoughtful poetry. Here he uses the same source of imagery to castigate and attack Queen Victoria for the chasm between rich and poor she represents. There is no denying the radical and subversive tone of these poems but, when we look at the volume in its entirety, socialism is not a prominent or sustained theme. Burgess' evolution into an influential Shetland socialist has perhaps been read back into his early work. Retrospective interpretations of his poetry by critics such as Graham, Burgess' own comments about his political development, and the additions to the third edition of *Rasmie's Büddie* have all contributed to the conception of Burgess as a left-wing poet. But, despite his later political position, *Rasmie's Büddie* does not set out to propagate socialist doctrine. His later verse, in a rather crude way, does do this, but it is in his debut volume of poems that we find his most significant contribution to local writing.

In terms of its thematic range and its level of intellectualism, *Rasmie's Büddie* goes beyond anything a Shetland writer had produced before. Despite the sometimes less than favourable view of contemporary society, the poems are full of optimism and energy, of linguistic adventure and willingness to experiment with what, in 1891, was still a relatively young poetic idiom. This sense of exploration and fun is perhaps surprising when we bear in mind that the poems were written soon after Burgess had lost his sight, given up on the ministry, and returned to Shetland. But, despite these difficult personal circumstances, *Rasmie's Büddie* is a major step forward in the development of Shetland's literature.

Novels

Rasmie's Büddie is the book that has sustained Burgess' reputation and, until William J. Tait started to write in the 1930s, it represents the most inventive and intelligent use of the Shetland language by any writer. It is, however, only one component of Burgess' work and, for the rest of this chapter, I would like to concentrate on the four novels he wrote: *The Viking Path* (1894) and *The Treasure of Don Andres* (1903), which are both historical novels; and *Tang* (1898) and the unpublished *A Temporary Marriage* (undated), which are both set closer to Burgess' own time.

The Viking Path and *The Treasure of Don Andres*

In Burgess' obituaries, *The Viking Path* was given a high position in his oeuvre. The notice in the *Shetland News* said:

> *The Viking Path: A Tale of the White Christ*, was the next important work [after *Rasmie's Büddie*] undertaken by Mr Burgess. It was published by Messrs Blackwood, Edinburgh, in 1894, and may be said to be the crown and glory of all his writings.[18]

Burgess, unlike Saxby, does not utilise old Norse themes to make a point about the political or racial status of contemporary Shetland. Instead, he draws on his extensive reading of the sagas and, perhaps, his reading of the many Viking novels which were appearing at the time, to create a thematically complex and exciting historical novel.[19]

The Viking Path is set in the ninth century, at a time when King Harald Fairhair was engaged in the unification of Norway. It focuses on a group of Vikings under the rule of Jarl Alsvid who, unwilling to submit to the new king, travel to Shetland to live as outlaws. While there, they continue to behave as they have always done, setting out every summer to raid and pillage. But, on the night they leave for Shetland (or Hjaltland, as they call it) Alsvid's brother Sigmund is slain, along with his wife and ship's crew, by the king's man Jarl Aegir. This act instigates the necessity of revenge – something which will eventually come to influence the life of Sigmund's son Hermod, who survives the attack and is brought up in the household of Aegir, Alsvid's nemesis. The theme of obligation to vengeance runs through the novel. The Viking way of life, with the need for retribution and the impossibility of forgiveness, envelops the individual and leaves no room for independence or agency. The only way to break free from this cycle comes through belief in a different god than Odin, and it is Burgess' investigation of the confrontation between faiths which makes the novel into something more than a blood-and-thunder Viking romp.[20]

When the Vikings come to Shetland they discover that a former comrade, Thorvald, is living there as a Christian convert. Instead of a longhouse, he lives alone in a hut, grows vegetables and worships Christ. As time goes on he gains influence in Alsvid's home and starts to preach the new faith to some of the lower-status members of the community. There is an irreconcilable gap established between Thorvald's beliefs and the faith of Jarl Alsvid. The Jarl has worshipped Odin, Thor and Frey all his life and will never change. He reproaches the new faith as unmanly and fit only for 'nithings', as the cowardly are termed by the Vikings. Thorvald, who was a mighty warrior, has, in the Jarl's view, become pitiful and womanlike and, because of his conversion, is now at the very bottom of the Viking hierarchy. The beliefs of Thorvald will always be antithetical to those of Alsvid and there can be no mediation between the two positions. Alsvid's faith in the old gods and the Viking way of life remain unshakable and many of the most memorable (and violent) scenes in the novel are constructed around him. For example, his death scene:

> Then Gudbrand trimmed the great sail for the last time and tied the steering-oar. With a flint he passed into the hold. In a little he came aft, placed Sigr [Alsvid's sword] in the Jarl's hand, and knelt beside him for a moment on the deck, but no one ever knew what was his final act of homage to his chief. He stepped on shore, and with his own hand set the dragon free.
>
> Solemnly the great ship moved out in the darkness from the lee of the high shore. Then she felt the breeze and her broad sail bulged. She had passed a good way from the shore when the first long tongue of flame shot out into the blackness, lighting up her gilded, gleaming sides, her gilded mast and yard, her white, gold-bordered sail with its bright symbol of a blazing sun in red and gold, and flinging on the sea a shimmering path of fire. Then the four watchers saw an unexpected sight.
>
> With the last pulse of life the Jarl sprang erect, waved Sigr till the sword flashed in the lurid light, gave forth one great war-shout, and fell dead on the poop, his sword grasped in his hand.
>
> The watchers stood spellbound. Urged by the strengthening breeze, the fair Gardrofa flew, a ship of fire, towards the open sea. Gradually they saw mast and sail succumb to the enwrapping flames that shot towards the sky. To Gudbrand and his sons it seemed as though they saw the messengers of Odin – the dark Valkyr maidens – hovering above the ship.[21]

Alsvid cannot forsake the pagan gods. He cannot accept the new deity and he cannot accept the inevitable rule of the new king. As the White Christ's influence becomes stronger, Geira the prophetess (who falls in love with

Thorvald) and Alsvid's daughter Dagmar become converts. Alsvid, in the face of this, has no choice but to accept their choice and tacitly permit the new kind of worship within the society he rules. Personally, however, he is resolute. The only possibility for him, in the face of certain spiritual and political defeat, is glorious death in a flaming longboat.

His world may be changing, but Alsvid cannot change with it. He cannot, like Scott's heroes, accept a world that is less colourful, romantic and heroic. It is hard for a Viking Jarl to be a pragmatist. In the character of Thorvald, however, Burgess gives us someone who, in the face of a metamorphosing world, is unable to see things in quite such a straightforward way. When the Vikings first arrive in Shetland, one of their number, Arvak, meets his former companion in the hills around Lerwick. They go to Thorvald's hut and Arvak sees his former comrade's sword and helmet placed, symbolically at rest, beneath the cross. Arvak taunts Thorvald about his conversion:

> 'Art thou then turned *nithing*?' asked Arvak quickly, with a keen contempt.
>
> Thorvald stood looking towards the cross and the Viking gear; but he did not know how strong within him yet was the old life. He heard the terrific epithet. In an instant, almost ere he could think, he snatched his sword down from the wall and turned on Arvak.
>
> Arvak sprang to his feet, kicking aside the bench on which he had been sitting, and his blade flashed in the sunlight that fell through the doorway. Thorvald's sword was raised. His blue eyes that had been so calm were now ablaze with rage. For a moment Arvak saw before him his old Viking comrade complete in everything but battle-gear. He seemed about to strike.
>
> Then suddenly Arvak, as he grimly watched him, saw a strange new sight. The wild light faded out of Thorvald's eyes. The war-sword dropped by his side.
>
> 'Tyr is dead,' said Thorvald, hoarsely. (pp.74-75)

Thorvald believes in Christ and wants to become more deeply devoted, but the old ways are still with him. He can still be enflamed by conflict but strives to overmaster his will, eventually regaining self-control. Alsvid's Viking ways and the new faith Thorvald aspires to are competing elements. Christian humility and forgiveness, however, are the things which ultimately triumph.

The dualism here is straightforward: pantheistic paganism or monotheistic Christianity. But Burgess, in the character of Arvak, who has 'not a single scrap of sympathy with either faith' (p.125) introduces an idea which contrasts with the positions of both Alsvid and Thorvald. Arvak is a man without religion. He believes in no deity, pagan or Christian, and relies only on his own will-to-power to control his environment. Fifteen years after the novel's publication, Burgess told L.G. Scott:

> He said he finished the book rather hurriedly and would have liked to have had another page in before the last one. The last page had been thought out before he started the book and he intended it to set forth anarchic philosophy – that every man shall ultimately become a law unto himself, but he added of course that cannot come to pass until every man wills to do right.[22]

For most of the novel, Arvak is a law unto himself. He participates enthusiastically in Alsvid's raids, but does so as an independent man who stands outside the bulwark of religion. But, unlike Alsvid, he does become a follower of the new faith. The character who most represents the desire to move beyond the two opposing positions is eventually inscribed into one of them. Had Burgess, as he discussed with Scott, added an additional page, perhaps the Nietzschean ideas he is circling around may have been more prominent. But, as it stands, although the pagans may get the best scenes, Christianity is what the novel affirms. As with later readings of Burgess' poetry, there is perhaps a subtle re-positioning which is difficult to confirm when looking closely at the work. Graham reads Burgess' socialism back into *Rasmie's Büddie*, and, here, one wonders if Burgess is trying to make the novel appear slightly more radical than it really is. In *The Viking Path*, Burgess does not try to go beyond Good and Evil, but investigates the way to the Good through a relationship with Christ.

Thorvald and Arvak have to struggle against their Viking inclinations, but access to Christ is, ultimately, a straightforward thing. For them, the Church, in an organised form, hardly exists. There are no ecclesiastical structures to regulate admittance to the Almighty. As is the case for Rasmie, Burgess' Viking characters have to find their own way to God. These are very Presbyterian ideas, and, in his second historical novel, *The Treasure of Don Andres*, Burgess attacks what he saw as the most cabbalistic of institutions, the sixteenth-century Catholic church and the Spanish Inquisition.[23] In *The Viking Path*, Burgess gives us a pure, uncomplicated religion but, in this novel, the people who are meant to be closest to God, like the devil in 'Scranna', are the most hellish, conniving, and malign characters of all.

The novel, like *The Viking Path*, utilises events from Shetland's past. Following the defeat of the Spanish Armada, one of its ships, the *El Gran Grifón*, was wrecked on Fair Isle, and Burgess uses this as the basis for his tale. The first half of the novel is set in Lisbon before the Armada departs. It concentrates on the treasure of a dying conquistador, and the love of his daughter, Ana, for a young nobleman, Don Sebastian. Ana and the treasure are pursued relentlessly by the evil Don Jago, a trainee priest and officer of the Inquisition. Like Arvak, Jago is a Godless man. But, as he is a southern European Catholic nobleman and

J. J. HALDANE BURGESS

J. J. Haldane Burgess.   *Courtesy of Shetland Museum and Archives*

not a Viking, he is Godless and evil, rather than Godless and good. Jago displays his individualistic worldview here:

> 'Human nature is still human nature, let your creed be what it may. Each man is simply a hot mass of nerves and passions, no matter whether he wear helmet, cowl, or crown.' [24]

Man is a creature of appetite and desire. Jago's will-to-power is untempered by religion and, as we see here, is made into something dreadful by the institution he is part of:

> 'The Christian faith is silly, Tizon. Holy Church is rotten to her core. There are a few fools who are really sincere, and trust her with an honest faith, but wise men understand how they can use her to advance their own designs. I may say I have made her serve my turn, and she shall serve me still a little further, and then I mean to bid farewell to her for ever. Your Moorish faith is somewhat better, though it is also very stupid. The only true faith is the faith of wealth and women.' (p.284)

The Catholic church, when allied with a rapacious appetite, supports and fosters evil. Access to Truth, as Burgess suggests with his Viking characters, is available to the individual standing before God, and the complexity and abstruseness of the Catholic church is an anathema to this idea.

The Treasure of Don Andres is a less complex and layered novel than *The Viking Path*. In the latter, we see competing ideas and belief systems struggle for supremacy in the characters of Thorvald and Arvak. Burgess' Armada novel, however, is more of a potboiler. Padre Juan, brother of Don Andres, is driven insane by the treasure he cannot find. Jago, at what seems to be his moment of triumph, is undone by a cross-dressing manservant. And, in a cataclysmic final chapter, the island in the Azores where the treasure is buried is partially destroyed by a volcanic explosion. Burgess breathlessly piles events on top of each other and, enjoyable as this is, the novel is less considered and thoughtful than his Viking story. That said, both novels, like *Rasmie's Büddie*, represent Burgess as an innovator. Jessie Saxby may have introduced her ideas about Vikings into stories about contemporary Shetland, but Burgess was the first local author to use Shetland's past as a basis for his novels.

A Temporary Marriage and *Tang*

In his other two novels, Burgess moves way from history and uses settings his readers would have recognised immediately. *A Temporary Marriage*, which is undated and unpublished, is divided between expatriate Shetlanders in late-nineteenth century Edinburgh, and the home and business of a merchant in Lerwick. The first half, set in the capital, tells the story of two young lovers, Mary Reid and John Angus. The villain of the tale, a boorish Shetland merchant

J. J. HALDANE BURGESS

called George Adamson, takes a liking to Mary and, through the power he has gained over her father due to a financial irregularity, marries her and returns to Lerwick with his prize. Mary is brought back to Adamson's house against her will and appears destined for a miserable existence. The house and situation she finds herself in become claustrophobic and imprisoning. Adamson controls the financial affairs, including the secret of Mary's father's dubious business dealings, so has power over her. His domination is financial, emotional and, as we see here, sexual. In this scene, a stratagem of Mary's has failed to secure her freedom, and Adamson then asserts what he sees as his right over her:

> Without a word or cry, Mary sank down into the big armchair, and stared at him with eyes full of amazement and despair.
>
> 'I think now, Mary,' he went on quietly, but with an expression of malignant triumph on his face, 'that we have got round very beautifully to the special point from which you started, which was, that we must clearly understand each other. It is a splendid notion, and I'll show you how we'll work it out. For the future, you can make a chum of Maggie Ness as much as you desire in ordinary ways; but you'll remember that you're not to breathe a single word to her or any other living soul regarding anything of this that I have told you. You will have no need now of intimate acquaintances for you and I are certainly not going to be strangers any longer. You are going to fulfil your obligations and be my sweet wife indeed. If you fail in any way to do as I have said, your father's doom is sealed; I'll ruin him without mercy. I make this plain as a foundation. But I don't mean to be a tyrant, unless you force me to it, Mary. I want to be your lover, as I have been since the first time I saw you. By heavens, Mary, that is my desire, and I'll seal the bargain with a kiss, as I proposed at first.'
>
> He rose, and, crossing to her, took her in his arms. He kissed her brow, her cheek, her neck, her lips. A shudder was the only sign that she was conscious of his nearness to her.
>
> The clock on the mantelpiece struck twelve.
>
> 'Midnight,' ejaculated Adamson, 'Come Mary. It's time for decent folk to be in bed.'
>
> She rose mechanically, and went with him.[25]

Mary is a powerless woman in a world controlled by men. Adamson's hold of the legal and financial reins allows him a sexual hold over his wife. Adamson's claim for himself as one of society's 'decent folk' is not an ironic one. As a successful merchant with a beautiful wife, he believes he is a respected member of the community, and this makes his treatment of Mary more shocking. He sees nothing wrong with a man of his social position forcing his wife to have sex.

Society gives men the power to act in such a way and, in Adamson's eyes, he is performing his allotted role. The character of Maggie Ness, however, shows that it is possible for women to resist. Maggie is a radical, outspoken figure. She never accepts her status as second-class citizen or, as Mary perhaps does here, as victim. The character of Maggie, who is the only person in the novel who can stand up to Adamson, shows Burgess' interest in progressive politics and, once again, in the ways in which an individual can find some kind of liberation.

A Temporary Marriage is an unusual part of Burgess' oeuvre because it has an urban setting. In *Tang*, however, he situates his story in a small Shetland crofting community. Burgess was in the habit of sending copies of his books to well-known authors and sent *Tang* to John Buchan. Buchan wrote back saying:

> I read *Tang* and enjoyed it very much. It has a curious freshness, coming I suppose from the strangeness of the locale to an ordinary Scotsman. It seems to me much better than the stories of village life that the Kailyard writers are producing.[26]

In his recent reassessment of the genre, *Kailyard and Scottish Literature* (2007), Andrew Nash argues that the work of Barrie, Crockett and Maclaren is more complex and worthwhile than has been recognised hitherto. Their novels are sentimental, they do present an idealised picture, but they can also be read as presenting an affirmative, celebratory view of their rural communities. Despite their deficiencies, as Edwin Morgan, after cautioning readers 'against lashing themselves into a fury over the Kailyard', points out: 'there is an important place for sentiment and pathos in any literature'.[27] We have no way of knowing if Burgess wrote his novel in self-conscious opposition to the Kailyard writers (although the publication date of 1898 certainly opens the possibility), but *Tang* is neither affirmative nor celebratory. Instead, it is an unsentimental, even cruel, portrayal of a small Shetland community. None of the characters are idealised. Peter Mann the minister is weak and inconstant. Hakki Perk the schoolmaster is cutting and rebarbative. Inga Bolt, the central female, is a manipulative coquette. Bob Ertison, who is in love with Inga, is honest but dim. And, in addition to these main characters, Norwick is full of people whose raison d'être is to spread malicious gossip as far and as wide as they can.

The novel is contained within the microcosm of Norwick. There is no glimpse of anything from outside the community, and this enclosure produces a claustrophobic insularity. In the first two thirds of the novel there is hardly any movement or action. Even the notorious Shetland weather is calm and unchanging. The community is static and every small occurrence, speech, or sign is amplified and speculated upon until it becomes an event. In this situation of inertia, even the gaze of certain characters becomes significant. For example, here we see Peter Mann in his bedroom, looking across at the home of Inga Bolt, who he has fallen for:

> He glanced across at Taft. The thick mistbank had gathered down behind the house, which stood out dark against it, and seemed much bigger than it really was. He saw the small, black window on the gable, and stood looking at it till it vanished in the fog.[28]

This seems innocent enough. But, as the novel progresses, we see that, because of his position in the community, Mann cannot court Inga openly. In the face of this difficulty, his gaze becomes rather more sinister:

> There was lying on his windowsill a big, old telescope, which had formed part of the assets of the late Rev. Mr. Wood, and through which Mr. Mann had often looked for long whiles at a time. It had been wont to lie in the window of the drawing-room, next to his own room, but for a week or two it had been lying on his bedroom windowsill. His hand touched it now. He took it up. He pulled down the sash and adjusted the glass upon the lighted window.
>
> Inga was in her room. She was feeling her right ankle rather sore, probably, she thought, from having twisted it, when she had slipped down from the steps. She had taken off her shoe and her stocking and was looking at it.
>
> Mr Mann saw a small lamp standing on the little table between the window and the chest of drawers. Then he saw suddenly, full in its light, Inga's white leg, from the rounded knee down to the pretty foot. Once or twice her brow came in sight as she bent forward. (pp.153-154)

The minister, afraid of gossip, is reduced to voyeurism. Passion and desire are frustrated by the oppressive social structures of Norwick. People cannot be unrestrained and Burgess shows the difficulties individuals can encounter in insular communities. As Buchan points out, Burgess does not idealise, sanitise or romanticise his fictional township. Norwick is no rural idyll. Writing of the most famous anti-Kailyard novel, *The House With the Green Shutters*, Nash states that:

> Barbie [...] emerges as a town filled with spiteful gossip and petty hatreds. The familiar characters of the minister, the dominie and the local "bodies" are the antithesis of their Kailyard counterparts. All community spirit is broken [...].[29]

Nash's description could equally be applied to *Tang*. Surprisingly, for a man who had, by the time of writing the novel, become an enthusiastic and fervent Marxist, it is not the economic structures of the society which oppress its residents, but the social and psychological constraints people place on one another. As is the case with Saxby's *Rock Bound*, in *Tang* (and *A Temporary Marriage*), Burgess is concerned with difficult human relationships and the pressures created by social norms, rather than the socio-economic structures of the societies he is writing about. In *Rasmie's Büddie*, he uses the world of the croft as a source of metaphor and intellectual possibility. Secure in his world, Rasmie draws on everyday things for his philosophical and theological speculations and, for him, the croft is positive and enabling. In *Tang*, however, we are dealing with a rural community and, when people become involved with one another, things become vicious. *Rasmie's Büddie* does not idealise the rural environment, but it does see the croft in an optimistic way. The world of *Tang* is a far less hopeful place.

Conclusion

In an article in *The Scottish Educational Journal* Hugh MacDiarmid writes of 'the pioneer work of Mr J. Haldane Burgess', and it is this view of Burgess as innovator which describes him best.[30] The writers studied in Chapter Two all produced significant contributions to Shetland's literature, but Burgess, despite sharing several ideas with Anderson, Angus and Saxby, really sets the agenda for what comes next. He opened new ground. His historical novels were a first for a Shetland author and, in *Tang*, he produces a resolutely non-idealised picture of a Shetland community. But it is with his early poetry that Burgess' real contribution lies. As we saw in Chapter Two, 'Auld Maunsie's Crü' is a poem of intellectual complexity, but Burgess' use of the local language represents a new level of ambition and intelligence in local writing. But, challenging as these poems are, they are also rooted in everyday things and everyday words. Later writers, as we shall see, followed Burgess' lead and utilised the croft as a central motif, and, as William J. Tait was to do a few decades later, Burgess, more than any of his peers, took the local language into new places and made it speak in new ways.

Notes

1. Laurence Graham, 'Haldane Burgess', *New Shetlander*, 10 (May-June 1948), 10-12 (p.10).
2. Brydon Leslie, *Borgar Jarl: J.J. Haldane Burgess and Up Helly Aa* (Lerwick: Shetland Amenity Trust, 2012), p.72.
3. Jack Peterson 'J.J. Haldane Burgess: An Appreciation', *New Shetlander*, 164 (Simmer 1988), 7-10 (p.10).
4. Brian Smith, 'Burgess, (James John) Haldane (1862-1927)', in *Oxford Dictionary of National Biography* <http://oxforddnb.com/view/article/68951> [Accessed 3 Aug 2009].
5. John J. Graham, *A Vehement Thirst After Knowledge: Four Centuries of Education in Shetland* (Lerwick: Shetland Times, 1998), p.172.
6. Laurence Graham, 'Profiles from the past xv – J.J. Haldane Burgess', *New Shetlander*, 61 (Simmer 1962), 14-16 (p.14).
7. See Leslie, *Borgar Jarl*, pp.25-26.

8. SA, D2/54, Esperanto translation of *Rasmie's Büddie*, 1906.
9. Smith, 'Burgess'.
10. SA, D2, Papers of J.J. Haldane Burgess.
11. L.G. Scott, Reminiscences of Haldane Burgess', *New Shetlander*, 16 (May-June 1949), 13-16 (p.15).
12. J.J. Haldane Burgess, *Rasmie's Büddie: Poems in the Shetlandic* (Lerwick: T. & J. Manson, 1891), p.87.
13. Laurence Graham, Preface to *Rasmie's Büddie*, by J.J. Haldane Burgess, 4th edn (Lerwick: Shetland Times, 1979), pp.xix-xxii (p.xix).
14. Graham, Preface, p.xxi.
15. Quoted in Graham, 'Profiles', p.16.
16. J.J. Haldane Burgess, *Rasmie's Büddie: Poems in the Shetlandic*, 3rd edn (Lerwick: T. & J. Manson, 1913), p.12.
17. SA, D2/17/2, J.J. Haldane Burgess, 'Onward: Labour Lines', undated.
18. [Anon.], Obituary of J.J. Haldane Burgess', *Shetland News*, 20 January 1927, p.5.
19. For a discussion of Burgess' uses of Norse myth see Leslie, *Borgar Jarl*, pp.61-72.
20. Blackwoods put the novel's poor sales down to its religious element. See SA, D2/19/3, Letter from William Blackwood and Sons to J.J. Haldane Burgess, 12 May 1905.
21. J.J. Haldane Burgess, *The Viking Path: A Tale of the White Christ* (Edinburgh / London: William Blackwood and Sons, 1894), pp.362-363. The book was later released, in an abridged form, as *The White Christ: A Story of the Vikings* (London: Horace Marshall & Son, undated), as part of a series called The Masterpiece Library, Penny Popular Novels. It also came out in German as *Der Vikinger Pfad* (Dresden: E. Pierson's Derlang, 1906).
22. SA, SA2/256, Notes by John Graham, undated, from jottings by L.G. Scott of conversations with J.J. Haldane Burgess in January-February 1911.
23. In a letter to L.J. Nicolson, dated 6 July 1901, Burgess wrote that 'The plot deals with the Inquisition and other matters which may strike the public fancy in connection with the demonstration against Romanism'. Quoted in typescript of Peter Jamieson, *Haldane Burgess: Poet of Shetland*, c.1971. SA, D9/187/p.109.
24. J.J. Haldane Burgess, *The Treasure of Don Andres: A Shetland Romance of the Spanish Armada* (Lerwick / Edinburgh: Thomas Manson / Oliver and Boyd, 1903), p.133.
25. SA, D2/55, Typescript of J.J. Haldane Burgess, *A Temporary Marriage*, undated, pp.186-187.
26. SA, D2/78/2, Letter from John Buchan to J.J. Haldane Burgess, 3 March 1898.
27. Edwin Morgan, 'The Beatnik in the Kailyard', in Essays (Cheadle: Carcanet, 1974), pp.166-176 (p.168).
28. J.J. Haldane Burgess, *Tang: A Shetland Story* (Lerwick / London: Johnson & Greig / Simpkin, Marshall, Hamilton, Kent & Co., 1898), p.64.
29. Andrew Nash, *Kailyard and Scottish Literature* (Amsterdam / New York: Rodopi, 2007), p.203.
30. Hugh MacDiarmid, 'Færöerne', *The Scottish Educational Journal* (12 January 1934), 54-55 (p.54). Reprinted in *The Raucle Tongue: Hitherto Uncollected Prose* vol.2, ed. by Angus Calder, Glen Murray and Alan Riach (Manchester: Carcanet, 1997), pp.354-365 (p.355).

CHAPTER FOUR

SONS OF RASMIE

Introduction

Rasmie has proved one of Shetland's most fertile literary progenitors. After Burgess created him, there was a proliferation of crofters in the work of local authors and, as we shall see in later chapters, subsequent generations continued to evoke what has become an archetypal character. In Burgess' own time we find crofters in Peter Greig's couthy dialect serial *Fireside Cracks*, which appeared in the *Shetland Times* from 1897-1904,[1] in Thomas Manson's three-volume novel *Humours of a Peat Commission* (1918, 1919, 1924), in Joseph Gray's still-popular comic sketches, *Lowrie*, first published in the *Shetland Times* in 1929, then in book form in 1933, 1949, and 1991, and, as we shall see, in the voluminous work of James Inkster. Like Rasmie, these crofters are always older men, as much a part of rural Shetland as crüs or peat hills, and are always assured in their use of the local language. Inskter's work represents the most extensive use of the character but, in the first few decades of the twentieth century, crofters were very often figures of fun. In Manson's three books, and especially in Gray's short stories, the crofter is an anachronistic figure in a modernising world. He struggles to cope with cheque accounts, motorised transport, electricity, synthetic manure, the cinema, and most of the other things which arrived in Shetland in the first half of the century. Rasmie was an intelligent man who could express himself eloquently in the Shetland tongue, but many of the crofters he begat were dim-witted and backward, floundering in a world that was changing. The influence of Burgess was large, but the innovations he brought into the literature became increasingly hackneyed and impoverished. The period of flourishing discussed in Chapters Two and Three was at an end. Shetlanders continued to write and publish, but new ideas and fresh impetus were required.

At the end of Burgess' life, Hugh MacDiarmid was busy introducing new energy and impetus into Scottish letters. In Shetland, however, the movement he engendered did not begin to influence local writers until after the Second World War. In the 1920s, although he did not take his cues from MacDiarmid, only John Peterson, a writer from Gruting on Shetland's west side, was travelling in different directions than his island contemporaries. In his work we find themes, often very unsettling ones, that no other Shetland writer was drawing on. His oeuvre is not large, but, especially in his early work, we see him move away from the croft, and from Shetland, in ways no other local author of his time was doing. By the time of the First World War Burgess was still alive, but his major works were behind him. James Inkster's important dialect serial *Mansie's Röd*, which represents the last highpoint of Shetland literature's late-nineteenth century golden era, ended in 1916. In the early decades of the century, Shetland's literature was in transition. Peterson was doing something new, but none of his peers followed his lead. One significant period was over and, as we shall see in Chapter Six, another was yet to begin.

James Inkster (1850-1927)

James Inkster, originally from the remote township of Sandvoe in the north of the Shetland mainland, produced the longest piece of writing in the Shetland language. Married to the sister of publisher and *Shetland News* editor Thomas Manson, Inkster, as author of the enormous serial *Mansie's Röd*, became a long-term contributor to his brother-in-law's paper. The serial appeared every week and consists of (fictional) reports of rural life, sent to the paper by an old crofter, Mansie Jamieson. It ran during three different periods – 1897-1904, 1907-1908, and 1914-1916 (a selection was published in book form in 1922) – and represents a substantial cultivation of the ground cleared by Haldane Burgess.[2]

Mansie is a close kinsman to Rasmie. His place on earth is the croft but, unlike the characters of Thomas Manson and Joseph Gray, his foibles are not used to make him seem idiotic. Like Rasmie, Mansie is meditative and thoughtful. His ruminations may not have the theological and philosophical sophistication of Burgess' character, but Inkster follows the older writer's principle of using the vernacular in a serious-minded and intelligent way.

What *Mansie's Röd* amounts to is an enormous, extremely detailed anatomy of rural Shetland in the late nineteenth century – a slowly moving catalogue of how life was. There is no central narrative but, as we read, we see stories continue for a few weeks, slide into new stories, and *da Röd*, as Mansie calls it, rolls on and on, a bit like a modern soap opera. The rhythms of *Mansie's Röd* are those of working life, of the innumerable small tasks – tarring boats, tending sheep, planting crops, mending roofs, cutting peats – the croft demands of its inhabitants. Inkster is interested in the minutiae of rural life – of fishing, of saving a choking cow, of impromptu nights of drinking, of the courtships of young people, and of the rivalries and tensions of a small insular community.

Mansie is the writer of the piece but his voice is not the only one we hear. Here we see his report of a sheep caa or drive:

> We could noo hear da hoochs an' skriechs o' da folk, an' da barkin' o' da dugs, sae awa' Arty an' I gengs ta meet dem. He didna get da hog, bit he took up ower da hill, sae Arty tought he wid geng in wi' da rest o' da caa, an' sae he wis.

'Berry, come in ta my fit,' I says ta wir dug. 'Arty, doo'll need ta keep dy ane close bi dee. I see he's still livin' efter layin' my barimskin in his stamack!'

'Man, Magnus, I wis vexed aboot dat,' Arty said, an' wis gaen ta –'

'Men, come up an' meet yon lowermost sheep,' cried Willie Anderson. 'Dü ye tink he's fair fur some folk ta rin till der fit ta fa' doon aboot idder folks' sheep as well is der ain? bit dat's been da pranks o' a lock o' fok. Dey're nae rules among da aaners noo-a-days, sae muckle is da waur.'[3]

Mansie introduces the scene then lets the dialogue take over. Throughout the huge length of the *Röd*, Mansie's is the organising hand, but he is not a domineering narratorial presence. Dialogue makes up an overwhelming percentage of the serial. Although Mansie is the writer, his voice is one of many. No hierarchy is established between him and the other characters. He reports what his neighbours say and, in his juxtaposition of their voices, we hear the speak of the place. A comparison with Lewis Grassic Gibbon (1901-1935) invites itself here but, in *Sunset Song* (1932), we hear the speak of the Mearns in the exhilarating flow of the narrator's voice. We hear Scots, English, the voices of the Kinraddie folk, with no hierarchy implied between the different idioms. The narrator's voice is the voice of the community and, in the cadences, textures and rhythms of Grassic Gibbon's prose, all language is given equal validity. But, in Inkster's text, Mansie, as narrator, is hardly present at all. The serial bears his name, but he is a more of a recorder than a narrator. Both *Mansie's Röd* and *Sunset Song* give us democratic, collegial views of their communities but, where Grassic Gibbon does this with his unique narratorial style, Inkster places his narrator at the margins. Mansie writes down what he hears around him and, by giving us the speech of his neighbours, a holistic, inclusive vision of the place is brought into being.

But what do Inkster's people say? Mansie reports on everyday things like herding sheep or harvesting corn, but the *Röd* does not simply relate commonplace events and routines. As Brian Smith, the only critic to recognise the value of Inkster's work, writes:

> it is [the] movement from the particular to the abstract, from the reality of day-to-day life to a discussion of the world, that is so impressive about these productions.[4]

As well as recording, in precise detail, how people lived in rural Shetland, Inkster weaves the histories and stories of his characters into their speech. In one of many social gatherings, Mansie's friends and neighbours (who call him Magnus) recount his days at the fishing to his daughter Sibbie:

'Magnus wisna lang pittin' doon da helm, an' I can tell you da *Livelihorn* cam' up ta da wind in shorter time den A'm taen ta tell hit. I tell'd Robbie agen ta jimp i' da fore head an' mak' himsel' handy. As shüne as dy faider ran da sheet I lows'd da halyards an sang oot ta Robbie ta 'tak' awa'. As shüne as da rudder wis drawn, Magnus cried, "Noo boys clear up da boat, an' lat wis get wir maean i' da watter. Tak' da efter aer apo' da backward side, Aandrew, an' dü as doo's tell'd. Rowin' is da first 'at'll pit life in ta dee. Could doo tak' a moothfoo' o' bread? If doo can dü dat der nae faer o' dee." Aandrew shook his head, bit niver answer'd. Be dis time, Lowrie wis begun ta' mak' reddy for bendid' da inner cappie. "Don't ye tink, men," Robbie cried frae da fore head, as he wis rowin' up da sail, "at we're innerly." "Howld dy tongue man. Doo toughtna dat a moment fraesyne," Magnus answer'd, luikin i' da airt, "I doot afore a' is düne, doo'll fin 'at doo's fram eneugh?'" 5

This is Mansie as crew member of a fishing boat in a storm. He is in control of a desperate situation and saves both men and vessel from disaster. The telling of the tale is, as one expects from Inkster, an extremely detailed picture of the kind of fishing which was common in Mansie's youth, filled with local words for parts of the boat and pieces of fishing gear. But this is more than an ethnographic catalogue. This is a move into the world of story, of story drawn from raw experience. As Walter Benjamin puts it:

> Experience which is passed on from mouth to mouth is the source from which all storytellers have drawn. And among those who have written down the tales, it is the great ones whose written version differs least from the speech of the many nameless storytellers.[6]

In this passage, Inkster allows the voice of the storyteller to occupy centre stage. The narrative moves back in time and makes a heroic figure of the modest old man who sits and smokes and listens to the tale he is starring in. The focus of the writing moves away from the everyday world of the croft and into a different narrative space. This is a telling, or, more probably, for tales like this are part of the warp and woof of a place, a retelling of one of the myths of the community.

Later in the book we see the boat in the story, the *Livelihorn*, lying outside Mansie's house. It has not been to sea for many years. Mansie's young neighbour, Tamy, comes to ask if he can buy the boat to use as a roof for his lamb house (a common building technique at the time). But Mansie cannot part with his old boat, and reads Tamy a poem he has written about it. After the reading he says:

> 'Noo, Tamy,' I says 'sell dee da auld boat A'll no. Laek mesel, shü widna fetch muckle money; at da same time, kens doo 'at I couldna baer da idee o' pairtin' wi' her brucks even for siller. Shü's aboot da only link noo 'at connecks da past wi' da present, remindin' me o' happy days, as weel as days an' nights o' doot an' danger.'[7]

The boat has come to symbolise the past and, in its rotting boards, the stories of a seagoing community can be found. The movement here is from the quotidian to the mythical, from the commonplace into the history of the place and its people.

The narrative, on other occasions, moves away from the everyday world in a different direction. The milieu of *Mansie's Röd* is the self-contained environment of the croft but, occasionally, the outside world intrudes at its margins. In a moment of despair at the life of hard work she has to endure, Mansie's daughter Sibbie says:

> As fur da young lasses, der a' noo earnin' mair at service, an' at da gippin' dan dey could dü be day's warks; an' a'm beginnin' ta tink 'at I'd better geen ta da gippin [...].'[8]

The characters in Mansie's reports are mostly concerned with the work which has to be done in their own community. But, here, we see how alternative sources of employment – herring gutting, working as a servant – might attract one of that community's members. When Inkster was producing his work, Shetland was experiencing a huge boom in the herring fishery. Many Shetlanders had been very poor during the nineteenth century but, with thousands of tons of herring passing through the ports of Lerwick and Baltasound, there were new ways for people to make money. In the face of these social changes, Sibbie begins to question the traditional life her father catalogues so extensively. The twentieth century is beginning to push up against the nineteenth.

Mansie himself is well aware of the changes which have happened in Shetland in his lifetime. Here he speaks about compulsory education:

> i' my young days da Güverment haedna wauken'd ta da fact dat eddication maun come ta da front, – mair dan dat, is desteen'd ta be da motiv-pooer in guidin' da actions, helpin' oot da genius, an' generally spaekin', controllin' da idees o' mankin' ower da universe at lairge. Da Eddication Scotlan' Ack, Schule Brods, an' compulsory rules! Da very wirds wid hae come wi' mair surprise ta my auld fayder an' midder, an a' idders o' der day an' generation, wi' as grit a gluff, as der auld midders got whin da Press Gang cam seekin' da men an' dey at da eella! [9]

Mansie is a progressive man who, like Rasmie, is not afraid to discuss politics, or any other subject, in his own tongue. His political opinions often emerge when he is in conversation with the schoolmaster, Mr McLeod. Here they discuss various state interventions in Shetland, and Mansie speaks about how the Crofter's Holdings (Scotland) Act (1886) has been perhaps the greatest boon the island folk have ever enjoyed:

> 'Well, well, Magnus, if your statements are correct, and I have no reason to think otherwise, the Crofter's Act certainly didn't come too soon to Shetland,' said Mr McLeod.

'Na sir, bit foo many broken herts did da greedy villains pit till an oontimely grave, an foo mony saut taers is run doon ower puir widows faces, afore he cam' tink ye?' [10]

Mansie may call the schoolmaster sir, but his tone is polemical. He is sharply aware of past injustices and, despite being a generally modest and thoughtful character, is not afraid to vent his ire when the subject warrants such treatment. But what is particularly notable here is that the vernacular is placed on an even footing with English. The use of English by the learned schoolmaster does not privilege his views over that of the unschooled demotic voice of Mansie. But neither does Mansie's native voice privilege his opinion of local affairs over the non-native voice of Mr McLeod. No hierarchy of languages is set up, and both ways of speaking are seen as valid means of discussing, in an intelligent way, social and political affairs. The English voice can also be part of the speak of the place.

Mansie's Röd is a highpoint in Shetland's vernacular prose. No other writer had used the language at such length, and the longevity of Inkster's work shows that, by the turn of the century, a widespread readership had developed for Shetland dialect writing. Ultimately, however, it is something of a dead end. The work tends towards the minute, the small detail, the DNA of the small community. The world outside the community does sometimes appear but, for most of the piece, the gaze is directed inwards. *Mansie's Röd* is an intensely local piece of writing.

A local focus also characterises the work of Inskter's contemporaries. Writers such as Christina Jamieson, W.A.S. Burgess (brother of J.J. Haldane), T.P. Ollason, William Moffat, Jane Saxby (daughter-in-law of Jessie), W. Fordyce Clark, and John Nicolson took for their subjects the folklore, language, historical events, and people of their archipelago. They address a local audience (expect, perhaps, Moffat who was producing easy-to-digest stories of Shetland, published mainly in England) and their work represents the growing popularity of reading and writing in the archipelago. In the work of John Peterson, however, we find a Shetlander writing about things very far from the crofts and townships of his native isles.

John Peterson (1895-1972)

Most of the writers in the first half of the century took their lead from Burgess. We have seen how he came to be a kind of intellectual and political paterfamilias in Lerwick and, after the First World War, Peterson was one of the young men who would come to his house at 4 Queens Lane where discussions of Marx were taking place. In political terms, both were on the far left, but Peterson's writing moves away from the influence of the older man. Inkster, and the other writers we have mentioned in this chapter, all belong to the Victorian flourishing of Shetland's literature, but Peterson's work is firmly part of the twentieth century.

In a letter to local antiquarian E.S. Reid Tait, Peterson gives a rather sardonic account of his life:

> Passed through Gruting School and Anderson Institute (the latter alleged to be an educational institution). Army: Sea. Hgrs. 1916/1919: rose to rank of private. Drifted into Civil Service, Customs and Excise, 1920, and to date have not drifted out again. Published *Roads and Ditches* 1920. Published *Streets and Starlight* 1923. Thereafter developed sufficient sense not to do it again.[11]

The central theme of Peterson's writing is the appalling experiences he endured during the First World War. Like thousands of other men, he embarked on these experiences at a young age, finding himself in the trenches in 1916 after only one month of training. He was wounded more than once, but managed to survive. During his years in Europe, Peterson sent letters to Robert Blatchford's socialist journal *Clarion*, under the nom de plume Private Pat, a name he used in his first collection of verse, *Roads and Ditches* (1920). Following the war he became a Customs and Excise officer, working in Speyside and Orkney before settling back in Shetland.[12] He combined this job in the civil service with a lifelong attachment to the extreme political left. The story goes that, when the Soviet Union sent tanks into Czechoslovakia in 1968 to crush attempts at reform, *New Shetlander* editor John Graham happened to be visiting Peterson. As the two men watched these depressing events on television, Peterson commented to Graham that he shouldn't pay attention to what he was seeing as the footage was nothing but CIA propaganda! He remained an unreformed Stalinist until his sudden death in 1972.[13]

Three years before his debut collection appeared, Peterson was thinking about the new directions Shetland poetry would have to take. In 1917, while in hospital in Liverpool recovering from shrapnel wounds, he wrote to Ms. J.J. Campbell of Lerwick, who had sent him a copy of a poem called 'The Isles of Thule'.[14] Peterson discussed the poem rather generously:

> 'The Isles of Thule' is wonderfully fine. I have again felt that Shetland Might be the subject of a really great poem, and the more I knock about – or get knocked about – the more I feel it. There have been many poems 'Thule' but this one you send me comes nearest of all I think of deserving the title, I'm sure we can feel proud a Shetland boy wrote it – but, who but a Shetlander could write 'The Isles of Thule'!

> This poem, however, deals rather with an aspect – the wild majestic grandeur of west-side cliffs and west-side ocean breakers. There is yet the Shetland twilight, the Shetland summer-night – if you may call it night. It calls for such a poet as wrote 'The Lake Isle of Inisfree'. Thule – the wrath of the gods; aspects and the contrast of aspects: it is something I am waiting for. And the poem you send me gives me to think I may not have to wait for ever.[15]

John Peterson. *Courtesy of Shetland Museum and Archives*

The kind of poetry he wants is a poetry in which all aspects of Shetland are present, but which also incorporates influences from outside the isles. By invoking Yeats, Peterson shows a desire to weave the work of a poet who has nothing to do with Shetland into the fabric of local literature. He realises, as a young poet trying to find his own voice, that something new has to be done, that the gaze cannot always be directed inwards.

The influence of Yeats or, to be more specific, the Yeats who existed before the modernising influence of Ezra Pound, can be detected in *Roads and Ditches*. The first section of the book frequently employs the Yeatsian images of roses and beggars, as we see in 'The Beggarman':

> Of bread the world gave him
> To soothe his hunger-throes,
> But the beggarman he sold it:
> And bought himself a rose.[16]

The rose represents beauty in the midst of squalor. It is an object of solace but, as we shall see, by the end of the book, there is nowhere left in which to find consolation.

There are also distinct Yeatsian echoes in 'The Vagrant Kiss': 'But wandered on from summer noons to winter nights / Through faery lands and wondrous sights' (pp.3-4). And, in 'The Surge', we see an even more Romantic glow, where Keats can also be heard: 'Sweet are hills and valleys, sweet are fields / Where sultry vineyards sleep for suns to drape / Their drowsy greenery in clustered grape' (p.1). As we shall see, the gentle, comforting luminescence of these poems does not form the main tenor of his work but, by the time of his second collection, *Streets and Starlight* (1923), he was still working through the influence of Yeats. 'The Gutter-Artist' once again features the character of the beggar or vagrant:

> And yet you stoop to pity me,
> My trembling limbs a monstrous travesty, –
> Was it your god of love and beauty shaped
> An ugly, grotesque, goblin parody? [17]

The gutter-artist, unlike his counterpart in 'The Beggarman' is not offered any comfort. The tone is much more caustic and the poem never answers its own question. Readers have to draw their own conclusion. We can work towards an answer by looking at the kindred figures in another poem from *Streets and Starlight*, 'The Monument':

> They crawl out from dim alleys of the slums,
> Pale, human refuse hung with filthy rags;
> To crouch, and leer, and spit
> Upon the sunlit, dusty flags. (p.17)

The monument of the title is a 'statued soldier', and the 'grotesque, goblin, parod[ies]' are bodies twisted and broken by the ravages of war.

The First World War hit Peterson's writing, and his life, with dreadful force. If some of his verse displays the influence of Yeats and the fin de siècle, the brute reality of war altered his writing in grim and powerful ways. The things he had experienced meant his writing had to change, as he says in a poem from *Roads and Ditches* titled, simply, 'War':

> The songs I've sung are futile,
> Of little futile things,
> Of foolish dreams and fancies
> On feeble faltering wings;
> So I will cease my singing,
> And take you by the hand,
> Down days and darksome ditches
> To the night of No-man's-land.

> Where the day is full of horror
> That words may never tell,
> And the twilight full of terror,
> And life is laughing hell. (p.11)

After surviving the trenches, Peterson is aware that the Yeatsian glow of the poems quoted above is no longer adequate. The poems from *Streets and Starlight* we have mentioned still display something of that influence, but their tone is much more bitter, their grotesques much less benign. The first half of *Roads and Ditches* contains Peterson's most romantically inclined work but, with its placement in the middle of the book and its self-referential opening line, this poem emphatically distances Peterson from what has gone before. He has to take a different path, and the rest of the collection is a gruesome litany of war. Some of the most well-known, and the most horrendous, events of the conflict are documented:

> Out by Arras in the day-time
> There lay bare the sun-parched sand,
> Where together men and torture
> Lived with foul dead hand in hand,
> Horror-stricken, God-forsaken
> Stretches broad of war-cursed land. (p.17)

'In Flanders', in contrast to 'The Beggarman', suggests that beauty can no longer be found:

> Long years ago, ere came
> Red war with ruthless hand
> And slew young Love, and drove
> Reluctant Beauty from the land. (pp.25-26)

The same thing occurs in 'The Plinth': 'And all the beauty we have known / Lies buried in war's tomb' (p.24). The rose of the 'The Beggarman' has been trampled and lost in the mud and the slaughter. Beauty has been destroyed by war. In his introduction to the anthology *In Flanders Fields*, a collection in which Peterson could easily have been included, had his verse been better known, Trevor Royle writes:

> When peace came in November 1918, concepts like honour, heroism, patriotism, duty and glory had changed utterly, not just through the experience of a dreadful war, but also through the response of the poets to that experience.[18]

As well as destroying bodies, war changes words. Poets are forced to think of words differently and Peterson shows that beauty can be added to Royle's list. After Flanders, after Arras, there is nowhere for the poet to find solace. The experience of battle demands a plainness, a straightforwardness, and not the romantic glow of the verse we find in the first half of *Roads and Ditches*. In 'Billets' he achieves the kind of clarity the situation requires:

> Rifles feebly flung
> Against the walls; and here and there about –
> Helmets, and bandoliers and bayonets,
> Box-respirators dropped amongst the straw [...]. (p.31)

The alliterative relationship between 'bandoliers' and 'bayonets' – objects of attack which could be used to represent the heroic escapades of the soldier – is continued with 'box-respirators', thus undercutting the relative glamour of the weapons with a much more utilitarian and defensive object. This is documentary description, bare realism, but a realism which skilfully constructs a subtle symbolic relationship between the objects being described. Peterson is more than just a cataloguer of war. He is direct in his descriptions of battle, but he is also interested in how war alters the consciousness and character of those forced to participate in it. In 'My Lady of the Night', we see this interest made explicit in one of the most startling passages in his oeuvre:

> For years, it seemed, I dragged through mud and clay,
> A lost, forlorn, a helpless soul in nightmare
> Among the dead and long-dead scattered there:
> And I was wet, and cold, and hunger-grey.
> For one red hour I lived to curse and slay,
> To shoot, and stab, and bite, and brain, and tear [...]. (p.22)

The speaker here is made into a beast, into an extension of the weapon he holds. The 'it seemed' in the first line distances the speaker from the things he has done, from the loss of humanity he has suffered. He looks at himself and finds it hard to believe he has experienced these things. He objectifies himself within the frame of his own recollection, and sees a thing made less than human by the bloodlust and desire to survive that war engenders.

Roads and Ditches is unlike any other work in this study. Unlike much of the writing local authors were producing around the same time, it does not take Shetland's history, culture, folklore or language as its theme or starting point. By drawing on his war experiences, Peterson creates a powerful series of poems which, in their directness and often savage realism, move in similar directions to those travelled by more well-known war poets such as Roderick Watson Kerr, Siegfried Sassoon, and Wilfred Owen. The work of Peterson and these writers gives us a picture of war written by men who have had their feet caked in mud and have felt the air around them made to vibrate by exploding shells. Poet and critic C.H. Sisson writes of the war poet:

> He should regard war as apocalyptic. It is not enough to think that there is in any case life and death, but that some men die in battle. That would be to place, relatively, too high a value on the ordinary

life of man. The 'war poet' must reflect popular sentiment about war – whether the initial enthusiasm or the sated disgust. He must, moreover, send back reports from the front, for the benefit of civilians, though one can see this role being taken over by the television camera and by commentators, so much more lyrical than any poet would be.[19]

The poems in *Roads and Ditches* are precisely 'reports from the front', without any sentimentality or hollow patriotic ardour. And, when we combine this willingness to confront the events of 1914-1918 head on with the avoidance of his native isles as a thematic or symbolic source, Peterson emerges as a new kind of Shetland poet.

Peterson's second collection, *Streets and Starlight*, lacks the immediacy and documentary feel of its predecessor. *Roads and Ditches* is the war from the point of view of a man in the trenches but, in *Streets and Starlight*, the focus is wider. In 'Famine' for example Peterson writes:

> Dawn,
> And the sun rising over the steppes,
> And the sun rising out of the sea,
> And the ground parched, and the hills bare,
> And the waves wild, and the winds free;
> And seven hundred sailing ships,
> Golden in dawn's glory;
> And seven million souls,
> And death;
> And this, a story. (p.24)

The repetition hammers home the images and, as the poem progresses, those images become increasingly apocalyptic. We read how:

> The hot winds blew over the plains
> And blanched the straggling wheat.
> The sun's fierce devastation brought
> Starvation and defeat;
>
> And moaning over the tortured waste,
> And over the sun-parched sand,
> The wail of the hunger-stricken came
> Out of the famished land. (p.24)

And, in the final stanza, the speaker gives us an image which comments on the ruined landscape he has anatomised: 'And tier on tier the rotting food / Rears high on wharf and quay' (p.26). Famine and drought may be the cause of hunger but, by ending his poem in the commercial setting of 'wharf and quay', Peterson, as a communist, shows his disgust at the economic system which allows this to happen.

War, however, remained a central concern. There are the shattered men, as we have seen in 'The Monument'. In 'The Unknown' (p.18) we return to the battlefield and see how a soldier can find sympathy for a dead enemy. And, in 'Bones', we find another apocalyptic landscape, but this time the ruination has been caused not by drought, but by war:

> Bones, and bones, like pebbles on the shore,
> On shores that round the earth for ever run,
> An hundred million bones that heed
> Not rain, nor snow, nor sleet, nor fiery sun;
> A myriad bones of all our martyred men,
> Laid in the lap of all things dead;
> Raised in the splendour of their glorious youth,
> And lashed a-smother in one grisly bed. (p.21)

The speaker is a woman, or, to be more precise, all the women, from both sides of the conflict, who are left behind while their men go away to fight. Loss unites them all:

> They are our dead – our dead, my many mothers,
> O German, Belgian, British mothers mine,
> Our sons, our husbands, and our brothers
> All lulled to slumber in one sorry shrine […]. (p.21)

Peterson, by his second volume, is beginning to assess what the war means. He no longer takes his readers into the trenches to show them the mud and the rats and the slaughter, but rather, in the war-inspired poems of his second collection, he widens his gaze and tries to work out what has changed.

But the volume is not entirely pessimistic about the state of the world. The landscapes ravaged by war, and left starving by capitalism, are terrible, but several poems in the book find solace in Peterson's native isles. *Roads and Ditches* hardly featured Shetland at all but, in *Streets and Starlight*, we see Peterson begin to look north. In 'A Hill-Song', for example, although a Shetland location is not made explicit, the setting is a rural one:

> So come; we'll leave the City
> To the crowds that haunt the street;
> And hand in hand, we'll clamber
> To where the winds come sweet. (p.33)

Conventional, perhaps, but also more hopeful than some of his other poems. We see Shetland come more sharply into focus in the Viking-themed 'A Norland Song':

> Here about the city I am lost and lonely,
> Here amid the bustle down the dusty way;
> I can stay no longer, for I dare not linger
> With the Norland calling, calling night and day. (p.37)

And, in the sequence of dialect poems at the end of the book, we see Peterson work in areas that Burgess and Inkster would have understood. In 'Aatim' for instance, we read: 'Sön ower stubbly rigs A'll waander / Doon da glimmer, Luv, wi dee' (p.56). In 'Aald Boat', the speaker, like Inkster's characters reminiscing about the *Livelihorn*, looks back wistfully at a vessel that has not been in the sea for a long time:

> Aald boat, doo's idy last noost noo,
> Da waandrin sea nae mair doo'll ken,
> Nae mair sall I, dy capten, crew,
> Set up dy aald broon sail agen. (p.58)

In 'Shetlan', we see Peterson identify with the isles more closely and fondly than anywhere else in his work:

> Doo may waander on for iver,
> An seek idder laands dee lane,
> Bit someday doo'll come driftin
> Ta da laand a laands agen. (p.61)

Shetland is seen in these poems as an idyll, as a place where the modern world can be escaped from. These poems do not have the visceral impact of Peterson's writing about war but, after what he had been through, can we blame him for sometimes displaying the kind of nostalgia about the isles that many of his peers spent their lives drawing on? After surviving the trenches, it is hard to criticise somebody for being sentimental.

But Peterson's engagement with Shetland in these poems, however much we can understand it, is, in the general context of his work, fairly insignificant. His real contribution to local literature is as a poet who moved outside the increasingly hackneyed world of the croft and into the vicissitudes of a radically changing world. We see this journey played out in a third work of Peterson's, an unpublished, undated, and untitled novel which exists only in typescript in the Shetland Archives.

The novel is divided into three sections. The first section gives us a picture of a small Shetland township, and follows the formative years of the novel's protagonist, Hakkie Isbister. Hakkie does all the things we would expect of a young Shetlander – he goes off in boats, guddles trout, works on the croft and so on – until, directed by his father's desire for him to become educated, he goes to school in Lerwick and then away to university. Unlike Sibbie in *Mansie's Röd*, Hakkie does break away from the croft. Before he is very far into his studies, however, he signs up and goes to war. In section two, the first picture we get of the battlefield, after the rural imagery of section one, hits hard:

> An ocean of mud. Hakkie's body was swathed and slothed in it. His mind smothered in it. It accumulated geologically in layers, the older strata caked and hard as a brick, the newer layers soft and clammy

as glue. [...] Occasionally it froze and chafed his legs raw. There was mud in his food, mud in the petrol-tainted wash called tea. He scraped mud from mud-stained biscuits with a mud-caked jack-knife, until he became indifferent to mud in his food and accepted it as an article of diet.

There was nothing in sight that was not drowned in mud. The living and the dead were alike in its clutch, and life had become a constant grovelling in mud in a wilderness of ruin and decay. Yet men continued to live in it, in a dull, desperate, mechanical way, performing the routine of trench-life in a numbed, stolid manner.[20]

By section three, the war is over. Hakkie drifts around, trying to find some kind of direction. He finishes his studies but, after what he has seen, academia seems empty and pointless. He has come out of the war in a better state than the ruined men in 'The Monument', but he is changed nonetheless: 'In five years Hakkie had dispensed with the illusions which take many men a lifetime to discard, and others more than a lifetime' (p.165). With nothing else on the horizon, he gets a job in India, which allows him to return to Shetland as a rich man. He gives his parents money to enlarge their little croft house and he brings one of the first cars to the community. But heading east on a colonial adventure has not satisfied Hakkie, and he ends the novel by moving to a very different kind of country.

During his war service, while recovering from a shrapnel wound in an English hospital, Hakkie meets a man called Sidman who introduces him to communism. On his return from India, he becomes reacquainted with Sidman and, encouraged by him, sets off for the Soviet Union, which turns out to be an unqualified vision of a workers' utopia. The novel ends with Hakkie working hard for the Soviet cause:

Months passed, and this vast land struggled and fought heroically in the face of almost soul-destroying obstacles and difficulties, and gradually it became evident that it was making measurable progress towards better times. (p.239)

This seems distasteful and naïve today but, for Peterson, who travelled to the Soviet Union in 1932, communism, and the implementation of it in the Soviet Union, was the great hope he turned to after the destruction caused by war.[21]

The war may have been devastating, but it also allowed new possibilities to emerge:

Just as war had shaken the foundations of civilization and produced a world situation of which instability was the most stable characteristic, so did this characteristic express itself in almost every phase of life. (p.170)

The crofts and townships which prevailed in Shetland's literature after Burgess, despite, as we saw in Inkster's work, feeling some pressure from new industries, are places of tradition, insularity and routine. Even in Kailyard incarnations like Gray's Lowrie, the crofter and the croft represent a way of life that has been settled for a long time. We have seen how Peterson's war poems largely ignore this rural milieu and move outside Shetland in a way no other local author was doing and, in his novel, by sending Hakkie to the Soviet Union, he again places a Shetland character in the tide of world events.

Having said this, it is not in the parts set in Soviet Union that we find the novel's real value. Its most striking scenes draw on the battlefields Peterson writes about in his poetry:

> And so Death raged and devoured that day, and Hakkie was his sergeant-at-arms, his faithful equerry, with the strength of the strong singing in his veins, the ruthlessness of the slayer and the scathlessness of the all-daring. (p.142)

We can compare this with the passage from 'My Lady of the Night' quoted above. Hakkie is turned into an agent of death, a human weapon. Later in the novel, during a battle in a town, Hakkie comes across a number of half-drunk soldiers in a music shop. He picks up a fiddle, starts to play, and a different kind of madness takes hold: 'Round him reeled and swayed the victims of a private Hades, a medley of dark, lurching figures' (p.147). This scene, lit by the burning spars of a smashed piano, is hellish. The men are turned into figures from Dante's *Inferno*, unable to escape the world that war has created around them. The documentary focus of his poems is present in Peterson's prose, as is the question about how the war changes those caught up in it. War has irrevocably changed people and the world they live in, and Peterson, in his fiction and his verse, attempts to take stock of both.

The works we have looked at so far are those of a young writer, albeit one who was old in experience. They rarely take Shetland as their subject, and are, for the most part, attempts to put into words what their author has undergone, and to think about how things – men, language, landscapes – have been changed. But these were to be Peterson's only two books of verse, and his novel was never published. He did not publish another poem until 1958, when his 'Elegy in a Country Churchyard', a Shetland dialect rendering of G.K. Chesterton's poem, won first prize in a poetry competition run by the *New Shetlander*.[22]

The *New Shetlander*, where Peterson's politics were looked on sympathetically, was his main place of publication for the late literary renaissance he enjoyed. In these late poems, often published under the initials S.R. or H.H., the war still appears, as we see in 'Great Wars':

> And after all those years
> Of deadlier strife and spurious peace,
> I look, but cannot see

> The broken dynasties,
> The tumbled crowns,
> The millions buried
> Where they fell;
>
> Only the momentary flash
> Of Robbie, crofter,
> Caught up in war,
> Passing with firm tread,
> His rifle slung
> Over an island graciousness,
> Smiling a courteous greeting
> As he passed
> Into the history of an age.[23]

We now see the battlefield of *Roads and Ditches* as a 'momentary flash' of memory. We are back with the soldier in the trenches, 'Alert, war-stained', 'Clad in the courtliness / Of other days', but this poem has none of the bitterness or nihilism of his earlier work (not that these things are necessarily detrimental). There are signs of hopefulness in the image of 'Robbie striding to the banks / And Mary standing by the door'. This is a soldier who survives unscathed, who comes home to his Mary, who retains something good in the midst of destruction.

In the figure of Robbie, Peterson introduces into his verse the archetypal figure of the crofter. We opened this chapter with a panoply of literary crofters and, here, we see him appear in Peterson's work. But Peterson's crofter is not a nostalgic character, and he is not used for ridicule. There is a nobility in the glimpse we get of him. As we have seen Peterson do in other works, he places this man in the tides and currents of the world, but, this time, he is not turned into a beast by what he encounters. He is in the middle of Hell, but he retains a sense of his self, a sense of hope, that we do not find in the rest of Peterson's war poems. At a distance of almost half a century, Peterson was perhaps coming to terms with the things he had lived through.

The final poem I will mention in this chapter is Peterson's 'Seine-Netters' which, according to John Graham, 'stands high among the best of Shetland poetry.'[24] It was first published in the *New Shetlander* in 1966 but, unlike the work we have looked at so far, it does not draw on the battlefields of Europe. Instead, it is about the sea:

> Black aa roond, an da steep seas makkin;
> Gunwale to gunwale, til da decks rin white;
> Mast-head licht in a swirlin moorie
> Loopin aboot laek a thing geen gyte.[25]

We launch straight into the world of the ocean and of seafaring. The boat fights its way through 'steep seas makkin' and contains generations of men who have sailed the waters around Shetland:

> Swein, an Hal, an da Bare-legged Magni,
> Brusi da black, an Kol Brokkenbanes,
> Day an nicht, wi der een ta da wastward,
> Strampin da seas laek dir ain briggiestanes.
>
> [...]
>
> Androo John an Grace Ann's Robbi,
> Willi by Nort and Hugh frae da Hadd,
> Day eftir day, i da hert-hol a winter,
> Shuttin, draggin an guttin laek mad.

We see here both Norsemen of the ninth century and fishermen of the twentieth. The use of names at the beginning of the first two lines of each stanza, the repeated 'day' in the third line, and the partial alliteration in the first word of each closing line, make one stanza mirror the other and, despite the thousand years that separate the characters in each, the men are united and made kin on the ocean that sustains them.

Setting the poem at sea also allows Peterson to introduce another kind of voice:

> Hullo! – Hullo! – Hullo! –
> *Daybreak* callin *Venture* –
> *Venture* – *Venture* – *Venture* –
> *Daybreak* callin *Venture* .
>
> [...]
>
> *Venture* callin *Daybreak* –
> *Daybreak* – *Daybreak* – *Daybreak* –
> What's da price a haddocks
> In Aberdeen da day? ...

What we hear in these stanzas, which are interspersed through the poem, is the utilitarian, staccato chatter of the trawler band, a radio channel used by the fishing fleet. The use of this electronically modulated voice, 'Throbbing out of the black box', as MacDiarmid puts it in 'The Wreck of the Swan', places the poem firmly in the present, but, with the saga-like names, we also move far back in time.[26] The contemporary and the ancient are brought together in the final stanza:

> What's da price, an da squall comes dirrlin;
> Black aa roond, nor ever a glaem –
> Compass, wheel, an a ee ta windward,
> Haddin da rodd da Norsemen cam haem.

The poem tacks through centuries and encapsulates a relationship with the sea which islanders have always had to form and negotiate.

'Seine-Netters' was a new kind of poem for Peterson. In it, he moves away from the dreadful experiences which characterise most of his writing and into a setting which appears surprisingly seldom in Shetland's literature: the ocean. As we have seen, the croft came to be the most popular setting for Shetland writers. These crofts, and the people who live on them, are often faced with a changing world. Whether the crofter is a serious figure, like Burgess' Rasmie or Inkster's Mansie, or a comic one like Gray's Lowrie, the certainties of their communities are often under threat. Their environment is increasingly malleable in the face of modernity. The sea is not like this. Land, society, and community can change, but the sea looked much the same to the Vikings as it did to trawlermen in the middle of last century. The croft represents tradition, but, like Auld Maunsie's crü, it is also mutable and unstable. Inkster's Sibbie feels the pull of new opportunities and begins to question the environment her father represents. Rasmie is secure in his world, but despairs at 'dis deevil's din' of the world.[27] Gaps open up between generations as tradition comes under pressure. The ocean, on the other hand, is eternal and draws together generations of seafaring men.

If 'Great Wars' shows Peterson coming to terms with both his own past and with aspects of Burgess' legacy, 'Seine-Netters' marks a coming to terms with the tradition of dialect writing that Burgess is such an important part of. As we shall see in Chapter Six, dialect writing underwent a renaissance after the Second World War, and 'Seine-Netters' was a major contribution to that second flourishing. We have looked at the vernacular poems in *Streets and Starlight*, but 'Seine-Netters' is a much more substantial piece of work. In those earlier poems, the language became a vehicle for all the bad things about Shetland dialect writing – nostalgia, sentimentality, an idealised view of the islands – but, in this poem, Peterson uses the language to write a poem which moves through a millennium of seagoing lives. Most of Peterson's work is about how life and history were shattered by the war but, in his late poem, he finds a way of reconciling the past with the present. He does not exalt the old to the detriment of the modern but, by setting his poem on the unchanging ocean, manages to unite the two.

Conclusion

This chapter has concentrated on a transitional period in Shetland's literature. Inkster's work marks the culmination of themes and ideas which had been circulating from the 1870s onwards, whereas Peterson eventually became part of the literary community that emerged around the *New Shetlander*. Like George Stewart, Basil Anderson, and Haldane Burgess, Inkster focuses on rural Shetland and, in Mansie, we find one of Rasmie's close literary kinfolk. But, in the first quarter of the century, the freshness, ambition and energy of the Victorian writers was beginning to ebb away. Peterson's work marks a new departure for a Shetland writer. The themes of his early writing were far from pleasant, but, in breaking away (or being broken away) from the literary world of the croft, Peterson stands at a distance from his contemporaries. His two books of war poems do not represent a new literary movement in the way the *New Shetlander* writers would after the Second World War, but he was working in very different areas to any of his peers. In the 1920s he was a solitary figure, working through his own terrible experiences. The writers of the *New Shetlander* generation, who came to prominence after World War Two, were accepting of Peterson's politics and enthusiastic about his work. As his late period suggests, he found common ground with them and, in the poems he published in the magazine, we see him begin to take account of his literary forebears. He may have found political kindred-spirits amongst some of Shetland's younger litterateurs but, in the 1930s, he was not the only writer and communist living in Shetland. He published nothing in that decade but, in a little cottage in Whalsay, another poet was engaged in one of the most difficult, but also the most productive, periods of his life.

NOTES

1. For a brief discussion of Greig's work see Brian Smith, 'Wir Ain Auld Language: Attitudes to the Shetland Dialect Since the Nineteenth Century', in *Dialect 04: Two Day Conference and Public Debate on the Development of the Shetland Dialect* (Lerwick: Shetland Arts Trust, 2004), pp.10-15 (p.13).
2. James Inkster, *Mansie's Röd: Sketches in the Shetlandic* (Lerwick: T. & J. Manson, 1922). The book version uses Röd, whereas the serialised text has Rüd. For the sake of consistency I will use the title of the book. Also, because I will be quoting from both versions, giving page numbers in the text may be confusing. References to the work will, therefore, be provided in endnotes.
3. James Inkster, 'Mansie's Rüd', *Shetland News*, 31 July 1897, p.8.
4. Smith, 'Auld Language', p.13.
5. Inkster, *Mansie's Röd*, p.87.
6. Walter Benjamin, *Illuminations* (London: Pimlico, 1999), p.84.
7. Inkster, *Mansie's Röd*, p.100.
8. Inkster, *Shetland News*, 26 June 1897, p.7.
9. Inkster, *Mansie's Röd*, p.1.
10. Inkster, *Shetland News*, 29 May 1897, p.8.
11. SA, SA4/3000/9/11, Copy of Peterson's *Streets and Starlight* with, pasted in, letter from Peterson to E.S. Reid Tait, 15 April 1934.
12. [Anon.], Obituary of John Peterson, *Shetland Times*, 22 September 1972, p.11.
13. Brian Smith, pers. comm., 3 May 2010.
14. Probably the poem by William Porteous (1887-1917), rather than the poem of the same name by L.J. Nicolson. Porteous' poem can be found in the *New Shetlander*, 1 (March 1947), 1. A posthumous collection of Porteous' verse, also titled *The Isles of Thule*, circa 1955, remains unpublished. See SA, D9/105.

15. SA, SA2/618, Copy of letter from John Peterson to J.J. Campbell, 23 May 1917.
16. John Peterson, *Roads and Ditches* (Lerwick: T. & J. Manson, 1920), p.2.
17. John Peterson, *Streets and Starlight* (London: Erskine MacDonald, 1923), p.30.
18. *In Flanders Fields: Scottish Poetry and Prose of the First World War*, ed. by Trevor Royle (Edinburgh: Mainstream Publishing, 1990), p.23.
19. C.H. Sisson, *English Poetry 1900-1950: An Assessment* (Manchester: Carcanet, 1981), p.80.
20. SA, D1/219/1, Untitled typescript of novel by Jack Peterson, undated, p.88.
21. Peterson became a well-known local photographer, publishing several collections of his work. He took a series of photographs during his trip to the Soviet Union (including one of an enormous floral mural of Stalin's head) and these photos are now in the online archive of the Shetland Museum and Archives. See <www.shetlandmuseumandarchives.org.uk> [Accessed 21 July 2009].
22. John Peterson, 'Elegy in a Country Churchyard', *New Shetlander*, 46 (March 1958), 14.
23. [John Peterson], 'Great Wars', *New Shetlander*, 73 (Summer 1965), 16.
24. John J. Graham, '"Seine-Netters" by John Peterson: An Appreciation', *New Shetlander*, 212 (Simmer 2000), 7-8 (p.8).
25. [John Peterson], 'Seine-Netters', *New Shetlander*, 79 (Yule 1966), 6.
26. Hugh MacDiarmid, *Complete Poems*, vol.1, ed. by Michael Grieve and W.R. Aitken (Manchester: Carcanet, 1993), p.730.
27. J.J. Haldane Burgess, 'Nazarene', in *Rasmie's Büddie: Poems in the Shetlandic* (Lerwick: T. & J. Manson, 1891), p.14.

CHAPTER FIVE

HUGH MACDIARMID

Introduction

Despite their kindred political sympathies, there is no evidence that C.M. Grieve and John Peterson ever met. In a small place like Shetland they might well have done so, but, even if MacDiarmid did know Peterson's work, one wonders if he would have seen it in the same way as he saw the rest of the archipelago's literature:

> It is a Brobdingnagian country peopled by Lilliputians, and, in addressing oneself at all to a description of it, one is burdened by a sense of the fact that not one of its people through all the centuries of human history has ever achieved expression on any plane of literary value whatever […].[1]

What MacDiarmid is saying, despite his bombast, is that, in looking at the place in which he lived in the 1930s, he was presented with a landscape that had few literary associations. He would not have known Chalmers' work (even if he had done he would no doubt have thought little of it), and much of the writing which had emerged from the 1870s onwards was concerned, not with the landscape, but with the microcosm of the croft and, perhaps more than anything else, with the local language. But, as we shall see, in some of MacDiarmid's Shetland poetry, especially the work in his 1934 volume *Stony Limits*, the Shetland landscape was one of the fundamental components.

We have seen how MacDiarmid had a good word to say about Haldane Burgess, but, as the above quotation shows, he was not very generous about the writing discussed in previous chapters. In later years, as we shall see in chapters Six and Seven, he was supportive of the *New Shetlander*, and of William J. Tait in particular but, in the 1930s, he did not see much to pique his interest. And, if MacDiarmid was generally unkind about the literary efforts of Shetlanders, writers and critics from the isles have been rather unwilling to recognise his contribution to their literature. He was an early contributor to the *New Shetlander*, but his work, like that of the writers studied in Chapter One, does not appear in any anthology of Shetland writing.[2] A number of his Shetland poems, however, as Kevin MacNeil's pioneering anthology *These Islands We Sing* (2011) recognises, are straightforwardly about the isles. As we are about to discuss, some of the writing MacDiarmid did in Shetland investigates the idea of extreme isolation but, in poems like the 'Shetland Lyrics',[3] 'Off the Coast of Fiedeland' (*CP*1, p.723), and in the essay 'Life in the Shetland Islands',[4] he was engaged with the society – its people, its ways of life, its language – in ways that much of his Shetland-era writing is not. In 'With the Herring Fishers' (*CP*1, p.437), for example, although MacDiarmid has misheard the dialect pronunciation of 'grow' as 'growl', we hear the fishermen speak and the rhythm of the poem captures the excitement of the hunt. These poems, in my view, can be incorporated unproblematically into the canon of Shetland writing we are working through in this book.

These Shetland poems, as MacNeil's anthologising of them suggests, are easy to appreciate. Their speaker is in an unexplored world, curious about what he is seeing, 'wholly engaged in the new experience', as critic, and publisher of MacDiarmid, Michael Schmidt puts it.[5] But these poems (and this is not to denigrate them) do not represent the prevailing trajectories MacDiarmid's work followed while he was living in Shetland, and present rather less of a challenge than much of what he wrote in his humble cottage at Sodom in Whalsay.

MacDiarmid was extraordinarily productive in that house. According to Ruth McQuillan, all the poems from page 385 to 1035 in MacDiarmid's *Complete Poems* were written there.[6] He also produced *Scottish Eccentrics* (1936), *The Islands of Scotland* (1939), *Lucky Poet* (1943), the unpublished *Red Scotland*, and hundreds of essays, reviews, and letters. MacDiarmid's prodigiousness during these years is impressive, heroic even, but, as McQuillan asks at the end of her essay, 'What are we to make of it all?'.

Some critics, to put it bluntly, might answer: not much. Schmidt, for example, writes of 'the problem of the immense, Siberian tundra of the later works',[7] and, much more coruscatingly, Seamus Heaney writes:

> If Burns and Dunbar are tributaries in the stream of Lallans, the portentous and absurd shadow of William McGonagall sometimes haunts MacDiarmid's English. The epic voice goes epileptic. [...] In attempting a poetry of ideas MacDiarmid can write like a lunatic lexicographer. [...] When his brow furrows with earnest ambition and his pedantic Scottish pipe begins its relentless drone we witness the amazing metamorphosis of genius into bore.[8]

Heaney would later concede that he had 'underprized' MacDiarmid's 'far-out, blethering genius', but his condemnation of much of the work produced in the isles remains explicit.[9] In the MacDiarmidian oeuvre, readers have generally preferred the Scots lyrics of the 1920s, the extraordinary performance of *A Drunk Man Looks at a Thistle*, and the masterpiece 'On a Raised Beach' (which, as I will discuss, is central to his early experience of Shetland), to the slowly moving, accumulative later poems such as *In Memoriam James Joyce* (1955) or *The Kind of Poetry I Want* (1961).[10] But these poems, although at times overly verbose, tedious, formless, and arcane, are also poems with serious aims and aspirations. They are big poems, and in them MacDiarmid was trying to accomplish big things.

In dealing with MacDiarmid's work, it is necessary to make our approach in a different way than we have done for the local writers looked at so far. Until now (with the exception of Scott) we have been considering authors who, in terms of Scottish literary scholarship, are relatively unknown. As well as providing necessary introductory material on these people, I have attempted to show the ways in which they engage with their native archipelago – through the language, through the self-contained milieu of the croft – and have discussed how they contribute to the literary tradition we have seen develop. MacDiarmid, as I say, has not been seen as part of that tradition. The work he did in his early Shetland years could easily be included in an anthology of local writing but, when we consider his Shetland output as a whole, these poems do not form a major part. So, instead of concentrating on these poems, I want to explore the main directions MacDiarmid's writing took while he lived in Whalsay. To do this, I will divide his Shetland-era work in two. Firstly, I will look at the work in *Stony Limits* which circulates around what Scott Lyall calls 'The stripped-to-first-principles philosophy of "On a Raised Beach"', and will consider the ways MacDiarmid saw the landscapes which surrounded him in the 1930s.[11] His later poems largely leave the islands behind but, in the first half of the decade, he was vitally engaged with austere landscapes of the archipelago. These poems are intellectually expansive, but they are also, in some ways, predicated on the place their author was living in. They move outward, into the world of ideas, but also inward, towards the harsh, stony landscapes and coastlines of Shetland. The divisive later poems are different. They rove far and are concerned with the world in an encyclopaedic way, but Shetland is no longer a recognisable presence in the way it is in the earlier work. Some critics, as we have seen, feel their interest in MacDiarmid wane at the sight of these poems, but this chapter, by reading MacDiarmid's Shetland work alongside that of a poet who was a 'key figure for MacDiarmid in the 1930s', Charles Doughty, will try to look at them, and the *Stony Limits* poems, in a new way.[12] The creative relationship between the two writers has not been much explored, but, by looking at MacDiarmid's writing in the light of Doughty's, we open up a context which helps us to better understand, and appreciate, a great deal of the writing MacDiarmid did between 1933 and 1942.[13]

To a Raised Beach

In our discussion of Scott's Shetland-set work, we explored how his reading of Scandinavian literature was a major factor in how he saw the isles. Similarly, when we consider the poetry in the first part of our division of MacDiarmid's

Christopher Murray Grieve (Hugh MacDiarmid) with wife Valda and son Michael in Whalsay.   *Courtesy of Edinburgh University library*

Shetland-era writing, we can see how his reading of Doughty influenced his conception of the archipelago. Before we explore this idea, however, some introductory paragraphs on Doughty who, in both MacDiarmid's time and our own is an obscure figure, may be useful.

Like the cliffs in Shetland, the works of Charles Montagu Doughty (1843-1926) are huge, forbidding, austere, difficult to access, and visited by only a few hardy adventurers. He is best remembered, if he is remembered at all, for his gigantic prose work *Travels in Arabia Deserta* (1888) which, in more than 600,000 words, relates his two-year sojourn in the Arabian peninsula in the 1860s. For Doughty, however, what has become his best-known book was only a precursor to what he saw as his major literary contribution – the writing of epic poetry.[14] His poems which, in terms of scale, are just as prodigious as MacDiarmid's, were published between 1906 and 1923, and in them, to use Ezra Pound's phrase, Doughty was consciously and resolutely 'out of key with his time'.[15] In *The Dawn in Britain*, a six-volume epic dealing with the early history of the British isles, Doughty writes:

> Now, after sundered from the Continent;
> This Isle lay empty, a land of cloud and frost,
> And forest of wild beasts; till creeping time
> Brought man's kin forth. Then Fathers of the World,
> Begate the nations. Last few fisher folk,
> Passed, driven by tempest, from the Mainland's coast.
> They feeble of stature, clad in fells of beasts;
> (Whose weapons, in their hands, were sharp flint stones,)
> The river strands possessed, and wild salt shores.
> To them were holes, delved underground, for bowers:
> Trees were and streams and hills and stars, their gods.[16]

These portentous, archaic lines were published in 1906. Doughty was an anachronism in a metamorphosing world. He wrote like an Old Testament prophet in the era of the moving picture; like a pre-Renaissance epic poet in the era of the wireless.

He was also, however, a presence for some of the major poets of the twentieth century. In 'Canto lxxxiii' Pound recalls the period from 1913 to 1916 when, working as Yeats' amanuensis at Stone Cottage in Sussex, he would read aloud to the Irishman after they had finished their day's work:

> did we ever get to the end of Doughty:
> *The Dawn in Britain*?
> perhaps not
> Summons withdrawn, sir.) [17]

Several decades later, in the 1940s in Italy, W.H. Auden was met by his young secretary James Schuyler. Schuyler remembered the meeting in his poem 'Wystan Auden':

> When he got off
> the liner at Naples, in black and
> a homburg, he said, 'I've just
> read *all* of Doughty's *The Dawn
> in Britain*.' [18]

And, in 1933, MacDiarmid wrote a little poem called 'To Charles Doughty', which includes this stanza:

> And slow as the movements
> O' continents in the sea
> Risin' and fallin' again
> Is your influence in me.[19]

References to Doughty become increasingly common in MacDiarmid's writing in the 1930s and, by 1952, his enthusiasm was undimmed. We see this in a letter to Edith Trelease Aney:

> Finally you ask what poet has influenced me most. That is a difficult question to answer. I am not easily influenced. I have read enormously and known many great poets of many lands, but I think I have not been influenced directly very much, though of course I have learned technical devices and found myself impelled towards certain types of subject matter and forms of treatment by many very diverse poets, e.g. Yeats, Pound, Hopkins, Rilke, Rimbaud, Mayakovsky. Probably the best answer to your question is Doughty.[20]

The question of influence, in a man so single-minded as MacDiarmid, is complex and difficult to pin down. In all phases of his career we can point out influences – John Davidson,[21] Jamieson's dictionary, the writers Peter McCarey discusses in his book *Hugh MacDiarmid and the Russians* (1987), for example – but MacDiarmid never writes very like anybody. Nobody writes like Doughty either. On the surface, it is easy to point out their differences: Doughty is archaic, MacDiarmid incorporates modern scientific terminology; Doughty's poems are narratives, MacDiarmid's are not; Doughty was an extreme political conservative, MacDiarmid was a communist.[22] But, by drawing parallels between their lives and work, we can begin to answer the same kind of questions that we have previously asked of Scott. What did Shetland mean to MacDiarmid? How did he see the isles?

Although some of MacDiarmid's Shetland work leaves us with the impression of extreme isolation, he was, especially in his early years in the archipelago, more engaged with island life than we might imagine. He went to the fishing, visited uninhabited islands, played bridge with the laird, walked around Whalsay, tried (and failed) to learn how to cut peat, wrote letters to the local papers, and was involved in a campaign against the County Assessor to try and stop the rates of Whalsay cottars being increased unfairly.[23]

In Arabia, Doughty also went among the people and his book, in exhaustive detail, reports what he experienced. Doughty had an unimaginably hard time in the desert. As a Christian he was constantly in danger and, throughout the course of his wanderings, he was attacked, threatened, abandoned in the desert, robbed and imprisoned. He was also, however, sometimes treated kindly, especially by women and, although he never accepted any of them, several offers of marriage did come his way. Much of his rough treatment was exacerbated by his own rebarbative, haughty, and unyielding personality (adjectives which many people would apply to MacDiarmid). In a 1980 review of a reprint of *Arabia Deserta*, Reyner Banham writes:

> It is difficult to think of anything in the whole history of European exploration to match this stiff-necked bloody-mindedness of Doughty's, his cast-iron self-righteousness, his condescending compassion for his adversaries – or his stoical endurance of the penury, ailments, frustrations and desert dangers to which his inflexibility dooms him in this land of Wahabi-Revival fanaticism.[24]

Although he gives us an unparalleled view of the Arabian people, Doughty was always an outsider. In Whalsay, despite his involvement with the community, MacDiarmid – as a writer (and as somebody who sometimes spoke about his neighbours in a disparaging way) in a place where almost every other man was at the fishing – remained an outsider too. MacDiarmid was never in physical danger in Shetland (although he was monitored by the security services)[25] but the figure of Doughty in the desert – as a Christian in a hostile Muslim country, as a book-learned scholar and writer among unlettered people – must have resonated. One can imagine MacDiarmid finding something of his own situation in lines such as 'How might we other days continue thus? / In cragged coast, where now decays our force', from Doughty's 1908 poem *Adam Cast Forth*.[26] Biographer D.G. Hogarth says of Doughty that, in Arabia, 'he was absolutely alone, thrown on his own sole resources in a most uncertain adventure.' [27] MacDiarmid wasn't quite alone – he had Valda, Michael, Grant Taylor – but, such was the state of his personal life in the early 1930s, that finding himself in Whalsay must have felt like 'a most uncertain adventure' indeed.[28]

But Doughty's book, like MacDiarmid's Shetland work, is much more than an ethnological and anthropological picture of the people and places he saw. Both *Arabia Deserta* and *Stony Limits* represent a deep and fundamental engagement with their respective landscapes. As an undergraduate at Cambridge, Doughty studied geology, going on to do fieldwork on a glacier in Norway. His interest in the science is evident on almost every page of *Arabia Deserta*:

> We look out from every height, upon the Harra, over an iron desolation; what uncouth blackness and lifeless cumber of vulcanic matter! – a hard-set face of nature without a smile for ever, a wilderness of burning and rusty horror of unformed matter. What lonely life would

not feel constraint of heart to trespass here! the barren heaven, the nightmare soil! where should he look for comfort? [29]

As well as living with (and criticising) the people of Arabia, Doughty pushes his mind into the barren earth and the ancient rocks. He deplored any signs of literary sentimentality – something which, in his view, there was plenty of in the late nineteenth century, Swinburne being a particular figure of opprobrium[30] – and he avoids that pitfall by allowing the landscape to mould and define his work. As Edwin Morgan writes:

> I supervised
> a thesis on Doughty, that great Englishman
> who brought all Arabia back
> in his hard pen.[31]

The desert and its hardships demand a tough response and Doughty avoids any hint of romantic sensuousness, as Mohamed Kaddal, in the thesis Morgan refers to, shows:

> He was not concerned with the mysterious, the marvellous, the picturesque, or the grotesque. In his insistence that *Arabia Deserta* was no 'milk for babes' he was the deliberate rebel, reacting against the fanciful romantic world of the *Arabian Nights*.[32]

Although *Arabia Deserta* is full of people and packed with life, it is the image of Doughty alone in the desert that stays in the reader's mind. When, on the final page, Doughty is 'called to the open hospitality of the British Consulate' (vol.2, p.539) in Jidda, he has encountered, and survived, some of the most elemental and unforgiving places in the world.

If we can make a comparison between MacDiarmid and Doughty's social positions, we can also see them as having something in common in terms of their respective landscapes. As Morgan puts it:

> The figure of Doughty in the Arabian desert exerted a strong appeal for MacDiarmid. Doughty was explorer, geologist, word-collector, epic poet, man of independent mind – everything that MacDiarmid admired – but he was also a man who exposed himself to the elemental things, to the most ancient and unassimilable part of the human environment.[33]

In *The Islands of Scotland*, MacDiarmid wrote of Shetland that 'Only the pen of the author of *Arabia Deserta* could do justice to this depopulated and derelict archipelago' (p.84). The harsh and austere rocks of Shetland, in MacDiarmid's mind, had something in common with the bare and unforgiving landscapes of Doughty's Arabia. Both men stood at a remove from the people they were living amongst, and, in encountering the rocks of Whalsay and the deserts of Arabia, Doughty and MacDiarmid found themselves contemplating the essential matter of the world. As he puts it in 'On a Raised Beach':

These bare stones bring me straight back to reality.
I grasp one of them and I have in my grip
The beginning and the end of the world [...]. (*CP1*, p.432)

It would be easy to dismiss a comparison between a little island like Whalsay and the Arabian desert but, for MacDiarmid, contemplating the rocks and stacks of the isle allowed him to access the same fundamental components of the planet that Doughty found in the desert.

MacDiarmid's symbolic journey to, and into, this rocky landscape is enacted in the sequence of elegies in *Stony Limits* which precede 'On a Raised Beach'. These are, firstly, to Scottish nationalist Liam Mac'Ille Iosa, then to Rainer Maria Rilke, and finally to Doughty. T.J. Cribb writes of the elegies:

> Their progressive denudation of landscape, hardening of language and tightening of form can be read as an increasingly difficult attempt to wrest meaning from deaths whose finality becomes more and more relentlessly realized. They are shadows cast by eternity.
>
> All three poems, while independent in themselves, can be seen as preparing for the definitive achievement of 'On a Raised Beach'.[34]

They are certainly 'an increasingly difficult attempt to wrest meaning from deaths', but the movement through the poems also leads to a landscape no more willing to yield up meaning than the brute, cold fact of mortality. Morgan writes of the prospect this stony landscape presents to the poet:

> the rock, the desert is a challenge not only to man's physical exploration and endurance but also in a curious way to his intelligence. Looking around the subhuman forms of life, we can make something of a monkey, a dog, a frog, even an oak-tree or a sunflower; but what about a stone?[35]

In Chapter One we explored how Margaret Chalmers found ways of incorporating the Shetland landscape into her verse and, in the *Stony Limits* poems, MacDiarmid had to do the same. He had to learn how to see these places, how to read them, how to make something of them. 'On a Raised Beach' answers Morgan's question. It is a supreme achievement in wresting meaning from an ungiving landscape, and it is in the two poems which precede it in the volume that the journey towards this definitive statement is made.

Nothing of the Shetland landscape is to be found in the Mac'Ille Iosa poem and MacDiarmid first lands on the archipelago in his elegy to Rilke, 'Vestiga Nulla Retrorsum'. In the volume, Shetland has perhaps been hinted at in 'In the Caledonian Forest' (*CP1*, p.391) and 'Ephphatha' (*CP1*, p.393), but we arrive in the islands dramatically in the Rilke poem with the strong stresses of the opening line: 'Halophilous living by these far northern seas' (*CP1*, p.416). The *Oxford English Dictionary* gives halophilous as 'salt loving' and, when we know what the first word means, the image is one of a precarious life, of the kind of life that exists, like the Bedouin tribes Doughty lived with, in a difficult and hostile environment.

The Shetland landscape is also very much an ingredient in MacDiarmid's elegy to Doughty, 'Stony Limits'. MacDiarmid draws himself and Doughty towards each other here:

> I belong to a different country than yours
> And none of my travels have been in the same lands
> Save where Arzachel or Langrenus allures
> Such spirits as ours, and the Straight Wall stands,
> But crossing shear planes extruded in long lines of ridges,
> Torsion cylinders, crater rings, and circular seas
> And ultra-basic xenoliths that make men look like midges
> Belong to my quarter as well, and with ease
> I too can work in bright green and all the curious interference
> Colours that under crossed nicols have a mottled appearance.
> (*CP*1, p.421)

The geological language, which Doughty would have understood, is used as an offering.[36] MacDiarmid is saying that he, like Doughty, has experienced tough and elemental landscapes – not the sands of Arabia, but the rocks and stacks of Shetland. It is geology, looking at the oldest and most impenetrable things there are, which, in MacDiarmid's mind, unites him and the poet he is elegising.[37]

In the penultimate stanza, we see MacDiarmid identify himself with the Shetland landscape explicitly:

> I know how on turning to noble hills
> And stark deserts happily still preserved
> For men whom no gregariousness fills
> With the loneliness for which they are nerved
> – The lonely at-one-ment with all worth while –
> I can feel as if the landscape and I
> Became each other and see my smile
> In the corners of the vastest contours lie
> And share the gladness and peace you knew,
> – The supreme human serenity that was you!
> (*CP*1, pp.421-422)

The 'stark deserts' he turns to are the rocky places, 'Geology's favourite fal-de-lals' (*CP*1, p.421), that he has described in the previous two stanzas and they, like Doughty's Arabia, elicit a certain response from the person who encounters them. They do not permit 'gregariousness', but what the solitary contemplator finds in these places is of immense value and worth.

The poem closes with the startling image of MacDiarmid sitting next to Doughty's empty skull, 'whose emptiness is worth / The sum of almost all the full heads now on Earth' (*CP*1, p.422). It is, as Cribb has it, an attempt to predicate poetic meaning on death. But the image, and the poem, is not a morbid one. The final word, 'friend', is one of affirmation and connection. As in the geological section, this word brings Doughty and MacDiarmid together, but this time the connection is a human one, not one mediated through landscape. MacDiarmid has symbolically passed though that stony, difficult landscape and can, by the end of the poem, call Doughty his friend. They are comrades in topographical adversity. And, as he finds his way to Doughty, he also finds his way to the central poetic masterpiece of his career.

Although 'On a Raised Beach' ranges far, it is also a very locatable poem. Alan Riach writes:

> No modern Scottish text is more significantly located in a memorable landscape than 'On a Raised Beach'. The very title tells us that location is the governing idea.[38]

The triumph of the poem is that, from this place, from the tiny uninhabited island of West Linga on Shetland's east side, MacDiarmid produces something of great philosophical and spiritual reach. For anybody familiar with the coastline of Shetland, the kind of landscape evoked is instantly recognisable. It is, in a sense, a very local poem, but one which is, emphatically, not confined by that location. It is also the poem in which the movement begun in the Rilke elegy is completed when, in the opening stanza, MacDiarmid, taking the reader with him, sinks deep into geological strata that have formed over millennia. In a late interview, MacDiarmid said of the poem:

> I was trying to define my own position generally in terms of my environment at that time which was the Shetland Islands where, of course, geology is the prominent feature. You've got none of the resources for illustrative material you'd have on the mainland of Scotland. There are no trees, no running water. You're thrown back on the bare rock all the time. So I was trying to re-shape my ideas of poetry, identifying myself in terms of the Shetland landscape. That's what I was doing. I think it's one of my very best poems, either in Scots or English.[39]

MacDiarmid's creative enterprise is moulded by the place he is writing about and, like Doughty's Arabia, the landscape does not allow a picture-postcard response. As Riach puts it, '"On a Raised Beach" evokes landscape in ways which disrupt the nineteenth-century Romantic sense of the "scenic"'.[40] The stones, the bare rock that MacDiarmid found himself thrown back on, demand that the poet does not write about them sentimentally. To make his stony poem, MacDiarmid's pen needed to be as hard as Doughty's was when he sat down to write about the desert.

By passing through the symbolic figure of Doughty – the solitary man in the wilderness, the anti-Romantic writer, the geologist – MacDiarmid finds his way to, and into, his raised beach. In his 1927 study, Barker Fairley writes that 'Doughty is not a landscape artist, his mind goes through the external detail to the puny life of man, measured against the elemental world', and it is this placing of man against wilderness which MacDiarmid takes up in the poem.[41] From his vantage point next to Doughty's empty skull, MacDiarmid makes a covenant with the landscape he found himself in during the 1930s and was able to write that he was 'enamoured of the desert at last' (*CP*1, p.431).[42]

But, despite the idea of isolation, of the man alone in the desert, 'On a Raised Beach', like the elegy to Doughty, is a poem which affirms connection, not separation. As Riach puts it:

> Here [in Shetland], physical and mental breakdown followed a period of intense isolation, introspection and psychological anxiety. [...] 'On a Raised Beach' begins with the poet utterly alone on a Shetland stone beach but it ends with him lifting a stone, understanding that life is an act of participation in a way the lonely observer never could comprehend. [43]

MacDiarmid advocates 'Contact with elemental things' (*CP*1, p.428) as a way 'Into a simple and sterner, more beautiful and more oppressive world / Austerely intoxicating' (*CP*1, p.428) but, having come to understand (in a line that echoes the last line of the penultimate stanza in 'Stony Limits') that 'The abode of supreme serenity is necessarily a desert' (*CP*1, p.431), the speaker is not cast forth from the world. MacDiarmid continues:

> the capacity for solitude
> Is its test; by that the desert knows us.
> It is not a question of escaping from life
> But the reverse – a question of acquiring the power
> To exercise the loneliness, the independence of stones [...].
> (*CP*1, p.431)

The isolation MacDiarmid finds on his raised beach allows him to reach a position where he can become more vitally engaged with the world:

> Detached intellectuals, not one stone will move,
> Not the least of them, not a fraction of an inch. It is not
> The reality of life that is hard to know.
> It is the nearest of all and easiest to grasp,
> But you must participate in it to proclaim it. (*CP*1, p.432)

Being alone in this landscape, with the figure of Doughty in the desert haunting the view we get of it, does not leave MacDiarmid in a position of extreme spiritual or intellectual isolation. He is, literally, alone (except for one bird),

C. M. Grieve (Hugh MacDiarmid) in Whalsay.
Courtesy of Edinburgh University library

but, after contemplating the stones, he achieves an independence of mind, a calmness and a tranquillity, that bring him to a position of engagement, not separation. Just as Doughty came back from the desert, MacDiarmid finds in his own stony landscape, in his own solitude, a state of being that allows him to take part in the world. He does not draw back from his isolation, he embraces it. Being alone is not a way of avoiding the world, it is a way of finding a more profound connection with it.

This initial period of MacDiarmid's Shetland years, culminating in 'On a Raised Beach', represents a symbolic journey into the landscape. That journey finds many parallels in Doughty's great book. In the quotation at the beginning of this chapter, MacDiarmid spoke about how the Shetland landscape had, for him, no literary associations but, by invoking Doughty, he could learn to read that landscape and find a way of using it in his verse. But the work MacDiarmid produced from the mid-1930s onwards moves in a rather different direction. The *Stony Limits*-era poems are engaged with the people of Shetland and their lives and, more deeply and significantly, with the strange and austere landscapes MacDiarmid experienced in the isles. These poems are certainly not insular, but they do have a very definite sense of the place MacDiarmid was living in when he wrote them. The epic work(s) which later occupied MacDiarmid are not engaged with Shetland in the same way, if they are engaged with it at all. In the poem 'In the Shetland Isles' (*CP1*, p.574) MacDiarmid confidently shrugs off his physical distance from cultural centres and, as we have seen, in 'On a Raised Beach' he finds a way of being both utterly alone *and* engaged with the world. But, in the 1930s and early 40s, Whalsay was a very remote place. His 'exile', as he puts it in the following passage from *Lucky Poet*, became increasingly wearisome:

> As the years of my exile on this little Shetland island stretch out, it becomes increasingly strange to have my rare interludes back in Edinburgh or Glasgow or Manchester among civilized people. They are to me like sparkling water in a thirsty land, these comings into relationship again with minds keen, alert, attuned to beauty. I realize that I had almost forgotten that there were people who had thoughts and could clothe them in words not only worthy of rational beings, but even make such words interesting, eloquent. (I do not want to be unfair to Shetland in the least. If there are no such people in Shetland, there are exceedingly few in Scotland or England either – not more than one per 100,000). Except for these brief visits in Scotland and England, and the rare occasions in the summer-time when I have friends – authors, artists, and students – to stay with me in Shetland, I see nobody who has read widely enough to possess grounds on which to base, if not opinions, at least reasonable speculations. I hear nothing but the inane phrases of women.[44]

In Whalsay, at a distance from publishers, editors, and other writers, MacDiarmid was undeniably limited. In later years, as Alexander Moffat's famous painting *Poets Pub* represents, he became the central figure of a literary and intellectual community but, in Whalsay in the 1930s, nothing like this was available.[45]

His life of 'exile' and isolation may have started to weigh heavily but, in terms of the intellectual and linguistic ground they cover, the later poems are far from closed-off from the world outside the isles. I do not want to overestimate the influence his isolation had on the later poetry, but it does seem to me a factor. MacDiarmid had travelled as far into the landscape as he was going to and, for the rest of his time in Whalsay, his gaze was directed outwards. And, as the huge number of Shetland-born merchant sailors suggests, people from small islands are often the most enthusiastic explorers.

A Vision of World Language

'On the Ocean Floor', the opening poem from MacDiarmid's 1935 collection *Second Hymn to Lenin*, gives us a good way into the later verse:

> Now more and more on my concern with the lifted
>   waves of genius gaining
> I am aware of the lightless depths that beneath them lie;
> And as one who hears their tiny shells incessantly raining
> On the ocean floor as the foraminifera die. (*CP*1, p.535) [46]

In 'On a Raised Beach' we are presented with a fundamentally anti-Romantic landscape, but the poetic persona which experiences that landscape remains a recognisable individual. It is a solitary poem and, although it engages with complex and esoteric geological terminology, with contemporary debates about culture and leisure,[47] with religious themes and imagery, it is also very quiet, especially when compared with the noise and clamour of the later works. In 'On the Ocean Floor', silence and loneliness are present but, in the last two lines, we see and hear a prefiguring of what MacDiarmid wrote in the second phase of his Shetland period. He says that he must go below the 'waves of genius', below the central, lyric consciousness which animates *A Drunk Man Looks at a Thistle*, below the individual poetic persona we find in 'On a Raised Beach', and that he must listen to the almost imperceptible sounds of 'tiny shells incessantly raining'. In 'On a Raised Beach' he ends by advocating engagement with the world and, here, he suggests that, to do this, he must leave behind his subjective self and listen to what that world has to say. He must leave behind introspection and direct his attention outwards. The sounds he wants to hear are the voices in different languages, the scientific facts, the digressions into eastern religion, the arguments and theories about economics, politics, biology, geology – in other words he must open himself to the hundreds of grace notes that make up his later poems. The unusual word in the final line 'foraminifera', according to the *Oxford English Dictionary* is 'an order of *Rhizopoda*, furnished with a shell or test, usually perforated by pores'. As these marine organisms die, their tiny shells float to the sea bed and, over millennia, accumulate to form massive cliffs and crags. From the smallest, most individually insignificant things, huge structures are formed. MacDiarmid's epic poems work in this way – they are vast edifices formed from his omnivorous and magpie-like reading. This poem partakes of the same silence as 'On a Raised Beach', but in it we can also hear, from the bottom of the sea, the noise that would grow louder and louder as MacDiarmid's work grew and grew and grew.

To write this inclusive, accumulative poetry (and the landscape-based poetry we have already looked at), MacDiarmid turned away from the Scots he used in the 1920s. A few years after arriving in Shetland, however, he was still thinking about what could be done with the language, as we see in a letter of 13 December 1935 to William Soutar. Once again, MacDiarmid's enthusiasm for Doughty is clear:

> If you haven't read Anne Treneer's *C.M. Doughty* (Cape) and Barker Fairley's *Selections from Doughty's Dawn in Britain* (Duckworth) may I strongly urge you to. I'll lend you them if you like. I expect to have an essay on them in the next *Modern Scot* and, a little later, 2 or 3 consecutive articles on Doughty in *The New English Weekly*. I am convinced that he is our line to take.[48]

The final sentence here is a curious one. What 'line' is MacDiarmid writing about? An earlier passage from the letter sheds some light on the matter:

> I do not know if you've seen Power's *Literature and Oatmeal* [...] but if you have you may have noticed what he says of me – viz. my non-realisation or only partial realization of my original declared purpose with the language [Scots]. I agree with him – in that point. And I propose now to resume my task where I let that bigger task slide in order to accomplish what I have in the meantime accomplished. In other words, I am now addressing myself to epic in Scots [...].

But this projected Scots epic never materialised. To allow his readers to hear the sounds of the foraminifera or, as I am suggesting, the multiplicitous sounds of the world, MacDiarmid extended the kind of English – a language filled with scientific terms, a language that moves into different areas of knowledge and experience – he had started to use in *Stony Limits*. *In Memoriam James Joyce*, published in 1955 but begun in the late 1930s as part of the unfinished 'Cornish Song to Valda Trevlyn' can be taken as paradigmatic of this later work. In the poem we encounter a bewildering array of references, from Sanskrit literature, to 'the American-Indian languages, / The Algonquian, Athabascan, Iroquoian, Muskogean and Siouan groups / With the possible addition of the Uto-Aztecan'

(*CP2*, p.751), to radio variety shows, to Norn words that MacDiarmid found in Jakob Jakobsen's *An Etymological Dictionary of the Norn language in Shetland* (1928-1932).[49] It is a poem which reaches very far from the tiny island MacDiarmid was living in when he wrote it – an island, we should remember, at a considerable distance from any libraries or centres of learning. Bearing this in mind, the fact that the long poems were written at all is a substantial achievement in itself.

David Daiches says of this period in MacDiarmid's career:

> In MacDiarmid's later poetry he largely dropped Scots and wrote in standard English, sometimes in English with such a wide-ranging vocabulary (culled sometimes from technical dictionaries) and so different in tone and movement from anything being written in England, that it almost becomes a language of its own.[50]

Daiches' statement about an English 'so different in tone' could equally be applied to Doughty who, with just as much ambition as MacDiarmid, set about reinventing the English language of his day. Anne Treneer, in her 1935 book on Doughty, writes of her subject's philological enthusiasm:

> He liked dictionaries. He knew the fascination of words as mere words; he studied their origin and relationships; but above all he studied their use in the English writers up to the beginning of the seventeenth century. He learnt Old English by reading Latin-Saxon versions of the Psalms and Gospels. There are long extracts in his notes from the *Anglo-Saxon Chronicle*, and from Aelfric's *Glossaries*; and Doughty's own glossaries have been preserved. He read Middle English, especially Chaucer, the lyrics, *Piers Plowman* and Gavin Douglas, whose *Æneid* he admired; and he was widely read in early Tudor and Elizabethan literature, especially Skelton and Spenser. He studied particularly the drama and sermons, where the written word comes nearest to the spoken.[51]

Doughty, like MacDiarmid, was a very well-read man. His range of influences, from the earliest English writers, to Spenser, to literature in Dutch, German, Arabic and Hebrew is, as Kaddal shows in his thesis, as bewildering and impressive as the huge catalogues of knowledge MacDiarmid amassed in Whalsay.

For Doughty, the English language of his day was a debased shadow of the glorious thing it had once been. In his 'Post Illa' to *The Dawn in Britain*, he writes:

> In this North-lying island soil, Geoffrey Chaucer kindled the first bright beacon-lamp, at the hearth of the divine muses. [...] But only to Edmund Spenser, darling of the divine muses; those, (with their companion Graces, of blissful lips,) revealed their own golden

> intimate tongue; and taught him, without spot or stain, to devoutly perceive the harmony of the Spheres. Yet even, in his brief lifetime, English speech began somewhat to decay [...]. (vol.6, pp.241-242)

Doughty loathed the way his peers used the English language, so reached back to earlier authors in an attempt to capture some of the grandness, nobility and distinction he found there. He saw the language as reaching an early highpoint in Chaucer (in Arabia, to save luggage space, Doughty buried a number of his books but retained his volume of Chaucer) and found its most full and brilliant form of expression with Spenser. He goes on to outline what he sees as the poet's responsibility to the language:

> it is the prerogative of every lover of his Country, to use the instrument of his thought, which is the Mother-tongue, with propriety and distinction; to keep that reverently clean and bright, which lies at the root of his mental life, and so, by extension, of the life of the Community: putting away all impotent and disloyal vility of speech, which is no uncertain token of a people's decadence. (vol.6, p.243)

For Doughty, by the end of the nineteenth century the English language was hopelessly decadent and corrupt, and the language he created for his poetry, which may seem eccentric to us today, was a serious and wholehearted response to this. As Herbert F. Tucker puts it: 'Doughty's lifelong commitment to the project of linguistic reinvention cannot be overestimated.'[52] For MacDiarmid, the nationalist and patriot, the poet who had already set in motion one linguistic revolution and was trying to produce another, the commitment Doughty advocates must have been very attractive indeed.

MacDiarmid's use of English can also be seen as a reaction against what he saw as a contemporary linguistic degeneracy. But his objection was not to the airy decadence Doughty objected to (although MacDiarmid would have had little time for that) but to the imperial associations the language held for him. In his 1931 essay 'English Ascendancy in British Literature', MacDiarmid writes:

> It is absurd that intelligent readers of English, who would be ashamed not to know something (if only the leading names, and roughly, what they stand for) of most Continental literatures, are content to ignore Scottish Gaelic, Irish, and Welsh literatures, and Scots Vernacular literature. Surely the latter are nearer to them than the former, and the language difficulty no greater. These Celtic and Scots dialect poets were products of substantially the same environment, and concerned for the most part with the same political, psychological, and practical issues, the same traditions and tendencies, the same landscapes, as poets in English to whom, properly regarded, they are not only valuably complementary, but (in view of their linguistic, technical, and other divergencies) corrective. Confinement to the English central stream is like refusing to hear all but one side of a complicated case.[53]

The essay passionately and persuasively argues for the value of non-standard and minority languages in poetry. For MacDiarmid, an ideal British poetry would allow equal status to Welsh, Gaelic, Scots, and all kinds of dialects from all parts of the islands. There would be no dominant tongue and poetry would be made richer by allowing all the available tributaries to flow into it. But this ideal, because of the overbearing position of England and the English language, could not emerge. The English language was, in MacDiarmid's view, in such a position of ascendancy that no other voices could make themselves heard.

But, as we have observed, by the time he wrote this essay, MacDiarmid's great period of writing in Scots was over and he was beginning to turn towards English. He said of this change in linguistic direction:

> I was becoming increasingly preoccupied with political and scientific matters, and there was no vocabulary for them in Scots. There's no vocabulary in English either; you had to use the international scientific jargon, you see, which I did use.[54]

He perhaps overstates the case when he claims that he was not using English, but, as we have seen, it was a wide-ranging and unique kind of English. The language of the English ascendancy, because it had closed itself off from any other language, had become narrow and impoverished. When a language is in a position of dominance, as English was all over the world in the nineteenth century, when it refuses to recognise the validity of so-called minority languages, it becomes provincial. In MacDiarmid's conception, the English language had refused to allow any outside influence to penetrate it and was all the poorer as a result. And, in his later work, allowing outside influences to penetrate his English was a key principle for MacDiarmid.

In his 1936 essay, *Charles Doughty and the Need for Heroic Poetry*, MacDiarmid wrote:

> Doughty alone foresaw and understood it all thoroughly and realized that the English ascendancy policy must go – that England must relapse on its native basis and let its dialect and minority language elements at long last resume their proper function after the tremendous misdirection of a policy by which England had gained the whole world and lost its own head. Great Britain, or better still, England might inspire an epic, but not the British Empire.[55]

The Doughty essay provides the answers to the problems identified in 'English Ascendancy in British Literature'. The thing holding back English poetry was the imperial associations the language had gathered. MacDiarmid continues:

> Doughty's idea was to make a fresh channel for English from the upper reaches, from the vernacular as it was before the Renaissance, and so freshen and purify the corrupt main Flood [...].[56]

MacDiarmid saw Doughty as a vernacular poet par excellence. In his creation of a synthetic English which reached back into the roots of the language, which predicated itself on the ways the language was used before the time of English world-domination, MacDiarmid saw something fundamentally anti-imperialist in Doughty's project. Doughty's English went back to the rich fundamentals of the tongue, therefore avoiding the imperial parochialness which MacDiarmid saw as having become inherent in the language. By going back to these constituent parts, Doughty's poetry could go forward. By avoiding the linguistic atrophy caused by imperialism, Doughty created a unique, rich and vital poetic idiom. Doughty's writing may have been archaic but, for MacDiarmid, it was a credible alternative to the impoverished language of the English Ascendancy. By reaching back 'before the Renaissance', MacDiarmid suggests that Doughty was able to create a rich and venerable national language that remained unsullied by the British Empire's enormities. The language of the English Ascendancy was exclusive, but Doughty's language, in a wholly committed way, was open to all kinds of older English words, registers, and alternative forms of speech. Writing like a sixteenth-century poet may seem reactionary but, in MacDiarmid's mind, Doughty's project was radical and cosmopolitan.

In MacDiarmid's own English-language work (and his Scots) he refuses to limit language to place, and one of the achievements of his poetry in both tongues is the way it reaches out to other cultures and literatures. As Heaney puts it, 'What was great about his effort in Scotland was the inclusiveness of it.'[57] Unlike many of the Shetland writers looked at in this study, MacDiarmid's Scots is not a local language (not that there is anything wrong with local languages), but an attempt to create a modern, cosmopolitan and international poetic idiom. Although the words and sounds of Langholm are perhaps privileged, MacDiarmid allows no authority or prominence to the local. His Scots is a deterritorialised Scots, and so is the English he used from the early 1930s onwards. *In Memoriam James Joyce* is subtitled *From A Vision of World Language* and, in the poem and in his other epic works, MacDiarmid seeks to create a language which ranges through the languages of the world. He was aiming at an international poetic vernacular – not the atrophied standard English of the imperial ascendancy, but an English which would be inclusive, multi-faceted, and willing to open itself to different languages and areas of experience. C.H. Sisson says of MacDiarmid:

> Not only has his mind been open to an uncommon variety of influences, from a variety of quarters, but having made a success of a curious version of his local speech, he abandoned it altogether for the English required by his wider later subject-matter. And so it will be, with any serious writer. The openness to foreign influences, so far from causing the drying up of the genuine native spring, helps it to flow.[58]

One suspects MacDiarmid might have taken issue with Sisson's idea that his Scots was 'a curious version of his local speech', or that the shift to English was inevitable, but the recognition of MacDiarmid's cosmopolitanism sums up the situation well. In his striving to construct a poetic language able to accommodate all the areas of experience he wanted to write about, MacDiarmid was reacting against a provincialism he saw as inherent in a language placed in a position of imperial dominance. To construct their poetry, Doughty looked back, MacDiarmid looked out from Whalsay into innumerable intellectual and linguistic avenues, but both men were aiming at nothing less than the reinvention of the English language their times confronted them with.

'Harbinger of the epical age'

If we can draw linguistic parallels between Doughty and MacDiarmid, we can also find points-of-contact in their attitudes to poetry. In our discussion of 'On the Ocean Floor' we saw MacDiarmid suggest that the subjective personae of lyric poetry must be left behind. It is a tiny poem but, in its image of accumulation, it leads us to the gigantic, amorphous epic that MacDiarmid spent many of his Shetland years building. For the rest of this chapter, again taking Doughty as a crucial precursor, I would like to discuss the creative possibilities opened to MacDiarmid by the use of the genre of epic.

The Dawn in Britain is Doughty's most substantial epic statement. In it, as well as trying to achieve a linguistic revolution, he attempted to provide a unifying series of histories, myths and legends for the nation he loved. But, according to Laura Riding, another of Doughty's twentieth-century advocates, his ambition went even further:

> Doughty tried to bring poetry within the frame of cosmic actuality as the setting of human actuality. Poetry, for Doughty, made possible the use of language for the spiritual deciphering of human existence – *and* of the essential phenomena of being, as viewed with poetic vision.[59]

Doughty is not a poet concerned with the self. *Arabia Deserta* is fundamentally opposed to Romantic notions which had developed about the Arabian peninsula during the nineteenth century and, in his poetry, Doughty disavows Romantic ideas about the centrality of the poet's consciousness. In his verse, as well as producing a national epic, Doughty is concerned with human existence itself. He is not aiming at a poetry which springs from an inspired subjective consciousness, from an overspilling of inspiration or emotion, but attempts to produce a poetry which listens to the world, which can allow us to hear the 'tiny shells incessantly raining'.

In his book on MacDiarmid's later poetry, Alan Riach writes:

> Individuality [...] is broken down in MacDiarmid's epic work, as it foregrounds the methods of its own construction. The text reveals itself as a construction, and not the unmediated outflowing of a Romantic sensibility. It works to deny the traditional bourgeois sense that the author is the exclusive owner of what he or she produces, yet at the same time the authorial function of the name 'MacDiarmid' is not relinquished.[60]

Like Doughty's work, MacDiarmid's epic poetry does not flow from the self. These works seek to gather all kinds of knowledge, and to bring together the diversity of human language and knowledge within a gigantic epic space. In 'On a Raised Beach' we can identify a single human presence that experiences the landscape but, in the later poems, this person is not to be found. As Riach puts it:

> What is perhaps most surprising (and in some ways, confusing) about MacDiarmid's use of the first person singular is the distance at which it stands from a consistently identifiable persona, or personae.[61]

The 'I' in MacDiarmid's later poetry functions as a kind of conduit through which the multifariousness of the world flows. It is a poetry which, instead of establishing the primacy of the poet's subjective self, attempts to integrate a multitude of voices. For MacDiarmid, it was epic, as opposed to lyric, in which this move away from subjectivity could be achieved. In his essay on Doughty, he makes the idea political:

> It is epic – and no lesser form – that equates with the classless society. Everything else [...] belongs to the old order of bourgeois 'values', to the nebulous entities described by terms like 'spiritual' and 'soul', in short, it stands for the old romantic virtues, which is to say, pragmatically, for nothing. Doughty, as against Auden and Day Lewis, say, is the only English poet who belongs to the new order, that is to say, to our own time.[62]

Epic poetry, in MacDiarmid's conception, is opposed to subjective, bourgeois lyric. Lyric poets, in their concentration on the self, cannot be the poets of a classless society. Their concern is with the individual, and this is a concern which leads to separation, not integration. Epic poetry, on the other hand, is concerned with the collective – with the country, the nation, the racial or ethnic group. Epics, for MacDiarmid, and for Doughty, are works which peoples and cultures can unite around.

Doughty's disavowal of the self and concern with the collective, and his grand use of epic prompted MacDiarmid, in *In Memoriam James Joyce*, to call him a 'Harbinger of the epical age of Communism' (*CP*2, p.740). The kind of epic poetry MacDiarmid wants is a poetry fit for an age of achieved communism, a political system which, for him, was able to bring together and synthesise the elements of a stratified society. In his epics Doughty sought to unite a nation and, in his, MacDiarmid attempts to create a utopian space in which he can unite the diversity of life. For both men, the poet's responsibility is not to express the self, but to use poetry to bring together things in the world, to, in Riding's terms, 'use language for the spiritual deciphering of human existence'. They are both concerned with the primary role of poetry in society. As MacDiarmid puts it:

> Poetry matters. I regard poetry as one of the things that matters most in the world. The organic apprehension that can only be achieved through poetry seems to me sadly lacking. There has been a playing down of the increasing complexity and pace of modern life and so on, playing down the role of the imagination. The seer, the foreknower, has been displaced in a hierarchy of human beings. It requires to be replaced there.[63]

The poet has a special place in the world, but their responsibility is not to express their own subjective self. Epic poetry, because it is concerned with the collective, and because it allows the poet to work on a very large scale, has the flexibility and potential for inclusiveness necessary to unify an infinitely varied world. For both Doughty and MacDiarmid, poetry was the central force in that world. And, as with their use of landscape and their attitudes to language, this returns to fundamental ideas about what poetry is for. Morgan writes of MacDiarmid's epics:

> It has something to do with a man who is looking at everything and trying to find a way of talking about everything. It's important because he's looking back to the old, the very ancient and respectable idea of poetry as not just feeling but knowledge, and just because knowledge is so difficult, so specialized nowadays, doesn't mean to say that an artist, a poet, can't attempt to grapple with it. I think it's got something to do with that – a man casting his eye over the available knowledge of his time, and seeing what he can make of it in poetry, and there's a pathos about that I think which is very interesting indeed.[64]

Morgan's view is echoed by Sisson:

> they [MacDiarmid's later poems] represent a heroic effort – too heroic perhaps – to use verse with a discursive freedom which was new to the twentieth century and recalls rather the sixteenth and early seventeenth centuries, before prose had become capable of handling a whole range of materials with its modern ease.[65]

In Sisson's 'too heroic perhaps' there is a subtle indication that MacDiarmid's project was never ultimately realised and, indeed, 'Cornish Heroic Song for

Valda Trevlyn', as MacDiarmid conceived it, was never completed. But, from the sections which were published, the ambitious and utopian aims of the work are clear. MacDiarmid aims at a poetry which, although endlessly varied, tries to achieve the impossible omnific one. It is a poetry of intellectual curiosity and reach, but it is also a poetry which strives for unity. It does not move towards closure – as he says to Norman MacCaig in *In Memoriam James Joyce* 'behind Leviathan / There's still the kraken / And no end to our "ontological heroics"' (*CP2*, p.851) – but represents an always-open fusion of disparate material.[66] It is constantly changing, leading readers down surprising, often bewildering, paths, but it is also a democratic poetic environment in which, like a jazz collective, all constituent parts are allowed to coexist, no matter how different they are.

The epic poetries of Doughty and MacDiarmid disavow what they see as a narrow focus on the self. Their epics present a considerable challenge to the reader but, in them, we see each poet trying to do big things. These are poems of participation – participation in the nation's past, participation in the world's variety – and, in the way they engage with existence, both MacDiarmid and Doughty try to reassert the poet's place in the world. Both men react against a Romantic sensibility in which poetry emerges from the poet's subjectivity. They do not look inside, but wrestle with the complexity of life in order to write something which has unification – of the nation, of the world – at its core.

Conclusion

MacDiarmid's time in Shetland can easily be seen as one of isolation, solitude and personal difficulty. Indeed, as we have seen, MacDiarmid himself came to see his residency in Whalsay as one of limitation and exile. He suffered a breakdown in 1935, was unable to see his two children from the marriage to Peggy, he struggled financially, and was engaged in producing an enormous, amorphous epic poem that was unlikely to find a publisher. But, as I have suggested, the poetry he wrote in Shetland is more often about engagement with the world than it is about a disavowal of it.

From his actual engagement with Shetland's people, to his creative use of its landscapes, to the later poems which some critics have tended to see less than favourably, MacDiarmid's invocation of Doughty proves illuminating. The *Stony Limits* poems represent what is perhaps the most significant engagement with the Shetland landscape by any poet. As we have seen, Margaret Chalmers aside, those landscapes have not been utilised much by local authors but, by seeing them through the lens of Doughty's book on Arabia, MacDiarmid was able to write what is, in my view, the central poem of his career.

In the poetry he wrote in the latter segment of his time in Shetland, MacDiarmid became much less concerned with the islands. If *Arabia Deserta*, with its adamantine picture of the places Doughty travelled through, provided an important context for *Stony Limits*, MacDiarmid drew some of his later coordinate points from what he found in Doughty's epics. MacDiarmid's later poetry strives to be linguistically inclusive and, in writing it, he was aiming at a poetry which engaged, not with the place in which he was living, but with the world of human knowledge and experience. There is, perhaps, a typical MacDiarmidian perversity in using a poet like Doughty – jingoistically English, an extreme political conservative, completely out of touch with the twentieth century – as a source of influence, but MacDiarmid's championing of him was much more meaningful than that. In Doughty he saw a man who, as he perhaps saw himself as having done, had gone through terrible adversity, completely alone, and had survived. And, in Doughty's attitude to language, and in his belief in poetry's importance, he also saw a writer who, with huge ambition, swam against the tide of English literature in the first quarter of the century.

When Grieve sailed from Shetland in 1942, a large amount of the poetry he had written there was stuffed inside forty tea-chests which were left for Valda and Michael to deal with.[67] As Ruth McQuillan points out, the last great creative effort of his life was at an end.[68] Despite what he was doing in his years in Shetland, however, local writers paid little attention. William J. Tait, whose work I will look at in Chapter Seven, and who, more than any other Shetland writer, took his cues from MacDiarmid, was later to rue the fact that a poet of such stature had been living in Shetland in such obscurity. Speaking about his school days in the 1930s, Tait said:

> I am still appalled to think that during part of those years one of the greatest living poets was resident in Shetland, and, if we knew of his existence at all, it was as a subject for cheap gibes [...]. [69]

But, when the first edition of the *New Shetlander* appeared in March 1947, the movement MacDiarmid kick-started in the 1920s finally arrived in the isles.

Notes

1. Hugh MacDiarmid, *The Islands of Scotland: Hebrides, Orkneys, and Shetlands* (London: B.T. Batsford, 1939), p.88.
2. MacDiarmid's first contribution to the magazine was in no.4 (June 1947) and his last in no.20 (January-February 1950).
3. Hugh MacDiarmid, *Complete Poems*, vol.1, ed. by Michael Grieve and W.R. Aitken (Manchester: Carcanet, 1993), pp.437-443. Page numbers given in text as CP1.
4. Hugh MacDiarmid, *The Uncanny Scot: A Selection of Prose*, ed. by Kenneth Buthlay (London: MacGibbon & Kee, 1968), pp.80-92.
5. Michael Schmidt, *40 Tea Chests: Hugh MacDiarmid and Shetland* (Lerwick: Shetland Amenity Trust, 2010), p.6.
6. Ruth McQuillan, 'Hugh MacDiarmid's Shetland Poetry', in *MacDiarmid in Shetland*, ed. by Laurence Graham and Brian Smith (Lerwick: Shetland Library, 1992), pp.4-17.

7. Michael Schmidt, *Lives of the Poets* (London: Weidenfeld & Nicolson, 1998), p.644.
8. Seamus Heaney, *Preoccupations: Selected Prose 1968-1978* (London: Faber and Faber, 1984), p.197.
9. Seamus Heaney, 'An Invocation', *London Review of Books*, vol.14, no.15 (6 August 1992), 16.
10. Despite the dates of publication, substantial portions of these poems were written in Shetland. See McQuillan, 'MacDiarmid's Shetland Poetry'.
11. Scott Lyall, 'MacDiarmid, Communism, and the Poetry of Commitment', in *The Edinburgh Companion to Hugh MacDiarmid*, ed. by Scott Lyall and Margery Palmer McCulloch (Edinburgh: Edinburgh University Press, 2011), pp.68-81 (p.68).
12. Alan Bold, *MacDiarmid: Christopher Murray Grieve, A Critical Biography* (London: Paladin, 1990), p.336.
13. See also Mark Ryan Smith, 'Two Explorers: Charles Doughty and Hugh MacDiarmid', *PN Review 202* (November-December 2011), 60-63.
14. For a detailed study of Doughty's work see Mohamed A.M. Kaddal, 'Charles Montagu Doughty: His Life and Work' (unpublished doctoral thesis, University of Glasgow, 1962).
15. Ezra Pound, 'Hugh Selwyn Mauberley (Contacts and Life)', in *Selected Poems, 1908-1969* (London: Faber and Faber, 1975), pp.98-112, (p.98).
16. Charles M. Doughty, *The Dawn in Britain*, vol.1 (London: Duckworth & Co., 1906), p.4.
17. Ezra Pound, *The Cantos of Ezra Pound* (New York: New Directions, 1996), p.554.
18. James Schuyler, 'Wystan Auden', in *The New York Poets*, ed. by Mark Ford (Manchester: Carcanet, 2004), p.190.
19. Hugh MacDiarmid, *Complete Poems*, vol.2, ed. by Michael Grieve and W.R. Aitken (Harmondsworth: Penguin, 1985), p.1294. Page numbers given in text as CP2.
20. *Hugh MacDiarmid: New Selected Letters*, ed. by Dorian Grieve, Owen Dudley Edwards and Alan Riach (Manchester: Carcanet, 2001), p.291.
21. For a discussion of Davidson and MacDiarmid see Hazel Hynd, 'The Authority of Influence: John Davidson and Hugh MacDiarmid', *Scottish Studies Review*, vol.2, no.2 (Autumn 2001), 77-93.
22. In a letter dated 8 march 1936, Doughty's widow, Caroline, writing to thank MacDiarmid for sending her a copy of his essay 'Charles Doughty and the Need for Heroic Poetry' (1936), said: 'Thank you very much for sending me your article on my husband's poetry, you are wonderfully generous in your praise but I must say my breath was quite taken away by the first sentence!! The U.S.S.R. was anathema to my husband! & how you can think of Lenin and C.M.D. at the same time passes my comprehension. I think if you had *known* my husband you would have thought differently.' See *Dear Grieve: Letters to Hugh MacDiarmid (C.M. Grieve)*, ed. by John Manson (Glasgow: Kennedy & Boyd, 2011), p.147.
23. See Brian Smith 'Stony Limits: The Grieves in Whalsay, 1933-1942', in *MacDiarmid in Shetland*, ed. by Graham and Smith, pp.42-72.
24. Reyner Banham 'Arabia Revisita', *London Review of Books*, vol.2, no.23 (4 December 1980), 16.

25. See Scott Lyall, '"The Man is a Menace": MacDiarmid and Military Intelligence', *Scottish Studies Review*, vol.8, no.1 (Spring 2007), 37-52.
26. Charles M. Doughty, *Adam Cast Forth* (London: Duckworth & Co., 1908), p.52.
27. D.G. Hogarth, *The Life of Charles M. Doughty* (London: Oxford University Press, 1928), p.37.
28. See Bold, *MacDiarmid*, pp.276-323.
29. Charles M. Doughty, *Travels in Arabia Deserta*, vol.1 (Cambridge: Cambridge University Press, 1888), p.405.
30. See Kaddal, 'Doughty', pp.56-57.
31. Edwin Morgan, 'Epilogue: Seven Decades', in *Collected Poems* (Manchester: Carcanet, 1990), p.595.
32. Kaddal, 'Doughty', pp.129-130.
33. Edwin Morgan, 'MacDiarmid at Seventy-Five', in *Essays* (Cheadle: Carcanet, 1974), pp.214-221 (p.219).
34. T.J. Cribb, 'The Cheka's Horrors and "On a Raised Beach"', *Studies in Scottish Literature*, vol.xx (1985), 88-100 (pp.89-90).
35. Morgan, *Essays*, p.219.
36. On 26 June 1936 Caroline Doughty wrote to MacDiarmid to thank him for sending her a copy of *Stony Limits* and a series of explanatory notes to the elegy for her husband. Of 'On a Raised Beach' she wrote that 'although I do not understand the geological terms, still, I see so much in it that he loved & wondered about, I wish you could have met him.' See *Dear Grieve*, ed. by Manson, p.156.
37. MacDiarmid gleaned some of his geological material from Tom Robertson, a geologist he spent time with in Shetland. See Glenn Bard, 'Between a Rock and a Hard Place: Science and Art in Hugh MacDiarmid's *Stony Limits and Other Poems*', *New Shetlander*, 254 (Yule 2010), 29-35.
38. Alan Riach, 'The Idea of Order in "On a Raised Beach": The Language of Location and the Politics of Music', in *Terranglian Territories: Proceedings of the Seventh International Conference on the Literature of Region and Nation*, ed. by Susanne Hagemann (Frankfurt: Peter Lang, 2000), pp.613-629 (p.613).
39. Hugh MacDiarmid, 'MacDiarmid at Eighty-Five', interview with George Bruce, 11 August 1977, in *The Thistle Rises: An Anthology of Poetry and Prose by Hugh MacDiarmid*, ed. by Alan Bold (London: Hamish Hamilton, 1984), pp.274-285 (p.279).
40. Riach, 'Idea of Order', p.614.
41. Barker Fairley, *Charles M. Doughty: A Critical Study* (London: Jonathan Cape, 1927), p.59. MacDiarmid read Fairley's book, and his *Selected Passages from the Dawn in Britain of Charles Doughty* (London: Duckworth & Co., 1935) in the mid-1930s and the two men later became acquainted. See letters in *The Letters of Hugh MacDiarmid*, ed. by Bold (London: Hamish Hamilton, 1984), and *New Selected Letters*, ed. by Grieve, Edwards and Riach.
42. MacDiarmid says something similar in 'The War with England': 'I was better with the sounds of the sea / Than with the voices of men / And in desolate and desert places / I found myself again' (CP1, p.454).
43. Alan Riach, 'Hugh MacDiarmid: Put it to the Touch', in *Dear Grieve*, ed. by Manson, pp.xiii-xxiii (p.xviii).

44. Hugh MacDiarmid, *Lucky Poet: A Self-Study in Literature and Political Ideas* (Manchester: Carcanet, 1994), p.xxvii.
45. See Grieve's letter to the *Shetland News*, 7 August 1941, p.2, for an example of his disdain for what some local people interested in encouraging Shetland dialect writing were trying to do: 'Mr Stewart and others need have no fear that I have any intention of intruding on their particular little cabbage-patch.' For a description of this spat see Smith, 'Stony Limits', in *MacDiarmid* in Shetland, ed. by Graham and Smith, pp.63-64.
46. For a discussion of the poem see Edwin Morgan, *Hugh MacDiarmid* (Harlow: Longman, 1976), p.21-22.
47. See Michael H. Whitworth, 'Culture and Leisure in Hugh MacDiarmid's "On a Raised Beach"', *Scottish Studies Review*, vol.9, no.1 (Spring 2008), 123-143.
48. *Letters*, ed. by Bold, p.155.
49. For a discussion of MacDiarmid's use of Jakobsen see Ruth McQuillan, 'MacDiarmid's Other Dictionary', *Lines Review* 66 (September 1978), 5-14.
50. David Daiches, *A Critical History of English Literature*, vol.2 (London: Mandarin, 1994), p.1146.
51. Anne Treneer, *Charles M. Doughty: A Study of His Prose and Verse* (London: Jonathan Cape, 1935), p.17.
52. Herbert F. Tucker, 'Doughty's The Dawn in Britain and the Modernist Eclipse of the Victorian', *Romanticism and Victorianism on the Net* no.47 (August 2007) <http://id.erudit.org/iderudit/016705ar> [Accessed 12 July 2010].
53. Hugh MacDiarmid, 'English Ascendancy in British Literature', *The Uncanny Scot*, ed. by Buthlay, pp.115-134 (p.121).
54. Interview by Bruce in *The Thistle Rises*, ed. by Bold, p.279.
55. Hugh MacDiarmid, 'Charles Doughty and the Need for Heroic Poetry', in *Selected Essays of Hugh MacDiarmid*, ed. by Duncan Glen (London: Jonathan Cape, 1969), pp.75-85 (p.79). The essay first appeared in *The Modern Scot*, vol.6, no.4 (1936), as a review of Barker Fairley's *Selected Passages from the Dawn in Britain*. It was then published in pamphlet form later that year by the journal's editor J.H. Whyte.
56. MacDiarmid, 'Heroic Poetry', p.85.
57. Dennis O'Driscoll, *Stepping Stones: Interviews with Seamus Heaney* (London: Faber and Faber, 2009), p.363.
58. C.H. Sisson, *The Avoidance of Literature: Collected Essays* (Manchester: Carcanet, 1978), p.562.
59. Carcanet Press Archive, CPA/2/3/125/40, Laura (Riding) Jackson, Introduction to unpublished selection of Doughty's work, Carcanet Press Archive, John Rylands University Library, undated.
60. Alan Riach, *Hugh MacDiarmid's Epic Poetry* (Edinburgh: Edinburgh University Press, 1991), p.162.
61. Riach, *Epic*, p.158.
62. MacDiarmid, 'Heroic Poetry', p.76.
63. Interview by Bruce in *The Thistle Rises*, ed. by Bold, p.285.
64. Edwin Morgan in 'Hugh MacDiarmid: A Disgrace to the Community', ed. by Robert Crawford, BBC Radio 1992. Reprinted in *PN Review 89* (January-February 1993) <http://www.pnreview.co.uk/cgibin/scribe?file=/members/pnr089/articles/089ar02.txt> [Accessed 25 November 2010].

65. C.H. Sisson, 'MacDiarmid's Sticks', *London Review of Books*, vol.6, no.6 (5 April 1984), 16-18 (p.17).
66. MacDiarmid's reference is to a letter from Herman Melville to Nathaniel Hawthorne, 29 June 1851. See *Melville's Letters to Hawthorne* <http://www.melville.org/letters5.htm> [Accessed 23 May 2012].
67. Michael Grieve, 'Hugh MacDiarmid: The Man', in *The Hugh MacDiarmid Anthology: Poems in Scots and English*, ed. by Michael Grieve and Alexander Scott (London: Routledge and Kegan Paul, 1972), pp.xi-xvi (p.xiii).
68. McQuillan, 'MacDiarmid's Shetland Poetry', in *MacDiarmid in Shetland*, ed. by Graham and Smith, p.5.
69. Quoted in Lollie Graham, 'W.J. Tait, 1919-1982: A Tribute', *New Shetlander*, 181 (Hairst 1992), 14.

Chapter Six

THE NEW SHETLANDER

Introduction

In the last quarter of the nineteenth century, as we observed in Chapter Two, writers in Shetland were given a new platform when local newspapers first appeared. Similarly, when Peter Jamieson (1898-1976), a writer, antiquary and communist from Lerwick, founded the *New Shetlander* in March 1947, another generation of island writers gained a publication dedicated to their work.[1] The journal was fundamental to the post-war development of the archipelago's literature and, today, it continues to be the most important publication for anybody who wants to read or write about Shetland's history, language, literature, or culture.

The magazine grew from two local precursors, both of which Jamieson was involved in – the *Shetlander*, a Marxist journal, and the Shetland Poetical Circle. The *Shetlander*, which ran for six issues, was produced by members of the Economics Club (including John Peterson), a socialist group which met in Lerwick in the 1920s.[2] The *New Shetlander*, despite its ideologically inclusive editorial policy, was also to the left, albeit in a less doctrinaire manner than the earlier magazine.[3] The willingness to discuss local affairs, in radical and serious ways, however, was a principle both journals shared. As for what concerns us here – creative writing – the earlier magazine did carry a small number of poems acceptable to a far-left editorship, but its focus was almost entirely political and ideological. The *New Shetlander* covered much wider cultural ground.

A more significant coming-together of creative writers can be seen in The Shetland Poetical Circle, an organisation which was active from 1941 until 1947. This group of writers, from all across Shetland, never met and, because there was no local journal (the newspapers no longer carried literary work as they did in Burgess' time), they circulated a notebook. When a member received the notebook, they had two weeks to write their contribution and post the book to another member. When everybody had contributed, the journal was kept by Walter John Robertson of Whalsay, one of the circle's founders (the other was Bertie Deyell from Semblister), and a new book was sent out. Three volumes of the journal, named *Shetland Writings*, were produced.[4] In the first year there were ten contributors and, by the third volume, this had increased to twenty-seven.[5] The journal allowed writers to form a kind of virtual literary community,

THE NEW SHETLANDER, NUMBER ONE. MARCH, 1947. 6d.

The New Shetlander

WITH da voar, and da maas klaagin ower da rigs, this journal makes its appearance, in sixteen modest pages. We feel confident, however that before our Hairst number is out, another sixteen pages will be added.

THE NEW SHETLANDER is a non-party political and literary paper. Space for the ideas of all progressive trends is at the disposal of those interested. Believing that Shetlanders should take a more intelligent interest in Shetland, we support schemes for the improvement of conditions, and the development of new industries. The growth of the S.H.K.A. and similar organisations, and the remarkable success of the S.C.W.S. branches, are significant, as showing a welcome approach to the problems of the day. While still proud of their independence, the Shetland crofter and his wife are not above selling dir oo an hosiery through "da Shak," and buying seed taaties and manure through da Crofters' Supply agency. Co-operation is, in our opinion, the solution to the problems facing the islands.

Writers, poets, critics and others interested in northern tradition and letters, and with a regard for our Shetlandic heritage, will get space for their work in these pages. In the past all too little encouragement has been held out to writers and poets. This paper gives a welcome to all who feel they have something to contribute to Shetland thought. Send your contributions, and we'll try and get them into print. For the present we are not able to pay for contributions, but intend to arrange competitions for work by writers on themes of northern interest, with special reference to writing in the dialect.

THE NEW SHETLANDER wants to "get around," so we invite readers to send letters with their criticism and advice. Suggestions for improving the format and contents will be appreciated. Readers willing to sell copies, or give subscriptions or donations, should lose no time in sending letters, as this new venture in northern journalism depends largely on their generosity.

OUR COMPETITIONS

IN order to encourage writers, three sets of prizes are offered for the best entries in the following classes:

1. For the best stories or articles in the Shetland dialect, written by competitors under 20 years of age: 1st, £1 1/-; 2nd, 10/6; 3rd, 5/-. Length should not exceed 2000 words.

2. For articles, up to 2000 words, dialect or English, on "The Shetland I'd Like to See," by writers under 30 years of age. Prizes as above.

3. For poems in the dialect by writers under 45 years of age. Same prizes.

Contributions should reach us by the 30th April. Please mark envelopes "Competition."

CONTENTS

The Ghost Walks, By Hagmark	Page 2
The I.W.W. Paul Bunyan and Other Things	3
Shetland at the Cross-Roads, By Prophet Smith	4
The Isles of Thule, Poem, By William Porteous	5
Co-operation in the Highlands and Islands, By Elizabeth Orr	5
Housing I.—Town and Burgh Council Houses, By J. W. Hay	6
At the Exhibition	7
Shetland's Future? By Freedom	7
The Shetland Scene	8
Poems—	
Makar's Sang, By Alexander Scott	8
Sonnet in Time of War, By W. J. Tait	
Shadows Gather, By Vagaland	
Lux in Tenebris, By W. J. Tait	9
Suspense, from the Persian, By H. Marouf	
Daal Scene	9
A Northern Notebook	10
South Georgia, by A. B. Robertson	11
A Gael Looks at Shetland, By Neil Matheson: I.—Ceilte Influence	12
Book Reviews, By Hans	14

First issue of the New Shetlander. *Courtesy of Shetland Museum and Archives* and the *New Shetlander* plugs into their need to share work and ideas. In the first notebook, however, Jamieson discussed the need for a more conventional magazine:

> There is no proper magazine, or periodical, in Shetland today, that can be said to give expression to various matters of Shetland interest, such as literature, poetry, criticism, art, music, progressive politics and culture generally. [...] The S.P.C. [Shetland Poetical Circle] and S.W. [*Shetland Writings*] are the first attempts at an organised Shetland school of thought. More is needed, however, before the movement can become really strong and influential. One way of rallying all Shetlanders to the flag of Shetland would be by the appearance of a magazine. [...] It would be a literary and critical review, appearing at first in a small way, say, either duplicated or printed, and either monthly or quarterly, printing costs permitted. [...] It is suggested that the magazine should have a title, either *Northern Writing*, or *Northern Review*. The latter title might be most suitable, with perhaps a sub-title such as *A Shetland Magazine*.[6]

Jamieson foresaw that something significant could be built around the group of writers brought together by the circulating journals.

The ideas, energy, and desire for publication represented by the *Shetlander* and the Shetland Poetical Circle crystallised in the new magazine. But the *New Shetlander* can also be seen as part of a general emergence of periodicals that took their bearings from the Scottish Literary Renaissance. Margery Palmer McCulloch, in her book *Modernism and Nationalism*, writes of the kind of publications which started to appear from the 1920s onwards in Scotland:

> An essential ingredient in any such exchange of ideas [i.e. those of the Scottish Renaissance] was the creation of a small magazine culture in Scotland, something noticeably absent in the period immediately after World War One. The great days of the *Edinburgh Review* and *Blackwood's* were over, and although these magazines were to continue for a few years longer, it was clear that they were in decline.[7]

In its first decade, the *New Shetlander* attracted contributions from Alexander Scott, Eric Linklater, Naomi Mitchison, Douglas Young, Maurice Lindsay, Helen Cruickshank and Ian Hamilton Finlay. Issue four included a letter of support from MacDiarmid, he contributed the poem 'Happy on Heimaey' to number seven, and a three-part essay 'The Scottish Renaissance Movement after 25 Years' to numbers eighteen to twenty. And in number six, the first of George Mackay Brown's numerous contributions to the magazine appeared. In its early years, although primarily a local journal, the *New Shetlander* was on the radar of a number of writers from outside the isles. Jamieson's magazine, like Derick

Peter Jamieson.   *Courtesy of Shetland Museum and Archives*

Thomson's Gaelic periodical *Gairm* perhaps, had its roots in a particular place, a particular linguistic community, but was willing to admit influences from outside the bounds of its region.[8] As well as drawing on local antecedents, the *New Shetlander* was part of the 'small magazine culture' McCulloch describes.

Jamieson's editorship lasted for forty-two issues. For number 43, after the magazine experienced some severe financial difficulties, John and Laurence (Lollie) Graham took over. Their tenure lasted for four decades, to number 203. The brothers, as Jamieson had done, were unafraid to tackle social and political issues – the years of Shetland's oil boom in the 1970s and 80s, where a gigantic processing terminal was constructed at Sullom Voe in the north of the isles, occasioned several pungent editorials – and, most importantly from the point of view of this study, they continued to encourage local writers. After its first decade there were fewer contributions from well-known Scottish authors, but, under the Grahams' editorship, and under the subsequent hands of librarian John Hunter and Alex Cluness (nos.204-219),[9] and writer Laureen Johnson and historian Brian Smith (no.220-present), the magazine has been the central place of publication for every Shetland author. The appearance of the *New Shetlander* allowed the second period of flourishing in Shetland's literature to begin.

Vagaland (T.A. Robertson) (1909-1973)

Of all the writers who appeared in the magazine in its formative years, the poetic career of Thomas Alexander Robertson best exemplifies the importance of the magazine to local authors. His first published poem appeared in the first issue and he had at least one poem in every number until his death in 1973. An extremely shy and reserved man, would he have been published as often were it not for the *New Shetlander*? He was published outside the isles, in magazines like *Lines Review* and *Lallans*, and also in John MacQueen and Tom Scott's anthology *The Oxford Book of Scottish Verse* (1966), but his readership was primarily local. In the first issue to appear without a contribution from Vagaland, John Graham wrote:

> There is a void in this number of the *New Shetlander*. For the first time in 107 numbers, over a period of 27 years, the *New Shetlander* is without a poem from Vagaland. And just as this magazine is somewhat incomplete without a Vagaland poem so is Shetland diminished by the recent death of T.A. Robertson, whose poetry under the name of Vagaland was but one of his many contributions to our local life and culture.[10]

Since his death, Vagaland's reputation and local popularity have remained high. Excerpts from his verse greet visitors to one of the galleries in the recently built Shetland Museum and Archives. A recent anthology of local writing, *Bright Pebbles* (2010), borrows from one of his best-known poems for its title. He (alongside Rhoda Bulter) is the most frequently used poet in Shetland dialect learning resources for schools.[11] Kevin MacNeil's anthology of island verse, *These Islands, We Sing*, states that Vagaland 'is widely regarded as the greatest Shetland poet of the 20th century',[12] and, in the introduction to Vagaland's *Collected Poems*, the Orcadian scholar Ernest Marwick called him 'Shetland's unofficial poet laureate'.[13] Vagaland, today, and during his own life, is seen as one of the foremost poetic representatives of his archipelago.

Robertson was born in the remote township of Westerwick on Shetland's west side. Less than a year after his birth, his father, a merchant sailor, was lost at sea, and his mother moved with her two sons to the village of Walls. It was the ancient Scandinavian name for this area that gave Robertson his nom de plume. He later attended the Anderson Educational Institute in Lerwick and, after struggling with homesickness (because of the distance from Walls to Lerwick it was necessary to board), went on to flourish, both in the classroom and on the sportsfield. Later, when he came to write, however, he remained utterly a poet of the countryside. After leaving school, he went to Edinburgh University to study English and History, graduating M.A. in 1932. He trained as a teacher and found a job at Lerwick Central School, remaining there, despite being tormented terribly by his pupils, from 1937 until his retiral in 1970. In 1953, he married Martha (Pat) Andrew, who he had known since childhood, and she became the most important figure in his life. Together they produced *Da Sangs at A'll Sing ta Dee* (1973), a collection of local songs and, after his death, Martha edited his *Collected Poems* (1975), which brought together the work from his volumes *Laeves fae Vagaland* (1952), *Mair Laeves fae Vagaland* (1965) and the many poems that first appeared in the *New Shetlander*.

Vagaland's central theme and inspiration was Shetland – its folklore, its history, its flowers and plants, its weather, its music, its wildlife, its language, its traditions. In Chapter Seven, we will discuss how Robertson's contemporary William J. Tait redefined what Shetland dialect verse could be made to do, but Vagaland's concern was to preserve what he saw as essential and good in Shetland. And, if his project, in terms of theme, was a conservative one, his verse is formally conservative too. His poems are always regular, balanced and, as we are about to discuss, they often owe something to song.

The anthology of music that Robertson co-edited, *Da Sangs at A'll Sing ta Dee*, contains both traditional songs and songs written by him and his peers.[14] The foreword outlines the burgeoning interest in folk culture in Shetland during the late nineteenth and early-to-mid twentieth centuries. This movement eventually led to the formation of the Shetland Folk Society, an organisation which sought to preserve, research and make more widely known all aspects of Shetland's folk culture. Robertson became the society's secretary and his interest in traditional culture and song are central to his verse. A number of his compositions – 'Da Sang o Da Twa Breider',[15] 'Da Skeld Man's Sang' (p.77), 'Da Sailor's Sang' (p.85), 'Simmer Sang' (p.130) – are straightforwardly song lyrics and, indeed, a number of them have been set to music by local composers.

T. A. Robertson (Vagaland).   *Courtesy of Shetland Museum and Archives*

The regularity of structure demanded by song is evident in much of Vagaland's poetry. His work shows no enthusiasm for alternative or irregular verse forms, and he is, I think it fair to say, more a poet of the nineteenth century than the twentieth. His verse is stable, balanced and formally straightforward. In this technical conservatism we find a point of comparison with the Orcadian poet Robert Rendall.[16] In *The History of Orkney Literature* Simon Hall says of Rendall:

> Uncomfortable with the difficult content and bewildering forms of high modernism, Rendall has as his primary interest the re-vivification – within traditional poetic frameworks – of his native language.[17]

This could equally be said of Robertson, but Hall's statement is problematic. The use of standard poetic forms is not necessarily anti-modern – MacDiarmid's early work is formally conventional, for example – but, for Vagaland, the point was to write in a way that did not jar the reader's sensibilities. MacDiarmid's early verse reached back to the ballads as a reaction against 'the bad tradition of post-Burnsian Scottish poetry'.[18] He reached back in order to subvert what he detested in contemporary verse. But, as Margery McCulloch shows in Chapter Two of her book *Scottish Modernism and its Contexts*, MacDiarmid combined these traditional sources with avant garde European ideas.[19] Vagaland, on the other hand, was not reacting against anything. His influences were not Mallarmé and Pound, but conservative poets like A.E. Housman and John Betjeman – writers we might see as being opposed to the disruptive, fragmentary approaches of high modernism.[20] Like them, Vagaland is a traditional, perhaps even an unadventurous, poet. Stability is one of the key terms we can use of his work. As we shall discuss, by invoking Shetland's folk traditions, and by concentrating on the local environment, Vagaland was seeking constancy. For him, old stories and songs, and the land that generations of Shetlanders have shared, were things that provided continuity and, in his prosodic conservatism, we see an extension of his desire for stability. For him, and for several of his peers, as we will discuss, the modern world was disruptive and, in his formal conventionality, we find something which is fundamentally opposed to disruption.

Robertson, as his long involvement in the Folk Society suggests, was passionate and knowledgeable about Shetland's folk culture. 'Da Selkie Wife' (p.46), for example, again in the form of a song, tells the kind of strange, ancient seal story that David Thomson writes about in *The People of the Sea* (1996). 'Peerie Folk' (p.52), like several of Robertson's poems, draws on stories of Shetland's nocturnal little people, the trows.[21] 'Da Swan's Gaet' (p.26) moves back to Viking times, another staple source for local folk tales, and 'Da Sneug Wal' (p.21) is a story about a well with magical healing powers. In the work we have looked at so far, with the exceptions of Stewart's *Shetland Fireside Tales* and Saxby's later work, folklore has not been a prominent concern but, in Vagaland's verse, it provides a copious poetic fountainhead. In this chapter, especially in our discussion of the Grahams, we will trace a growing awareness of a local literary tradition and, in Vagaland's work, we see the general interest in folk culture, exemplified by the Folk Society, find expression in verse.

In his use of folklore, Robertson celebrates a rich part of island culture. But, as was the case with Burgess' Rasmie, when the modern world is brought into the picture, that culture is seen as being under threat. In 'Da Trolligirts', for example, we see how ominous the modern world can be:

> Der naethin faersim here ita da hill;
>   da Trows'll never budder folk nae mair.
> Da folk at's livin noo haes atom bombs
>   an pöshon ida sea an laand ta faer;
> An, if dey ruin what's eftir o da past
>   da wirld'll be a poorer place, dat's clear.
> Nane o hit sood be needlessly destroyed
>   an sae I trust dey'll no destroy what's here
> aroond da Trowie Knowes. (p.121)

Nuclear weapons ruin the environment, but the loss of what the past has left us is equally devastating. The trows are gone, but the stories and legends they have bequeathed – the things 'aroond da Trowie Knowes' – are what enrich the world. For Vagaland, traditional culture was not just a series of colourful stories and songs, but was a fundamental component of what it meant to be a Shetlander. For him, traditional culture provided a communal set of stories and songs which could bring people together. As John Graham, in a lecture on Vagaland, puts it: 'He came to see the old traditions and customs as the continuing link between past and present, giving people a sense of stability'.[22] By drawing on the past, Vagaland was seeking to affirm the cultural narrative of the Shetland community. Traditional culture provided a shared storehouse of meaning for Shetland people, but he also saw it as something which could easily disappear. Anxiety about atomic weapons is entirely understandable but, in his verse generally, Vagaland always values tradition over modernity. For him, the modern world was unsettling and, in his evocation of traditional culture, he finds a source of consolation. He looked back to try and make the centre hold.

If Vagaland's verse finds solace in songs and stories, an equally comforting set of images is drawn from the natural world. His poetry is overwhelmingly rural and, on page 133 of his *Collected Poems*, when we find a mention of streets and pavements and traffic, the images jar, after dozens of poems filled with pretty plants, idyllic lochs, mischievous trows, cute animals and the golden glow of cornfields. Vagaland is as much a poet of nature and of landscape as he is a poet of tradition. Marwick writes:

> What Bredon Hill was to Housman, Stoorbra Hill [near Walls] was to him – the unchanging symbol of a countryside that was indescribably dear, and of a way of life so natural and good that he coveted for future generations a perpetuation of its essential features.[23]

The natural world, and the way generations of Shetlanders have lived in that world, are central ideas for Vagaland, and his poetry often finds peace and consolation in those valleys, lochs and hillsides. Unlike William J. Tait, Vagaland is not an outward-looking writer. His gaze is always towards the places that meant most to him. Despite his main place of publication being a magazine that, in its early years, was engaged with wider themes and ideas circulating in Scottish letters, Vagaland remained, proudly and passionately, a local writer.

His focus on the natural world often produces a rather idealised pastoral landscape. In 'Beach of Bright Pebbles', however, something harder is evoked. The poem is set on a stony beach and, although it 'lies flooded in a soft Summer light' (p.182), the scene is not bucolic. Like MacDiarmid, Vagaland uses the stones as a way to imagine the past – not the geological past, but a time in prehistory where ancient Shetlanders walked on the same beach. Vagaland, however, does not stand on his beach in extreme isolation. He feels the comforting presence of his ancestors. The stones on the beach are 'An ornament, an aid to memory' (p.182), and they allow the person who contemplates them:

> to feel that we are not alone,
> That there are others with us on this beach,
> Not seen, sensed rather in the misty haze,
> Bare-footed, strangely-clad, and searching too
> For hard quartz-pebbles with a gem-bright glaze. (p.182)

The poem then offers the land as a source of comfort:

> And doubtless, too, these bare-limbed Stone-age folk,
> Walking like us upon the sun-warmed sand,
> Bathed in the rainbow light of happiness,
> Saw beauty in this Summer-scented land;
> Forgot the times of hunger and of cold,
> As we forget the threats of death and wars;
> Felt themselves part of all the pulse of life –
> Night, day, Earth's seasons, and Time's circling stars. (p.182)

'On a Raised Beach' begins with a solitary figure, but concludes with a desire for involvement and participation. In Vagaland's poem, however, the community is not something he has to struggle towards. It is present from the start. He visits the beach and, prompted by the stones' age, thinks of past generations of Shetlanders who have stood in the same place. For Vagaland, the land, the shared environment, like traditional culture, unites an island community that has existed for centuries.

Vagaland is a poet of solace. His voice is one which, through his use of tradition and the shared natural environment, seems to speak for and affirm the values of the community. In his poem 'Kwarna Farna?', however, we find less to comfort us:

Kwarna Farna? *

A laar o Wast wind blaain
Keeps doon da warm ön;
I hear da Baas o Huxter
An hear da laevrik's tön
Ita da lift abön.

Da lochs trowe bricht daals lyin,
Spreads wide dir sheenin net;
Da simmermil is mirrlin
By skerry, stack, an klett;
Bit shön da sun will set.

You see noo, every saison,
Run waas o barns an byres,
An riggs an cuts fast shangin
Ta burra an ta mires,
An little reek fae fires.

Eence Dale ta Brouster mustered
A thousand folk an mair
Ta dell, an draa da boats doon,
An cast, an maa, an shair;
Bit noo da laand is bare. (p.1)

* Norn for 'where are you going?'

The question the title poses is addressed to people who have been forced from their homes. Unlike 'Beach of Bright Pebbles' this poem is about the disruption of community. The first two stanzas give us a conventional rural scene, but the last line of stanza two signals that this world is going to change. In stanza three, like Maunsie's Crü, we see agricultural buildings begin to crumble and the wildness of the land begin to encroach on cultivated spaces. Nature is not the benign force it usually is in Vagaland's verse. It offers nothing but destruction to anybody who looks at what is left of the once-busy community. 'Kwarna Farna?' is perhaps Vagaland's most bleak and powerful statement. In his verse generally, as we have seen, the community's traditions, stories and ways of life are often under threat. But something usually persists – the kernel of a story, a stone which can invoke kindred people – to allow us to retain what is in danger of disappearing. Yet in 'Kwarna Farna?', community fails and is irrevocably swept away.

This dislocation of community is, however, the exception rather than the rule. Vagaland is much more interested in finding continuity and connection than he is in showing how communities can sometimes become untenable. And, if he often tries to bring the community together by drawing on common traditions and a shared environment, he also attempts to unite the people of his archipelago through language. His poem 'Shetlanrie' (p.68) does this in a rather simplistic way, but his most eloquent and imaginative use of language as a means of bringing people together is to be found in 'A Skyinbow o Tammy's'. The poem, in which many of the themes we have discussed are present, opens with an invocation of Shetland's musical tradition:

> Oh, man, Tammy, dis is vexin,
>   hearin what du haes ta say;
> Boy, I tink du'll tak da fiddle –
>   I wid laek ta hear dee play
> As du played at rants an haemfirs
>   mony a time afore dis day
>
> Yun's *Da Mirry Boys o Greenland*,
>   bit da Greenland men is geen;
> *Underhill*, fae first I heard him
>   mony a heavy day A'm seen.
> Whin du plays *Aald Swaara* ta me,
>   boy, da taers come ta my een. (p.2)

This is the voice of an old man looking back, lamenting the halcyon days he and Tammy have shared and, again, traditional songs are invoked as markers of a common culture. The next two stanzas employ the same voice but, in the first line of stanza five, the poem widens out from the reminiscences of a single person and speaks explicitly for the Shetland community.

> Trowe wir minds wir ain aald language
> still keeps rinnin laek a tön;
> Laek da laverik i da hömin,
> sheerlin whin da day is döne;
> Laek da seich o wind trowe coarn
> at da risin o da mön. (p.2)

For Vagaland, it is the Shetland language, a language which is inextricably wedded to the local environment, that carries 'Things at maks dis life wirt livin' (p.3) and brings the community together. It runs through the minds of its speakers 'laek a tön'. It is the music which has played during the lives of generations of Shetlanders and, for Vagaland, it is this language which must be preserved. If the language is allowed to die, not only is a means of communication lost, but the shared experiences and heritage of the community. The speaker in 'A Skyinbow o Tammy's' realises that many of the old ways are in the past, but he urges that these things must not be forgotten. They, embodied in the language, are like the 'strainin-post' (p.3), the part of a fence that takes all the tension and stops the whole thing from collapsing. For Robertson, the dialect of his native islands symbolised a culture and a way of life and, through his use of that language, his poetry is an attempt to resist the loss of 'da aald true wyes' (p.3) he cared so much about.

We have seen how Burgess' influence permeated Shetland's literature in the first half of the twentieth century. Vagaland is a less groundbreaking poet than Burgess – he is more concerned with preservation than innovation – but Robertson's influence has been, and continues to be, pervasive. In Chapter Eight we will trace echoes of his work in the writing of contemporary authors, especially Christine De Luca and Laureen Johnson, and, in his own time, we see many of his peers following similar literary paths. His quiet concentration on the rural environment is a salient feature in the work of Unst poet Jack Renwick (1924-2010), who first contributed to the *New Shetlander* in its second issue. The verse in his debut volume *Rainbow Bridge* (1963), is formally conventional, sometimes wistful, nostalgic and gentle – all things which characterise much of Robertson's writing. Vagaland is immediately brought to mind in the opening stanza of 'Hjaltlandia', the first poem in the volume:

> Sweet heritage o hedder hills
> An broon burns singin ta da sea,
> Lang windin voes, wi skerries swart,
> Whaar waaters wild mak melody.[24]

But, and this is a theme we also find in Rhoda Bulter and Lollie Graham's work, when Shetland's oil boom started in the 1970s, a satirical, critical tone emerges in Renwick's writing.[25] His 2007 collected poems *The Harp of Twilight*

T. A. Robertson and Martha.   *Courtesy of Shetland Museum and Archives*

contains many of these later, oil-inspired, poems.[26] In poems like 'Sullom Voe, 1976' (p.51), 'Decline and Fall' (p.14), 'Grund Ebb in Eden' (p.63), 'Tammie Tinkin' (p.53), 'High Flyer' (p.66), and 'Jet Set' (p.67), Renwick castigates the oil industry for the damage he thought it was doing to the natural environment, and for the way the new wealth and opportunities it introduced made people get ideas above their station. We will see in the next chapter how a younger writer, Robert Alan Jamieson, takes a more nuanced and complex look at these radical developments but, as we will discuss below, for writers of Renwick's generation, the modernising and industrialising force of oil was something entirely negative.

Vagaland's role as tradition bearer is also a key principle in the work of George P.S. Peterson (b.1933), a writer from the island of Papa Stour on Shetland's west side, who first contributed to the *New Shetlander* in issue thirteen. Growing up in Papa Stour has had a lifelong effect on Peterson, as we see in a 2007 interview where he describes his uncle and neighbours coming to visit the family home:

> He would speak non-stop, tellin stories, an I wid listen. Dey wir highly dramatic stories bit lichtsome eens too. When folk wir in aboot da night dey wid aye spin yarns, tell aboot shipwrecks and folk at wis awa. When I wis aulder I cam ta feel at you wir grippin da soul o da isle wi da stories an da fiddle music.[27]

Peterson, like Robertson, believes in the value of traditional culture and, having learned from old men like his uncle Willie, is one of Shetland's most respected storytellers. His writing, which was collected in the 2009 volume *Aald Papa, I'm Dine!* is a celebration of the stories, place-names, nature, language, folklore, and people of his native island. Thematically and formally, his verse is reminiscent of Vagaland, as we see in his poem 'Da Hairst Is In':

> Dan draa up dy feet ta da fine warm fire;
> We're shoarn an we're ripit as alwees we're dön;
> Ta Göd be da tanks at we're aa hale and weel –
> Come, oot wi dy fiddle, an strik up a tön! [28]

And his respect and love for the older man is clear in his poem 'Ta da Memory o Vagaland':

> I hae nae hert ta write, for hit's dat lonnlie noo –
> No only me, bit Shetland murns for him as weel.
> An dem oonboarn wi love, respect, admire him too –
> An so fareweel! My göd an true aald freend – Fareweel! [29]

If his dialect verse (almost all his poetry is in dialect) is perhaps somewhat derivative, Peterson has also produced a significant amount of vernacular prose. Many of these pieces take their cue from the kind of stories he listened to as a young boy. For example, in *Aald Papa, I'm Dine!*, we find lengthy and complex stories such as 'Nannie Georgedaughter'[30] and the Viking-themed 'Saint Magnus Isle' (pp.165-218). Several stories, 'Karl Boakie's Skinship' (p.20) for example, features Vagaland's favourite creatures, the trows. There are couthy little folk tales such as 'Da Time da Laverik Lost Her Sang' (p.122). 'Emergency' (p.155), a story about Peterson breaking his leg at the age of three, captures the peculiarities of life on a very small island in late 1930s. And there are dramatic stories, both fictional and true, about the many shipwrecks which have occurred around Papa Stour. Robertson was associated with Walls and Renwick with Unst but, for Peterson, the culture and landscape of his island can be traced in almost everything he has written. Like Robertson, it is the community – its stories, its songs, its wildlife, its language – that his writing celebrates and affirms.

All the writers in this chapter find something essential in their local environment. We have mentioned how the *New Shetlander*, especially in its early years, attracted contributions from well-known Scottish writers but, for authors like the ones we are discussing here, its importance as a platform for local literature is key. The work we have covered in this chapter so far emerges from particular regions of Shetland, but it was disseminated across the isles, and to the Scottish mainland, by the magazine. To readers outside Shetland, Peterson's intense concentration on Papa Stour may seem inward, parochial even, but, for someone who was so fundamentally part of the place, the ability to publish in a journal that was read all over the archipelago, and which was on the reading-list of poets and critics from further afield, was a way to speak about his community to a very wide audience. Would Vagaland or Peterson have found a journal so receptive to their work had the *New Shetlander* not come into existence? Their writing is rooted in a particular part of the islands, but the readership they address is relatively large. If they did not have a micro-regional focus, their work would lose much of its character. If the outlet of the *New Shetlander* had not been available, they would have published far less than they did. Very localised environments, and the encouragement offered by the magazine, were crucial to these writers, and to the subject of our next section.

Rhoda Bulter (1929-1994)

After Vagaland's death, Lerwick poet Rhoda Bulter stepped into his shoes as Shetland's unofficial laureate. In a short essay on Bulter, poet and novelist Robert Alan Jamieson, who read her work in the *New Shetlander* as he was growing up, writes:

> I think I recall my father reading out 'Fladdabister', and telling us with some pride that she was sib ta wis, a distant cousin. So Rhoda felt like one of the family as, during the seventies, she inherited Vagaland's mantle as Shetland's favourite poet [...].[31]

Like Vagaland, Bulter's poetry is dedicated to Shetland and to its language, in which she worked exclusively and considered one of her 'gret loves' and her 'midder tongue'.[32]

For somebody who only started to write and publish in their 40s (her first contribution to the *New Shetlander* came in 1965 in number 74) and who had no literary background, this position as the most popular poet in the isles is remarkable. Although she was not part of the magazine's first decade, Bulter became a regular contributor. Compared to many of the periodical's writers, she was relatively uneducated (in that she had not been to university), and it cannot have been easy, as a Lerwick housewife and mother, to have put herself forward as an author. But, when she got into her stride, she was prolific. She produced four collections of poetry, *Shaela* (1976), *A Nev Foo a Coarn* (1977), *Link-Stanes* (1980), and *Snyivveries* (1986), the first two books being republished in the combined volume *Doobled-Up* (1978). For almost ten years she contributed the long, James Inkster-like dialect prose sequence, 'Laeves fae Beenie's Diary',

Rhoda Bulter, c.1976.   *Courtesy of the Bulter family*

to *Shetland Life* magazine.[33] Alongside her friend, broadcaster Mary Blance, she was one half of the dialect-speaking comedy duo Tamar and Beenie, a staple of local radio broadcasts from 1982 until shortly before Bulter's death. And, as what we might call Shetland's first performance poet, she appeared hundreds of times at concerts and shows in community halls all over the islands.

Despite being born and living most of her life in Lerwick, Bulter's work, like that of the poets discussed above, has a rural focus. During the war, Bulter and her mother spent two years living with her Aunt Joan in the parish of Lunnasting, on a croft called Da Horn. This sojourn had a significant effect on Bulter, turning her gaze towards a way of life she saw as slipping away. Her long poem 'Macarism' evokes the world she experienced in those two years:

> Salist for a meenit again wi me,
> For I fin at I man turn roond
> An look at da hoose a da Horn again,
> Noo wir wun ta da Floddens toon.
> I hear a yowe yarmin doon at da Aestdaek,
> An da scraep o a keel ower da linn;
> A whaap cries fae his hert ower Murron,
> Dan heads for da hill in Packinn.[34]

Bulter, like many of the post-Burgess Victorian writers, utilised the croft as an imaginative, symbolic and moral space. For her, the croft represented a way of life that consisted of hard but wholesome work, respected tradition, was filled with humour, and was fundamentally in tune with nature.

Like the poets discussed above, Bulter always celebrates, and sometimes idealises, rural communities. In her poem 'Fladdabister', for example, which first appeared in the voar edition of the *New Shetlander* in 1970, she focuses on a place which, despite having no family associations in the way Lunnasting did, she held in great affection:

> Whin da sun clims higher idda sky,
> An da hidmist fans trow da ditches lie,
> Dan comes da time I feel dat I
> Man geng an see
> Da place, whaar nedder kith nor kin
> O mine is ever bidden in,
> Yit every time A'm dere I fin
> Dearer ta me.[35]

In our discussion of Vagaland we commented on his prosodic stability but, in Bulter's work, there is none of the careful regularity we find in his writing. In Bulter's poem, the words, especially where the fourth line runs into the fifth, seem to fit the verse pattern rather awkwardly. But it is this awkwardness, the speechlike artlessness, which provides some of the poem's appeal. Vagaland's verse was accessible partly because of its regularity, but Bulter's is easy to appreciate because of the relatively unsophisticated diction. She is closer to speech than Vagaland. People in Shetland had immediate access to her voice and tone. As Jamieson writes:

> Rhoda was not the careful "versifier" Vagaland was. Her poetic lines seem to run breathlessly across the page, like clouds scudding across the sky on a gale. But when read aloud there is a tonal assurance in her work, a natural feel for da dialect that gives her poetry a rhythm and cadence quite natural and unforced. I always think I can hear her speak when I read her work, and that is the highest compliment to be paid to any poet.[36]

The colloquial, down-to-earth, speech-like nature of the language, was a significant factor in Bulter's widespread appeal. Vagaland, in 'A Skyinbow o Tammy's', invokes the language of the community as a carrier of tradition, as something which provided stability in the face of change. In Bulter's verse, however, the voice we hear is one that might be shared by any member of the community. Vagaland often seems to speak *for* the community, but Bulter's less prosodically formal voice is perhaps closer to the voices of the people who were reading her work.

The poem goes on to root the speaker firmly in the place she is writing about: 'Whin idder laand is lyin weet, / Dere da aert is springin aneath me feet' (p.11). The land she stands on is not sodden and unproductive, as it is in other places, but shows all the signs of new spring life. The speaker and land are then brought even closer together: 'Bit da time I tink I laek da maest / Is whin da maa'in girse is tae me waist' (p.11). It is now late summer and the long grass partially envelops her, drawing her into itself. In the final stanza the harvest is complete, with 'rigs o stubble, aert dow'd an bare' (p.12) and, in a surprising and original image which shows Bulter's ability for instinctive description, 'da dockens staand laek bolts o roost' (p.12). We have moved from early spring to the brink of winter, and, with the final words of the poem, 'At Fladdabister', Bulter reaffirms the poem's connection with the place she was so fond of.

In poem after poem Bulter returns to rural Shetland and to its agricultural communities, past and present. Her focus on what she saw as a prelapsarian world makes her poems tend towards nostalgia but, occasionally, she moves away from the country and turns her sharp observational eye on the kinds of things she experienced in Lerwick. 'Observations in a Bar' (*Doobled-Up*, p.29) is a straightforward description of a night in a pub. 'Da Bargain Book' (*Doobled-Up*, p.67) shows the speaker studying a mail order catalogue, which makes her look unfavourably at the paucity of fine things in her own house. 'Da Essy Kert' (*Doobled-Up*, p.84) is an encomium for weekly rubbish collections. 'Clearin Oot Da Handbag' is an amusing catalogue of the things the speaker finds when her bag becomes almost too heavy to lift, making her decide to empty its contents on to the table for a clear out. The poet's delight in the language is obvious in the rumbustious inventory she creates:

> Dey wir asprins an liniment for doctorin spaigied hochs,
> A wharter a clatchy caramels an twartree peerie mochs,
> Tree entirely different aer-bells an a brocken string a beads,
> A scorie's pen an showin gum an umpteen aiple seeds.
> (Doobled-Up, p.86)

The poem then concludes with the speaker shovelling everything back into the bag. This is good fun and, in poems like this, one can see why Bulter was always in demand as a performer of her verse.

In both her rural and urban poems, there is a concern with the everyday lives of working people. In the poems mentioned in the previous paragraph, she writes about the experiences of a working-class woman in Shetland – experiences which were her own – and this concern with women's lives is something we also find in 'Neeborly Feelin'. In this poem the speaker looks at a family living nearby and reflects on the differences between them and her own household. Her house is tidy and everything is carefully maintained, whereas the neighbouring house is poorly cared for, its occupants more concerned about 'hae'n a spree' (*Doobled-Up*, p.33) than keeping things in order. The speaker believes her house is 'a credit to be seen' (p.33) and disdains as extravagant the man next door's lavishing of presents on his wife. The voice of the speaker verbalises the pressure exerted on a housewife in a small society. She is worried about how her house looks to others and, as far as next door is concerned, she acts as the person looking in and finding the place wanting. But there are hints throughout the poem that the slatternly neighbour perhaps has things right after all. The neighbours' children 'Grew up ta be dat helty, an content wi little things' (p.33) and, when the speaker looks in the door to see the neighbours' house in its usual state of upheaval, she remarks 'Yit hit niver seemed ta budder her, bit if yun hed been me / I'd been dat black affrontit for a neebor wife ta see' (p.33). The neighbour does not care what society thinks of her and, rather than constructing for the eyes of the community the perfect image of order, she and her husband pay attention to one another. The speaker concludes the poem with the line 'Dan Guid forgie me for tinkin dis – bit I wist it hed been me' (p.33). Despite the picture of good domestic organisation she presents to the world, in the end the speaker wishes she could, as her counterpart does next door, shrug off the need to accede to society's pressures.

As with many of Bulter's poems, 'Neeborly Feelin' is a comic piece, but it is also a poem which discusses what it means to be a woman in a small community. The poem does not idealise that community and, unlike much of Bulter's work, it also avoids the technique of juxtaposing (unfavourably) the modern with the old, something she does in poems like 'Gjaan ta da Doctor' (*Doobled-Up*, p.82), 'Gjaan for da Airrents' (*Doobled-Up*, p.4), 'Dey wir Days Dan-A-Days',[37] 'Whin

We Wir Young' (*Doobled-Up*, p.22), and, unusually for Bulter, in an urban setting in 'Bidin ida Kloss' (*Doobled-Up*, p.68). In Bulter's work, much more than in Vagaland's, the modern world is present, but the poems constantly turn the reader's eyes to the past, as Jamieson points out:

> Considering Rhoda's early writing now, what is most noticeable to me is the predominance of what I might call "the backward glance". So many of those early poems seem to muse on a way of life departed, or departing, evoking the absence of not only da fok but the very ethos they embodied.[38]

Although Jamieson suggests this 'backward glance' is most obvious in Bulter's early work, it is, in my view, characteristic of her oeuvre as a whole. Tradition, the past, the ways and rhythms of life Bulter saw as being central to Shetland, are what her poems bring into the light. And, as was the case with Vagaland, if these things are perceived to be under threat, the need to write about them becomes acute. Idealising the past at the expense of the present is a rather reductive technique but, in several poems, it is a weapon Bulter yields with powerful results.

In 'Da Maara', for example, she asks a series of questions about the disappearance of an idyllic rural environment. Like Vagaland's 'Da Trolligirts', atomic weapons are to blame. In asking where 'da boannie hedder' (*Snyivveries*, p.29) and other features of the countryside have gone, the poem invokes an absence of beloved things, leaving 'Jöst silence, wi a soond at A'm niver heard, / Laek da kyist lid lockin an da last breath sighin' (p.29). The two lines are inhabited, simultaneously, by silence and by the sound of a dying person's final gasp. The imagery then becomes savage and explicit as we are told by the speaker that she is starving and that her flesh is rotting. Another question, which makes clear the reason for the devastation, is posed in the penultimate stanza:

> Is did whaat man kyempit for sae lang?
> Is dis da prize for da conquerin nation
> At wis iggit on ta mak nuclear war,
> An wan a world a devastation? (p.29)

Bulter locates the reason for the ruination of the environment with the competitive nature of human beings. Progress (always a word looked on suspiciously by Bulter), which emerges from man's need to triumph over other men, has led the world towards a terrible epoch where it is possible to obliterate everything.

But Bulter cannot leave us in such a terrible place and concludes by making the deathly images disappear:

> Dan da maara sklents wi da rive a dim.
> Da fresh wind blaas i me face eence mair.
> Life wins til its fit for anidder day,
> Wi a chance ta dö right or wrang still dere. (p.29)

Despite the hell of nuclear war, life continues. In the second line, the speaker asks where 'da mödoo girse idda fresh wind dancin' (p.29) has gone and, at the end, as the nightmare is left behind, it is 'Da fresh wind' (p.29) which blows in her face, bringing hope and new life with it. Despite what man has become capable of, Bulter reasserts the natural environment and the potential of people to do good.

If nuclear war was a threat to the environment she loved, for Bulter, as was the case for Jack Renwick, the arrival of the oil industry in Shetland during the 1970s also brought with it the possibility of ruin. She saw the discovery of north sea oil and the use of Shetland as a location to process it as an urgent threat to the place and its way of life. Her world of little crofts and 'hamely Shetland fok' (*Doobled-Up*, p.61) came under severe pressure with thousands of workers arriving in the isles to build one of the largest oil terminals in Europe. In 'Da Blight', for instance, she writes:

> An eftir da bonanza time is ower
> An da money's geen, d'ill staand whaar idders stüd;
> An hae naethin left bit ta buks among the ruins
> At da oil men left ahint dem whin dey guid.
>
> Da girse ill growe in ower an hoid da biggins,
> An da sea-birds nest again apu da stack;
> Bit lat wis keep a hadd apu wir wye a livin,
> For dat eence lost is ne'er again browt back.
>
> (*Doobled-Up*, p.95)

Oil brings with it greed and the desire to make a fast buck. But, compared to the timelessness of culture and tradition, the boom is transitory and superficial.

The oil industry is also in Bulter's sights in 'Wir Inheritance':

> Juist bore an dreel an gurm an shap,
> Roog in da siller athin dir lap,
> Dan birze da aert for da hidmist drap
> Dey tink is tane.
> An sae up anchor an pit ta sea,
> Rubbin dir oily hands wi glee,
> Laevin da brucks ta da twa or da tree
> At widna geng. (*Doobled-Up*, p.49)

The repetition and single syllables in the opening line of this stanza hammer at her target and invoke the hammering of the land at Sullom Voe. The oil conglomerates perform a smash-and-grab on the islands, leaving destruction in their wake. Unlike 'Da Blight' and 'Da Maara', however, it is not a re-emergent nature which provides hope at the end:

Dir aye da twartree at hae da care
Ta bide an bigg up whaat lies wasted an bare,
Ta lave something livin for idders ta share,
Laek dey hed wance.
Tho da gaet might be herd an da night be lowng,
Lat it be lightened wi word an sowng,
Aye uttered idda midder towng –
Wir inheritance. (p.49)

Despite the destruction, it is culture, community and, most importantly, language which provide constancy. As was the case in Vagaland's 'A Skyinbow o Tammy's', it is language, the speech of the people, which, in its words, syllables and cadences, encapsulates tradition. The spoken word is what binds members of a community together. It weds them to their shared heritage and, if Bulter's verse has an overarching mission, it is to affirm the culture of her archipelago and the validity of her community by advocating pride in her 'midder towng'.

Laurence (Lollie) Graham (1924-2008)

For Bulter and others, as we have commented, the *New Shetlander* was a vital platform, and its long-term editors, Lollie and John Graham, crucially important literary facilitators. Under their editorship, hundreds of writers were encouraged into print, many of whom had never published anything before.[39] In previous chapters, we have seen both men comment on several of the authors under discussion and, as was the case with Shetland's folk culture, the period we are looking at in this chapter witnessed an increased awareness of the archipelago's literature. The Grahams were important in the creation of new writing, but they are also key figures in the appreciation of what had gone before. Both John and Lollie were universally respected teachers and, in their classrooms, hundreds of Shetland children were given their first glimpses of local writing. John co-edited with T.A. Robertson the Anthology *Nordern Lichts* (1964) for the Shetland Islands Council Education Committee, a volume which, for the first time, placed contemporary Shetland writers alongside those from the nineteenth century. And, in 1998, the brothers co-edited the most substantial collection of Shetland verse to date, *A Shetland Anthology*. In his introduction to the volume, Lollie Graham writes:

> Three writers laid the foundations of modern Shetland poetry. First we have James Stout Angus who hailed from Nesting and wrote some of the finest examples of the old speech we have. Next comes Basil Anderson, a poet from Unst who died tragically young at the age of 27, leaving behind his masterpiece, 'Auld Maunsie's Crü', a superb description of Shetland life last century. The third writer was

Lollie Graham. *Courtesy of Brian Smith*

J.J. Haldane Burgess, poet, novelist, and linguist whose popular book of poems *Rasmie's Büddie*, broadened the scope of dialect verse to include satire, political comment and philosophical speculation.[40]

In the anthologies the Grahams were responsible for, these earlier writers and people from the second half of the twentieth century were seen as part of a literary continuum (Chalmers and her contemporaries never come into the picture). Neither Chalmers' nor Angus' generation could look back on local literature in the way the Grahams' could and, in the era of the *New Shetlander*, for the first time, Shetland writers saw themselves as part of a literary tradition.

That tradition was one in which the local language was central, and in which rural, working-class life was revered. These things are fundamental to many of the poets we have covered, and they are found in Lollie Graham's work too. As we have seen, Graham lionised Haldane Burgess, and the croft, that salient motif of Rasmie's creator, is something that Graham, who worked a croft his whole life, respected enormously.[41] We see this in 'What Ken Dey?', a poem from his only book, *Love's Laebrack Sang*:

> What ken dey o da traachle an swaet o da crö,
> Da helpin, willin haands
> Caain, markin, crugsettin, clippin,
> Drenchin, sortin, dockin, and dippin,
> Till dayset comes an we braethe wis a bit,
> An aise wir wearied banes? [42]

The poem takes as an epigraph a statement by the then Historiographer Royal Gordon Donaldson. Donaldson had claimed that 'The [1886 Crofters] Act has led to the virtual death of crofting', and this denigration of what is generally considered an important emancipatory milestone in Shetland raised Graham's ire.[43] 'Dey' are learned men like Donaldson who, despite their theoretical knowledge, cannot understand rural life because they have not lived it. Although he was an educated and highly literate man, Graham's sympathies, like those of Haldane Burgess, are with the working people of rural Shetland.

During his university years in Edinburgh, as well as becoming a socialist (something he remained for the rest of his life) and associating with other writers, Graham started to contribute to the magazine he was later to co-edit. He first appeared in the *New Shetlander* in number nine, with two poems and a short story (all of which, unlike the bulk of his writing, were in English), and, like his brother, he became a regular contributor and enthusiastic supporter of the magazine. At first glance, his early verse, like Renwick's and Peterson's, brings Vagaland to mind:

> Da wind flans in fae Fitful Head
> Whaar dayset in a glöd
> Hings ower da far haaf's western rim
> Reeb'd red as yatlin blöd.

> An flannin in fae dat black ert,
> Borne in on flans o faer,
> Come caald black tochts at numb da hert
> An slock da emmers dere. (p.75)

Reminiscent of Vagaland perhaps but, in images such as 'red as yatlin blöd', and 'caald black tochts at numb da hert', there is a rather blunt note we might not expect to find in Robertson's work. The poem, like James Stout Angus' 'Da Lad 'at Wis Ta'en in Voar', shows us a woman who wants her man back from the sea. But in Graham's poem it is the weather, not the Press Gang, that has taken the man away. In stanzas three to five we hear the woman appeal to God to calm the sea before it gets dark but, in the final stanza, there is an ominous note:

> Da wind flans in fae Fitful Head
> Wast ower fae blatterin seas,
> Bit never da lang, lang lippen'd sail
> Whaar lycht an lippnin dees. (p.75)

Her voice seems to fade away and, as the more objective, authorial voice re-establishes itself, we realise the situation is hopeless.

'Flans fae da haaf' offers no solace. Graham is not, as Vagaland was, a poet who gives us comfort. He can be tender, but he is at his best, like Jack Renwick, when on the attack. And, as with Renwick and Bulter, his target is often the oil industry. In 'Delting Disaster' for example, we hear how the new source of employment has disrupted traditional ways of life:

> I eence hed a croft up in Delting
> At keepit baith Lowrie an me,
> Bit he up an selt oot ta Nordport –
> Fae syne he's been on da spree:
> Hit's Graven Hotel every helly,
> Except whin he hadds owre ta Brae
> Whaar da Nordern Lights wi dir blinkin
> Leds Lowri still farder astray.
>
> Chorus –
>
> Oil! Oil! Oil! I wiss dey'd never fun it,
> Bit left it at da boddom o da sea,
> Oil! Oil! Oil! My curse be seen upon it,
> For aa da grief at's brocht ta you an me! (p.47)

And, adapting Haldane Burgess' poem 'Hiss! Sigg Him!' to the oil era, we hear the lamenting voice of another old crofter:

> O! wir dey ever fail'd aald man
> At hed sic ills ta dree,

> As Oil an aa its cuttanoy
> Is lowsed on da laeks a me? (p.48)

These poems attack what Graham and his peers saw as a destructive influence. As we have observed, poems which set up a straightforward opposition between an idealised traditional society and a demonic industrial interloper tend, perhaps, to be rather simplistic. This technique does not open the investigation of social change, but in his poem, 'Da Ill Wind' (named after William J. Tait's poem of the same name), the criticism meted out to the oil industry is hard to disagree with:

> Da wind blaas aff a Quandal
> An da smell at it brings along
> Is no fae a Quandal midden
> Or a beach a rottin tang
> It comes fae da banks a Gerts Ness
> Fae da guts o a battered hull,
> A forty-thousand-ton tanker
> At's spewin her mogie a oil. (p.51)

The poem is about the oil tanker *Braer*, which grounded in Shetland in January 1993, causing a major oil spill. The above stanza maintains the opposition between traditional, rural imagery and the sullying impact of the oil industry but, in stanza two, the opposing forces begin to slide and seep together:

> Da wind blaas aff a Quandal,
> You can smell it miles awa,
> For he's blaain a gell fae da suddert
> An da spöndrift's gyaain laek snaa.
> It's drenchin da rigs an da toonships
> Wi hydrocarbons an dirt –
> Detergents labelled "top secret"
> Pollutin da sea an da eart. (p.51)

In stanza one, the smell is not from a midden or a beach of rotting seaweed, but is from the tanker. In stanza two, however, the spöndrift, or spray from the sea, is itself a deadly chemical brew. The ocean spray is not just tainted by oil, it *is* oil. The opposition between the two things breaks down. The oil penetrates the natural environment to such a degree that it actually takes it over. Graham handles deftly this idea of co-mingling. Lines 3-5 of this stanza, for example, if we try to think of them independently of the rest of the poem, might have been written by Vagaland. But, with the short, abrupt fourth line, and the word 'hydrocarbons' (not a word one hears often in dialect poetry) the impact of the disaster on the natural world is rendered powerfully. 'Da Ill Wind', because it is written in response to an actual, seemingly cataclysmic, event, avoids the simple opposition of tradition and industrialisation. It does not set up an idealised rural culture and show how that culture is endangered: rather, it is an angry and pungent reaction to something which really did pose a grave threat to the islands.

Graham's salvos against the oil industry are poems in defence of his community. As a socialist, he abhorred the invasion of big business and the threat of pollution that invasion brought with it. He also abhorred the political leader who would have welcomed this kind of development. When Margaret Thatcher was elected prime minister, Graham was 55. But, in his poems about her, there is no hint of a mellowing into middle age and, even more so than his oil poems, she was on the receiving end of his most eloquent and biting scorn.

Often, as we have seen him do with his oil poems, when railing against Thatcher and her government, Graham adapts the work of other writers. Here he rewrites Haldane Burgess' Up Helly Aa song:

> Fae graand owld Viking centuries, Jarl Thatcher's surely come,
> Ta shaa at Britons still can fecht, an sort yon Argie scum,
> So wave da flag, parade da streets, an baet da Falkland drum,
> Da Iron Lady Rules! (p.57)

Burns is utilised to withering effect in 'Holy Maggie's Prayer':

> What was I, or my Thatcherites
> That we should rekk sic dizzy heights?
> We, wha sae mony human rights,
> Hae see dung doon,
> Wi dole-queues, slums and shut-doon pits
> Raaed aa aroon. (p.60)

And, in 'Twa Wirlds', although not using a model as he does in these other poems, he widens his assault to decry oppression of all kinds:

> No da steeket nev o greed an strife
> grinndin da poor among da stoor,
> bit da oppen haand at heals da wound
> an lifts war's curse fae dis wirld o wirs,
> da human haand, unwearied, kind –
> da gifts a life an love in its löf. (p.65)

The final line here is awkward, but the genuine commitment to humanitarian principles and the will to resist oppression are explicitly and powerfully expressed.

Unlike the oil poems, these poems castigating the figures of the political right are not about Shetland. But Graham, as did Burgess, as did Bulter, sees the vernacular as the language of the people, and his poetry, like theirs, assumes a class position through its use of that language. The poems are written in a spirit of solidarity with working-class people from all over the country, and the fact they are in the vernacular highlights that allegiance. They are poems of common resistance, in the voice of working people from Shetland. Bearing in mind a great deal of the verse looked at in this chapter, especially that of Vagaland, we find in Graham's poetry a piquancy that is not often seen in Shetland dialect verse. He is the most political poet of his generation and he shows none of the sentimentality we can sometimes detect in the work of his peers.

John Graham (1921-2008)

Before the brothers became editors of the *New Shetlander*, and central figures in the period of growth this chapter is looking at, both men, as students at Edinburgh University, experienced a different kind of literary scene. John, who had embarked on a career in the merchant navy (something he abandoned after a terrible trip on the *St Magnus*) and had joined the RAF in 1941 to train as a pilot in Alabama, went to university after the war as a mature student. While there, as well as sending poems to the *New Shetlander*, he got his first taste of editing when he helmed the literary journal *Jabberwock*.[44] A letter from Lollie to Peter Jamieson, on 14 January 1948, gives us a glimpse of John's life in the city, and a clue as to how the *New Shetlander* was regarded by some well-known Scottish writers:

> You may be interested to know that my brother John – who is at Edinburgh meantime – has met Alex Scott there. He says that the *New Shetlander* is regarded quite highly by the literary coteries there. Sydney Goodsir Smith in fact places it above the *Scots Review*. He also saw and spoke to Hugh MacDiarmid who seemed quite elated over the first literary earnings of his son.[45]

Graham revelled in the literary atmosphere in Edinburgh and, like his brother, was excited about the new developments back home.

But, despite being an early contributor of poetry to the *New Shetlander*, John Graham's most important creative project took place in the latter years of his life, when he wrote the novels *Shadowed Valley* (1987) and *Strife in the Valley* (1992). As this chapter has shown, the *New Shetlander* generation concentrated heavily on poetry but, in the books Graham wrote after retiring as a teacher, we find two of the most intelligent and substantial novels to have come from a Shetland author since Haldane Burgess.[46]

Shadowed Valley

Shadowed Valley, like Iain Crichton Smith's *Consider the Lilies* (1968) and Neil Gunn's *Butcher's Broom* (1934), takes for its subject the clearances. It is based on an actual series of evictions which occurred in the district of Weisdale, on Shetland's west side, in the mid-nineteenth century.[47] Clearances were less

169

widespread in Shetland than in other parts of Scotland, but that was probably of little consequence to the people driven from their homes. Graham's novel, backed up by methodical research, looks at how these events devastated a small, insular district of Shetland, and in particular how they came to bear on the novel's main protagonist, Hakki Hunter.

The novel is a work of historical fiction, but there is an element of it that goes beyond the straightforwardly historical. Here we see Hakki in the hills that form the valley of Weisdale:

> He ignored the hill-grind and cleared the daek with a bound. He was now in open scattald, ahead of him the long brown shoulder of the hill. He climbed quickly, heading for Da Mossy Flat where sheep gathered to graze.[48]

In a Shetland township of this time, the land was divided into the 'toon' – what was inside the hill dykes, where people had their houses and grew their crops – and the 'scattald', the communal pasture, generally of poorer arable value, outside the boundary wall. In the novel, agricultural improver David Dakers Black, a real historical figure, is responsible for clearing families in order to make way for sheep. Looking at the lands he has acquired, where people scrape a living from tiny plots, Black sees himself as a progressive force. His modern ideas, however, come into conflict with an older, more traditional way of life, and the results are devastating. These two opposing forces, when they meet, do so in the toon, in the parts of the land where people live. But, in the scattald, the more primal, open lands that lie further up the hills, the modern world, with its instinct to "improve", cannot penetrate in the same way. We see this in the novel's closing scene, where an ancient woman, Aald Mallie, and Hakki meet. She says to him:

> 'Du's no laek dis brutes noo at's sweepin folk oot o der hames.' She squinted up at him. 'But does du ken dis? Dey canna pit Aald Mallie oot, na dat in trath! For I'm ootside da hill-daek an dey canna touch me.' (p.193)

She then performs a strange ritual:

> As she spoke she bent her head and shoved back the black napkin until the white hair tumbled down to cover her face. She placed the point of her stick firmly on the ground and moved slowly around it, muttering some strange words. She stopped and a clear, high-pitched voice said:

> 'Da Soaroo sit annunder him – an aa his kind!'

> She raised her head slowly and he could see her closed eyes through the sway of floating hair. Then her eyes opened as if from a trance. (pp.193-194)

John Graham. *Courtesy of Beryl Graham*

Mallie is from a different world than the other characters. She has different, much older, forces flowing through her and represents some kind of primal, perhaps pagan, spirit of the land. Unlike Scott's Norna, however, her more ancient, more strange, more colourful way of being, is not exposed as a fraud, and she is the only character who is not damaged by the new agricultural methods. Like the open scattald she lives on, she will not be affected by the jarring influx of modernity. Mallie lives outside the dykes which enclose the world in which the agricultural experiments are being conducted. She cannot be touched by what David Dakers Black is trying to do. Mallie is both part of the community – people like and help her, she is a carrier of traditional knowledge – but also outside the reach of what is being done to that community.

Since the nineteenth century, as we have seen, agricultural communities have been a staple component of Shetland authors' work but, here, Graham reaches back to something much older. James Inkster, for example, is interested primarily in the social life of the croft, but Graham's conception of his agricultural community includes something much less definable. In the closing scene of his novel, even in the midst of devastation, there is something ancient, some kind of indigenous, elemental, timeless force which cannot be destroyed by greed and avarice.

Strife in the Valley

Graham's second novel, also set in Weisdale, deals with events in the 1780s, a generation or two before the evictions of *Shadowed Valley*. Like that book, *Strife in the Valley* depicts a society in which poor people are made to suffer by rich and powerful ones. The novel opens with the Press Gang removing two teenage boys from the local school, and the first third of the story follows the young teacher, George Clunies, as he tries to get men of influence to help return his pupils. He visits the Tingwall parish minister, then goes to Lerwick, where he meets several prominent men, but the Press Gang are a powerful institution and the boys end up in the navy anyway. After these events, the novel changes tack and deals with a social-class-straddling love affair between George and Elizabeth Ross, the sister of Weisdale landlord and merchant Robert Ross. As with Graham's first novel, we are dealing with a historical novel which, as one expects, is based on extensive and diligent research. In this later work, however, unlike *Shadowed Valley*, Graham's concern is not only with history, or some kind of primal, spiritual pre-history, but with language.

Most of the *New Shetlander* writers were poets, but Graham was the only novelist of his generation. The poets we have looked at, by working primarily in the Shetland language, saw themselves as upholding something essential in their identity as Shetlanders. We saw in Bulter's 'Wir Inheritance' and in Vagaland's 'A Skyinbow o Tammy's' how the language, the spoken utterance, carries with it a culture and ethos. The way these poets wrote, as their popularity suggests, was accepted as authentic and representative by a local readership and, when they did publish outside the isles, their language was a marker of their distinctiveness. The way people speak defines them and, if we accept the idea that poetry is closer to spoken utterance than prose, we can see why many of these writers, because of their concern with identity and culture, gravitated towards verse.

George P.S. Peterson, in his short stories, is one of the few post-war writers to have worked substantially with dialect prose. But, were this work to be extended over several hundred pages, might the patience of readers be somewhat stretched? Even for a dialect speaker, the language in print can appear alien, requiring close attention. Because poetry is, in general, relatively short, the difficulties presented by unusual orthography are more easily overcome than they would be if the same idiom was used for a work tens of thousands of words long. Rhoda Bulter, as we have seen, also produced a significant amount of dialect prose, but, like Inkster's *Mansie's Röd*, 'Laeves fae Beenie's Diary' was a collection of short, serialised pieces and not a novel. Collectively, both works are of considerable length but, because they were published in short sections, they do not require the sustained concentration that a dialect novel would.

John Graham would not have argued against the idea that the local language is a salient marker of identity and, in his dictionary, and in the book he co-authored with T.A. Robertson, *Grammar and Usage of the Shetland Dialect* (1953), he was an important scholar of the language. In *Strife in the Valley*, he is interested in finding a way to take account of the vernacular in his prose. The novel opens in George Clunies' schoolroom:

> George Clunies stood behind the tall plain desk, leaning lightly on an elbow, watching his pupils appear one by one through the door and shuffle barefoot across the earthen floor.[49]

The school, as many in Shetland were, is run by the Scottish Society for the Propagation of Christian Knowledge and, when children attend, they must leave their local speech at the door. We see the tension between the two tongues, English and Shetlandic, a few paragraphs later:

> It was amazing they came to school at all in these terrible times of hunger. But there was something else this morning. He felt the concentration of eyes and leaned slightly over his desk:
> 'Well, what is it?'
> A few tentative hands waved.
> 'Yes, John,' he said, nodding towards a tall, fair-haired lad at the back.
> 'Please sir, Rasmie Peterson's faider winna let him come to the school.'
> 'Won't let him! Why?'
> 'Please, sir, da Press Gang.'

'The Press Gang!'

'Yes,' and as the voice grew in confidence, the local speech became more pronounced. 'He says at der news o a navy ship apo da Wastside an da men are takkin ta da hills.'

'Nonsense. Just one of those rumours. And how often do I have to remind you that you speak proper when in the school.' (pp.1-2)

George accepts the dictum that the vernacular should not be used in the classroom. He is a young man from the island of Yell and, although a dialect speaker himself, has learned to suppress this way of talking when in front of the class. This opening sequence, despite the pupils' occasional lapses into dialect, reads much like *Shadowed Valley*, with the narrative voice largely an English one. After the Press Gang take the boys, however, George dismisses the class and is left alone. As he ruminates over what has happened, we see the narrator's voice begin to sound a little different:

> Left alone, he looked round the empty room. By the standards of the time it was a good classroom – about fifteen feet square with peerie windows in each of the side walls. On the same level was a kitchen and upstairs a reasonably big living-room and three peerie bedrooms. This place, this classroom, was the fulfilment of his dreams. Here he had found the deepest satisfaction, not only seeing bairns learning and developing under his care, but forbye finnin ithin himsel qualities he had never kent he had. Here he had established, in his ain hesitant wye, a kind o relationship wi the young folk o the place. And, maist important, here in this bare, simple room, he had a standing he had never had afore. Noo, within a few terrible moments, all that had been laid in bruck – his peerie world invaded, scholars riven awa, himsel treated laek dirt. The very tocht sent a spasm o rage through him.
> (p.7)

With the children gone, dialect words begin to appear. When describing the building, English words are the most prevalent but, when the narrator starts to deal with George's thoughts and feelings, dialect comes to the fore. We are not listening to George's voice but, rather, we see Graham modulate the narrator's voice to show how George, like his pupils, has the local tongue running through his mind.

This prose style – not entirely English or Shetlandic, but a careful blend of both – is used throughout the novel. When the narrator takes us inside George's mind, there is a profusion of local words but, because of his vocation, he has trouble articulating himself in the same tongue. We see this difficulty when the mother of one of the impressed boys comes to see him:

> He knew the torment she was going through and wanted to comfort her, to get closer to her. To speak to her in the old Shetland tongue

would be hamelier. But somehow he found it difficult to depart from his classroom English. (p.16)

To get on professionally, George has schooled himself to speak English, but that language becomes a barrier when he tries to speak to his neighbours. The narrator may show us how George often thinks in Shetlandic, but the fact that he cannot express himself in that tongue impinges on his ability to connect with people from similar backgrounds as him. 'Wir ain aald language' may run trowe George's mind but, because he cannot exclusively use it to communicate, he lies slightly outside the community. In other words, some of the things Shetland dialect came to represent in the verse of Graham's peers – identity, class, community – can be read in the way he combines the two languages in his prose. George, because of his inability to speak to people in dialect, cannot be the same as them. He, as the schoolmaster, is a central member of the community, but his education and social position, which brings with it a linguistic shift, also places him at a distance from that community. Vagaland and Bulter assert the salience of the language to the place – its ethos, its culture – and, here, Graham shows how the loss of that language severs somebody from those things.

Graham's use of this hybridised language is a new development for a Shetland writer. The work of Graham's peers has the local speech at its core and, in *Strife in the Valley*, Graham finds a style that takes account of that speech, while at the same time opening the narration to a readership unused to reading dialect prose. His language acknowledges the tradition of vernacular writing this study has traced, but also, through its subtle combination of registers, extends that tradition to produce an accesible, but still recognisably Shetlandic, narratorial voice.

Graham, despite working in prose, is just as concerned with language as his contemporary writers. Another central concern in their work, as we have seen, was the appearance of the oil industry in Shetland. Might we also see *Shadowed Valley* as a response to these unsettling forces? Bulter and Renwick explicitly deride the new developments and, sometimes in a rather reactionary way, retreat into an idealised rural past. But, in his historical novels, might we see Graham as also responding to oil in a different, rather more complex, more subtle way?

Writing in the late 1980s and early 1990s, slightly after the big period of controversy and upheaval that the building of Sullom Voe Terminal occasioned, Graham gives us the unwritten stories of people who lived on the land. Shetland had been changed by new wealth and new opportunity and, in the wake of these changes, Graham displays a need to conserve and to record. Would he have used history as he did if oil had not come to Shetland?[50] Trawling through documents in the archives and writing the stories of these characters is, perhaps, a response to the changes happening in Shetland in the 70s and 80s. Ways of life were changing, and by bringing into the light events which had left only faint traces, Graham enriches a culture which many people saw as being in a precarious state.[51]

Stella Sutherland (b.1924)

This chapter has seen several common ideas and motifs emerge. The writers we have looked at are often concerned with place (both their own locales and Shetland itself), with traditional culture and a way of life they saw as fading into the past, and, perhaps more than anything else, with language. Vagaland has been a pervasive influence in this group but, in their focus on crofting communities, we can see a clear link with Burgess and his contemporaries. Stella Sutherland, the final writer we will look at in this chapter, despite sharing certain characteristics with her peers, is less pre-occupied with questions of place, culture or identity. Like the poets discussed above, she is deeply connected to the rural environment, but her verse is more interested in the personal, in the self, than it is in holding up that rural culture as an ideal.

That she is not a poet of place, when we consider her life, is perhaps surprising, for Sutherland has lived in some of the most exceptional places in Shetland. She was born Stella Smith, in the island of Bressay, moving in 1933 to Foula, one of Britain's most remote places, where her mother ran the local school. She stayed in Foula until the age of eighteen, witnessing the filming of Michael Powell's film *The Edge of the World* (1937), and, around the time she left the isle, her first published poem appeared in the 1942 edition of *Manson's Almanac*. In 1949 she married Lollie Sutherland, a crofter from Bressay, and, for the next twenty-one summers, the couple, with their two daughters, tended to a flock of 450 ewes on the otherwise uninhabited island of Noss, a place we have already seen in the verse of Margaret Chalmers.[52]

In her early years away from Foula, Sutherland, sometimes using the pseudonym Veng, started to publish in the *New Shetlander*. Her first contribution to the magazine was to number nine and, under the by-line 'A Crofter's Wife', she went on to write a series of intelligent and sharply observed articles titled 'Through a Croft Window'.[53] These lightly fictionalised diary entries give us a detailed picture of crofting life, and are also willing to discuss wider affairs – nuclear war, for example – in a serious and considered way that sat well with the ethos of the magazine. Although it is more than forty years since 'Through a Croft Window' ceased, Sutherland continues to publish in the *New Shetlander*, her most recent contribution coming in issue 263 (Voar 2013). She is not the most prolific of poets, releasing only three small collections (several poems appear in all three), *Aa My Selves* (1980), *A Celebration* (1991), and *Joy o Creation* (2008) and, partly because her work has not been published in an expansive way, but also because of the challenges it presents, she has not had the popular appeal of the other major female poet of this generation, the more extrovert Rhoda Bulter.

Although, as I will discuss, Sutherland is primarily a poet of the self, her poem 'At da Croft Museum' is one of the century's major statements on the rural culture her contemporaries were so inspired by. The poem, set in a restored

Stella Sutherland. *Courtesy of Stella Sutherland*

crofthouse in the south of Shetland which now operates as a museum, opens with what seems like a deliberate echo of Vagaland's 'A Skyinbow o Tammy's':

> Robbie, whin I wis alang a while sinsyne,
> du med me wylcom; I cam in trow, sat
> i da hoodie shair i da shimley neuk.
> Du played *Da Sodger's Joy*, *Da Fairy Dance*,
> *Da Mirry Boy's o Greenland*, *Kail an Knockit Coarn*,
> fit aye nuggin, bow an fingers fleein.[54]

The speaker, sitting in the kind of house she used to live in, listens to Robbie play the fiddle and, as is the case in Vagaland's poem, the music carries Shetland's way of life in its tune. Being in a crofthouse makes the speaker look back, and she imagines Robbie and herself doing some of the little jobs – making straw ropes, baking scones – that crofters would have done at the fireside. She realises, however, that this is a 'makadu' (p.20) or pretence, and the poem, despite its respect for an older way of life, refuses any hint of nostalgia or sentimentality:

> For da truth is, Robbie, dat day is by,
> an aa dis gear sae lately wint wi use
> Time's flick is frozen lifeless, still as stane;
> only da fiddle's no ootdune, da tune,
> da tune plays on; da draem, da draem moves on […]. (p.20)

The dream is the one that past generations held, of moving into the future, of striving ahead despite adversity, and the poem's focus, despite its invocation of bygone days, is on going forward. The speaker, despite coming from a time when houses like the one she is in were common, despite her reverence for the people who 'clang tae dis rock, loved, toiled, failed, wure awa' (p.20), does not only look back. She takes account of the past but is not beholden to it, and it is the stoic, optimistic spirit of past generations she admires.

This stoicism, and the symbolic tune, however, come under threat in stanza seven as the people, like the Weisdale folk in John Graham's novels, are:

> grund doon wi poverty an idders' greed!
> Dir mortal frames could nedder win nor want,
> sair riven wi fant, wi toarns o need an pride.
> Schaested, debateless, driven benon dir strent,
> some o dem geed, an some wis kerried oot;
> some bedd, tho toom da hoose, da hert, da press,
> da fiddle hingin sangless on da waa. (p.21)

As people are cleared from their houses, the tune and the dream, are forced into abeyance. What the people represent, however, is lasting. The spirit evoked by Sutherland persists:

> Dey yearned forever upward, laek da flooers
> bund i da seed under black tons o time –
> draemin o light, strivin towards da light,
> an dybin on an on becaase dey most [...]. (p.21)

Generations of island people have had to, simply, keep themselves going and, despite being 'gaddered noo in eart's green band' (p.21), as the poem closes we see them triumph over all the adversity they have had to endure. The tune keeps playing: 'till dis caald eart sood tak a warmer cant, / an da frost melt an lat da simmer trow, / an burst dir laef, dir blossom an dir sang!' (p.21).

'At da Croft Museum', like many of the poems looked at in this chapter, has its roots in a fundamental regard for the kind of place Shetland used to be. But, despite evoking this crofting culture, it is the human ability to keep going that Sutherland is writing about. Like the voice at the end of Beckett's *The Unnamable*, the poem honours the ability of people to say, despite the difficulties they face: 'you must go on, I can't go on, I'll go on.'[55] Her ultimate object of affirmation is not traditional culture, but the people themselves.

In her poem 'Da Allover' we see a similar movement towards the personal and subjective. An allover is a knitted jumper, and the poem begins by moving through the ways in which one is made. In stanza three, however, knitting is compared to a different creative act:

> Your mind haes a joy o creation
> laek writin a rhyme – hit's nae lee –
> whin your fingers an wires in relation
> maks da colours an patterns agree. [56]

Writing a poem, or making a jumper with a complex pattern, are crafts which require skill, care and precision. But, despite the work required, there is joy in the making when the finished article is on the jumper-board or on the page. As with 'At da Croft Museum' the poem engages with traditional culture, but its real concern is with human beings. The garment is a fundamentally Shetlandic symbol but, despite the jumper being the central physical object in the poem, it is the 'joy of creation' that the reader is left with. The object itself is celebrated, but it is the impact the making of it has on the creator that the poem affirms. The jouissance comes from the creative act. In other words, we have here a celebration of subjective consciousness. Sutherland places the 'I' at the centre of the poem.

We see both these things – craft and the importance of the 'I' – in one of her finest poems, 'Aa My Selves'. The poem opens with this stanza,

> Mony a different body, I:
> him at spoils, him at creates,
> him at loves an him at hates;
> dem at slew an mocked ta see,

> him at bure da agony –
> aa athin me creep an cry:
> mony a different body, I! (*Aa My Selves*, p.8)

The syntax of the first line is rather unusual. What would, in normal speech be 'I am many different bodies' becomes 'Mony a different body, I'. By making a line with strong stresses on the first syllable and the last, Sutherland highlights the 'Mony' and the 'I'. She is saying, and emphasising this through rhythm, that the 'I', that she, is multiple. Like Whitman in 'Song of Myself' she is saying that 'I celebrate myself, and sing myself',[57] but also that 'I contain multitudes' (l.1325), that the self she celebrates is a complex and multi-facetted thing.

The skilful use of pronouns is what moves the poem forward. The 'I' of line one quickly gives way to 'him' and lines four and five suggest that Christ is present within the speaker. But, because the masculine pronouns are not capitalised, as they would conventionally be when used to represent Christ, the speaker suggests that He is not the only source of her different selves. Stanza two, with its use of the collective pronouns 'folk' and 'dem' gathers together these identities, but the speaker still maintains, rather uneasily, her multiplicity:

> O da folk at bides in me
> what ane haes da upper haand?
>
> […]
>
> I can nedder fend nor flee
> aa da folk at bides in me. (p.8)

But by the final stanza, the 'I' is absent entirely and the poem finds a way to unify the numerous selves it has invoked:

> An, whin aa is laid ta aa,
> wha can redd, far back da reel,
> if he's come o sant or deil?
> Fae what coorse or kirsen kin
> twined da boady he bides in –
> an da mind at guides, fae wha?
> Goad hae da full pooer o aa! (p.8)

God is now the central presence in the poem. The speaker recognises the composite, accumulative nature of her being but, like the speaker in Donne's 'Batter my heart, three-personed God' she wants to give this complexity up to God.[58] At the end of a life, no matter if you come from 'coorse or kirsen kin', in the final reckoning it is only God that has 'da full pooer o aa'.

In her focus on the self, Sutherland is a much more introvert poet than some of her contemporaries. Her writing is utterly unsentimental and, despite being rooted in Shetland, her movement is towards the personal, and not to an idealised rural community or to ideas about how the local speech defines a Shetland identity. Her 'Through a Croft Window' pieces combine dialect and English words unconcernedly and, in her verse, she is willing to use either tongue. Her two poems 'Midder' (*Aa My Selves*, p.38) and 'A Celebration' highlight this versatility well. The first of these, a tribute to her own mother, is in dialect, whereas 'A Celebration', which is about her father, is in English. Sutherland accepts that English is as much part of her literary and linguistic inheritance as Shetlandic, and she refuses to close herself off from what that language can bring to her poetry.

A Celebration

The cage my father wore was made,
that crippled all his day,
before his parents ever met
and close together lay:

a web in wait, a snare, a net
of intricate design,
a tender fret that closed and cut,
of filigree too fine.

He was caught and set at naught,
confined without reprieve,
without avail, to toil and fail,
and little to achieve.

But in one poignant surge of bliss
he let me here begin:
my world, as I uncurled, to his,
converse and yet akin.

For me, the cruel filigree
sprang jewels at the tips;
the gift he gave that's mine to have,
they shine without eclipse.

And now, too late, I celebrate
him and his cripple day:
he never had a gift so glad
as that he gave away.[59]

This is a poem about confinement, and the moments of possible escape from it. In the first three stanzas, the punctuation, especially in the first line of stanza two and the third of stanza three, does not allow the language to flow smoothly. The poem seems to confine itself, and the release comes at the start of stanza four when the 'one poignant surge of bliss' elongates the line and flows into the next. There is a fluency here, an opening out, that results in the conception of the speaker, of the 'I' that inhabits the rest of the poem. Once more, Sutherland places human beings – her father and herself – at the centre and, filtered through the consciousness of her speaker, a poem of confinement becomes joyous and affirmative. 'The cruel filigree' is transformed into a thing of beauty and, despite the celebration coming 'too late', as she says in the final stanza, at least it has come.

Although Sutherland is a central member of the *New Shetlander* group, her work moves in different directions to that of her contemporaries. Alongside William J. Tait, she is the most talented and original poet of her generation. She utilises many of the same sources of imagery as her peers, but, in the attention she gives to the self, her poetry stands out as particularly intricate, complex and intelligent. Her milieu, like Bulter and Vagaland's, is rural Shetland, but Sutherland is not interested in creating a Shetland identity or in using verse as a medium for cultural conservation. She does not place her writing at the service of the community. Instead, she uses her poetry as a way of trying to understand the human subject.

Conclusion

The *New Shetlander* had a galvanising effect on a number of young Shetland writers. Although, in the late nineteenth century, there were authors with similar themes who came to prominence at the same time, Basil Anderson, Haldane Burgess and their contemporaries were not a group in the same way as the writers in this chapter were. Often taking their cues from Vagaland, the writers of the post-war period, with the exception of Stella Sutherland, were concerned with Shetland itself – its culture, the idea of community, its language as a mark of identity. This dual focus of celebrating, sometimes romantically and sentimentally, an agrarian culture, and of creating a poetry which looked to the speech of working people, draws on the work of Burgess and, in the late twentieth century, especially after the arrival of oil, the need to retain what was distinctive about Shetland's language and culture seemed more important than it had ever done before. With this mission in mind, there is a conservatism that runs through much of the work covered in this chapter. There is a need to look back and take account, to give due respect to what has been, and to use literature as a means of preservation.

If the *New Shetlander* had not emerged, much of the work discussed above would not have been published. It gave local authors an encouraging platform and opened their work to a wider readership. The *New Shetlander* allowed Shetlanders to read the writing of their island compatriots and, in its formative years, as we have seen, the magazine was also part of a culture of journals that grew around the writers of the Scottish Renaissance. But, as it became an established part of Shetland's cultural life, contributions from more well-known

Scottish authors started to peter out and the journal became more of a local magazine. The early numbers of the *New Shetlander* may have placed famous authors like MacDiarmid and Naomi Mitchison alongside unknown ones from Shetland but, as we saw in our discussion of Vagaland, the cosmopolitan and avant garde ideas that MacDiarmid incorporated into his poetry are not to be found in Robertson's highly influential work. In the poet who is the subject of our next chapter, however, we find Shetland dialect verse brought into contact with things it had never encountered before.

NOTES

1. Jamieson had been active as a writer since the 1930s. He published two works of non-fiction, *The Viking Isles* (1933) and *Letters from Shetland* (1949), and gathered thousands of pages of notes about Shetland's folklore, language, place-names, fishing, literary figures, politics and other subjects. See SA, D9.
2. For the *Shetlander* see SA, SA4/590. Peter Jamieson's unpublished essay 'William Morris, Socialist' gives a vivid picture of the Economics Club. See SA, D9/99.
3. The editorial in the first issue stated that 'The *New Shetlander* is a non-party political and literary paper. Space for the ideas of all progressive trends is at the disposal of those interested.'
4. SA, D9/174, *Shetland Writings*.
5. See Stella Sutherland, 'Some Shetland Literary Work of the 20th Century', *New Shetlander*, 248 (Simmer 2009), 23-25. Sutherland was a member of the Shetland Poetical Circle.
6. SA, D1/174/1, *Shetland Writings* vol.1.
7. Margery Palmer McCulloch, ed., *Modernism and Nationalism: Literature and Society in Scotland 1918-1939: Source Documents for the Scottish Renaissance* (Glasgow: Association for Scottish Literary Studies, 2004), p.xiii. For another discussion of this culture of little magazines see Glen Murray, 'MacDiarmid's Media 1937-1978', in *The Raucle Tongue: Hitherto Uncollected Prose*, vol.3, by Hugh MacDiarmid, ed. by Angus Calder, Glen Murray and Alan Riach (Manchester: Carcanet, 1998), pp.xiv-xxxiv.
8. For discussions of *Gairm* see Iain Crichton Smith, 'Modern Gaelic Poetry', in *Towards the Human: Selected Essays* (Edinburgh: MacDonald Publishers, 1986), pp.97-107 (p.97), and Michelle Macleod and Mary Watson, 'In the Shadow of the Bard: The Gaelic Short Story, Novel and Drama Since the Early Twentieth Century', in *The Edinburgh History of Scottish Literature*, vol.3, ed. by Ian Brown (Edinburgh: Edinburgh University Press, 2007), pp.273-282 (p.273).
9. Cluness was the first literature development officer for the publically funded organisation Shetland Arts Trust. He also established the pamphlet publisher North Idea, which has published nine volumes by local authors who may have found it difficult to get a book published elsewhere.
10. John J. Graham, 'T.A. Robertson: An Appreciation', *New Shetlander*, 107 (Voar 1974) 6-7 (p.6).
11. I am indebted to Shetland Islands Council Dialect Co-ordinator Bruce Eunson for this information.

12. Kevin MacNeil, ed., *These Islands, We Sing: An Anthology of Scottish Islands Poetry* (Edinburgh: Polygon, 2011), pp.256-257.
13. Ernest W. Marwick, Introduction to *The Collected Poems of Vagaland*, ed. by Martha Robertson (Lerwick: Shetland Times, 1975), pp.xvii-xxvi (p.xxvi).
14. *Da Sangs at A'll Sing Ta Dee: A Book of Shetland Songs*, ed. by T.A. Robertson and Martha Robertson (Lerwick: Shetland Folk Society, 1973).
15. T.A. Robertson, *The Collected Poems of Vagaland*, ed. by Martha Robertson (Lerwick: Shetland Times, 1975), p.20.
16. George Mackay Brown met Robertson once in Stromness. He claimed that Robertson and Rendall had an uncanny facial resemblance. See 'A Shetland Poet: A Tribute', *Orcadian*, 29 May 1975, p.4.
17. Simon W. Hall, *The History of Orkney Literature* (Edinburgh: John Donald, 2010), p.121.
18. Hugh MacDiarmid, *Lucky Poet: A Self-Study in Literature and Political Ideas* (Manchester: Carcanet, 1994), p.59.
19. Margery Palmer McCulloch, *Scottish Modernism and its Contexts: Literature, Identity and Cultural Exchange* (Edinburgh: Edinburgh University Press, 2009), pp.30-52.
20. Housman was Robertson's favourite poet. See Martha Robertson, *Night-Scented Stock in Bloom?* (Edinburgh: Pentland Press, 1993), p.47-53. He also knew and corresponded with Betjeman. See SA, D22/1/1/4/1.
21. Many of Robertson's ex-pupils remember fondly his telling of trowie stories in class. Pers. comm. Bobby Robertson, 5 September 2009.
22. SA, D22/2/3, John Graham, Unpublished lecture on Shetland's literature, undated.
23. Marwick, 'Introduction', p.xx.
24. Jack Renwick, *Rainbow Bridge: A Collection of Poems in English and Shetlandic* (Lerwick: Shetland Times, 1963), p.1.
25. For a survey of the oil developments in the isles see James R. Nicolson, *Shetland and Oil* (London: William Luscombe, 1975).
26. Jack Renwick, *The Harp of Twilight: An Anthology of Poems in English and Shetlandic* (Baltasound: Unst Writers Group, 2007).
27. Mary Blance, 'George P.S. Peterson: A Profile', *New Shetlander*, 239 (Voar 2007), 11-13 (pp.11-12).
28. George P.S. Peterson, 'Da Hairst Is In', in *A Shetland Anthology: Poetry from the Earliest Times to the Present Day*, ed. by Laurence L. Graham and John J. Graham (Lerwick: Shetland Publishing Company, 1999), p.168.
29. Peterson in *A Shetland Anthology*, ed. by Graham and Graham, p.170.
30. George P.S. Peterson, *Aald Papa, I'm Dine!: A Collection of Stories, Tunes, Poetry and Paintings* (Lerwick: Shetland Times, 2009), pp.233-245.
31. Robert Alan Jamieson, 'Rhoda's Voice', *Shetland Life*, 315 (Jan 2007), 32.
32. Rhoda Bulter, 'Letter to the Editor', *Shetland Life*, 70 (August 1986), 21.
33. The sequence ran from April 1982 to March 1991.
34. Rhoda Bulter, *Snyivveries: Shetland Poems* (Lerwick: Shetland Times, 1986), p.4.
35. Rhoda Bulter, *Doobled-Up: All the Shetland Poems from Shaela and A Nev Foo A Coarn* (Sandwick: Thuleprint, 1978), p.11.
36. Jamieson, 'Rhoda's Voice', p.32.
37. Rhoda Bulter, *Link-Stanes: Shetland Poems* (Lerwick: Shetland Times, 1980), p.8.

38. Jamieson, 'Rhoda's Voice', p.32.
39. See Mary E. Blance, 'John and Lollie Graham and the *New Shetlander*', *New Shetlander*, 221 (Hairst 2002), 4-7.
40. Laurence Graham, Introduction, in *A Shetland Anthology*, ed. by Graham and Graham, pp.xv-xxiii (p.xvi).
41. For an account of Lollie Graham's life see Brian Smith, 'A tribute to Lollie Graham, Teacher, Poet and Scourge of Capitalist Life', *Shetland Times*, 13 November 2009, p11.
42. Lollie Graham, *Love's Laebrak Sang* (Lerwick: Shetland Library, 2000), p.36.
43. Graham uses the Donaldson quote as an epigraph. For a discussion of the Crofters Act see Brian Smith, 'Shetland and the Crofters Act', in *Shetland Crofters: A Hundred Years of Island Crofting*, ed. by Laurence Graham (Lerwick: Shetland Branch, Scottish Crofters Union, 1987), pp.1-9.
44. Brian Smith, 'A Man of Vision and Influence' *Shetland Times*, 22 February 2008, pp.14-15.
45. SA, D9/259/1, Letter from Laurence Graham to Peter Jamieson, 14 January 1948.
46. In addition to his novels, during his retirement Graham wrote an account of education in Shetland and worked on several new editions of his Shetland dialect dictionary. See John J. Graham, *A Vehement Thirst After Knowledge: Four Centuries of Education in Shetland* (Lerwick: Shetland Times, 1998), and John J. Graham, *The Shetland Dictionary* (Stornoway: Thule Press, 1979).
47. See John J. Graham, 'The Weisdale Evictions', *New Shetlander*, 130 (Yule 1979), 29-31. For a general study of the subject see David Cooper, '"Da Fiends at Drave Da Tenant Furt": A Study of the Clearances in the Shetland Islands' (unpublished M.A. (Hons) dissertation, University of Glasgow, 2011).
48. John J. Graham, *Shadowed Valley: A Novel Based on the Weisdale Evictions* (Lerwick: Shetland Publishing Company, 1987), p.64.
49. John J. Graham, *Strife in the Valley: A Novel Set in 18th Century Shetland* (Shetland Publishing Company, 1992), p.1.
50. Graham was a key figure in the establishment of museum and archives services in Shetland.
51. For a discussion of the cultural responses to oil see Thomas Simchak, 'Oil, Culture and Economy: The Reinvention of the Shetland Way of Life' (unpublished masters thesis, University of Oxford, 2008). *Shadowed Valley* was the only local novel taught in my own years at school (1981-1992), some of which took place in Weisdale. It served as both an introduction to local writing and as a way of telling pupils about historical events.
52. Karen Eunson, 'Stella Sutherland at Eighty', *New Shetlander*, 229 (Hairst 2009), 4-6.
53. The series commenced in the June-August 1953 number and ended in Voar 1966. See nos.36, 37, 39, 45, 46, 47, 48, 49, 51, 53, 60, 63, 67, 71, 76.
54. Stella Sutherland, *Aa My Selves: Poems 1940-1980* (Lerwick: Shetland Times, 1980), p.20.
55. Samuel Beckett, *Trilogy: Molly, Malone Dies, The Unnamable* (London: Calder Publications, 1994), p.418.
56. Stella Sutherland, *Joy o Creation: Favourite Poems Old and New in Shetland Dialect and English* (Stromness: Hansel Cooperative Press, 2008), p.2.

57. Walt Whitman, 'Song of Myself (1881)', in *The Norton Anthology of American Literature*, vol. C, 6th edn, ed. by Nina Baym and others (New York / London: W.W. Norton & Company, 2003), pp.122-166 (l.1).
58. *John Donne: The Complete English Poems*, ed. by A.J. Smith (Harmondsworth: Penguin, 1973), pp.314-315.
59. Stella Sutherland, *A Celebration and Other Poems* (Bressay: Stella Sutherland, 1991), p.13.

CHAPTER SEVEN

WILLIAM J. TAIT (1918-1992)

Introduction

Of all the writers associated with the *New Shetlander*, William J. Tait, or Billy as he was more commonly known, was the most challenging, innovative and brilliant. As Tait's friend and contemporary Lollie Graham wrote in his introduction to *A Shetland Anthology*: 'Among recent Shetland poets, W.J. Tait has been the most ambitious, in choice of theme, technical skill and use of language.'[1] In Tait's verse, as we shall see, the local tongue was stretched further than it had ever been before. He is the most important twentieth-century Shetland poet and, alongside Haldane Burgess, the second major native figure in this study.

William John Tait was born in the island of Yell, later moving to the township of Sandwick in the south of the Shetland mainland, where his father was the schoolmaster. Like Burgess, he was a high achieving scholar, becoming the top pupil in Shetland during his time at the Anderson Institute in Lerwick and, after leaving school in 1936, he also went to Edinburgh University, where he studied English and joined the Communist Party. He remained a political man for the rest of his life but, as we shall see, his verse is not heavily influenced by politics. After leaving university, like the Grahams and T.A. Robertson, Tait became a teacher but, unlike them, he did not spend the rest of his life in Shetland. He taught for a few years at the Anderson Institute in the 1940s, also helping Peter Jamieson to revive the Shetland Labour Party and found the *New Shetlander*, but left in 1949, going on to work in schools and colleges across Britain, before returning to Shetland in the mid-1980s.[2] As we are about to discuss, his writing has a different relationship with his native isles than that of his contemporaries. Their writing gravitates towards the archipelago – its language, its culture – and to what they saw as a Shetland identity, but Tait's terms of address are different. Vagaland and Bulter wrote for a local audience but, for most of his career, Tait, despite contributing many poems to the *New Shetlander*, was part of a different literary scene. He is one of the most important members of the literary tradition discussed in this book, but he is also an atypical Shetland writer. His contemporaries in Shetland addressed a local readership but Tait, as part of what Roderick Watson, in his book *The Literature of Scotland*, categorises as the 'second wave' of the Scottish Literary Renaissance, was the only poet of his generation to conduct his literary career outside the isles.[3] As well as his portrait hanging on the wall of Milne's bar in Edinburgh, his work was published, alongside many of his more well-known peers, in the journals *Akros, Aquarius, Chapman, Life and Letters, Poetry (Scotland), Scotia Review, Scottish Review, Scottish International,* and *The Voice of Scotland*; and in anthologies such as Alexander Scott's *Modern Scots Verse 1922-1977* (1978), and John MacQueen and Tom Scott's *Oxford Book of Scottish Verse* (1966). According to the short biography on the cover of the only book Tait published during his lifetime, *A Day Between Weathers* (1980), he was a 'well-known and much-liked feature of the Edinburgh public-house circuit', and he featured, alongside Sorley MacLean, Norman MacCaig, Robert Garioch, Tom Leonard, Liz Lochhead and others on Heritage Records' 1975 album *An Evening with the Heretics*. His poem 'The Makar Fou', his first composition in Scots, is addressed to W.S. Graham, who Tait met for the first time in Soho in the mid-50s.[4] 'Aubade' relates how Tait 'stoater[ed] hame thro Drummond Place / At ten tae five o an April moarnin' (p.53) after a night with his friend Sydney Goodsir Smith. 'Racial Characteristics', which ends with the self-deprecating image of Tait as 'An overweight deracinated Shetlander' (p.47), relates a different bibulous adventure in Edinburgh's pubs. 'Faustus in Heevin' (p.93) is a sequel to Robert Garioch's poem 'Faustus in Rose Street'. George Elder Davie appears as the 'second figure who I better knew' (p.119) in the long war poem 'Scorched Earth', and 'I Belang to Glasgow' (p.45) is a parody of Tom Leonard.[5] And, in the final poem in the first section of his book (the volume is divided in three parts), Tait produces an elegy for his friend Chris Grieve:

> Chris deid! What nou – sen immortality
> Was his afore? Shouthers aff his load
> An snugs him doun, the darg an trachle by,
> Tae feenish his lang airgument wi Goad. (p.54)

In 1949 Grieve wrote a testimonial for Tait which places the younger poet at the centre of literary developments in Shetland after the war:

> During the past two to three years a group of young writers has come into existence in the Shetland Islands and have done a great deal to create a modern literature, alike in poetry, prose, and drama in the Shetland speech. They have gone about this task in an admirably systematic and scholarly fashion and, along with the linguistic aspect of their work, have manifested a splendid spirit of local patriotism, based upon diligent research into Shetland history and its Scandinavian origins and affinities, a thorough grasp of the economics of the local industries and potentialities of development, and a consistent concern with the highest journalistic and literary virtues. Their organ – the *New Shetlander* – is a model of its kind and ranks as one of the most interesting literary periodicals in Great Britain today.

In all this work Mr Tait has played the part of a leader, and in respect both of his work in English and in the Shetland dialect, is the most distinguished poet of the group, and unquestionably deserves a high place in the ranks of contemporary British poets generally.[6]

It should be pointed out that Grieve is writing a reference for Tait to help him get a job, but his summing up of Tait's position in Shetland at the time is cogent and accurate. Tait was part of the post-war Scottish literary milieu that circulated around MacDiarmid, but he was also a new voice in Shetland's literature.

One of the things that makes Tait stand out from his Shetland peers is that, more than any other Shetland poet of the time, he avoids the pitfalls which can present themselves when using a language closely associated with a particular place. Poet and critic Jim Mainland, in a 2010 interview with fellow poet Sheenagh Pugh, discusses the problems facing a writer who chooses to write in the Shetland vernacular:

> there is […] a particular voice that dialect gravitates too easily towards: a kind of matter-of-fact, self-satisfied conservatism. This also lends it a certain charm, and regional distinctiveness, but a certain parochialism, too. […] The Shetland poet Billy Tait transcended all the limitations I have mentioned here […].[7]

Tait transcends these limitations because Shetland is only one element in his poetic make-up. He does not privilege his local speech over other tongues, and he does not turn his back on the cultures which exist outside his native isles. He is not, as many of his peers were, a nostalgic writer, and he does not idealise the culture of his native isles. He does not travel, as, for example, James Inkster and Rhoda Bulter do, into Shetland's rural communities, but, in his frame of reference, moves out from the isles in an expansive and adventurous way. His terms of engagement with the world are symbolised in his poem 'The Contracting Universe':

> Mount Palomar's parabola,
> Swinging its pole-wide span,
> Finds in a reddening spectral light,
> Launched before time began
> Across five thousand million years,
> The proper scale for man.
>
> But I have held the farthest star
> Within my elbow's crook;
> And bathed in pure galactic seas
> Without let or rebuke;
> And seen the last sun gutter out
> In one tormented look. (p.89)

There are perhaps echoes of MacDiarmid's 'The Watergaw' here, but the poem also seems to owe something to the body of science fiction writing and film developing in the 1960s. Whatever the inspiration, the poem travels far from Tait's native archipelago. He wants his poetry to rove outwards. He does not want to write only about Shetland but, following the internationalist strain in the Scottish Renaissance, Shetland, when it does appear in his poems, is often his point of departure and not the raison d'être of his writing, as it is for Vagaland or Bulter. Shetland, for Tait, is a linguistic resource and a source of imagery, and his voice, while taking account of what Shetland can bring to his poetry, does not limit itself to the islands and their culture.

Villon: Le Testament and Other Translations

This outward-lookingness is apparent in the first poem Tait wrote in the Shetland dialect, a translation of Villon's 'Les Regrets De La Belle Heaulmiere'. He first translated the poem, in a different version to that which appears in *A Day Between Weathers*, in 1936 or 1937, for a reading at an Edinburgh University Orkney and Shetland Society magazine night.[8] In 1947 he revised the translation and the final version appeared, in September of the same year, in volume 4, number 1 of Grieve's *The Voice of Scotland*. Following this early experiment, Tait went on to become Shetland's most significant literary translator. His collected translations, recently published as *Villon: Le Testament and Other Translations* (2011), include Shetlandic versions of the French poets Alfred de Magny, Paul Scarron, Ronsard, Tristan Corbière, Baudelaire, and George Brassens, and of the Scandinavians Gunnar Heros and Martin Melsted. The most extensive translations Tait produced, however, as the title of the book suggests, were from François Villon. The Villon translations, which amount to approximately a third of *Le Grand Testament*, and include several of Villon's shorter poems, were produced during a long period of Tait's life. Laurna Robertson, who became acquainted with Tait in the late 1970s, loaned him the French text he used to complete his typescript,[9] which was subsequently rejected by Polygon in 1987.[10] The translations, therefore, were completed during the 1980s, almost fifty years after Tait's engagement with the French poet began.

Tait's versions of Villon are unique in Shetland's literature and, in them, the local tongue was taken in new directions. 'Fat Marget's Ballade', a rude and rambunctious poem, gives us a good way into the work. In this section we hear how a man and his prostitute partner make up after their latest falling out:

> Dan we mak pace; shoe slips a monstrous fart.
> (Shoe's ey as blaan-up as a bloed-swalled bug.)
> Laachin, shoe lays her haand on me, an: 'Start!
> Vite! Vite!' shoe says, an gies my prick a nug
> Syne, baith daid drunk, we sleep as soond's a clug.

> Bit, whin shoe waakens an still feels da yuck,
> Shoe climms on tap, fur faer her seed wants muck;
> I gron below, as ony plank pressed flat.
> Wi sic bed-wark, shoe's laid me fair in bruck,
> Here i dis hoorhoose whaar we had wis at.[11]

In his Villon translations the local dialect is not held up, as it is in the work of Tait's contemporaries, as a marker of an ethos or an identity. Despite working in a language associated with a particular place, he does not allow his poetry to be limited to that place. Vagaland, for example, who translated a small number of poems, mostly Scandinavian ones, but also two of Horace's *Odes*, draws his source texts into the rather idealised vision of rural Shetland that provides the background for much of his verse.[12] Tait, however, reaches out from the islands and inhabits the medieval world of the originals. He does not relocate his source texts into a world of crofts, but-and-bens, and little fishing boats, but takes his words into the brothels, jails, and inns that Villon knew well. Vagaland's translations sound much like the rest of his work, but Tait, in his versions of Villon, combines the source text and the local language to produce a series of semi-pornographic, funny, bawdy, and European poems. Tait's approach to the Shetland dialect, especially in his Villon poems, is always a cosmopolitan one.

In his 2010 collection *Bho Leabhar-Latha Maria Malibran*, Gaelic poet and literary scholar Christopher Whyte offers a straightforward solution to the possible limitations a so-called provincial poet is at risk of being trapped by:

> My stance at the time [of writing] was to approach Gaelic like any other European language. This meant that it was suitable for dealing with all kinds of subjects, no matter how unprecedented or unusual, and I was happy to accept the implied challenge.[13]

Tait's approach in his Villon poems parallels that of Whyte in his use of Gaelic. For Vagaland, Bulter and others, the local language encapsulated a culture and a way of life. For them, and for some Shetland poets today, the speech of the community was of fundamental importance for a local identity. As poet Laureen Johnson puts it in a radio programme about Shetland's literature: 'I naturally speak da Shetland dialect, it's my native tongue, and I don't mak any great effort to write in any other way except the way I speak.'[14] For these writers, authenticity with the spoken word is a key element in their verse. Their literary mission is to allow the authority of print to a speech community which is, to use poet John Ashbery's phrase, 'Barely tolerated, living on the margin'.[15]

Tait's approach, his attitude to the language, is different. In his hands the Shetland dialect becomes a language fit to carry the spirit, vigour and, like Peter Dale's English versions, the formal properties of Villon's work.[16] He does not place his language in service to the community but creates a new kind of idiom for Shetland poetry. The Villon translations begin with the lines:

> Foo I repent my days o yoeth,
> Whin mair as maist I med a splore,
> I kentna dey wir gien, in troeth,
> Till aald age chappit at my door.
> Goed dey on fit or horse, I spoer?
> Na feth dey! Less wid sair dir turn.
> Dey vanished an, ithoot a stoer
> Ta bliss mysel wi, here I murn. (p.1)

The word 'splore' is not a common usage in Shetland (although George Stewart does use it in *Fireside Tales*), whereas 'Na feth day!' is a typical spoken exclamation. The poem goes on:

> Dey left me in a paarlous state,
> Poer baith in midder-wit and lair,
> Doelfil, debateliss, black's a paet,
> Wi nidder rent nor rank nor gear.
> O dem at's sib ta me, I swear,
> Da laichist gledly wid deny
> At we wan raid bloed-drap did share
> If he cood hain a doit dereby. (p.1)

Again, an expression like 'midder wit' comes straight from Shetland speech, and 'black's a paet' draws on the archetypal Shetland image of peat, both phrases drawing close to the rural worlds that Vagaland and Bulter inhabit. The final line, apart from the initial 'd' in the final word, however, is pure Scots. Stanza four contains the obscure words 'twapert' (p.2), which Tait might have found in James Stout Angus' dictionary, and the word 'hoggleskew' (p.2), which probably came from Jakobsen. Stanza five combines Shetlandic and Scots in the phrase 'An lairned ta haag an hain' (p.2), then uses a down-to-earth Shetland expression, 'laek a witless bairn' (p.2), and, finally, contains the line 'At stangs me ta da very hert' (p.2) which, again, uses a Scots word not commonly used in Shetland, 'stangs'.

The point here is that, for his Villon translations, the language Tait created is a construction, a composite. He draws on Shetland speech, but also uses Scots words not commonly used in the isles and little-known and archaic words from Jakobsen's dictionary. His language takes account of the spoken tongue, but it is a dictionary Shetlandic, just as MacDiarmid's Scots is a dictionary Scots in which readers can hear the speech of Langholm and the Borders. The fidelity of Tait's poetic language is not to the spoken tongue. He does not, as Johnson does, try to write in the way he speaks, but creates a synthetic *literary* idiom which draws on all the poetic and linguistic elements available to him. He does not utilise the Shetland language as a badge of identity, but treats it as a rich linguistic resource. This is Scots poetry, Shetland dialect poetry, and European poetry all at the same time.

WILLIAM J. TAIT

Billy Tait. *Courtesy of Jeanette Novak*

Tait was not the only Scottish poet of his generation to translate Villon into Scots. Tom Scott's *Seevin Poems o Maister Francis Villon* appeared in 1953 and, although there is no direct evidence that Tait read this work, it is highly likely that he did. Both men were born in the same year, they were both graduates of Edinburgh University and, from the early 1950s until his death in 1995, Scott was resident in Edinburgh, a city Tait frequented on many occasions.[17] It is very probable that the two poets knew each other and may even have discussed their translations. William Cookson, in an obituary of Scott, says of his work on Villon:

> Scott found his voice in Scots by visiting Europe, in particular Sicily. He then realised that he belonged to the great tradition of Scottish poets (Dunbar, Henryson, Gavin Douglas) which was more European and less insular than much of English poetry. This led him to produce his great translations of the fifteenth-century French poet Villon [...].[18]

Scott was more than well-versed in the work of the Makars, publishing *Dunbar: A Critical Exposition of the Poems* in 1966, and it is on this rich foundation that his Villon translations are built.[19] He was working in the second half of the twentieth century, but the poetic lineage he locates himself within is one from the fifteenth. Tait, on the other hand, is self-consciously part of the tradition of Shetland dialect writing that this study has traced. Or, to be more accurate, he is writing in, but also against, that tradition. Nothing like his Villon translations had ever been attempted by a writer from the isles. J. Derrick McClure, in an introductory essay in the volume of Tait's translations, says of Shetland's literature, and of the contribution Tait made to it:

> it is quintessentially a literature of place: the astonishing range of local words from the domains of farming and fishing, and for the sea and land features, plants, birds and weather conditions of the archipelago, have been exploited with great skill by Shetland writers to bring the islands and their unique culture to vivid literary life. Using this dialect to translate a fifteenth-century French poet, and one at that whose literary persona is emphatically of his place and time, is in itself a breaching of the boundaries within which Shetland dialect literature has traditionally operated.[20]

Tait's Villon translations take Shetland dialect writing into new places. He does not, as many of the other *New Shetlander* poets did, use the language to symbolise Shetland's culture and community. Rather, he reaches out from the isles and, in doing so, in placing the Shetland tongue in contact with a key European text, expands the range of the literature of his native archipelago.

'A Hogmanay Sermon'

As these translations show, Tait was a major innovator in Shetland's literature. He does not gravitate towards the rural culture that his peers were concerned with, and he does not utilise the local language as a label of identity. Rural Shetland is visible in his work, and the use of Shetland dialect gives him a distinctiveness among his Scottish peers, but he also displays the cosmopolitanism and willingness to engage with European culture that would have met with MacDiarmid's approval. His Villon translations diverge from the general principles of the work traced in Chapter Six and, in a poem from *A Day Between Weathers*, 'A Hogmanay Sermon', he takes on those principles directly. Tait is not a didactic poet, but the poem is the closest he came to a manifesto for Shetland's writers.

Unlike many of the other pieces in the book, the poem is discursive rather than lyrical. It is conversational but it also references several literary texts throughout its three sections. It opens with a line from Yeats' poem 'Under Ben Bulben' – 'Irish poets, learn your trade' – and then the speaker goes on to complain about the lack of decent poetry in the *New Shetlander,* 'number Seeventy-Wan' (p.41), which he is reading. There are two poets included in that issue of the magazine, T.A. Robertson and George P.S. Peterson, and, in a note about 'A Hogmanay Sermon' Tait wrote:

> On 30 December 1964, I received the Yule number of the *New Shetlander* (No.71). The "Christmas" verse in it struck an all-time low [...]. To my surprise they printed it ['A Hogmanay Sermon' which Tait had submitted under a pseudonym]; and to my relief Tammie Alex Robertson (Vagaland) who was the author of some of the "poems" I attacked, still greets me as an old friend, though quite aware of my pseudonymous alter ego! [21]

Tait clearly sets himself apart from other Shetland poets of the day, but there was one item in the magazine which did elicit his admiration. This is a factual account by W.S.I. (Captain Willie Inkster, former harbour master of Lerwick), titled 'Muness Sixareens', which recounts a nineteenth-century fishing disaster. This account leads Tait into the second section of his poem, which is his own retelling of those events.

The final section of the poem, however, is where Tait really does his work. It is a major statement of what he sees as important for Shetland's literature. This section begins by continuing the Yeats quotation from the opening line of the poem: 'An wi dat I pick up my beuk an mind my text: / "Sing whatever is well made", an da sang sood be / Soond, clean-lined, shapely as da boats we bigg' (p.43). With the reference to native boat building, a craft which has existed in Shetland, in a unique form, for many generations, his wish is that Shetland poets should take account of local things in their verse, and that they should attempt to produce something as expertly constructed as a Shetland boat. He continues:

> No da roed o ee sleepless nycht. I wey mysel
> An fin short misser. Bit, still on on, dir mair
> Apo my beuk-brod yit. *Faber an Faber*,
> Da publishers. Noo, dere's a name! Da poet,
> Da Makar, *faber* – een 'ill doe my turn – 'a worker
> In hard materials', da dictionary says. Nae wird
> O plasticine or icin shuggar or tinsel on a tree. (p.43)

Tait criticises the mawkishness of the seasonal verse he has been reading in the *New Shetlander* and, in his references to boat building and to the poet as 'a worker in hard materials', he argues for a Shetland verse with a tough, clear edge – a modernist poetry to sweep away the cloying sentiment of what he is attacking. He then addresses Shetland poets directly: 'O Shetlan poets, fin your tred! Poo ower your een / Nae mair ooey blankets' (p.43, word emboldened in text). Shetland poets must define what their trade is going to be. It is necessary to shed the baggage of a nineteenth-century sentimentality which runs through the poems in the magazine, and through several of the poems we looked at in Chapter Six, and to create a modern Shetland poetry. The comfort Shetland writers find in tradition should be left behind and they should take on life in as direct a way as possible. They should, he says, write about things that 'as laek as no, / We canna mention i da *New Shetlander*' (p.44). He advocates a poetry that, like W.S.I.'s piece, takes life as its subject and which avoids romanticising or sanitising that life. Tait's peers, as we have discussed, often venerate their rural environments, but Tait argues for a less bucolic, less nostalgic view of the islands. 'A Hogmanay Sermon' is Tait's most explicit statement on what Shetland's literary culture meant to him and how he thought it should develop. And, as with his Villon translations, he is at odds with what other Shetland poets of the time were trying to do.

'Rumours of Wars'

'A Hogmanay Sermon' is engaged with Shetland's literary tradition and what it meant to Tait but, in his verse generally, Shetland is only one element. We have seen how, in his work on Villon, he marshals the resources available to him as a Shetland poet, but also how he moves outside the isles – to medieval France for his themes, to Scots for his words – in surprising and innovative ways. And, just as Shetland is only one of a number of ingredients (albeit a very important one) in those poems, the islands are not to be found in all the writing he did. The third section of *A Day Between Weathers*, for example, does not mention Shetland at all, and none of these poems are written in the local language. Titled 'Rumours of Wars ' (the quotation is from *Matthew* 24:6), Tait, in his foreword, writes of this part of the book: 'The third and last section consists of poems, mainly unpublished, which I felt required to be specifically set in the context of world events in the years 1938-1945.' The eighteen poems in this section are, as one might expect from the subject matter, rather more sombre than many of the other pieces in the book. 'Tattoo', for example, relates the viewing of a newsreel on which is shown 'The King at Lords, a train smash, the quarter-finals at Wimbledon, / And last, genteel emasculation, war in Spain' (p.101). The poem goes on to castigate the sanitised view of the civil war presented:

> Not the shambles at Badajoz, not the road
> To Almeria, but the siege of San Sebastian
> A century ago. Nor mud nor stench
> Of putrefaction mars the glorious game.
> The cannon vents its atrabilious spleen,
> But spills no entrails on the well-kept lawn. (p.101)

As he advocates in 'A Hogmanay Sermon' the poem does not seek solace or consolation in the face of terrible events.

Other poems move closer to Scotland, and to a different conflict. 'First Raid', for example, takes for its subject an aerial attack which was carried out on the Forth Bridge on 16 October 1939. Tait's note in the volume tells us how 'A bus trip from Bo'ness to Edinburgh was interrupted to provide a grandstand view of the Forth Bridge air-raid' (p.106). The poem, which suffers from a lack of clarity, is not one of Tait's best, but the image of the Forth Bridge under siege in an 'aerial pageant' (p.106) is a powerful one. It is an image which Tait uses again in the longest, and best, of the war poems 'Scorched Earth', which, told in the voice of what would now be called an embedded reporter, imagines a Fascist invasion of Scotland.

The report begins on the east coast, just north of the border, but the Scots are soon forced to 'withdraw across the Forth' (p.114). The battle rages around the capital and then we are given the image picked up from 'First Raid':

> 'And half through that disnatured night we saw
> The triple pyramids of steel which crowned
> The pillars striding deep into the Forth
> Convulsed, transfigured in a lightning flash,
> Then half-submerged beneath a sea of fire;
> For past Inchkeith, whose guns no longer spoke,
> The burning oil ran like a tortured snake.' (p.119)

The image is apocalyptic and hellish. The enemy strikes at one of the key symbols of industrial Scotland and, following this, during a Scots retreat toward the north:

> 'Suddenly, sprung from God alone knows where,
> A kilted figure clambered on a tank,
> Balanced, and as he stood upright, he strained

> His shoulders back and swung in a wide arc
> His clenched hands high and with them an old sword,
> But such a sword as dwarfed even his great frame.' (p.119)

Despite being a political man, Tait generally eschews politics in his verse. His writing does not advocate Scottish nationalism, and this image, which gathers the symbolic potential of Scottish nationalism in the face of a Fascist invasion, is, for Tait, an unusual one.

The Scots, as they have been forced out of the central belt of the country, move to the Highlands, and here we see the first glint of hope in the poem:

> 'Now once again I smile to think how we,
> The disinherited, have come to claim
> That Scotland which the deer and grouse have owned
> These many years, though empty names have filled
> The musty parchments in St. Andrew's Square.
> So from the playgrounds of the multitude
> To the arena of the favoured few,
> Our trail of ravage led, and, in death's teeth,
> Life has returned to Scotland's mountain heart.' (p.120)

The country has been sundered by the invading forces, but there is a hopefulness, a possibility of regeneration, which opens up when the Scots move north. The imaginary war is terrible, but the economic and cultural devastation of the Highlands, which has its roots in the clearances, can be overturned because large numbers of people have been forced to go there. The Scots' hold on these northern lands is, however, precarious:

> 'Even to name, as I have done, such hope
> Gives Hell a hostage; and to put our trust
> In anything except our willingness
> To die would surely breach a fortress that we hold
> More surely than the Grampians, from whose crests
> Our eyes strain southwards for the next attack,
> Southwards across the scorched and bleeding earth' (p.121)

The poem is a hopeful one, but that hope is tempered with the threat of a powerful Fascist force to the south.

'Scorched Earth' is a rather uncharacteristic work for Tait. It does not employ the first-person 'I' that animates both the Villon poems and the love poetry that will be looked at next, and the use of an impersonal, media voice opens Tait's imagination in the direction of narrative. This technique also brings to the poem an immediacy which makes the events exciting and dramatic. But, despite its grim subject matter , the poem is not ultimately pessimistic. Its sense of hope, however under threat that may be, is what the reader is left with at the end.

WILLIAM J. TAIT

Billy Tait by Jeanette Novak. *Courtesy of Jeanette Novak*

'Lux in Tenebris'

A similar sense of fragile hopefulness can also be detected in some of the poems in the second section of the book, which is titled 'the craft so long to lerne', a quote from Chaucer's *The Parliament of Fowls*. These poems take love as their subject or, as Tait rather chauvinistically puts it in his foreword, quoting H.L. Mencken, to 'the illusion that one woman differs from another'.[22]

One of Tait's earliest love poems, 'Lux in Tenebris', has become one of the most revered poems in the Shetland canon, a recent reviewer calling it 'one of the most arresting and beautifully rendered accounts of love by any writer of dialect or English' [23]:

> My daarlin, whin I canna tell
> Whaar my niest stramp mycht faa, what rod
> My wilt stravaigan fit mycht tak,
> A feddir in a mirkabrod;
> Whin every waa at croes me in
> Rins tae hits aishins i da staars
> An, hingin laich owerhaid, da lift
> Roefs in my soety haad an daurs

> Ee quick blyde tocht o dee ta smoot
> Trow da black gaird o nycht an time,
> An hert an sowl an boady seem
> Pickit wi aa da bloed an ime
> O History; dan sometimes I mind,
> As veevly as I mind da sea,
> Sunlycht an shedow o dy een,
> An aa da sunlycht meant ta me. (p.59)

This poem uses a sense of movement in a subtle way, and it is this which makes it work so well. In the first stanza, how the speaker wants to move is frustrated. He does not know where his steps will go and describes himself as 'A feddir in a mirkabrod'. 'Mirkabrod', a word drawn from Jakobsen's dictionary, meaning 'mist covering the hill-tops followed by wind', captures the struggle between stasis and movement perfectly. Mist is symbolically obscuring and static, but the word also introduces the wind, which is dynamic and able to clear the mist away. The next four lines play around this same sense of being simultaneously trapped and trying to move. The walls that confine him or, in an unusual use of the word as a verb, 'croe' him in, extend to the sky, and the sky itself, picking up on the word 'aishins', meaning the top part of a wall inside a building, becomes the roof which encloses him. But, despite these images of confinement, which, like MacDiarmid's early lyrics, combine domestic and everyday things – walls, roofs – with more cosmic images, there is a sense of hope and possibility of escape as the poem moves into the second stanza. The way the poem gathers pace here is superb. The strong stress on the verb at the end of the first stanza is continued in the first four words of the second, the quickness of the monosyllables sweeping the reader through the line, just as the speaker's thought is now free to move towards the lover he is addressing. This pace is maintained in the run-on into the next line and then, again like MacDiarmid, the poem retains a sense of larger forces as the individual is placed in touch with the ' bloed an ime / O History'. The final four lines are calmer, as the speaker and his love, within the space of memory, are reunited. He remembers both the 'sunlycht an shedow' of her eyes, but it is the hopeful, affirmative image of sunlight he hangs on to at the end. The title means light in darkness and, in the way the poem moves, that idea is symbolically borne out.

This idea of happiness being reached when two lovers come together is also used in several of Tait's other pieces. 'The Gift' (p.71) and 'The Fault' (p.85), for example, both employ Edenic imagery to frame the contact of two lovers, and 'Sang', which combines images from Shetland with more urban ones – 'Da geo-face o da terrace backs' (p.78), for instance – ends with the similar ideas of light and love as 'Lux in Tenebris'. But Tait's most expansive statement on the possibilities of what love can do is found in 'A Day Atween Waddirs'.

'A Day Atween Waddirs'

'A Day Atween Waddirs', is Tait's masterpiece, and is one of the key Shetland poems. Like some of the other poems I have looked at in this chapter, it is discursive, lengthy, and moves away from the lyrical mode that Tait often employs. It is also his most local poem, in the sense that it is filled with identifiable Shetland places, but it is the poem in which Tait travels the furthest. In it he moves back and forth through time, discusses the kind of language suitable for his poem, and considers the big questions of death, history, and, most importantly, love. In 'A Day Atween Waddirs', as we saw Haldane Burgess do in Chapter Three, Tait produces a Shetland dialect poem which is unafraid to be philosophically and intellectually complex.

The poem is quick to locate itself, as we see in its opening lines: 'Twa days fae syne I cam dis sam gait, / Cut aff o da Cumlick rod an strack up da brae' (p.72). From the vantage point at the top of the brae, in the second stanza the speaker looks over the 'Sannick rigs' (p.72), with lines of poetry partially formed in his mind.[24] He speaks one of these lines, '"dissolve in emollient phrases"' (p.72) and the English words jar. They seem too fine, too heightened and poetic, to be placed here, and, as the speaker thinks back to another day when he was out walking, he tells us how his 'fine wirds wilt' (p.72). As he looks at an old house, a memory is triggered of another house which was built using parts of a standing stone:

> an I mindit da day
> An da place whaar I stoed. Eence a staandin-stane –
> A gibbet accoardin ta some – hed crooned dis broo,
> Bit dey caad 'im doon an his gey freestane flanks
> Dey shapit fur lintels fur yon sam aald hoose [...]. (pp.72-73)

This use of an ancient monument for building material, which perhaps recalls the kind of pragmatism we identified in 'Auld Maunsie's Crü', leads Tait into one of the main themes of his poem, death and ruin. The stanza then ends, rather ominously, with a borrowing from the 'East Coker' section of Eliot's *Four Quartets*, 'Gulga Golgotha, goelgreff, dung an daeth' (p.73).

But, ultimately, like 'Lux in Tenebris' the poem is not a bleak one. In the next stanza the speaker tells a story about the death of an old woman, 'A poer crazed craitir' (p.73) whose meagre possessions were auctioned off in a public sale. Again, like Maunsie's Crü, time takes its toll on the house and:

> Dan da roef fell in – or mebbe dey pooid 'im doon –
> An da rain washed da elt an da ime, da door
> Mooldered awa fae da haars an an orta glisk
> O da sun – a day atween waddirs – glansed
> Ithin neuks whaar da daylycht herdly wis coagit afore. (p.73)

What has happened to the woman, 'Da Crunter' (p.73), as she was nicknamed by the speaker and his boyhood friends, is fairly unpleasant. She has been shunned by the community because 'shu hed an ill-name wi some fock' (p.73), the implication being that she is in league with supernatural forces and, at the auction, people come to her house 'mair tinkin ta laach as ta buy' (p.73). Even in the horridness of this death, however, there are glimpses of new life and hope as the dark corners of the old woman's hovel feel, for the first time, the regenerating balm of the sun. Again, as with 'Lux in Tenebris', we see sunlight symbolically allowed into what seems like an all-confining darkness.

The poem speculates about death, but it is also about ways in which we might find solace in the face of that brute and inescapable fact. In the fifth stanza, from his hilltop vantage point, the speaker sees other members of the community, who he describes as like 'honticlocks' (p.74), or beetles, walking to church. He says of the sermon they are soon to hear:

> An I tink o da news d'll hear whin da shaar an clink
> O da kirk bell whites; an I tink o yon monstrous stane,
> Toorin hych i da lift, i da olament air,
> Castin a shedow, a grist, ower laand an ower sea [...]. (p.74)

Religion offers no comfort for the speaker. The 'monstrous stane' stands for the forbidding and oppressive power of the church. Light can find its way in to the bleak territory he is moving through, but none of that light comes from a pulpit, and he denigrates and makes trivial the minister's words as 'news'.

The stanza then ends with the aphoristic 'Friday's lill still faas afore Sunday's stoal' (p.74). The statement is a pithy one, and it juxtaposes the 'lill' or news that people exchange on a Friday with the 'stoal' or legend that they hear in the kirk two days later. And it is with people – the speaker and his love – that the poem remains until the end.

His memory moves to 'anidder day an anidder stane' (p.75), but this time the stone is used, practically, as a place for the two lovers to shelter from the rain. This section of the poem begins in the rain but, again, the sunlight finds its way through. The poem continues:

> (A staandin stane, toe, een o twa, da kind at dey caa
> Da Giant's Greff, alwies, whaarever you fin dem)
> At we hed fur a skoelbrugg an blissed ee Settirday moarnin,
> Taen oonawaars fur as lang as da shooir wis traetened.
> Fur a sae lang we cruggit, bit hit never wis leak ta geng aff,
> So we left Aald Grey Whiskers an took ta da hill.
> Hit wis nae rain ta spaek o, a grain o smaa smush,
> Mair makkin weet fae da mist, as we turned ta da wind,
> Bit hit gaddert in beads in her hair, on her eyelashes even,
> As shu laached up at me as we breestit da broo o da hill.
> Fur a lunk cam i da waddir, da sun brook trow,
> An dere, nearly rycht below wis, wis Mavis Grind [...]. (p.75)

The last of these lines is the point at which the poem thematically turns. Mavis Grind is one of the narrowest points of the Shetland mainland, but Tait does not simply use this place as a setting. Rather, it is the point at which the spiritual, historical, and philosophical territory the poem has wandered through achieves some kind of resolution. The speaker and his lover do not pass through Mavis Grind, but the poem does. It moves into a space which leaves behind the intense speculation of death and into a world of light and love and, once again, hope. The water 'gaddert in beads in her hair' then becomes a means of physically uniting the two lovers:

> An her hair wis weet on my sheek
> An I held her an said: 'We'll come back.' An da promise wis med.
> Dan we turned wis roond fae da loch an goed strecht up da hill
> Ta da Survey Cairn at da tap [...]. (p.75)

As at the beginning of the poem, the perspective is one from the top of a hill. The difference now, however, is that the view is a shared one.

Death is still a literal presence in this section, when we hear how another old woman is dying at the same time as the lovers take their walk, but it no longer has the ominous symbolic power it had earlier in the poem:

> An I kent we wir rycht, at da sunlycht wis wirs an no hirs;
> An I kent, and it seemed rycht toe, at da hoemin wid come

Fur wis twa as weel, an anidder pair someday wid link
Dis sam rod alang an ink een anidder da sun. (p.76)

Once again, it is in the sunlight that we see the lovers and, despite the fact that their own death will come, symbolised in 'da hoemin', there is a gladness in the fact that future lovers may walk in the same places and experience the same joy as they have. The speaker finds a way to free himself of the terrible fact of death which haunts the poem. He finds his solace, not in God, but in the simple experience of a day spent with somebody he loves. As the last words of the poem say, his resolution is complete when he realises he has to 'Gie tanks fur da day' (p.76).

Conclusion

Like Sorley MacLean's 'Hallaig', 'A Day Atween Waddirs' is firmly a poem of place. Both poems are fundamentally local in their settings and are filled with place-names which would be familiar to anybody acquainted with these locations. The triumph of the poems, however, is that they are not poetically, thematically, symbolically or metaphorically limited by their very localised topographies. Both Tait and MacLean prove emphatically that a poet from a small island, writing in a language closely associated with regions far from urban cultural centres, does not have to be parochial in his or her work. Their poetry transcends any limitations presented by their place of birth or choice of idiom.

It is worth noting that many of the key writers of the period had their own regional limitations to transcend. Whereas European modernism is often seen as an urban phenomenon, focused on the cultural centres of London and Paris, in Scotland there was a rather more rural element in the cutting-edge writing which appeared throughout the century. MacDiarmid began his revolution in the unlikely setting of Montrose, before writing many of his most ambitious and wide-ranging poems in Whalsay. Orkney is central to the work of both Edwin Muir and George Mackay Brown, and Iain Crichton Smith, despite being born in Glasgow, grew up in Lewis. Tait's position as a Shetland poet has several parallels, but it is perhaps the Raasay-born MacLean who provides the most apposite point of comparison. Marjory Palmer McCulloch in her book *Scottish Modernism and its Contexts* writes of MacLean:

> One of MacLean's many achievements in his poetry is to bring his Celtic inheritance together with European literary references, with classical poetry and with modernist poetry, thus transforming Scottish Gaelic poetry and bringing it again into the mainstream of contemporary European culture.[25]

If we were to replace 'Celtic' and 'Gaelic' with 'Shetland' and 'Shetlandic', McCulloch's précis could equally apply to Tait. His verse stands in contrast to that of his Shetland peers and, like MacLean, he was reacting against prevailing currents in the literature of his islands. Vagaland and Bulter's poems travel deep into the culture and the way of life of those islands, but Tait, in his engagement with European poetry and with the cosmopolitan and internationalist principles of the Scottish Renaissance, represents an opening of new directions for Shetland's writers. By creating a language less rooted in the isles than that of his peers, by advocating a more modern, less sentimental approach for Shetland writers and, like Haldane Burgess, by using Shetland dialect to investigate the big questions, Tait's work represents a major leap forward for the literature of the isles. More than anybody else, Tait showed what it was possible for a Shetland writer to achieve.

NOTES

1. Laurence Graham, Introduction, in *A Shetland Anthology: Poetry from the Earliest Times to the Present Day*, ed. by Laurence L. Graham and John J. Graham (Lerwick: Shetland Publishing Company, 1999), pp.xv-xxiii (p.xxii).
2. [Anon.], Obituary of William J. Tait, *Shetland Times*, 7 August 1992, p.8.
3. Roderick Watson, *The Literature of Scotland* vol.2 (Basingstoke / New York: Palgrave Macmillan, 2007) p.106.
4. William J. Tait, *A Day Between Weathers: Collected Poems* (Edinburgh: Paul Harris Publishing, 1980), p.39.
5. These references are discussed by Tait in a series of notes he made for the Shetland Archives in 1980 concerning the poems in *A Day Between Weathers*. See SA D1/122.
6. SA D30/43/1, Testimonial by C.M. Grieve for William J. Tait, 3 May 1949.
7. Jim Mainland, Interview with Sheenagh Pugh, *New Shetlander*, 253 (Hairst 2010), 14-17 (p.16).
8. SA, D1/122.
9. Letter from Laurna Robertson to me, 8 July 2010. The text she loaned was *François Villon: Ouevres* (Paris: Club Des Amis Du Livre, undated).
10. SA, D30/15, Letter from Murdo MacDonald, Polygon, to William J. Tait, 4 March 1987.
11. W.J. Tait, *Villon: Le Testament and Other Translations*, ed. by John Cumming and Mark Ryan Smith (Stromness: Hansel Cooperative Press, 2011), p.33.
12. For Vagaland's translations see T.A. Robertson, *The Collected Poems of Vagaland*, ed. by Martha Robertson (Lerwick: Shetland Times, 1975), pp.140-153.
13. Christopher Whyte, *Bho Leabhar-Latha Maria Malibran* (Steòrnabhagh: Acair, 2009), p.145.
14. Laureen Johnson in *Norn but not Forgotten: Sounds of Shetland*, presented by Kathleen Jamie and broadcast on BBC Radio 4, 29 August 2010.
15. John Ashbery, 'Soonest Mended', in *The New York Poets: An Anthology*, ed. by Mark Ford (Manchester: Carcanet, 2004), p.73.

16. *François Villon: Selected Poems*, ed. by Peter Dale (Harmondsworth: Penguin, 1978).
17. Tom Hubbard, 'Scott, Thomas McLaughlin (1918–1995)', *Oxford Dictionary of National Biography* <http://www.oxforddnb.com/view/article/57753> [Accessed 27 Aug 2010].
18. William Cookson, Obituary of Tom Scott, *Independent*, 14 August 1995 <http://www.independent.co.uk/news/obituaries/obituary-tom-scott-1596211.html> [Accessed 27 August 2010].
19. The common ground between the two poets is widely acknowledged, as A.M. Kinghorn outlines in his essay 'Dunbar and Villon: A Comparison and a Contrast', *Modern Language Review*, vol.62, no.2 (April 1967), 195-208.
20. J. Derrick McClure, 'The Translations of W.J. Tait', in *Villon: Le Testament*, by W.J. Tait, ed. by Cumming and Smith, introductory material unpaginated.
21. SA, D30/21/1, Drafts of and notes concerning 'A Hogmanay sermon', by William J. Tait, 1964-1965.
22. I have been unable to find an original source for Mencken's aphorism, but Tait makes it clear that the quotation comes from him.
23. Jordan Ogg, Review of *Bright Pebbles: Poetry and Prose from Shetland*, *New Shetlander*, 253 (Hairst 2010), 41.
24. These places are in Sandwick, where Tait grew up.
25. Margery Palmer McCulloch, *Scottish Modernism and its Contexts: Literature, National Identity and Cultural Exchange* (Edinburgh: Edinburgh University Press, 2009), p.212.

CHAPTER EIGHT

CONTEMPORARY WRITERS

Introduction

For Shetland's writers today, the legacies of the *New Shetlander* generation have been both inspiring and problematic. In the previous chapter I suggested that Billy Tait, whose work is a departure from that of his island contemporaries, was the most important poet of his era, but subsequent writers have not followed the paths he cleared. Instead, in much of the work we are about to discuss, we see writers preferring to take their directions from the group studied in Chapter Six. As we saw in that chapter, these authors share a deep attachment to their native isles and its language but, with the exception of John Graham and Stella Sutherland, they often display a rather inward-and-backward-looking conservatism. Sutherland and Graham utilise both English and Shetlandic to widen the formal and thematic ground of local writing but, in general, the idea of the Shetland dialect as an icon of culture and identity was a guiding principle for the *New Shetlander* generation. For writers today, many of whom were first published in the magazine alongside Vagaland, Bulter and their peers, the ideals and principles identified in Chapter Six are the literary inheritance that must be negotiated. These ideals and principles are still prominent in local writing but, as we shall see, there is also a need to expand and diversify them and, in some cases, to reject them entirely.

Christine De Luca (b.1947)

For Christine De Luca, the *New Shetlander* writers are crucial precursors. In a 2011 interview, she told me how important Vagaland was to her development as a poet:

> I was aware of dialect poetry from an early age. My parents were friends of both Tammie Alex Robertson (alias Vagaland) and his wife Pat (Martha Andrew). My mother and Martha had been at the Bruce Hostel in Lerwick together while at secondary school, and my father and Tammie Alex were of the same generation of teachers. So Vagaland's poems were known and loved in our house, particularly so as we lived in Waas [Walls], his stamping ground. A school concert,

The Literature of Shetland

Christine De Luca.   *Courtesy of Christine De Luca and Dawn Marie Jones*

or indeed any local concert, was not complete without someone reciting one or two Vagaland poems. He wrote of places round about us: Stoorbra Hill, Dale, Huxter, Sefster, Brouster, Vaila, Linga. He re-imagined the landscape for us, sometimes peopling it from earlier times. I still can't walk or drive around Da Wast Side without Vagaland getting under my skin. The link feels personal. His poem 'Water-Lilies' still touches me in its simplicity: 'I took my tushkar be Lungawater / An cöst a bank near Stoorbra Hill.' His peatbank was at the same place as our childhood peatbank. It was his loch. It was my loch.[1]

For De Luca, Vagaland's lyrics, which were part of the cultural life of her community, opened up and continue to define the local landscape as an imaginative space. The scenes described in her poem 'Lönabrack at Littlure', for example, would have been immediately familiar to T.A. Robertson:

> Laevin Burrastow, hills winter ochre
> we lean inta da wind, alang banks' gaets.
> Luckit bi da updraa, maas lift
> ta plane in silence.
>
> Drappin doon ta da loch o Quinnigyo
> April sun is warm.
> A pair o rain geese mak fur da hill
> an a laverock is a ringin string
> ta da lunder o ocean bass.[2]

The specific place-names (all from around Walls), the landscape, the sound of the ocean and the birds, bring Vagaland's work to mind. She uses similar locations in 'Gyaain ta da Eela', but this time the land is seen from the sea:

> Vaila darkenin fae aest ta wast,
> wind faa'n awa;
> eela nichts i da simmer dim.
>
> Abune da tide, lik a sel, wir boat wid lie;
> we hed ta tize her doon,
> bulderin an traan owre da ebb
> but nyiff i da sea.
>
> Rowin oot bi wir kent wirld
> ta da uncan moo o da Western Soond,
> holms lay black on a sea an sky o gowld.
>
> (*Voes and Sounds*, p.10)

Again, 'sea an sky o gowld' is reminiscent of Vagaland. De Luca, especially in her more recent verse, does not restrict herself to the isles, but here we see how she shares with Vagaland the close observation of the local environment, and a love for rural Shetland.

Her poetry often utilises Shetland's scenery but, unlike the writers looked at in Chapter Six, De Luca has lived outside the isles for most of her literary career. In the introduction to her 2010 collection *North End of Eden* she writes: 'Despite having lived in Edinburgh for more than 40 years, my Shetland identity is intact and my delight in my mother tongue as strong as ever.' [3] In her conflation of language and identity, De Luca stands in clear lineage to the *New Shetlander* writers and, indeed, the magazine remains an important place of publication for her. She also, however, has a readership outside the isles. Several of her volumes have been published in Edinburgh and reviewed in Scottish journals and newspapers, she is a member and former convener of the Shore Poets group in Edinburgh, and she appears regularly at Scottish book festivals.[4] Like Vagaland and Bulter, her work is a conscious attempt to preserve and celebrate Shetland's culture and what she sees as her mother tongue, but she is also concerned with bringing these things to new audiences. Her verse is traditional, both in the sense that it reveres what Vagaland in 'A Skyinbow o Tammy's' calls 'da aald true wyes', and in the sense that it often takes its cues from poets of an older generation. But she is also forward-looking in her willingness to use the Shetland language to write about things which may have seemed unusual, even exotic, to Vagaland and his peers. Despite this, however, the idea that the Shetland language and a sense of local identity are fundamentally entwined is a key component of her work. For De Luca, to write in the Shetland dialect is to give expression to an essential ingredient of what it means to be from the isles:

> if my poems do not speak to the average Shetlander, I might as well give up. It is their language, their heritage, and not there to be used as a literary device even if one is a fluent dialect speaker. The writing has to be authentic, should respect the dialect's cadence, the way it reflects the physicality of the environment. If writers do not take the speakers of the dialect with them on that journey the dialect will, I fear, become a literary artefact, of interest only to academics.[5]

De Luca, like many of the *New Shetlander* writers, takes the local speech as her litmus test. Her use of dialect may appeal to her non-Shetland readership as exotic but, here, she positions the 'average Shetlander' (whoever he or she is) as her linguistic arbiter. Any poem is a construction or literary artefact, but De Luca wants her writing to draw towards utterance. For her, the poem, as a made thing, is secondary to need to seek fidelity with the spoken tongue.

De Luca, like Vagaland and his contemporaries, believes that the local language encapsulates the ethos of Shetland. And, also like them, she sees it as providing a connection to the past. We see this in her poem 'A Shuttle o Soonds':

At da time at folk namit da nort end o Eden
a moothfoo o soonds gied frame tae da laand
every bicht, every knowe a wird pictir in Norn.

Dey hed böddies o wirds for da varg o da crofter
soonds o da crö, da crub an da hill: some lost
on da wind owre da flakki o years.

An a kyist-foo o soonds for aa kinds o sea wark
wi a hoidy-hol for queer luckin wirds
stowed far fae wir hearin ta keep herm awa.

Da Norn is lang gien, but hit's left a waageng
at keethcins a tongue at can hadd ony haert
can rowe up wir feelings, unreffel wir tochts.

[...]

Fur dey mak da warp in a pattern o livin, while
da weft comes fae places ootbye da Sooth Mooth.
Dey can blend i da waeve wi wir shuttle o soonds.

Da garb o wir language is pitten dagidder
in a wye at maks room fur da new an da auld
baith pipeline and paet-bank; rap artist an skald.[6]

De Luca's imagery – knitting, the croft – draws on the same sources as that of Bulter and her peers but, where these poets tend to emphasise the danger posed to the community by outside forces, De Luca is more optimistic. She accepts the influences that come from furth of the isles as things which can enrich the local language and, in a more conciliatory way than her predecessors, suggests that the language, as a changing, evolving, vital thing, can encapsulate both the traditional world of the peat-bank and the modernity of the oil age.

De Luca rarely writes about the disruption of her community, preferring to see contemporary Shetland, and its language, as able to accept, and even thrive, in the face of radical pressures. In a review of De Luca's 2002 collection *Plain Song*, Jim Mainland identifies this as one of the central ideas in De Luca's work: 'one theme that emerges strongly is that of continuity in the face of change, the way the past informs the present.'[7] In 'A Strynd o Sense', for example, the speaker encounters her father cutting corn with a scythe:

He wid see me is I roonded
da shooder o da Kloss
lift his een, but keep his sye
i da rhythm o centuries.[8]

The ancient is found in ways of life that the poet has been a part of. There are similar ideas about the congruity of ancient and modern in 'Da Fremd':

> Dem at brook oot laand,
> built and taekit doon da years at Aness, dey böst
> a sought some meaning fur hit's being dere.
> Dey laid a foond for generations still ta come,
> layer on layer, beddin planes o continuity.
> *(Wast wi da Valkyries,* p.43)

The poem goes on to say that change is inevitable, that people will be 'muv'd bi forces oot a wir control' (p.43), but that the foundations laid down by the ancestors will prove strong and substantial. The past, in De Luca's work, is rarely held up as an ideal in contrast to the perdition of the modern world. Rather, she looks on the past as something which shapes the ever-changing present. She does not, like some of the *New Shetlander* writers, privilege tradition and reject modernity, but tries to find ways of reconciling the two.

But it is not only continuity between ancient and modern Shetland that De Luca is interested in. She also uses her verse to build links with other places and communities. In 'Hoy fae Innertoon', for example, she finds common ground in Scotland's two northern archipelagos: 'Hoy fae Innertoon / could be Quarff fae Burra / majestic symmetry' (*Plain Song*, p.5). And, in 'Plainsong 1' and 'Plainsong 2', she compares the lives of women in Shetland in 1907 and in Natal, South Africa, in 1997:

Hit's a lang gaet ta Lerook, an me at da faain fit wi twins. A'll sell spencers and glivs fur linen. [...] I wid lik a widden flör i da but end an a peerie black stove. I could roast a duke, bake a curn lof. Whitna day!	On my back I tie my tenth child nameless as yet. I care for her but will not love her, name her till I know she will survive. [...] And I dream too of a square house with a tin roof and windows and a light switch, quick and clean, a tap to turn. One day it will come.

(Plain Song, pp.58-61)

This is a critique of a situation where people in the late twentieth century have to live in primitive housing, but it also finds a shared set of experiences in the lives of these women. De Luca is interested in the diversity of lives and places, but is also concerned with the things people have in common.

De Luca's willingness to draw diverse places and ways of life into her poetic orbit has been present since her first volume and, perhaps as she has travelled more widely, it has become an increasingly prominent feature of her work. Her recent verse includes a number of translations, mainly from Scandinavian poets, and, with her collaboration, a French-Shetlandic selected poems, *Mondes Parallèles*, appeared in 2007. Her 2005 collection *Parallel Worlds*, published, like *North End of Eden*, in Edinburgh, contains poems set in Turkey, Finland, British Columbia, Italy and Afghanistan. Similarly, *North End of Eden* ranges from Shetland to Brittany, Manitoba, and India. In 'Fire-Sang Cycle', a sequence from *North End of Eden* which encompasses Shetland and Rajastan, she again brings together the working lives of people from each place. Here she describes the cutting of peats in Shetland and the preparation of buffalo dung for fuel in India:

Finnin da harmony

Ripper an flayer,	Hent aa da sharn,
rhythm o tushkar,	*tagelia* head-heich,
pattern o paetbank;	mix hit wi strae,
wind wark an sun wark.	flatsh aa da *uple*;
Raise dem an roog dem,	lay dem ta dry,
borrow-foo, kishie-foo,	raise dem an roog dem,
hurl dem, rin wi dem,	lift dem an kerry dem,
a saeson's wark half dön.	a saeson's wark half dön.

(*North End of Eden*, p.98)

The clipped rhythms and repeated lines, as well as symbolising the work being done, make the stanzas reflect one another, drawing the two cultures together in a common need for physical work in a harsh environment. But the major difference between this sequence and the two 'Plainsong' poems is that, here, Shetland dialect is used to write about both places. This is a different approach to the one taken by De Luca in her earlier work. She writes of the formative part of her career:

> As a poet, I've always written in English as well as Shetlandic. Looking back now I realise that, unconsciously, for the first decade or so I tended to compartmentalise my writing: I wrote in Shetlandic when the location or theme of the poem seemed to fit; and everything else I wrote in English.[9]

De Luca's earlier work used Shetland dialect to write about the isles but, as her career has developed, she has used the language to write about things and places which have nothing to do with her native archipelago. As well as poems about India, for example, *North End of Eden* includes dialect poems about Albert Edelfelt (a Finnish painter), about Hiroshima, about artefacts in the Museum of the Royal College of Surgeons in Edinburgh, about folk dancing in northern France, and about the murder of prostitutes in Ipswich in 2006. The *New Shetlander* poets provide a foundation for De Luca, but, especially in her later volumes, she endeavours to expand the thematic boundaries of Shetland dialect writing. Her work, unlike Billy Tait's, is not a reaction against prevailing ideas in local literature, but it does represent a diversification of what she would have read in the *New Shetlander* as a young girl in Walls.

De Luca is unafraid to incorporate both traditional and contemporary themes in her work and, in this enlargement of the thematic ground covered by a Shetland writer, we see a growing confidence in a poet who has published frequently outside the isles. This burgeoning confidence has led De Luca to try her hand at a form not often taken up by local writers, the novel. In our discussion of Robert Alan Jamieson, we will look at what, alongside the work of Burgess and John Graham, is the most substantial group of novels in the Shetland canon but, in De Luca's first attempt at the form, we find themes that are also explored in Jamieson's most recent contribution, *Da Happie Laand* (2010).

Like much of Jamieson's fiction, and like Graham's two fictional works, De Luca's *And Then Forever* (2011), is (partly) a historical novel. In it, we are told two love stories: that of Gilbert Jamieson, a Shetlander living in Winnipeg in the late nineteenth century, and that of his granddaughter, Katherine Maitland, a middle-aged divorcee living in Edinburgh. Gilbert falls in love with Bridget O'Donaghue, an Irish Catholic, but, because he was raised as a Methodist, her father proscribes their relationship. Despite this, they continue to meet clandestinely and Gilbert even goes to a priest to discuss becoming a Catholic. But he finds it impossible to accept the faith and, eventually, because they can never marry, and because Gilbert has to go back to Shetland to see his dying mother, they are forced to accept that their relationship is at an end.

Katherine's present-day relationship with Peter MacPherson, another middle-aged divorcee, comes to a happier ending, with the couple deciding to marry. Peter's proposal comes during an idyllic sojourn in Winnipeg, where Katherine has gone to research her grandfather's time there, with Peter arriving unexpectedly to surprise her. Katherine remembers her grandfather but knows little about his past. In Canada she pieces together his story in the city archives and eventually contacts a descendant of Bridget, thus reconciling the two families broken apart more than a century earlier. Through this meeting, Katherine is able to complete the story of what happened to Gilbert and heads back to Scotland with several things that belonged to him – things which, alongside his story, will become heirlooms for his great grandchildren.

Katherine's relationship with Peter is a positive one but, for Gilbert, the impossibility of marrying Bridget destroys him and he returns to Shetland in psychological tatters. As Katherine and Bridget's niece look at a photograph of Gilbert, Katherine says:

> 'Well, seemingly he was quite depressed and strange when he got home. No one ever knew what was wrong. They didn't speak about things like mental illness then I suppose. Anyway when the First World War was declared he must have been called up. I know he was in France. He was one of the lucky ones, came back alive but I believe worse than ever.' [10]

Even more so than the war, emigration causes a rupture in Gilbert, but also in the story of Katherine's family. What, for Gilbert, began as an exciting and positive adventure turns into something appalling and, because of what happened to him in Winnipeg, his story has never been told. Here, Katherine tries to picture her grandparents, in order to tell her own daughter about them:

> The two of them would sit, one on each side of the Modern Mistress stove, the silence uncomfortable even to a child; the only noise the hiss of the Tilley lamp. Gilbert and Marion Jamieson. Yes, my grandparent's house had been a house of silence, tiny acres of it. (p.50)

This silence, the repression of Gilbert's story, is the legacy his involvement with Empire has left, and it falls to Katherine to become his narrator. In the Winnipeg archives, after making good progress with finding out about Gilbert, a research assistant Katherine has employed says to her: 'I often say this kind of research is for people who have a hole in their lives. Something needing to be filled, to be solved' (p.210). By constructing his story from archival documents, by visiting places in which he lived and worked, and by meeting the remaining members of Bridget's family, Katherine is able to find a way of reconciling the disruptive legacy her grandfather has passed on. As she does in her verse, De Luca's novel probes at the ways the past can influence the present and, again, we see her willingness to find conciliation, rather than irreconcilable rupture.

De Luca's work, despite its geographical roving, is rooted in Shetland. None of her novel is set in the isles, but Shetland is the location around which the stories turn. It is also is the core point of reference in her poetry. In a review of *North End of Eden*, poet Jen Hadfield points out this ability somebody from the islands has to redraw the map:

> "Liminality" (the phenomenon of the dangerous/alluring threshold or "edge") can be, as De Luca hints [in her poem 'Nae Aesy Mizzer'], a dated notion verging on the colonial, when it tries to explain why people are attracted to "edge communities" such as Shetland. Liminality as an idea can't help but treat those alluring "edges" as commodities, while overlooking the fact that for folk in Shetland, this is the centre.[11]

De Luca, despite living in Edinburgh, does not see the islands as being at the margin of her imaginative world. They are at the centre. The landscapes and language of the archipelago inform much of her work and, in her use of these things, she displays clear affinities with authors of a previous generation. The *New Shetlander* writers inform her poetic practice and, with a readership outside the archipelago, she continues to produce work which exports the principles and ideas these writers represent to a relatively wide audience. For her, Vagaland and his peers are not poets from one of the most remote parts of Scotland, as they would be to somebody not from Shetland. They are her formative influences. She takes her cues from these writers but, in her increasing willingness to use the local language to write about things unconnected to the isles, she expands the thematic boundaries of the literature she is part of. She is both a poet of tradition and a poet who is open to the globalised places in which we live.

Robert Alan Jamieson (b.1958)

Like De Luca, Robert Alan Jamieson has also lived outside Shetland for a large part of his life. He was born in the remote community of Sandness in the extreme west of the isles but, since the mid-1980s, has lived in Edinburgh, where he currently teaches creative writing at Edinburgh University. All his books have been published in the capital, but Shetland and, in his later works, Sandness, remain his central imaginative locations. His writing, as we shall see, has been constantly experimental, but the idea (and also, perhaps, the ideal) of community, which Jamieson experienced in his formative years, has become increasingly important. At first glance, particularly in his verse, he does not resemble any of the writers covered in this study but, when we look closely, we do find continuities with his literary forebears. Jamieson is a writer who is aware of the traditions he is working within, but is also consciously and single-mindedly trying to expand and contribute something new to those traditions. Like De Luca, Jamieson's work represents an extension of the writing covered in Chapter Six.

Poetry

Jamieson first started publishing poems in the *New Shetlander* in 1979, but his first collection of verse, *Shoormal*, did not appear until 1986, by which time he had already published two novels.[12] His second collection of verse, *Nort Antlantik Drift* (2007), was published more than twenty years later and, from one book to the other, although Jamieson's characteristic dialect orthography remains, there is a major shift in what he is trying to achieve.

Shoormal is not an easy volume to engage with, as we see in its opening poem, 'Avunavara':

>   Fae dis graet ledi I'll lukk dy glureks,
>   Skorpnin saat apo dy face,
>   Scravlin, lurrin da boo o wyrds
>   Apo dy tongue, norard t' Norn.
>
>   Dis goglit spaek, lackin da vynd
>   T'lowse dy hert fae ledli toons o døl,
>   Quhar avunavara rins dy glumpsin jaas
>   Wi wyrds o iddir laands.[13]

This is Shetland dialect poetry, but it is very far from anything Vagaland wrote. Even for someone used to reading Shetlandic, it is very challenging indeed. In his introduction, Jamieson says of his approach to dialect writing:

> Modern Shetlandic is an uneasy combination of English, Lowland Scots and Norroena or Norn, which was the language spoken in the islands from their settlement by the Norsemen in the early Viking age until well into the eighteenth century. By the year, English grows more dominant, as the least anglicised corners of the dialect are eroded by the hard rub of modern media.
>
> The poems which form *Shoormal* reflect this meld of tongues, ranging between the full flow of the coming tide and an ebbing artificiality, which is a synthetic Shetlandic using some Norn words and phrases bound together with Scots. (p.11)

The language in *Shoormal*, like Billy Tait's Shetlandic, is not an attempt to approximate speech. We do not hear the language of the community but, instead, we find an idiom which, perhaps even more so than Tait's, is constructed from the linguistic resources available to the Shetland poet, especially Jakobsen's dictionary. Not all Jamieson's dialect poems are this obscure but, by placing this poem at the start of the collection, he announces, jarringly, that the reader is about to be drawn into an alienating linguistic world.

In this use of language, two things seem to be at work. Firstly, we see a young writer reacting against his literary forebears. In a conference paper, which is a valuable key to his poetic practice, Jamieson writes of himself as a young poet looking at older Shetland writers and deciding to make the tradition new:

> Kompært wie da ræsint wark o Skots pojits, quhan I lookit at a lokk o da pojitrie inata *Nordern Lichts*, hit siemt t'me t'bie owir Engliesh in hit's forims an aftin owir Sjetlin in hit's subchek. I toght, o følish konfiedins o jooth, 'at I wid dø sumthin diffrint wie it.[14]

Jamieson is wry about his youthful attempts at poetic revolution but, alongside this reaction against established ways of writing, there is a symbolic point to be found in the abstruseness of the Shetlandic poems in *Shoormal*. Jamieson explains:

> In a lok o dat pojims, da langwiech is kynda unriedibil. Bit in a wy dat wis da pojint I wis maakin – dat da græt sjims o histrie furt o dis pierie gaddirie o land itada nort atlantik, dir kynda med da past unriedibil t'wis. We dønna hæ da wrytin o wir foarbærs bakk mær as twartree hundir jeir, an if we did we widna, forby twaartrie spesjilists be æbil t'makk mukkil o it. Quhit we dø hæ is fir da mæst pært choost da Norn-studdit Skots an Engliesh wrytin o da last kuppil o hundir jeir. In *Shoormal*, I wis t'sum ikstent enaktin dat, in da impenietriebil forims da pojims sumtyms took.[15]

More than any other author, Jamieson's work displays the influence of Jakobsen. Vagaland and Tait drew on Jakobsen's work, but Jamieson, as well as taking words directly from the dictionary, evokes Norn as a symbol of what has been lost. He does not only use the language as a lyrical or aesthetic resource, but as a way of analysing Shetland's peculiar linguistic history. As discussed in the introduction to the present work, there is virtually no extant Norn literature and, as Jamieson says in his conference paper, even if there were, modern Shetlanders would not be able to read it. In *Shoormal*, by making some of his Shetlandic poems close to unreadable, he symbolically represents the archipelago's disrupted linguistic narrative. He cuts off the reader from meaning, just as Shetlanders are cut off from the imaginations of their ancestors. Vagaland, in his poem 'Beach of Bright Pebbles', and De Luca in her work, emphasise continuity between modern and ancient but, through his evocation of Norn, Jamieson emphasises the fragmented story of Shetland's languages.

But a poetry that gives so little concession to the reader can only be taken so far. One must admire Jamieson's single-mindedness in making his point like this, but a poetry that is very hard to understand can cause a longing for something rather more easy to grasp. And, if *Shoormal* represents, in part, a reaction against Jamieson's literary forebears, his next collection *Nort Atlantik Drift*, a sequence of maritime-themed poems, reacts against the poetic methods of his younger self.[16]

Jamieson describes this collection as consisting of 'Simpl pierie pojims, o bærndæs in Saanis, wie næ græt mikkil unkan wirds', and, although the poems, in terms of orthography, look similar to the dialect poems in *Shoormal*, the later volume enters us into a much simpler linguistic environment.[17] The poems are easier to understand than those in *Shoormal*. They give ground to the reader by, firstly, eschewing the incorporation of obscure words and, secondly, by providing English prose cribs. Jamieson, as we have observed, is wary of giving too great a concession to English and, on the face of it, his use of translation in *Nort Atlantik Drift* would appear to do exactly what he seeks to avoid. But this use of English alongside every Shetlandic poem does several things beyond simply rendering an unusual-looking poem into an easier form for non-dialect speakers.

One of the things this technique does is to reflect the linguistic make-up of the society in which Jamieson was raised. In the 1960s in Shetland, English was the language of the classroom, and the local tongue was strictly outlawed in schools. Jamieson describes himself as 'gro[win] up apo a lingwistik fruntier', on which the educational system forced children to become bilingual.[18] The poems in *Nort Atlantik Drift* reflect this duality. In our discussion of John Graham's *Strife in the Valley*, we saw how the use of English placed a barrier between members of the community but, in Jamieson's conception, despite the oppression of the local language, something is gained when children are made to speak in two different ways. He accepts both tongues as part of his linguistic heritage. By providing English translations, Jamieson avoids any problem of impenetrability that a reader of *Shoormal* might expect to find and, once the simple story of each poem is grasped, the reader's eye is thrown back to the Shetlandic, without the worry of not being able to understand what is being said.

What the reader finds when encountering the Shetlandic versions is, essentially, phonetic poetry.[19] For example, in 'Da Boat Biggir's Nefjoo':

> Quhan da bærns chap da windoo
> he hadds up da sjip ati'da bottil,
> sjaaks his hed – awa!
>
> An da aald fokk sæ –
> 'Tink næthin o'it.'
> 'Tym'll tell.' 'Du'll fin dy nitch.'
>
> 'He tinks – Foo dæs'it kum t'gjing insyd?
> No a trikk, bit maachikk.
> Dønna shaa me, I want it ta happin.
>
> An da aald fokk sæ –
> 'Quhar dir's a will, dir's a wy.
> Aniddir skurtfoo fæ da skroo.' [20]

Which is given in English as:

> When the children tap the window, he holds up the ship in the
>   bottle, shakes his head – Away!
> And the old folk say – 'Think nothing of it.' 'Time will tell.' 'You'll
>   find your niche.'
> He thinks – How does it come to go inside? Not a trick, but magic.
>   don't show me, I want it to happen.
> And the old folk say – 'Where there's a will there's a way. Another
>   armful from the haystack.' (p.17)

In his introductory note to the volume, Jamieson writes of this bilingual approach: 'I felt I could show something of the unique dialect of my village at that time [i.e. during his childhood]' (p.11). The easy rendering of meaning allows the reader to tune their eye and ear to the Shetland tongue. Unlike *Shoormal*, in this volume Jamieson does attempt to represent the spoken language of his community and, by sidestepping any difficulties in understanding through his use of English translation, tries to let non-dialect speakers hear what the language sounded like to him as a boy in Sandness in the 1960s. In the earlier collection, he attempts to weave together a literary idiom which draws on all the roots of the modern Shetland dialect, but which also laments what has been lost. In *Nort Atlantik Drift*, however, Jamieson is much closer to the *New Shetlander* poets. Bulter and her peers drew their poetry towards the spoken tongue and, in *Nort Atlantik Drift*, Jamieson does the same.

Novels

Language is the most prominent concern in *Shoormal* and *Nort Atlantik Drift*, but Shetland's history is also of crucial importance to both works. The earlier volume, as we have seen, makes a point about Shetland's linguistic past and, in the later book, it is the world of Shetland's merchant sailors – a world that Jamieson, in the figures of his older sea-going relations, glimpsed as a boy – which provides inspiration for many of the poems. In Jamieson's novels, apart from *A Day at the Office* (1991), the history of the isles is a central concern. His first novel *Soor Hearts* (1983) is a relatively short, conventional tale (Jamieson's introductory note calls it a 'yarn'), which concentrates on an unsolved murder in a small Shetland community in the nineteenth century, but his 1986 novel, *Thin Wealth*, which takes the arrival of the oil industry in Shetland as its subject, is a much more complex affair.

The novel investigates the impact that the oil-related developments at Sullom Voe have on a large group of characters who are connected by the tiny fictional township of Glimmerwick. Many lives are glimpsed in the novel but the two most important characters are the crofter Lowrie a' Wurlie, and the orphaned girl Linda, who came to Glimmerwick as a child.

The figure of the crofter, as we have seen, is a key figure in Shetland's writing. He is one of the archetypes of the literature and Lowrie a' Wurlie is a contemporary incarnation. Here we see Lowrie performing a ritual he has observed all his life:

> Lowrie a' Wurlie leaned heavily on his tushkar. He lit a roll-up and paused a while in the midst of cutting the year's supply of peat. The metal blade of his home-made cutter glistened with moisture from within the peat hill, was smeared with fragments of decaying vegetation. Behind him stretched a wall of fresh-cut fuel stacked in brick-like uniformity on the edge of the peat bank, soon to dry in the summer sun, to be carried to the settlement below, and burned in the Rayburn stove at Wurlie.
>
> The bank he was cutting had been in the Manson family as long as they had lived at Wurlie. It was tied to the house with unwritten legality, and contained the kind of peat most highly prized – the bluish variety which would burn as fiercely as any coal.
>
> Each year he cut another two feet of turf to allow extraction. Each year the peat bank moved further from the distant green land below, deeper into the territory of the hare and the curlew. Into the silent high ground, the moors.
>
> Lowrie's inner voice spoke intimately here. Above the immediate world he knew so well, time swung in circles and stopped anywhere he desired – back in the age of the Pict and the Broch, the Celtic time before time.

Robert Alan Jamieson.   *Courtesy of Robert Alan Jamieson*

> He was not a religious man. He had no patience with ministers or churches, no love of people when they dressed up in self-importance. But he was a spiritual man, in touch with the rhythmic pulse of his environment, a Celtic man himself.[21]

Lowrie bears the weight of history on his shoulders. He represents Shetland before oil, before the unsettling inrush of modernity. He knows many traditional stories about Shetland, is perfectly attuned to the rhythms of rural life, and has a deep, almost mystical, connection with the land. The scraps of vegetation on the blade of his tushkar are the last vestiges of the trees that once covered the islands. Over centuries, these boughs and branches have slowly decomposed, leaving the moors, an ancient landscape which, in places, has not changed for millennia. It is to this landscape that Lowrie is fundamentally connected. In the rituals of the work he performs, in his innate understanding of the changing of the seasons and the waxing and waning of the land, Lowrie is a part of that land. He represents a way of life which, as the oil industry arrives in Shetland, seems to be coming to an end.

But Lowrie is not simply an anachronistic figure, floundering in the modern world. He is secure in his way of doing things, and there is a quiet and resolute nobility in his adherence to 'da aald true wyes'. Just as so-called progress could not reach what Auld Mallie represents in *Shadowed Valley*, oil cannot affect all of what Lowrie symbolises and, ultimately, it is a connection with the land that the novel affirms. That affirmation, however, does not only occur with Lowrie, but with the most conflicted and troubled character in the book, Linda.

Lowrie is at one with his surroundings and way of life. Linda, however, has never felt at home in Glimmerwick, or been comfortable with life in Shetland. She has a chance to leave for art college but, when the oil-boom starts, she is drawn along in its jetstream and ends up staying in the isles. Lowrie keeps his distance from anything to do with oil or the modern world. His wife insists on them getting a TV, but the noise and the inanity of it irk him terribly. And, when she gets a job at one of the accommodation camps erected to house the oil workers, Lowrie is aghast. Of all the characters in the book, he remains the least changed by oil. Linda, on the other hand, is swept into the vortex of material gain that oil brings. She also gets a job as a cleaner at one of the camps, and moves into a caravan with her feckless boyfriend Heggarty. She soon, however, comes to see this new kind of life as empty and unfulfilling.

Unlike Lowrie, Linda is changed by oil and, after she gives up her job at the camp, she forms an unlikely friendship with the crofter. She visits him at Wurlie and hears stories about a Shetland which existed before the developments at Sullom Voe:

> He had hundreds of old stories to tell. She was glad that she had the chance to hear them now, before they were lost forever, buried along with the old man who was now sadly failing.

It was an important step forward in her quest. Lowrie knew things that were not recorded in any book. So Linda bought a little tape recorder and coaxed him to go deeper and deeper into the past.

Lowrie seemed to relish the opportunity to talk. It was the first time in Wurlie since the coming of television when conversation took the main role in the evening's entertainment. It reminded him of the old days, of gyaain aboot da night. (p.199)

Linda, with Lowrie as her guide, travels into the past of their islands. She is moving back, beyond the world of consumer capitalism and global trade, and into an entirely different symbolic space. She is trying to find a connection with some kind of indefinable, ineffable essence of Shetland. She has never felt at home in the isles, but tries to find a way to belong:

She knew life in Shetland inside out. But she didn't know the place itself. At school, her history lessons had been confined to Scottish kings and queens and the goings-on at court and in battle. She knew more about England and the continent than she did of Shetland's past.

Over the next few weeks Linda put time and energy into her quest for Shetland's history. She went to the local library and museum, to the archives, in search of something she wasn't quite sure of. Somewhere the answer lay waiting, the definitive statement of her belonging, the key to her reason for being. It was something she shared with all Shetlanders, she knew, but also something personal to each and every one.

[...]

Somewhere, the key lay waiting for discovery.

She had found her purpose. She was searching for the heart of ancient Shetland. (p.185)

But Linda does not find this ancient heart in the library or archives. Rather, when she does achieve the connection she is looking for (after taking magic mushrooms), it is when she is out in the land, at the Grind o da Navir, a spectacular coastal feature in the north of Shetland. As she tries to paint this place, she hears voices. The voices initially speak English, and then a female voice says:

'I dønna hing laek muswubs, sylken, lippenin dy hert's dim riv. Dead fokk's will gings wi dir bairns, lukkin dem as I lukk de t'da places qhuar da blue-mondet stonns'll crø wis. I'm glansin swarmin fleein; licht, dy meed in aa. Death vamms nothin, only lowses, slips de fae

223

> da lemskit mondi du caas "life". Hit's juist a stab athin a sea o wantin, wir spirits most ootgeng be understandin wings!' (p.207)

The narrator then explains that:

> The tongue she spoke with was old, containing fragments of the Norn language native in the islands before the coming of the Scottish influence. Linda knew few of the words she had heard – yet she understood. Some part of her which was not her, but a part of her belonging knew it all. (p.207)

In *Shoormal*, Jamieson used Norn to symbolise the impossibility of connecting with Shetland's ancient past but, here, Linda, in a mystical way, manages to cross that impossible border and find her way into what she has been circling around in her trips to the library and her conversations with Lowrie. The voice she hears is both the voice of her dead mother and the voice of the land which mothers her, and all Shetlanders, even in the midst of the radical influence of oil. The ancient Shetland it represents cannot be destroyed, and it is to both the known past and the time-before-time that Linda must connect before she can complete her spiritual journey and feel, like Lowrie, that Shetland is where she should be.

The need to discover and write about the history of Shetland is also central to Jamieson's most recent novel *Da Happie Laand*. This novel, his first since *A Day at the Office* almost two decades earlier, draws heavily on the actual history of Shetland, and of Jamieson's home community Sandness, but also moves out into the world to investigate the legacies left by emigration.[22] The novel, like *Thin Wealth*, has at its centre a small Shetland community. In a manuscript which eventually ends up in the hands of the novel's editor, Robert Alan Jamieson, we are given the (unfinished) 'A History of Zetland, with particular attention to the parish of Norbie, Valay and Thulay', which is partly written by a nineteenth-century Norbie community schoolmaster James Gabrielsen, and has been augmented by Archibald Nicol, a minister in Perth in the present day who came into possession of the script in rather mysterious circumstances.[23] Unlike *Thin Wealth*, the historical sections of the novel do not try to find their way towards ancient, unknowable things but, rather, in them we see a twenty-first century Shetland novelist attempting to address the absence of a large-scale literary view of Shetland's more recent past.

Interspersed with the historical material about Shetland (or Zetland as it is called), and the antipodean colony of New Zetland or Tokuma, is the first-person narrative of David Cunninghame, a scion of the lairds of Norbie, who comes to the islands to search for his missing father. These sections, which have a mysterious, noirish feel, follow David on this search but, as the narrative develops, his quest takes on a spiritual dimension. In the final part of David's section we see him back in his home city of Perth where, after learning that his father's body has been found in Zetland, he tells us:

I found some solace in the idea of an afterlife, and slowly I realised
that I was prepared to believe, prepared to follow, that I
   needed to
      believe
         in [24]

The sentence is never completed. We are never told what David needs to believe in and, because of the way he appears at the beginning of the novel (unkempt, incoherent and shoeless at the Rev. Archibald Nicol's house in Perth after he returns from Zetland), it is possible he has lost his mind. But, like the protagonist in James Robertson's *The Testament of Gideon Mack* (2006), a novel which, with its use of found manuscripts and spiritual turmoil, may be an influence on Jamieson's work, it is also possible that David is of sound mind and has reached some kind of spiritual transcendence or Happie Laand.

The world David encounters in Zetland, as well as setting him off on his spiritual (or perhaps mentally degenerative) journey, is a world which exists at the very end of Britain's imperial adventure. David says of Dr Hart, the laird of Norbie he stays with in Zetland:

> And thinking about this old laird who has brought the artefacts and the attitudes of imperialism to this northern island, I realise again just how huge a part of the history of this small country the British Empire has been. How emigration and immigration, departure and arrival, have been the pattern whereby so many of the rich folk of this country have captured or consolidated their estates. And the victims, those whose journeys led nowhere but the bottom of the sea. (p.203)

The legacies of Empire are disruptive and far-reaching. The father David is searching for, whose family once owned the estate he is visiting, was born in Australia but came to Scotland as a young man. In the laird's study David reads a book titled *Bendigo and Eastern Goldfields* and, seeing the Scottish names given to places in Australia, he has a moment of epiphany about his own background:

> All those Scottish names, next to native. I sit down in the laird's study, stunned by this. Why has it taken me so long to realise that this is important? Was it because I hated it for being the thing that marked us out as different from all the others on Abbott Street? Except the Singhs, of course. And there it is, clearly framed, what we and the Singhs shared. Products of Empire, of the Great British adventure, both our families. Of emigration and exile. (p.193)

David and his family are 'Australian as well as Scottish' (p.192) and this duality, this splitting of national identity, causes him anxiety. He has an ancestral connection to Shetland, but his family narrative also moves through Australia and mainland Scotland. As happens in Christine De Luca's novel, the mass emigrations that Scots took part in during the nineteenth century produce fragmentation and rupture. Like Linda in *Thin Wealth*, David cannot see himself as really belonging anywhere. Linda finds a way of reconciling herself to her native place but, at the end of *Da Happie Laand*, it is not clear if David manages to successfully negotiate the disrupted narrative he has inherited, or if he has simply gone insane.

Empire and its aftermaths are also causes of concern for a novelist writing about Shetland's history. Empire and emigration, Jamieson seems to suggest, have made that history too multi-faceted, too unwieldy and complex, to write about straightforwardly. The basic story of David coming to Shetland to look for his missing father is a relatively simple one, but, in telling the story of Shetland and the communities its emigrants have formed, Jamieson, as well as Gabrielsen's manuscript, utilises letters, pages from the internet, scraps of oral history and paragraphs glanced in books to compile a (sometimes confusing) historical montage. How this connects to David's story (or if it does) is unclear but, in his use of this accumulative method, Jamieson is perhaps suggesting that the only way to narrate the archipelago's history is through the use of disparate fragments and multiple voices. Because of emigration and empire, Shetland's story is plural, many-sided, and the need to capture it leads him to the kind of experimentation that characterises the novel.

This willingness to experiment with the formal properties of the novel is prefigured in Jamieson's earlier work, *A Day at the Office*.[25] This work, unusually for Jamieson, is not concerned with Shetland. Instead it follows the interlinked stories of three people from Edinburgh – Ray, Douglas and Helen – who are imagined by the novel's unnamed narrator as he or she spends their day at an office desk. The milieu of the novel is one of failed relationships, broken families, drug taking, and unemployment and, right at the start of the 1990s, we see Jamieson utilise themes that would become increasingly prominent in Scottish fiction as the decade wore on. But it is not the thematic aspect of the novel which is most striking. Rather, perhaps drawing on novels such as Janice Galloway's *The Trick is to Keep Breathing* (1989) and the work of Alasdair Gray, Jamieson experiments with typography and page layout.[26] Critic and novelist Rodge Glass says of Jamieson's approach:

> Pity the poor typesetter: each page of this book – a precursor to much modern experimental Scottish fiction – looks more like a work of art than a novel, with Jamieson jumping in and out of italics, different fonts and size of lettering, punctuating the main text with succinct, sad mini-poems that are part interior monologue, part theory on life's big questions. Once you adjust your brain not to expect words in a straight line across the page, this style of delivery really helps an understanding of the text, almost as if each page has been opened up to reveal the layers of meaning contained within.[27]

As Glass suggests, what appears, at first glance, as visual oddity, allows Jamieson to make more complex the view he gives us of his characters. We slip in and out of their thoughts, just as the text slips and slides into different fonts and layouts. We learn about Ray, Douglas and Helen from both the objective, narratorial point of view, and also from the subjective, internalised points of view of the characters themselves. The novel's engagement with drug culture is also symbolised by this trippy, disorientating style and, as Glass observes, once the reader leaves behind pre-conceived ideas about what a novel is supposed to look like, the three narratives are not difficult to follow. Like *Da Happie Laand* the story emerges from a set of, sometimes bewildering, fragments, but the earlier novel is much more personal in its focus. By flitting into the minds of the characters, and by being challenged to construct the narrative from the words and phrases which flash across the pages, Jamieson draws his readers closely into the lives of his protagonists. As Glass says, what might appear eccentric is actually an effective way of opening up levels of meaning in the text.

Jamieson has never been afraid to experiment. His early poetry was an attempt – perhaps not an entirely successful one – to create a new kind of language for Shetland dialect writing and, in his most recent book, as well as incorporating several hundred years of Shetland's history, he attempts to create a new kind of Shetland novel. Previous Shetland novels – Burgess' *Tang* and Graham's two books, for example – concern themselves with the life of the community but, in *Da Happie Laand*, although he places a small community at the centre of the book, Jamieson also attempts to produce a multifarious, technically radical, narrative which, like De Luca's novel, sets Shetland in a global historical context.

But, if *Da Happie Laand* tries to incorporate some of what we have seen Jamieson in his 'Saekrit Paetbank' conference paper call 'da græt sjims o histrie furt o dis pierie gaddirie o land itada nort atlantik', his latest volume of poetry is concerned with the community in a more closely focused way. In *Thin Wealth*, he uses Shetland's ancient language as a way of bringing together the past and the present, and of allowing his protagonist to finally become part of her community but, in *Nort Atlantik Drift*, it is the Shetland tongue as Jamieson has heard it spoken that interests him. In the use of Norn in the early part of his career, Jamieson makes a symbolic point about the unusual and disrupted linguistic history of the isles but, in his later dialect verse, the Shetland language becomes one of the defining components of the community – of his community – that he wants to portray. We have discussed how the *New Shetlander* writers, and how De Luca, see the representation of their speech communities as centrally important and, in *Nort Atlantik Drift*, we see Jamieson working towards the same ideal. Characteristically, however, he does this in his own idiosyncratic way. He goes further than any other Shetland poet in trying to produce a purely phonetic dialect poetry and, with his use of English, as well as reflecting what he sees as the bilingual nature of a Shetlander of his generation, he also has an eye on an audience outside the isles.

Incomers

Both De Luca and Jamieson stand in lineage to their local literary forebears but, as writers who have formed a literary career on the Scottish mainland, they are also engaged in broadening the legacies they have inherited. In *Nort Atlantik Drift*, for example, Jamieson is just as concerned with the speech of the community as Bulter but, with his English translations, he addresses a readership unaccustomed to reading Shetland-language poetry. His dialect renderings are less conventional than De Luca's, but both poets want to take the language of their native communities to new audiences. Apart from Billy Tait, the *New Shetlander* writers addressed a local audience but, as writers who draw extensively on the isles for their themes, images and words, De Luca and Jamieson have shown that there is a national readership for Shetland-related literature. For somebody from Shetland, the islands do not seem exceptional but, for readers who have never been to the isles, the farthest-north and most-remote place on the map may appear unusual and beguiling.

In the last few decades, what we might see as the exceptional nature of Shetland has formed a significant part of the work of several writers who were not born and raised in the archipelago. Margaret Elphinstone (b.1948), who was born in Kent, and the Welsh poet Sheenagh Pugh (b.1950), for example, both of whom have lived in the isles (Pugh still does), often write about Shetland's history. Elphinstone's 1994 novel *Islanders* is set in twelfth-century Fair Isle and, in Pugh's work, especially in her Lerwick-set novel *Kirstie's Witness* (1998), characters and events from Shetland's past frequently appear. In 'Comfort' and 'Baliasta Kirkyard', both from her 2005 collection *The Movement of Bodies*, for example, we find the story of a seventeenth-century Shetland man who was sentenced to death for bestiality, and, in 'Golden Rabbits' she describes what the incomer encounters when arriving in the isles: 'He came up for the peace, the scenery, / the stepping back in time'.[28] Stepping back in time is what characterises both Pugh and Elphinstone's engagement with the isles but, in the work of the most successful contemporary incomer, Jen Hadfield (b.1978), it is not Shetland's history which provides the primary inspiration, but the place as she sees it in the early twenty-first century.

When Hadfield won the 2008 T.S. Eliot Prize for her collection *Nigh-No-Place* (2008), Shetland was, for a short while at least, on the literary pages of newspapers and journals all over the UK. Jamieson and De Luca, as we have seen, utilise their island backgrounds in a way that appeals to a readership outside the isles but, in Hadfield's quite sudden fame, the unique nature of the archipelago reached a wider audience than it had done since MacDiarmid, or even Scott, was writing about the place. Jamieson and De Luca have built literary careers in Scotland, but they do not have quite the profile that Hadfield gained after winning an internationally publicised poetry prize. All three writers, however, show that people who are not from Shetland are interested in reading about it.

CONTEMPORARY WRITERS

Jen Hadfield. *Courtesy of Jen Hadfield*

In both her prize-winning volume and her debut *Almanacs* (2005), Hadfield, originally from Cheshire but resident in Shetland since 2004, displays a restless, lively curiosity about her island surroundings and conjures original, sometimes off-kilter, responses to things that may seem prosaic to somebody who has grown up with them. For example, in 'Fool Moon Fever' we see fleeing sheep described as 'foam to my breaker, / trickling into the camber',[29] and, also from *Almanacs*, 'Talking About the Weather', is Hadfield's version of that perennial topic for people living in such an exposed place:

> Haar climbs the Voe
> and fills the valley's pitcher.
> Fence posts barble it.
> The red and umber mosses
> drink it in. (p.29)

And in a third poem from the volume, 'Song of Parts' we feel the speaker's fascination when gutting fish:

> you diddle the knife down fatty silver,
> fingernail-deep, the broad blade's tip.
> Slow burgundies stain the enamel sink.
> Mackerel hoop and harden in your grip. (p.54)

These poems, all from her first collection, are by a poet who finds herself in a new, perhaps even exotic or alien, environment. We are given fleeting glances of Shetland as she moves through the landscape and her imagination is fired by what she finds. Writers brought up in Shetland cannot see it as exotic or different but, for Hadfield and other non-native writers, and for their readerships, the natural environment, language, and history of the place are exciting and new.

In *Nigh-No-Place*, despite being written after several years of Shetland residency, Hadfield has lost none of her curiosity about everyday things. In the prose poem 'Snuskit', for instance, the speaker walks along a shore on which 'all the rubberduckery of the Atlantic is blown up [...] – a bloated seal and sometimes skull, fishboxes and buoys, a cummerbund of rotting kelp.'[30] And in 'Blashey-wadder' we hear how:

> across Bracadale
> a gritter, as far as I could tell,
> rolled a blinking ball of orange light
> ahead of it, like a dungbeetle
> that had stolen the sun. (p.31)

Both these poems use dialect words for their titles and, throughout the collection, much more so than in her debut, we see Hadfield incorporate local words. In her note at the end of the volume she provides a short glossary of these words and describes how they 'flitted through [her] vocabulary' (p.64) when the poems were being written. In 'Burra Grace' for example, she writes 'I bide on this bit / of broken biscuit' (p.52) and, in 'Daed-traa', the second line subtly utilises a dialect verb form: 'I go to the rockpool at the slack of the tide / to mind me what my poetry's for' (p.35). Again, for an audience who may not know very much about Shetland (and for the judges of poetry prizes), the use of dialect words gives the verse an exoticism, an outréness that makes Hadfield's work stand out in the marketplace.

Both these poems, as well as dropping in dialect words, seem more rooted than many of the poems in *Almanacs*. The poems in that volume are poems of movement in which we catch images and impressions of Shetland, but, in *Nigh-No-Place*, the connection to place is more settled, the impressions slightly less fleeting and restless. In 'Daed-traa', mimicking the pattern of the tide, the first two lines repeat in the middle and at the end of the poem as the speaker returns to the rockpool. She no longer whizzes through the landscape – she is no longer 'the Girl Racer [...] the darling of the Sumburgh road' (*Almanacs*, p.31) – but constantly, even quietly, returns to a favoured place in that landscape.[31] Hadfield's Shetland poetry is full of zest, energy and fascination with her environment but, in 'Daed-traa' we see that environment become a reflective space in which a poet discovers something vital about her art. Hadfield has lived in Shetland for less than a decade but, in *Nigh-No-Place*, we can, perhaps, see signs that her engagement with the isles will continue to deepen and become increasingly meaningful.

Contemporary Local Authors

We have discussed in this chapter how writers have negotiated the legacies presented by their native literary tradition. Although they address a wider audience, and although they experiment with both theme and language, Jamieson and De Luca display distinct similarities with their literary forebears. The writers we will look at for the rest of this chapter are less well-known than those discussed above but, as predominantly local authors who grew up reading the *New Shetlander*, the question of how they place themselves in relation to their native literary tradition is a pertinent one. As we have seen, the *New Shetlander* writers and, reaching back a few decades, Haldane Burgess and his contemporaries, have defined Shetland's literature. Hadfield and other writers who have come to Shetland, although they may have picked up some knowledge of Vagaland, Bulter or Burgess, do not have to deal with the ideals and principles these writers have left in the way local writers have to do. How do contemporary writers negotiate the legacies of their literature? How does the tradition of writing discussed in this book influence writers today?

Laureen Johnson (b.1949), in terms of these legacies, is perhaps the most traditional contemporary Shetland author. In addition to her co-editorship of the

New Shetlander, Johnson is a founding member of the dialect advocacy group Shetland ForWirds, and her work (both literary and as an activist) constantly champions the local language in a way that the Grahams, Bulter and Vagaland would have encouraged.[32] In their advocacy of the Shetland language, Johnson and her ForWirds colleagues, by working in schools and in the community, formalise the literary principles identified in Chapter Six and, in her own writing, Johnson shares the *New Shetlander* writers' ideas about the importance of the spoken tongue. Her earliest writing was for the stage and, in works such as *Property Values* (1992) and *Choices* (1994), both of which are in dialect, we see Johnson concerned, as her work has continued to be, with domestic situations, everyday life, and, most importantly, everyday language.[33] Her novel *Shetland Black* (2002), a whodunit, is driven by dialogue and, in its extensive use of speech, draws on Johnson's experience of dramatic writing.[34] The foreword to her only collection of poetry to date, *Treeds* (2007), claims that 'Her poems reflect the speaking voice of contemporary Shetland' and, in these poems, we find quotidian glimpses of phones, storage heaters, 'da töd o wadder forecasts, / Wogan an SIBC', as she writes in her poem 'Moarnin Ida Kames'.[35] But, as we see in her poem 'Staandin Sten', in addition to these down-to-earth images we also find contemporary Shetland held up against its own ancient past:

> Staand ida lee o a staandin sten,
> look at da stars
> an tell yoursel it's da 21st century.
> Tak you radio,
> tune as you will.
> Tak your mobile,
> an 'phone a friend'
> fae da lee o a staandin sten.
> Mak a daet, phone hame,
> tell your midder you'll be laet
> fae da lee o a staandin sten. (p.4)

Like Hadfield's rock pool, the stone provides a place of contemplation and rootedness. The modern world of electronic communication reels around its solidity and, by standing in its shade, the speaker invokes the ancient past of Shetland, perhaps in a similar way to Linda at the end of *Thin Wealth* (but without the assistance of psychotropic fungi). In Johnson's verse, the modern world is often treated with wry humour. For example, in another poem from *Treeds*, 'Tap Flöd at da Marina', we see the speaker heading to his boat, which is tied up in a modern, all-mod-cons marina. The boat is kitted out with sophisticated electronic navigation equipment and the speaker makes sure to take a mobile phone, just in case. This safe, dry, modern way of going to sea is then contrasted with the rather more hazardous methods used by the speaker's grandfather. Here we see the speaker as a boy helping 'Jeemie and John' drag the boat towards the sea:

> Bulderin owre da cuggly stanes
> an dunderin doon da shingle we guid
> full belt, an me wi me hert i mi mooth,
> an right ida sea, swampin
> mi size two rubber böts,
> an Graanda smilin,
> haadin da stem o'er,
> 'Noo boy, win du in!' (p.23)

The rambunctious, careering rhythms and run-on endings of these lines contrast with the safety-conscious, insipid image in the opening stanza. The poem then concedes, somewhat regretfully, that taking a boat out is 'Less hassle noo' (p.23) but, as the speaker gets out of his berth and, in accordance with an ancient custom, 'turn[s] her / wi da sun' (p.22), we see that the world of his grandfather has not entirely passed into history. Like De Luca, Johnson is always respectful of tradition, of how the past informs the present, and, by learning the lessons of her forebears, and through her advocacy and use of the local language, her work seeks to preserve and keep alive what she sees as vital and true for all Shetlanders.

'Tap Flöd at da Marina', with its maritime setting and knowing glance of an experienced seaman, brings to mind the work of the Unst poet Paul Ritch (b.1967), a prolific writer, working mostly in dialect, who now publishes under the name Paolo Dante Ritch. Ritch's verse often takes for its territory the world of the fisherman, a world he knows intimately, having crewed on fishing boats for many years. In both his debut collection *Mother Wave* (1995) and his next, *Goodnight Gypsy Moon* (2004) Ritch draws heavily on these experiences. Unlike many other Shetland authors, he is not interested in the croft but, with a rollicking energy and rhythm which sometimes brings Bulter to mind, Ritch focuses on Shetlanders' relationship with the ocean. This environment is an almost exclusively male one and his poems often place the speaker alongside an older figure with much greater experience of maritime life. 'Gyaun Aff' shows us the speaker as a boy waiting to be taken fishing:

> fur here he comes noo
> platchin doon da park
> wi a flask o coffee
> an a creeshy bottle of fuel
> siphoned fae da Hillman Imp,
> an ah'm hoppin he'll understand
> at da lifejacket in my haund
> is een o yun things at a midder maks you wear,
> laek short breeks ida simmer,
> an a parka ida winter.
> An if a lifejacket isna sheem enyoch

Paolo Dante Ritch.   *Courtesy of Paolo Dante Ritch*

der's also da bottle o juice,
an da tub o chocolate biscuits an sandwiches,
made by a midder at canna tell da difference
atween a boy goin ta sea
an a bairn gyaun on a picnic.[36]

In the third stanza, the boy who can 'box da compass backwirds, / yitter in Morse laek a wireless / an sweem 500 lengths of the pool' finds himself dealing with a box of rancid bait. Contemplating the 'sluttery soor sly an guttery gub / o muck-rotten piltocks', the boy, despite his theoretical knowledge, quickly learns that:

> da first cruel lesson
> o guid seamanship learned
> is kiltin up da sleeves
> afore gyaun near da stuff.

Knowledge of the sea (and the ability to write about it) is gained on the sea, and cannot be acquired vicariously.

Experience of a seagoing life also turns men into storytellers. In '"While the Whisky Warms"', for example, we see the speaker listen to the tales of an old seadog, as Ritch no doubt did in Baltasound in the 1970s:

> This whisky-filled tumbler reminds me of
> The stories he span and the lies that I loved,
> Stormbound on the isle eating snipe for a week,
> Plucked where they cling to the grass with their beaks,
> A mermaid that throws him her scallop shell comb,
> He shouts on the crew, but the mermaid is gone.[37]

The stories are not true, but they are still captivating. And, despite being made up, the fact that they are told by a man who has sailed the globe gives them a touch of authenticity. Ritch's poems, like the tall tales of the old man, are frequently over-the-top and hyperbolic, but they are also often rooted in things he has seen and done. He is constantly aware of what older generations can pass on, but he is not a nostalgic writer. In a review of *Mother Wave*, Alex Cluness writes:

> Paul Ritch's poetry addresses one of the apparent contradictions of Nineties' Shetland life: trying to retain a cultural 'past' identity while at the same time attempting to embrace a frightening wider world of modernity and progress. Paul Ritch, then, is very much a poet of his time, trapped between the Mackay Brown-like world of our Island forebears and the encroaching twenty-first century.[38]

This need to take into account the lessons of previous generations, but also to produce new and vital work, is perhaps the central dilemma for any contemporary

Shetland author. Despite their thematic and orthographic innovations, De Luca, Jamieson (in his most recent verse), Johnson, and Ritch, all seek to represent the local voice in their writing. In the early twenty-first century, Shetland dialect writing, which this study has seen develop, is a tradition that all local authors find themselves having to address. In Ritch's work, for example, although the world of the fisherman is a relatively unusual concern for a Shetland poet, in his rambunctiousness, we are perhaps reminded of Bulter and, going back further, even of certain passages in Angus' 'Eels'. Johnson's work is engaged with the small, seemingly insignificant, domestic details of the modern world, but, in both her dialect activism and in her central idea of representing local speech in her verse, she is a writer who stands in clear lineage to previous generations. For these authors, the use of the local language defines their work. By drawing their writing towards local speech, they attempt to express something essential about what it means to be a Shetlander. They seek to represent their linguistic community, to give the voice of that community the validity of print. For some contemporary Shetland authors, however, this tradition of Shetland dialect writing is rather more problematic and, in the work which will occupy the rest of this chapter, there is an ambivalence about dialect and about the need of the writer to be at the service of a linguistic community.

The local language, for example, appears relatively seldom in the work of former *New Shetlander* editor, Alex Cluness (b.1969), who has published four short volumes to date – *Shetland and Other Poems* (2002), *Disguise* (2004), *2005* (2005), and *Mend* (2007) – or in the work of his late friend Jim Moncrieff (1947-2010). Moncrieff's writing does include some vernacular poems, but is characterised predominantly by the quiet, unshowy observation of his local environment and, in his two books, *Seasonsong* (1998) and *Beaten Gold* (2008), he generally prefers to write in English. Dialect words, as they do in Hadfield's poems, occasionally flit into his poems, but, unlike Johnson, De Luca or Jamieson, he is not interested in the language as a totem of identity or community. Like Hadfield, he has a keen eye for the natural world, and his poems are populated by animals, flowers and birds. And, like many other Shetland poets, he draws on the glimpses he has had of an older way of life, as we see here in 'Cutting Corn':

> Your hands made the blade sing
> In the morning sun
> Its arced length quivered
> Then danced among the corn.[39]

And, in 'Noost', like James Inskster's Mansie with the *Livliehorn*, he looks at what remains of an old boat:

> Sea-grass and meadow flowers
> Push through the gaps between the nails
> And sea-pinks flourish
> Bedded in the hinny-spot. (p.43)

This image of the rotting boat could be read as a metaphor for a fading culture, but Moncrieff does not seem to me to employ the boat as a symbol. The poem does not lament Shetland's seafaring past but, rather, what Moncrieff does, very simply and precisely, is give the reader a picture of something which can be found all over the isles. We have observed how Hadfield often incorporates everyday things in their work, not as symbols, but as visual, verbal, and auditory phenomena and, although he is much less exuberant than her, Moncrieff treats the world outside his door in a similar way. He is not interested in ideas of identity or of linguistic authenticity but, rather, tries to capture what he sees and hears as clearly, simply, and beautifully, as he can.

Jim Mainland (b.1952), like Moncrieff, also seems to be unsure about some of the linguistic ideas that have been prominent in Shetland writing, and of cultural norms in Shetland more generally. He writes of himself as a young man in the 1970s:

> When I left school I definitely wanted to escape. I was starting to get interested in music, in literature, in the avant garde, if you like. And I felt it was very difficult growing up in Shetland to get access to that. You really had to work hard, you had to listen to the right sort of radio programmes, look for the right sort of magazines. I was ready to get out to the wider world. And things in Shetland really didn't appeal to me at all. Certainly not the older fashioned Shetland, so to speak. It was something that was utterly moribund and laughable at that time. That's what I was ready to do.
>
> Shetland dialect, Shetland music – they weren't important to me. They never surfaced. I wasn't really aware of them at all.[40]

Mainland does not hold up the local language as a marker of identity and, as we see in his short story 'Brave New World', has been openly scornful of what he sees as a conservative ethos that surrounds the use and discussion of Shetland dialect. The story, like Aldous Huxley's novel of the same title, is set in a dystopian future and, in his vision of Shetland, Mainland aims his satire at the language preservers:

> Anyway, before long Shetland ForWirds had become an aggressively promotional pressure group, led with evangelical zeal. Their biggest break had come when they argued, with stupendous success, for World Heritage Status for Shetlandic, as they insisted on calling the dialect. This meant millions of pounds for the council, or Althing, as it was quickly renamed. The only condition was that Shetlandic should retain its linguistic distinctiveness, and be used, in written and spoken form, at all levels of society, and to the exclusion of any other, more recent, linguistic interlopers. In other words, everyone, from cradle to grave, Shetland by birth or not, had to speak Shetlandic at all times and in all places.[41]

Jim Mainland. *Courtesy of Jim Mainland*

The story then goes on to show us a computer called TIRVAL which translates everything, including *Eastenders*, into Shetlandic. At a secret meeting, we see a group of people listen to readings from Shakespeare and Dickens (in the original language), and we hear their surprise when they learn that these authors are not from the isles. The story is very funny and takes the promotion of the local language to an absurd extreme, but it makes the serious point that, for some Shetland writers, the use of that language is not a straightforward issue. Writers such as Jamieson, De Luca and Johnson are enlivened by it but, for Mainland, the local tongue, 'the dialect of the tribe' as Eliot puts it in 'Little Gidding', imposes a limitation, a parochialness, that he is constantly trying to escape.[42]

It is not the language itself that causes these limitations, however, but the uses that language has been put to. In our discussion of Tait's work, we saw a Shetland writer who used the language as a literary resource, and not as something which stands for the traditions and ethos of the community. Tait differs from most Shetland writers because he was self-consciously creating a synthetic literary idiom, rather than trying to approximate the way people sound or trying to represent a Shetland identity. Mainland, as we saw in Chapter Seven, has sympathies with Tait's project and, in his own recent work, we also find a number of translations – from Les Murray, Miroslav Holub, Charles Simic, Marin Sorescu, Zbigniew Herbert, Anna Akhmatova – into the local language.[43] Although his oeuvre is still developing, and although his interest in translating European and international poets is relatively new, are we perhaps seeing a Shetland poet beginning to work some of the ground cleared by Billy Tait?

It would be quite wrong, however, to give the impression that dialect writing is a major part of Mainland's work. In his collection *A Package of Measures* (2002) and in his frequent contributions to the *New Shetlander*, we see a writer who engages with poetry and culture that have nothing to do with Shetland, and who refuses to bow to any limitations which may be imposed by place, tradition or language. We also see, in poems such as 'Concerning Members of Parliament and Their Expenses', and 'My Travails in Ye Bigge Society' a writer who is unafraid to voice his anger about what he dislikes in contemporary Britain.[44] In 'Prestidigitator', for example, this anger is worked into an ingenious metaphor which sees the conjuring of an illusionist made to stand for the salacious, celebrity-obsessed, soundbite culture served up daily by the media:

> Watch this, watch my hands, look in my eyes:
> this is viral, this is fiending, this is Celebrity Smash Your Face In,
> I'm spooling tissue from an ear, I'm sawing her in half, no, really,
> I'm vanishing your dosh, I'm giving it makeover, giving it bonus,
> palming it, see, nothing in the box, check out
> your divorce hell text tease sex tape, whoops,
> gimme a tenner gimme your valuables this is a hammer this is an
>   explosive
> see the cleverdazzle off the microgleam, moat me that you peasant!
> over here, here, oy you, break-up Britain, toff off! watch this instead,
> it's my way, it's bodies out of the hat, watch out, that's had your legs off,
> this is brainsmear this is scorcher this is dying doing the job you loved
>   this is
> pure dead victim.[45]

The poem is fiercely angry and alert to the ills of the country and, in his verse generally, Mainland displays a political engagement which is unusual for a Shetland writer. Lollie Graham, the most political poet of his generation, would have relished Mainland's castigation of Cameron's Britain.

But, unlike Graham, the traditions, culture, and language of his native isles do not define Mainland's work. In his recent experiments with translation, however, we see him use the local language more than he has ever done before. It remains to be seen if he will become as significant a poet and translator as Tait. But, like Tait, his intelligence, inventiveness and originality set him apart from many of his peers and, in what may be a burgeoning engagement with the local tongue, we see a poet who is concerned not with preserving a language, but with putting that language to new uses and making it sing in new ways.

Conclusion

It is not easy to assess the work of writers who are still very much active. Any judgements we make are provisional. The ground is not quite stable. In previous chapters (with the exception of Stella Sutherland and George P.S. Peterson), we have been dealing with bodies of work that are complete but, here, we have been looking at writers who are still developing. Jamieson, for example, has, in his poetry, become closer to an older generation in what he is trying to achieve. Hadfield continues to live and work in Shetland, but we will have to wait until she writes another book to see how her engagement with her adopted home will evolve. And, in Mainland's work, which I think represents the most explicit contemporary rejection of the ideas of the *New Shetlander* writers, we are perhaps seeing a poet who will produce a wide-ranging, internationally inclined contribution to local writing. Nobody knows how the literature will develop and, because we are dealing with writers who are in the middle of their careers, it is easy to assume that Shetland's literature is in a period of transition. Despite this caveat, however, I think that the ideas which have been prevalent in local writing – language as a crucial component of identity, the croft as an imaginative, symbolic and actual space, the reverence for tradition in contrast to modernity – are ideas that some contemporary writers are beginning to question. For writers who have come to live in Shetland as adults, these questions are of little concern. They did not read the *New Shetlander* as they were growing up and, whatever their formative literary influences were, those influences are not from Shetland. Some of the local writers in this chapter, however, especially De Luca, Jamieson, Johnson and Ritch, clearly draw on the work of their predecessors and, especially in the case of De Luca and Jamieson, are actively trying to extend both the thematic and technical precepts, and the readership, of writing that has Shetland at its core. But, in the work of other writers, we see a refusal to write in ways that are recognisably part of that tradition.

The *New Shetlander*, however, whose contributors have done so much to shape and define local writing, continues to be Shetland's most important literary platform and, as it moves through its sixth decade, readers will have to wait and see what directions the literature will move in next. We are still waiting for a Shetland writer with the status of a George Mackay Brown or a Sorley MacLean but, with Hadfield winning a major poetry prize, with Jamieson and De Luca building reputations and records of publication outside the isles, with the publication of Kevin MacNeil's anthology *These Islands, We Sing* (2011), and with Shetland-related material appearing in journals such as *Archipelago* and *PN Review*, there are perhaps signs that writing from the isles is becoming more widely known.[46] If a Shetland writer does emerge who has the potential to command an international readership, the *New Shetlander*, as it has done for hundreds of other islanders, will be a key publication in their development. This book has tried to give a picture of Shetland's literature during the last two centuries, and readers of the *New Shetlander* are better placed than anybody to follow the trajectories Shetland's literature will take in the forthcoming decades.

Notes

1. Christine De Luca, interview with Mark Ryan Smith, 23 June 2011.
2. Christine De Luca, *Voes and Sounds: Poems in English and Shetland Dialect* (Lerwick: Shetland Library, 1994), p.21.
3. Christine De Luca, *North End of Eden: Poems in English and Shetlandic* (Edinburgh: Luath Press, 2010), p.13.
4. The Shore Poets are an informal group which provides opportunities for lesser-known poets to read their work alongside experienced writers. See <[http://www.marcabru.pwp.blueyonder.co.uk/> [Accessed 4 April 2012].
5. Christine De Luca, 'Language and My Poetry', in *Northern Lights. Northern Words. Selected Papers from the FRLSU Conference, Kirkwall 2009*, ed. by Robert Millar (Aberdeen: Forum for Research on the Languages of Scotland and Ireland, 2010 <http://www.abdn.ac.uk/pfrlsu/uploads/files/De%20Luca,%20Language%20 and%20my%20poetry.pdf> [Accessed 15 March 2012].
6. Christine De Luca, *Plain Song: Poems in English and Shetland Dialect* (Lerwick: Shetland Library, 2002), p.25.
7. Jim Mainland, Review of *Plain Song*, by Christine De Luca, *New Shetlander*, 221 (Hairst 2002), p.67.
8. Christine De Luca, *Wast wi da Valkyries: Poems in English and Shetland Dialect* (Lerwick: Shetland Library, 1997), p.34.
9. De Luca, 'My Poetry', in *Northern Lights*, ed. by Millar, p.110.
10. Christine De Luca, *And Then Forever* (Lerwick: Shetland Times, 2011), p.254.
11. Jen Hadfield, Review of *North End of Eden*, by Christine De Luca, *Shetland Times*, 5 November 2010, p.19.
12. Jamieson's first contribution to the *New Shetlander* was the story 'Fire Down Below' in no.127 (Voar 1979), and his first poem came in the next issue.
13. Robert Alan Jamieson, *Shoormal: A Sequence of Movements* (Edinburgh: Polygon, 1986), p.23.
14. Robert Alan Jamieson, '"Da Saekrit Paetbank": meditaesjins apo a Sjetlin poyit's responsibielitie t'dir middir tung', in *Dialect 04: Two Day Conference and Public Debate on the Development of the Shetland Dialect* (Lerwick: Shetland Arts Trust, 2004), pp.56-62 (p.58).
15. Jamieson, 'Saekrit', p.58.
16. The sea has become an increasingly prominent theme for Jamieson. See, for example, his sequence of ballads 'The Cutting Down of Cutty Sark', *Poetry Scotland* 52 (undated), pp.1-16.
17. Jamieson, 'Saekrit', p.60.

18. Jamieson, 'Saekrit', p.56.
19. Jamieson explains his phonetic spelling system in the endnotes to a privately published version of the 'Saekrit Paetbank' conference paper. See SA, SA4/2453.
20. Robert Alan Jamieson, *Nort Atlantik Drift*: (Edinburgh: Luath Press, 2007), p.16.
21. Robert Alan Jamieson, *Thin Wealth: A Novel from an Oil Decade* (Edinburgh: Polygon, 1986), p.70.
22. Like the rest of Scotland, thousands of people emigrated from Shetland in the nineteenth and twentieth centuries.
23. These place-names, like other names in the novel, are slightly altered versions of actual places in the isles. Norbie, for example, is taken from Norby, a part of Jamieson's native community of Sandness.
24. Robert Alan Jamieson, *Da Happie Laand* (Edinburgh: Luath Press, 2010), p.364.
25. Robert Alan Jamieson, *A Day at the Office* (Edinburgh: Polygon, 1991).
26. For a discussion of typographical experimentation by modern Scotish writers see Chapter Four, 'The Typographic Muse', in Cairns Craig, *The Modern Scottish Novel: Narrative and the National Imagination* (Edinburgh: Edinburgh University Press, 1999).
27. Rodge Glass, Entry for *A Day at the Office*, by Robert Alan Jamieson, in *The 100 Best Scottish Books of All Time*, ed. Willy Maley (Edinburgh: The List, 2005), pp.17-18.
28. Sheenagh Pugh, *The Movement of Bodies* (Bridgend: Seren, 2005), p.27.
29. Jen Hadfield, *Almanacs* (Tarset: Bloodaxe Books, 2005), p.34.
30. Jen Hadfield, *Nigh-No-Place* (Tarset: Bloodaxe Books, 2008) p.39.
31. The Shetland landscape is sometimes utilised in a similar reflective way in the work of the Indian-born, Manchester-raised poet Raman Mundair. Mundair came to Shetland in 2003, as writer in residence for the publically funded arts agency Shetland Arts Trust, as Hadfield was to do a year later. See Mundair's volume *A Choreographer's Cartography* (2007) for her Shetland-inspired work.
32. For a description of Shetland ForWirds' work see <http://www.shetlanddialect.org.uk/about-us> [Accessed 5 April 2012].
33. Johnson's plays are unpublished but I thank her for providing me with her typescripts.
34. Johnson and I discussed this influence via email on 14 September 2011.
35. Laureen Johnson, *Treeds: Poems in Shetland Dialect* (Stromness: Hansel Cooperative Press, 2007), p.3. SIBC stands for Shetland Islands Broadcasting Company, a local radio station.
36. *New Shetlander*, 246 (Yule 2008), 7.
37. *New Shetlander*, 180 (Summer 1992), 10.
38. Alex Cluness, Review of *Mother Wave*, by Paul Ritch, *New Shetlander*, 191 (Voar 1995), 39.
39. Jim Moncrieff, *Seasonsong* (Lerwick: Shetland Library, 1998), p.28.
40. Jim Mainland in *Black Gold Tide: 25 Years of Oil in Shetland*, ed. by Tom Morton (Lerwick: Shetland Times, 2004), p.57-58.
41. *New Shetlander*, 240 (Simmer 2007), 18-19.
42. T.S. Eliot, *The Complete Poems and Plays* (London: Faber and Faber, 2004), p.194.
43. See *New Shetlander*, 243 (Voar 2008), 9, and 245 (Hairst 2008), 15.
44. *New Shetlander*, 248 (Simmer 2009), 3, and 255 (Voar 2011), 6.

45. *New Shetlander*, 253 (Hairst 2010), 14.
46. See, for example, contributions by Tim Dee and Michael Longley in *Archipelago* 3 (2009), and my own and Malachy Tallack's pieces in *PN Review* 186 (March-April 2009), 193 (May-June 2010), and 195 (September-October 2010).

CONCLUSION

In the preceding eight chapters, we have moved from a small group of obscure local writers, through two significant periods of literary flourishing, to a discussion of Shetland's current literary scene. Haldane Burgess and Billy Tait have emerged as the two most innovative native writers, and we have discussed the ways in which dozens of authors have chosen to write about their island environment. The writers in Chapter One, Chalmers especially, approach the islands predominantly in terms of its unusual, and, in their eyes, unpoetic landscape but, from the 1870s onwards, rural life and the speech of working people, have been writers' most common concerns. For the two most famous non-native authors, the terms of engagement are different, with Scott and MacDiarmid mediating their view of the islands through different literary sources – Scandinavian literature and Doughty – to produce their own creative visions of Shetland.

What all these writers have in common, however, as this book has explored, is an engagement with a particular place. And, in engaging with this place, for the bulk of the writers we have covered, it is the local language which has provided the primary term of address. This use of Shetland dialect, as we have seen, makes Shetland's literature a regionally distinctive body of work, but we have also discussed how the centrality of the language for local writers is not always unambiguously positive. Some writers have built large bodies of work through their exploration of the tongue but, especially in recent years, other writers have begun to question the vernacular tradition they have been born into. Even so, this study has shown that the use of Shetland dialect is one of the salient aspects of the archipelago's literary tradition. This observation is one that would generally be seen as unproblematic by local critics. Lollie Graham, for example, quoting from Ernest Marwick's introduction to Vagaland's *Collected Poems*, writes:

> 'To make the living speech of their islands the vehicle of serious literature, and to create among their own folk a lively and sympathetic appreciation of its quality, has been the two-fold task of Shetland's poets and writers of prose.' [1]

Dialect may be central but, in suggesting that the use of the language is the defining characteristic of Shetland's literature, critics and anthologists have tended to exclude some writers. Any attempt at an encompassing definition has to leave something out, and this study has constantly striven to be inclusive. The view of Shetland's literature presented in collections like *Nordern Lichts* and *A Shetland Anthology* places the local language at the centre. For Lollie Graham and many others, the Shetland dialect is the most important component in local writing, but this idea has meant that writers such as Chalmers, Saxby, and MacDiarmid have not been seen as part of an island canon. This book presents a more catholic overview of Shetland's literature than has been attempted before. Shetland's literature, like any literature, is a multiplicity of voices and, in this work, I have tried to respect the right of every speaker to be heard, whether they are a dialect poet, a middle-class Lerwick woman writing in English, a famous Scottish poet attempting a world-encompassing language, or a contemporary Shetland writer who feels uncomfortable with their vernacular heritage. The Shetland dialect may be fundamental to many local writers, but focussing too closely on it stops us from telling the whole story.

After trying to tell the whole story, however, what are we left with? This book has clearly laid out the narrative of Shetland's literature – its periods of flux, growth, and slump – but what kind of literature has emerged? Is Shetland's literature a literature of place? Is it a rural literature? A literature without an ancient basis? A literature of community? Or, is it a literature which, more than anything, affirms the value of the local tongue?

All of these things are true, but I do not want to conclude by summing things up with a label. I am reluctant to do so, because literature resists closure. All writers are different. Every voice has its peculiarities and, in this book, while retaining a view of relevant social and literary contexts, I have tried to give a sense of each writer's individuality. To pithily sum up this large body of heterogeneous material with a tag or definition would be to countermand my own critical principle. Although I have been careful to take account of the network of evaluation that exists around Shetland's literature – the various anthologies which have appeared, the opinions of critics in the *New Shetlander*, for example – my readings, like those of any reader, are subjective and partisan. We cannot stand outside the poems and stories we read. They involve us. As Michael Schmidt puts it:

> Good readers, great readers – some of whom are writers – take intense pleasure from engaging with a poem, not as a resource for their own purpose but as a source of primary experience. Poems – if they're worth anything at all – are primary experiences. They make things happen, they adjust the ear, the tongue, the heart.[2]

This study shows how Shetland's writers have developed their literary tradition, and how their body of work intersects with wider literary currents and trends, but I have also tried to approach the poems and stories as 'primary experiences'. In a work such as this it is necessary to engage with an expansive corpus of criticism and scholarship, but the individual response to poems and stories also has an important role to play. Errors of judgement have no doubt been made, and another reader surveying the same material may have chosen to emphasise the work of different authors, but *The Literature of Shetland* is an attempt to break new ground. Not everybody will agree with me on the literary merits of Margaret Chalmers, James Inkster or Robert Alan Jamieson but, in telling the story of Shetland's literature, I have tried to open the territory for other people to think about the material in their own way. In the introduction to this book I advocated the study of so-called regional writing and, even if subsequent readers and critics disagree with my interpretations and evaluations, the existence of this work gives those readers and critics the opportunity to debate, discuss, and enjoy (or not) the work Shetland's writers have done.

In drawing attention to Shetland's literature, this book opens an area that has been neglected by mainstream literary scholarship. As we have seen, critics within Shetland, especially since the appearance of the *New Shetlander*, have been writing about the material we have covered for a number of years, but *The Literature of Shetland* redraws Scotland's literary borders. The material we have worked through is diverse, ranging from Chalmers' early verse, to Burgess' intellectualisation of the Shetland dialect, to Peterson's sombre work, to Billy Tait's atypical vernacular poems, and we have seen how the narrative these writers are part of intersects with wider literary movements and seams of influence. Tait was a friend and contemporary of many well-known Scottish poets in the second half of the twentieth century and, throughout this work, we have seen how literary developments in Shetland have had much in common with those further south.

The first significant period of flourishing in Shetland's literature, for example, which we covered in Chapters Two, Three and Four, can be seen as part of the upsurge of regional and vernacular writing that was happening across the country. As a great deal of this work was published in the popular press, building a comprehensive picture of the regional diversity of Scotland's literature at this time is challenging but, by showing how Shetlanders from the 1870s onwards were producing work that drew on their distinctive culture and language, this book helps us understand more fully that diffuse corpus of poems and stories. Similarly, in Chapters Six and Seven, we discussed how Shetland's literature was influenced by the wider cultural movement of the Scottish Renaissance. We commented how the *New Shetlander* emerged as part of a culture of little Scottish magazines and how, in encouraging local writers to explore their local environments, the journal provided the impetus for a resurgence, and in the case of Tait especially, a redefinition of Shetland's literature. As we observed at the end of Chapter Seven, the Scottish Renaissance had a peculiarly rural, regional geography, and by exploring the work of the *New Shetlander* writers, we add another set of co-ordinates to that cultural map.

Studying the poems and stories which emerged in Shetland in these periods broadens our understanding of well-known trends in Scottish literary scholarship and, taken as a whole, this volume makes our picture of Scotland's literature more pluralistic, varied, and, to use MacDiarmid's word, 'multiform'.[3] At the beginning of this book I suggested that the study of local literatures was a way to enrich our knowledge and enjoyment of literature. *The Literature of Shetland* is a demonstration of that principle. This book does not disrupt any existing picture of Scotland's literature but, in engaging critically with a large collection of material that finds inspiration in the country's northernmost archipelago, we perhaps find that those pictures have been embellished with an additional Shetlandic hue.

Notes

1. Laurence L. Graham, Introduction, in *A Shetland Anthology: Poetry from the Earliest Times to the Present Day*, ed. by Laurence L. Graham and John J. Graham, eds. (Lerwick: Shetland Publishing Company, 1998), pp.xv-xxiii (p.xv).
2. Michael Schmidt, *Lives of the Poets* (London: Weidenfeld & Nicolson, 1998), back cover.
3. Hugh MacDiarmid, *Complete Poems*, vol.2, ed. by Michael Grieve and W.R. Aitken (Harmondsworth: Penguin, 1985), p.1170.

BIBLIOGRAPHY

Archival sources

Shetland Archives
SA1, Microfilms.
SA2, Photocopies and transcripts.
SA4, Published material.
D1, Small gifts and deposits.
D2, Papers of J.J. Haldane Burgess.
D6, Papers of E.S. Reid Tait.
D9, Papers of Peter Jamieson.
D15, Papers of T. & J. Manson.
D16, Papers of Thomas Irvine.
D22, Papers of T.A. Robertson (Vagaland).
D24, Nicolson estate papers.
D30, Papers of William J. Tait.

John Rylands University Library
CPA, Papers of Carcanet Press.

Primary printed sources

Anderson, Basil Ramsay, *Broken Lights: Poems and Reminiscences of the Late Basil Ramsay Anderson*, ed. by Jessie M.E. Saxby (Edinburgh / Lerwick: R. & R. Clark / C. & A. Sandison, 1888).
Angus, James Stout, 'Eels', *Shetland Times*, 22 December 1877, p.3.
Angus, James Stout, *Echoes from Klingrahool: Poems: Mostly in the Shetland Dialect*, 3rd edn (Lerwick: T. & J. Manson, 1926).
Ashbery, John, 'Soonest Mended' in *The New York Poets: An Anthology*, ed. by Mark Ford (Manchester: Carcanet, 2004), p.73.
Beckett, Samuel, *Trilogy: Molly, Malone Dies, The Unnamable* (London: Calder Publications, 1994).
Bold, Alan, ed., The *Letters of Hugh MacDiarmid* (London: Hamish Hamilton, 1984).
Bulter, Rhoda, *Doobled-Up: All the Shetland Poems from Shaela and A Nev Foo A Coarn* (Sandwick: Thuleprint, 1978).
Bulter, Rhoda, *Link-Stanes: Shetland Poems* (Lerwick: Shetland Times, 1980).
Bulter, Rhoda, 'Letter to the Editor', *Shetland Life*, 70 (August 1986), 21.
Bulter, Rhoda, *Snyivveries: Shetland Poems* (Lerwick: Shetland Times, 1986).

Burgess, J.J. Haldane, *The White Christ: A Story of the Vikings* (London: Horace Marshall & Son, undated).
Burgess, J.J. Haldane, *Rasmie's Büddie: Poems in the Shetlandic* (Lerwick: T. & J. Manson, 1891).
Burgess, J.J. Haldane, *The Viking Path: A Tale of the White Christ* (Edinburgh / London: William Blackwood and Sons, 1894).
Burgess, J.J. Haldane, *Tang: A Shetland Story* (Lerwick / London: Johnson & Greig / Simpkin, Marshall, Hamilton, Kent & Co., 1898).
Burgess, J.J. Haldane, *The Treasure of Don Andres: A Shetland Romance of the Spanish Armada* (Lerwick / Edinburgh: Thomas Manson / Oliver and Boyd, 1903).
Burgess, J.J. Haldane, *Der Vikinger Pfad* (Dresden: E. Pierson's Derlang, 1906).
Burgess, J.J. Haldane, *Rasmie's Büddie: Poems in the Shetlandic*, 3rd edn (Lerwick: T. & J. Manson, 1913).
Campbell, D.P., *Poems* (Inverness: J. Young, 1811).
Campbell, D.P., *Harley Radington: A Tale in Two Volumes* (London: A.K. Newman and Co., 1821).
Chalmers, Margaret, *Poems* (Newcastle: S. Hodgson, 1813).
Dale, Peter, ed., *François Villon: Selected Poems* (Harmondsworth: Penguin, 1978).
Dante, Paolo [Paul Ritch], 'Gyaun Aff', *New Shetlander*, 246 (Yule 2008), 7.
De Luca, Christine, *Voes and Sounds: Poems in English and Shetland Dialect* (Lerwick: Shetland Library, 1994).
De Luca, Christine, *Wast wi da Valkyries: Poems in English and Shetland Dialect* (Lerwick: Shetland Library, 1997).
De Luca, Christine, *Plain Song: Poems in English and Shetland Dialect* (Lerwick: Shetland Library, 2002).
De Luca, Christine, *North End of Eden: Poems in English and Shetlandic* (Edinburgh: Luath Press, 2010).
De Luca, Christine, 'Language and My Poetry', in *Northern Lights. Northern Words. Selected Papers from the FRLSU Conference, Kirkwall 2009*, ed. by Robert Millar (Aberdeen: Forum for Research on the Languages of Scotland and Ireland, 2010) <http://www.abdn.ac.uk/pfrlsu/uploads/files/De%20Luca,%20Language%20and%20my%20poetry.pdf> [Accessed 15 March 2012].
De Luca, Christine, *And Then Forever* (Lerwick: Shetland Times, 2011).
Donne, John, *The Complete English Poems*, ed. by A.J. Smith (Harmondsworth: Penguin, 1973).
Doughty, Charles M., *Travels in Arabia Deserta*, 2 vols. (Cambridge: Cambridge University Press, 1888).
Doughty, Charles M., *The Dawn in Britain*, 6 vols. (London: Duckworth & Co., 1906).
Doughty, Charles M., *Adam Cast Forth* (London: Duckworth & Co., 1908).
Edmondston, Arthur, *A View of the Ancient and Present State of the Zetland Islands*, 2 vols. (Edinburgh: James Ballantyne and Co., 1809).
Edmondston, Biot, and Jessie M.E. Saxby, *The Home of a Naturalist* (London: James Nisbet & Co., 1888).
Eliot, T.S., *The Complete Poems and Plays* (London: Faber and Faber, 2004).
Graham, John J., and T.A. Robertson, eds. *Nordern Lichts: An Anthology of Shetland Verse and Prose* (Lerwick: Shetland Islands Council Education Committee, 1964).

Graham, John J., *Shadowed Valley: A Novel Based on the Weisdale Evictions* (Lerwick: Shetland Publishing Company, 1987).
Graham, John J., *Strife in the Valley: A Novel Set in 18th Century Shetland* (Shetland Publishing Company, 1992).
Graham, Laurence L., and John J. Graham, eds., *A Shetland Anthology: Poetry from the Earliest Times to the Present Day* (Lerwick: Shetland Publishing Company, 1998).
Graham, Lollie, *Love's Laebrak Sang* (Lerwick: Shetland Library, 2000).
Grieve, Dorian, Owen Dudley Edwards and Alan Riach, eds., *Hugh MacDiarmid: New Selected Letters* (Manchester: Carcanet, 2001).
Gunn, Neil M., *The Silver Darlings* (London: Faber and Faber, 1969).
Hadfield, Jen, *Almanacs* (Tarset: Bloodaxe Books, 2005).
Hadfield, Jen, *Nigh-No-Place* (Tarset: Bloodaxe Books, 2008).
Heaney, Seamus, 'An Invocation', *London Review of Books*, vol.14, no.15 (6 August 1992), 16.
Hibbert, Samuel, *A Description of the Shetland Islands* (Edinburgh: Archibald Constable and Co., 1822).
Inkster, James, *Mansie's Rüd*, *Shetland News* (1897-1916).
Inkster, James, *Mansie's Röd: Sketches in the Shetlandic* (Lerwick: T. & J. Manson, 1922).
Jamieson, Robert Alan, 'The Cutting Down of Cutty Sark', *Poetry Scotland* 52 (undated), 1-16.
Jamieson, Robert Alan, *Shoormal: A Sequence of Movements* (Edinburgh: Polygon, 1986).
Jamieson, Robert Alan, *Thin Wealth: A Novel from an Oil Decade* (Edinburgh: Polygon, 1986).
Jamieson, Robert Alan, *A Day at the Office* (Edinburgh: Polygon, 1991).
Jamieson, Robert Alan, '"Da Saekrit Paetbank": meditaesjins apo a Sjetlin poyit's responsibielitie t'dir middir tung' in *Dialect 04: Two Day Conference and Public Debate on the Development of the Shetland Dialect* (Lerwick: Shetland Arts Trust, 2004), pp.56-62.
Jamieson, Robert Alan, *Nort Atlantik Drift*: (Edinburgh: Luath Press, 2007).
Jamieson, Robert Alan, *Da Happie Laand* (Edinburgh: Luath Press, 2010).
Johnson, Laureen, *Treeds: Poems in Shetland Dialect* (Stromness: Hansel Cooperative Press, 2007).
Leonard, Tom, *Intimate Voices: Selected Work 1965-1983* (Buckfastleigh: Etruscan Books, 2003).
Low, George, *A Tour Through the Islands of Orkney and Schetland* (Kirkwall: William Peace & Son, 1879).
MacDiarmid, Hugh, 'Færöerne', *Scottish Educational Journal* (12 January 1934), 54-55.
MacDiarmid, Hugh, *The Islands of Scotland: Hebrides, Orkneys, and Shetlands* (London: B.T. Batsford, 1939).
MacDiarmid, Hugh, *The Uncanny Scot: A Selection of Prose*, ed. by Kenneth Buthlay (London: MacGibbon & Kee, 1968).
MacDiarmid, Hugh, *Selected Essays of Hugh MacDiarmid*, edited by Duncan Glen (London: Jonathan Cape, 1969).

MacDiarmid, Hugh, 'MacDiarmid at Eighty-Five', interview with George Bruce, 11 August 1977, in *The Thistle Rises: An Anthology of Poetry and Prose by Hugh MacDiarmid*, ed. by Alan Bold (London: Hamish Hamilton, 1984), pp.274-285.
MacDiarmid, Hugh, *Complete Poems*, vol.1, ed. by Michael Grieve and W.R. Aitken (Manchester: Carcanet, 1993).
MacDiarmid, Hugh, *Complete Poems*, vol.2, ed. by Michael Grieve and W.R. Aitken (Harmondsworth: Penguin, 1985).
MacDiarmid, Hugh, *Lucky Poet: A Self-Study in Literature and Political Ideas* (Manchester: Carcanet, 1994).
MacDiarmid, Hugh, *The Raucle Tongue: Hitherto Uncollected Prose*, vol.2, ed. by Angus Calder, Glen Murray and Alan Riach (Manchester: Carcanet, 1997).
MacNeil, Kevin, ed., *These Islands, We Sing: An Anthology of Scottish Islands Poetry* (Edinburgh: Polygon, 2011).
Mainland, Jim, in *Black Gold Tide: 25 Years of Oil in Shetland*, ed. by Tom Morton (Lerwick: Shetland Times, 2004), pp.57-58.
Mainland, Jim, 'Brave New World', *New Shetlander*, 240 (Simmer 2007), 18-19.
Mainland, Jim, 'Concerning Members of Parliament and Their Expenses', *New Shetlander*, 248 (Simmer 2009), 3.
Mainland, Jim, Interview with Sheenagh Pugh, *New Shetlander*, 253 (Hairst 2010), 14-17.
Mainland, Jim, 'Prestidigitator', *New Shetlander*, 253 (Hairst 2010), 14.
Mainland, Jim, 'My Travails in Ye Bigge Society', *New Shetlander*, 255 (Voar 2011), 6.
Manson, John, ed., *Dear Grieve: Letters to Hugh MacDiarmid (C.M. Grieve)* (Glasgow: Kennedy & Boyd, 2011).
Moncrieff, Jim, *Seasonsong* (Lerwick: Shetland Library, 1998).
Morgan, Edwin, *Collected Poems* (Manchester: Carcanet, 1990).
Nabokov, Vladimir, *Pale Fire* (London: Penguin, 2000).
Nicolson, L.J., and Thomas Manson, *Da Last Noost: A Shetland Folk Song* (Lerwick: T. & J. Manson, 1891).
Nicolson, Laurence James, *Songs of Thule* (Paisley / London: Alexander Gardner, 1894).
Nicolson, L.J., and William Yorston, *A Shetland Lullaby* (Lerwick: T. & J. Manson, 1896).
Peterson, George P.S., *Aald Papa, I'm Dine!: A Collection of Stories, Tunes, Poetry and Paintings* (Lerwick: Shetland Times, 2009).
Peterson, John, *Roads and Ditches* (Lerwick: T. & J. Manson, 1920).
Peterson, John, *Streets and Starlight* (London: Erskine MacDonald, 1923).
Peterson, John, 'Elegy in a Country Churchyard', *New Shetlander*, 46 (March 1958), 14.
[Peterson, John], 'Great Wars', *New Shetlander*, 73 (Summer 1965), 16.
[Peterson, John], 'Seine-Netters', *New Shetlander*, 79 (Yule 1966), 6.
Pope, Alexander, *The Poems of Alexander Pope*, ed. by John Butt (London: Methuen, 1968).
Pound, Ezra, *Selected Poems, 1908-1969* (London: Faber and Faber, 1975).
Pound, Ezra, *The Cantos of Ezra Pound* (New York: New Directions, 1996).
Pugh, Sheenagh, *The Movement of Bodies* (Bridgend: Seren, 2005).
Renwick, Jack, *Rainbow Bridge: A Collection of Poems in English and Shetlandic* (Lerwick: Shetland Times, 1963).

Renwick, Jack, *The Harp of Twilight: An Anthology of Poems in English and Shetlandic* (Baltasound: Unst Writers Group, 2007).
Ritch, Paul, '"While the Whisky Warms"', *New Shetlander*, 180 (Summer 1992), 10.
Robertson, T.A., and Martha Robertson, eds., *Da Sangs at A'll Sing Ta Dee: A Book of Shetland Songs* (Lerwick: Shetland Folk Society, 1973).
Robertson, T.A., *The Collected Poems of Vagaland*, ed. by Martha Robertson (Lerwick: Shetland Times, 1975).
Sandison, William, *Shetland Verse: Remnants of the Norn* (Privately published, 1953).
Saxby, Jessie M.E., *Daala-Mist; or, Stories of Shetland* (Edinburgh: Andrew Eliot, 1876).
Saxby, Jessie M.E., *Rock-Bound: A Story of the Shetland Isles* (Edinburgh: Thomas Gray and Company, 1877).
Saxby, Jessie M.E., *Viking Boys* (London: James Nesbit & Co., 1892).
Saxby, Jessie M.E., *Heim-Laund and Heim-Folk* (Edinburgh: R. & R. Clark, 1892).
Saxby, Jessie M.E., 'Notes on the Shetland Dialect', *Saga-Book of the Viking Club*, vol.4, pt.2 (1906-1910), 65.
[Saxby, Jessie M.E.], *Joseph Bell: An Appreciation by an Old Friend* (Edinburgh / London: Oliphant, Anderson & Farrier, 1913).
Schuyler, James, 'Wystan Auden', in *The New York Poets*, ed. by Mark Ford (Manchester: Carcanet, 2004), p.190.
Scott, Walter, *Northern Lights: or, A Voyage in the Lighthouse Yacht to Nova Zembla and the Lord Knows Where* (Hawick: Byway Books, 1982).
Scott, Walter, *The Pirate*, ed. by Mark Weinstein and Alison Lumsden (Edinburgh: Edinburgh University Press, 2001).
Stevens, Wallace, 'Anecdote of the Jar', in *The Norton Anthology of American Literature*, vol. D, 6th edn, ed. by Nina Baym and others (New York / London: W.W. Norton & Company, 2003), p.1241.
Stewart, George, *Shetland Fireside Tales; or, The Hermit of Trosswickness* (Edinburgh / London: Edinburgh Publishing Company / Simpkin, Marshall & Co., 1877).
Sutherland, Stella, *Aa My Selves: Poems 1940-1980* (Lerwick: Shetland Times, 1980).
Sutherland, Stella, *A Celebration and Other Poems* (Bressay: Stella Sutherland, 1991).
Sutherland, Stella, *Joy o Creation: Favourite Poems Old and New in Shetland Dialect and English* (Stromness: Hansel Cooperative Press, 2008).
Tait, William J., *A Day Between Weathers: Collected Poems* (Edinburgh: Paul Harris Publishing, 1980).
Tait, W.J., *Villon: Le Testament and Other Translations*, ed. by John Cumming and Mark Ryan Smith (Stromness: Hansel Cooperative Press, 2011).
Whitman, Walt, 'Song of Myself (1881)', in *The Norton Anthology of American Literature*, vol. C, 6th edn, ed. by Nina Baym and others (New York / London: W.W. Norton & Company, 2003), pp.122-166.

Secondary sources

Amis, Martin, *The War Against Cliché: Essays and Reviews 1971-2000* (London: Vintage, 2002).
[Anon.], 'Minor Scottish Poets – Laurence J. Nicolson', *Glasgow Weekly Mail*, undated.
[Anon.], Review of *Broken Lights*, by Basil Ramsay Anderson, *Shetland Times*, 14 July 1888, p.3.

[Anon.], Obituary of L.J. Nicolson, *Shetland News*, 6 July 1901, p.5.
[Anon.], Obituary of James Stout Angus, *Shetland Times*, 29 December 1923, p.4.
[Anon.], Obituary of J.J. Haldane Burgess', *Shetland News*, 20 January 1927, p.5.
[Anon.], Account of James Stout Angus tribute night, *Shetland Times*, 5 April 1957, p.7.
[Anon.], Obituary of John Peterson, *Shetland Times*, 22 September 1972, p.11.
[Anon.], Obituary of William J. Tait, *Shetland Times*, 7 August 1992, p.8.
Ash, Marinell, '"So much that was new to us": Scott and Shetland' in *Essays in Shetland History*, ed. by Barbara E. Crawford (Lerwick: Shetland Times, 1984), pp.193-207.
Banham, Reyner, 'Arabia Revisita', *London Review of Books*, vol.2, no.23 (4 December 1980), 16.
Bard, Glenn, 'Between a Rock and a Hard Place: Science and Art in Hugh MacDiarmid's *Stony Limits and Other Poems*', *New Shetlander*, 254 (Yule 2010), 29-35.
Barnes, Michael P., 'Jakob Jakobsen and the Norn Language of Shetland', in *Shetland's Northern Links: Language and History*, ed. by Doreen J. Waugh (Edinburgh: Scottish Society for Northern Studies, 1996), pp.1-15.
Barnes, Michael P., *The Norn Language of Orkney and Shetland* (Lerwick: Shetland Times, 1998).
Barnes, Michael P., 'The Study of Norn', in *Northern Lights, Northern Words. Selected Papers from the FRLSU Conference, Kirkwall 2009*, ed. Robert Millar (Aberdeen: Forum for Research on the Languages of Scotland and Ireland, 2010) <http://www.abdn.ac.uk/~wag020/uploads/files/Barnes,%20Tue%20Study%20of%20Norn.pdf> [Accessed 17 April 2012].
Benjamin, Walter, *Illuminations* (London: Pimlico, 1999).
Behrendt, Stephen C., *British Women Poets and the Romantic Writing Community* (Baltimore: John Hopkins University Press, 2008).
Blance, Mary E., 'John and Lollie Graham and the *New Shetlander*', *New Shetlander*, 221 (Hairst 2002), 4-7.
Blance, Mary, 'George P.S. Peterson: A Profile', *New Shetlander*, 239 (Voar 2007), 11-13.
Blind, Karl, 'Discovery of Odinic Songs in Shetland', *Nineteenth Century*, vol.5 (June 1879), 1091-1113.
Bold, Alan, *MacDiarmid: Christopher Murray Grieve, A Critical Biography* (London: Paladin, 1990).
Brown, George Mackay, 'A Shetland Poet: A Tribute', *Orcadian*, 29 May 1975, p.4.
Cluness, Alex, Review of *Mother Wave*, by Paul Ritch, *New Shetlander*, 191 (Voar 1995), 39.
Cooke, Peter, *The Fiddle Tradition of the Shetland Isles* (Cambridge: Cambridge University Press, 1986).
Cookson, William, Obituary of Tom Scott, *Independent*, 14 August 1995 <http://www.independent.co.uk/news/obituaries/obituary-tom-scott-1596211.html> [Accessed 27 August 2010].
Cooper, David, '"Da Fiends at Drave Da Tenant Furt": A Study of the Clearances in the Shetland Islands' (unpublished M.A.(Hons) dissertation, University of Glasgow, 2011).

Craig, Cairns, 'Scotland and the Regional Novel', in *The Regional Novel in Britain and Ireland, 1800-1990*, in *The Regional Novel in Britain and Ireland, 1800-1990*, ed. by K.D.M. Snell (Cambridge: Cambridge University Press, 1998), pp.221-256.

Craig, Cairns, *The Modern Scottish Novel: Narrative and the National Imagination* (Edinburgh: Edinburgh University Press, 1999).

Crawford, Robert, ed., 'Hugh MacDiarmid: A Disgrace to the Community', BBC Radio 1992, reprinted in *PN Review 89* (January-February 1993) <http://www.pnreview.co.uk/cgibin/scribe?file=/members/pnr089/articles/089ar02.txt> [Accessed 25 November 2010].

Cribb, T.J., 'The Cheka's Horrors and "On a Raised Beach"', *Studies in Scottish Literature*, vol.xx (1985), 88-100.

D'Arcy, Julian Meldon, *Scottish Skalds and Sagamen: Old Norse Influence on Modern Scottish Literature* (East Linton: Tuckwell Press, 1996).

Daiches, David, *A Critical History of English Literature*, 2 vols. (London: Mandarin, 1994).

Donaldson, William, *Popular Literature in Victorian Scotland: Language, Fiction and the Press* (Aberdeen: Aberdeen University Press, 1986).

Eunson, Karen, 'James Stout Angus – Our First Dialect Poet', *New Shetlander*, 203 (Voar 1998), 21.

Eunson, Karen, 'Stella Sutherland at Eighty', *New Shetlander*, 229 (Hairst 2009), 4-6.

Fairley, Barker, *Charles M. Doughty: A Critical Study* (London: Jonathan Cape, 1927).

Fielding, Penny, *Scotland and the Fictions of Geography: North Britain, 1760-1830* (Cambridge: Cambridge University Press, 2008).

Fielding, Penny, '"A Lady of the Isles": Margaret Chalmers' Letters to Walter Scott and Two New Poems', *Scottish Literary Review*, vol.2, no.2 (Autumn/Winter 2010), 23-44.

Fielding, Penny, 'Genre, Geography and the Question of the National Tale: D.P. Campbell's *Harley Radington*', forthcoming in *European Romantic Review*.

Findlay, William, 'Reclaiming Local Literature: William Thom and Janet Hamilton', in *The History of Scottish Literature*, vol.3, ed. by Douglas Gifford (Aberdeen: Aberdeen University Press, 1989), pp.353-375.

Glass, Rodge, Entry for *A Day at the Office*, by Robert Alan Jamieson, in *The 100 Best Scottish Books of All Time*, ed. by Willy Maley (Edinburgh: The List, 2005), pp.17-18.

Graham, John J., 'Basil Ramsay Anderson', *New Shetlander*, 57 (Summer 1961), 10-12.

Graham, John J., 'T.A. Robertson: An Appreciation', *New Shetlander*, 107 (Voar 1974) 6-7.

Graham, John J., *The Shetland Dictionary* (Stornoway: Thule Press, 1979).

Graham, John J. Graham, 'The Weisdale Evictions', *New Shetlander*, 130 (Yule 1979), 29-31.

Graham, John J., *A Vehement Thirst After Knowledge: Four Centuries of Education in Shetland* (Lerwick: Shetland Times, 1998).

Graham, John J., '"Seine-Netters" by John Peterson: An Appreciation', *New Shetlander*, 212 (Simmer 2000), 7-8.

Graham, Laurence, 'Haldane Burgess', *New Shetlander*, 10 (May-June 1948), 10-12 (p.10).

Graham, Laurence, 'James Stout Angus', *New Shetlander*, 15 (March-April 1949), 24-25.
Graham, Laurence, 'Profiles from the past xv - J.J. Haldane Burgess', *New Shetlander*, 61 (Simmer 1962), 14-16.
Graham, Laurence, preface to *Rasmie's Büddie* by J.J. Haldane Burgess (Lerwick: Shetland Times, 1979), pp.xix-xxii.
Graham, Laurence, 'W.J. Tait, 1919-1982: A Tribute', *New Shetlander*, 181 (Hairst 1992), 14.
Graham, Laurence, and Brian Smith, eds., *MacDiarmid in Shetland* (Lerwick: Shetland Library, 1992).
Graham, Laurence, 'Shetland Literature and the Idea of Community', in *Shetland's Northern Links: Language and History*, ed. by Doreen J. Waugh (Edinburgh: Scottish Society for Northern Studies, 1996), pp.52-65.
Grieve, Michael, 'Hugh MacDiarmid: The Man', in *The Hugh MacDiarmid Anthology: Poems in Scots and English*, ed. by Michael Grieve and Alexander Scott (London: Routledge and Kegan Paul, 1972), pp.xi-xvi.
Grundy, Isobel, 'Chalmers, Margaret (b. 1758)', in *Oxford Dictionary of National Biography* <http://www.oxforddnb.com/view/article/45839> [Accessed 2 November 2011].
Grundy, Isobel, 'Campbell, Dorothea Primrose (1792-1863)', in *Oxford Dictionary of National Biography* <http://oxforddnb.com/view/article/45837> [Accessed 2 November 2011].
Grundy, Isobel, 'Dorothea Primrose Campbell', in *Scottish Women of the Romantic Period* <http://www.alexanderstreet2.com/SWRPLive/bios/S7030-D001.html> [Accessed 20 August 2008].
Grydehøj, Adam, 'The Orpheus of the North', *New Shetlander*, 240 (Simmer 2007), 23-27.
Hadfield, Jen, Review of *North End of Eden*, by Christine De Luca, *Shetland Times*, 5 November 2010, p.19.
Hall, Simon W., *The History of Orkney Literature* (Edinburgh: John Donald, 2010).
Heaney, Seamus, *Preoccupations: Selected Prose 1968-1978* (London: Faber and Faber, 1984).
Hogarth, D.G., *The Life of Charles M. Doughty* (London: Oxford University Press, 1928).
Hubbard, Tom, 'Scott, Thomas McLaughlin (1918–1995)', *Oxford Dictionary of National Biography* <http://www.oxforddnb.com/view/article/57753> [Accessed 27 Aug 2010].
Hynd, Hazel, 'The Authority of Influence: John Davidson and Hugh MacDiarmid', *Scottish Studies Review*, vol.2, no.2 (Autumn 2001), 77-93.
Jamie, Kathleen, presenter, *Norn but not Forgotten: Sounds of Shetland*, broadcast on BBC Radio 4, 29 August 2010.
Jamieson, Robert Alan, 'Rhoda's Voice', *Shetland Life*, 315 (Jan 2007), 32.
Johnston, J. Laughton, *Victorians 60° North: The Story of the Edmondstons and Saxbys of Shetland* (Lerwick: Shetland Times, 2007).
Kaddal, Mohamed A.M., 'Charles Montagu Doughty: His Life and Work' (unpublished doctoral thesis, University of Glasgow, 1962).

Kent, Alan M., *The Literature of Cornwall: Continuity, Identity, Difference* (Bristol: Redcliffe Press, 2000).
Kinghorn, A.M., 'Dunbar and Villon: A Comparison and a Contrast', *Modern Language Review*, vol.62, no.2 (April 1967), 195-208.
L.S., 'Profiles from the past xxiv - Jessie M.E. Saxby', *New Shetlander*, 70 (Hairst 1964), 12-14.
Laing, R.D., *The Divided Self: An Existential Study in Sanity and Madness* (London: Penguin, 1990).
Leonard, Tom, *Outside the Narrative: Poems 1965-2009* (Buckfastleigh: Etruscan Books, 2009).
Leslie, Brydon, *Borgar Jarl: J.J. Haldane Burgess and Up Helly Aa* (Lerwick: Shetland Amenity Trust, 2012).
Lumsden, Alison, '"To Get to Live": Negotiating Regional Identity in the Literature of North-East Scotland', in *The Edinburgh History of Scottish Literature*, vol.3, ed. by Ian Brown (Edinburgh: Edinburgh University Press, 2007), pp.95-105.
Lyall, Scott, '"The Man is a Menace": MacDiarmid and Military Intelligence', *Scottish Studies Review*, vol.8, no.1 (Spring 2007), 37-52.
Lyall, Scott, 'MacDiarmid, Communism, and the Poetry of Commitment', in *The Edinburgh Companion to Hugh MacDiarmid*, ed. by Scott Lyall and Margery Palmer McCulloch (Edinburgh: Edinburgh University Press, 2011), pp.68-81.
Mack, Douglas and Suzanne Gilbert, 'Scottish History in the Waverley Novels', in *Approaches to Teaching Scott's Waverley Novels*, ed. by Evan Gottlieb and Ian Duncan (New York: Modern Language Association of America, 2009), pp.26-37.
Mack, Jane, 'Thomas Irvine of Midbrake', parts 1-3, *Shetland Life*, 91 (May 1988), pp.24-25; 92 (June 1988), pp.37-38; 93 (July 1988), 40-41.
Macleod, Michelle, and Mary Watson, 'In the Shadow of the Bard: The Gaelic Short Story, Novel and Drama Since the Early Twentieth Century', in *The Edinburgh History of Scottish Literature*, vol.3, ed. by Ian Brown (Edinburgh: Edinburgh University Press, 2007), pp.273-282.
Mainland, Jim, Review of *Plain Song*, by Christine De Luca, *New Shetlander*, 221 (Hairst 2002), 67.
Marwick, Ernest W., Introduction to *The Collected Poems of Vagaland*, ed. by Martha Robertson (Lerwick: Shetland Times, 1975), pp.xvii-xxvi.
McClure, J. Derrick, 'The Translations of W.J. Tait', in *Villon: Le Testament and other translations*, by W.J. Tait, ed. by John Cumming and Mark Ryan Smith (Stromness: Hansel Cooperative Press, 2011), unpaginated.
McCulloch, Margery Palmer, ed., *Modernism and Nationalism: Literature and Society in Scotland 1918-1939: Source Documents for the Scottish Renaissance* (Glasgow: Association for Scottish Literary Studies, 2004).
McCulloch, Margery Palmer, *Scottish Modernism and its Contexts: Literature, Identity and Cultural Exchange* (Edinburgh: Edinburgh University Press, 2009).
McQuillan, Ruth, 'MacDiarmid's Other Dictionary', *Lines Review*, 66 (September 1978), 5-14.
McQuillan, Ruth, 'Hugh MacDiarmid's Shetland Poetry', in *MacDiarmid in Shetland*, ed. by Laurence Graham and Brian Smith (Lerwick: Shetland Library, 1992), pp.4-17.

Montluzin, Emily Lorraine de, 'Attributions of Authorship in the *European Magazine*, 1782-1826' <http://etext.virginia.edu/bsuva/euromag/> [Accessed 18 January 2012].
Morgan, Edwin, *Essays* (Cheadle: Carcanet, 1974).
Morgan, Edwin, *Hugh MacDiarmid* (Harlow: Longman, 1976).
Mortensen, Peter, '"The Descent of Odin": Wordsworth, Scott and Southey Among the Norsemen', *Romanticism*, vol.6 (July 2000), 211-233.
Murray, Glen, 'MacDiarmid's Media 1937-1978', in *The Raucle Tongue: Hitherto Uncollected Prose*, vol.3, by Hugh MacDiarmid, ed. by Angus Calder, Glen Murray and Alan Riach (Manchester: Carcanet, 1998), pp.xiv-xxxiv.
Nabokov, Vladimir, *Lectures on Literature*, ed. by Fredson Bowers (New York: Harcourt, 1982).
Nash, Andrew, *Kailyard and Scottish Literature* (Amsterdam / New York: Rodopi, 2007).
Nicolson, James R., *Shetland and Oil* (London: William Luscombe, 1975).
O'Driscoll, Dennis, *Stepping Stones: Interviews with Seamus Heaney* (London: Faber and Faber, 2009).
Ogg, Jordan, Review of *Bright Pebbles: Poetry and Prose from Shetland*, *New Shetlander*, 253 (Hairst 2010), 41.
Peterson, John, 'J.J. Haldane Burgess: An Appreciation', *New Shetlander*, 164 (Simmer 1988), 7-10.
Pound, Ezra, *ABC of Reading* (London: Faber and Faber, 1961).
Rendboe, Laurits, *The Shetland Literary Tradition: An Introduction* (Odense: Odense University, 1985).
Riach, Alan, *Hugh MacDiarmid's Epic Poetry* (Edinburgh: Edinburgh University Press, 1991).
Riach, Alan, 'The Idea of Order in "On a Raised Beach": The Language of Location and the Politics of Music', in *Terranglian Territories: Proceedings of the Seventh International Conference on the Literature of Region and Nation*, ed. by Susanne Hagemann (Frankfurt: Peter Lang, 2000), pp.613-629.
Riach, Alan, 'Hugh MacDiarmid: Put it to the Touch', in *Dear Grieve: Letters to Hugh MacDiarmid (C.M. Grieve)*, ed. by John Manson (Glasgow: Kennedy & Boyd, 2011), pp.xiii-xxiii.
Riddell, Linda, 'Sir Walter Scott's Piano: The Life and Times of Dorothea Campbell' (unpublished paper given at the conference Shetland: A Women's Island, Shetland Museum and Archives, 2007).
Robertson, J.D.M., *The Press Gang in Orkney and Shetland* (Kirkwall: Orcadian, 2011).
Robertson, Martha, *Night-Scented Stock in Bloom?* (Edinburgh: Pentland Press, 1993).
Royle, Trevor, ed., *In Flanders Fields: Scottish Poetry and Prose of the First World War* (Edinburgh: Mainstream Publishing, 1990).
Schmidt, Michael, *Lives of the Poets* (London: Weidenfeld & Nicolson, 1998).
Schmidt, Michael, *40 Tea Chests: Hugh MacDiarmid and Shetland* (Lerwick: Shetland Amenity Trust, 2010).
Scott, L.G., 'Reminiscences of Haldane Burgess', *New Shetlander*, 16 (May-June 1949), 13-16.
Sigurðardóttir, Turið, and Brian Smith, eds., *Jakob Jakobsen in Shetland and the Faroes* (Lerwick / Tórshavn: Shetland Amenity Trust / University of the Faroe Islands, 2010).

Simchak, Thomas, *Oil, Culture and Economy*: The Reinvention of the Shetland Way of Life (unpublished masters thesis, University of Oxford, 2008).
Sisson, C.H., *The Avoidance of Literature: Collected Essays* (Manchester: Carcanet, 1978).
Sisson, C.H., *English Poetry 1900-1950: An Assessment* (Manchester: Carcanet, 1981).
Sisson, C.H., 'MacDiarmid's Sticks', *London Review of Books*, vol.6, no.6 (5 April 1984), 16-18.
Smith, Brian, 'Shetland and the Crofters Act', in *Shetland Crofters: A Hundred Years of Island Crofting*, ed. by Laurence Graham (Lerwick: Shetland Branch, Scottish Crofters Union, 1987), pp.1-9.
Smith, Brian, 'The Development of Literature in Shetland', *New Shetlander*, 174 (Yule 1990), 29-31 and 175 (Voar 1991), 18-19.
Smith, Brian, 'Stony Limits: The Grieves in Whalsay, 1933-1942', in *MacDiarmid in Shetland*, ed. by Laurence Graham and Brian Smith (Lerwick: Shetland Library, 1992), pp.42-72.
Smith, Brian, 'The Development of the Spoken and Written Shetland Dialect: A Historian's View', in *Shetland's Northern Links: Language and History*, ed. by Doreen J. Waugh (Edinburgh: Scottish Society for Northern Studies, 1996), pp.30-51.
Smith, Brian, Review of *The Pirate*, by Walter Scott, *New Shetlander*, 199 (Voar 1997), 46.
Smith, Brian, 'Udal Law: Salvation or Romantic Fiction?', *Shetland Times*, 3 October 2003, pp.18-19.
Smith, Brian, 'Wir Ain Auld Language: Attitudes to the Shetland Dialect Since the Nineteenth Century', in *Dialect 04: Two Day Conference and Public Debate on the Development of the Shetland Dialect* (Lerwick: Shetland Arts Trust, 2004), pp.10-15.
Smith, Brian, 'Eels: Strange Masterpiece', *New Shetlander*, 230 (Yule 2004), 29-30.
Smith, Brian, 'Saxby, Jessie Margaret Edmondston (1842-1940)', in *Oxford Dictionary of National Biography* <http://www.oxforddnb.com/view/article/55498> [Accessed 27 November 2008].
Smith, Brian, 'Burgess, (James John) Haldane (1862-1927)', in *Oxford Dictionary of National Biography* <http://oxforddnb.com/view/article/68951> [Accessed 3 Aug 2009].
Smith, Brian, 'A Man of Vision and Influence' *Shetland Times*, 22 February 2008, pp.14-15.
Smith, Brian, 'A Tribute to Lollie Graham, Teacher, Poet and Scourge of Capitalist Life', *Shetland Times*, 13 November 2009, p11.
Smith, Brian, 'Goings on at Grevavoe', *Unkans*, 41 (December 2013), 4.
Smith, Hance D., *Shetland Life and Trade, 1550-1914* (Edinburgh: John Donald, 1984).
Smith, Iain Crichton, *Towards the Human: Selected Essays* (Edinburgh: MacDonald Publishers, 1986).
Smith, Mark Ryan, '"Minstrel of the Mossy Isle": The Poetry of Thomas Irvine of Midbrake', *New Shetlander*, 244 (Simmer 2008), 29-34.
Smith, Mark Ryan, 'The Artist and the Wilderness', *PN Review*, 193 (May-June 2010), 8-10.

Smith, Mark Ryan, 'From Kafka to Maunsie's Crü: Willa Muir and Basil Ramsay Anderson', *Coontin Kin*, 79 (Simmer 2011), 13-15.

Smith, Mark Ryan, 'Two Explorers: Charles Doughty and Hugh MacDiarmid', *PN Review*, 202 (November-December 2011), 60-63.

Snell, K.D.M., 'The Regional Novel: Themes for Interdisciplinary Research', in *The Regional Novel in Britain and Ireland, 1800-1990*, ed. by K.D.M. Snell (Cambridge: Cambridge University Press, 1998), pp.1-53.

Sutherland, Stella, 'Some Shetland Literary Work of the 20th Century', *New Shetlander*, 248 (Simmer 2009), 23-25.

Swan, Annie S., *My Life: An Autobiography* (London: James, Clarke and Co., 1947).

Tait, Ian, *Shetland Vernacular Buildings 1600-1900* (Lerwick: Shetland Times, 2012).

Tait, William J., 'Basil R. Anderson and Auld Maunsie's Crü', *New Shetlander*, 16 (May-June 1949), 26-33.

Treneer, Anne, *Charles M. Doughty: A Study of His Prose and Verse* (London: Jonathan Cape, 1935).

Tucker, Herbert F., 'Doughty's The Dawn in Britain and the Modernist Eclipse of the Victorian', *Romanticism and Victorianism on the Net* no.47 (August 2007) <http://id.erudit.org/iderudit/016705ar> [Accessed 12 July 2010].

Watson, Roderick, *The Literature of Scotland*, 2 vols. (Basingstoke / New York: Palgrave Macmillan, 2007).

Wawn, Andrew, Foreword, in *The Pirate*, by Walter Scott, ed. by Andrew Wawn (Lerwick: Shetland Times, 1996), pp.i-xix.

Wawn, Andrew, *The Vikings and the Victorians: Inventing the Old North in Nineteenth-Century Britain* (Cambridge: D.S. Brewer, 2000).

Weinstein, Mark, and Alison Lumsden, Historical Note, in *The Pirate*, by Walter Scott, ed. by Mark Weinstein and Alison Lumsden (Edinburgh: Edinburgh University Press, 2001), pp.485-497.

Welsh, Irvine, 'Is There Such a Thing as a National Literature?', *Guardian*, 19 August 2012. <http://www.guardian.co.uk/books/2012/aug/19/irvine-welsh-a-national-literature> [Accessed 21 November 2012].

Whitworth, Michael H., 'Culture and Leisure in Hugh MacDiarmid's "On a Raised Beach"', *Scottish Studies Review*, vol.9, no.1 (Spring 2008), 123-143.

Whyte, Christopher, *Bho Leabhar-Latha Maria Malibran* (Steòrnabhagh: Acair, 2009).

INDEX

Akros 188
Amis, Martin 9
Anderson, Basil Ramsay 56, 63, **64-68**, 73, 90, 110, 163, 182, 202
Anderson Educational Institute 72, 147, 187
Andrew, Martha (Pat) see Robertson, Martha (Pat)
Aney, Edith Trelease 118
Angus, James Stout 41, **46-51**, 54, 59, 63, 68, 90, 163, 165, 166, 192
    'Eels' 49-51, 236
Aquarius 188
Arabia 117, 119-120, 122, 123, 130
Archipelago 241
Ash, Marinell 33
Ashbery, John 191
'Auld Maunsie's Crü' 64-68, 163, 202
Auden, W.H. 117-118

Ballantyne, R.M. 56
Baltasound 235
Banham, Reyner 119
Barclay, Archibald 39n
Bard of Thule, The see Nicolson, Laurence James
Beckett, Samuel 179
Bell, Joseph 55-56
Benjamin, Walter 95
Betjeman, John 149
Blackwood's Magazine 144
Blance, Mary 158
Blatchford, Robert 98
Blind, Karl 4-5
Braer 167
Bressay 176
Bright Pebbles 146
Brown, George Mackay 6, 144, 204, 240
Buchan, John 88
Bulter, Rhoda 154, **156-163**, 166, 168, 172, 173, 175, 176, 182, 189, 190, 191, 192, 205, 207, 210, 219, 231, 232, 233, 236

260

Burgess, J.J. Haldane 14, 33, 54, 68-69, **72-91**, 92, 93, 97, 105, 107, 110, 113, 142, 150, 154, 165, 166, 168, 169, 176, 182, 187, 201, 205, 214, 231, 244, 246
   Rasmie's Büddie 73-81, 165
   Tang 88-90, 227
   Temporary Marriage, A 86-88
   Treasure of Don Andres, The 84-85
   Viking Path, The 81-84
Burgess, W.A.S. 97
Burns, Robert 168

Campbell, Dorothea Primrose 2, 13, 14, 22, **23-27**, 28, 33, 37, 44, 45, 46
Campbell, J.J. 98
Chalmers, Margaret 13, **14-23**, 32, 33, 37-38, 48, 68, 113, 121, 136, 165, 176, 245, 246
Chambers, Robert 56
Chambers, William 56
Chapman 188
'Charles Doughty and the Need for Heroic Poetry' (MacDiarmid) 131
Chaucer, Geoffrey 129-130, 200
Chesterton, G.K. 107
C.I.A. 98
Clarion 98
Clark, W. Fordyce 51, 97
Clouston, J. Storer 33
Cluness, Alex 146, 235, 236
Communism 134-135
Complete Poems of Hugh MacDiarmid, The 114
Cookson, William 194
Craig, Cairns 7
Cribb, T.J. 121, 123
Crofter's Act (Scotland) 96, 165
Cruickshank, Helen 144
Czechoslovakia 98

D'Arcy, Julian Meldon 2
Daiches, David 35, 129
Dale, Peter 191
Dante 107
Dasent, George Webbe 55
Davidson, John 118
'Day Atween Waddirs, A' (Tait) 201-204
Day Between Weathers, A (Tait) 188, 195, 196
De Luca, Christine 154, **207-216**, 218, 225, 227, 228, 231, 236, 238, 240
Deyell, Bertie 142
Donaldson, Gordon 165
Donaldson, William 41
Donne, John 180
Doughty, Caroline 138n, 139n

Doughty, Charles M. 115, 117-126, 128, 129-130, 131-137, 244
Drunk Man Looks at a Thistle, A (MacDiarmid) 114, 127
Dunrossness 42

Economics Club 142
Edge of the World, The (Powell) 176
Edinburgh 197, 210, 215
Edinburgh Orkney and Shetland Literary Association 56
Edinburgh Review 144
Edinburgh University Orkney and Shetland Society 190
Edmondston, Arthur 3, 16-17, 32, 54
Edmondston Family 54-55
Education Act (Scotland) 41
'Eels' (Angus) 49-51, 236
Eliot, George 13
Eliot, T.S. 202, 238
'Elopement at Grevavoe, The' 69n
Elphinstone, Margaret 228
'English Ascendancy in British Literature' (MacDiarmid) 130, 131
Eyrbygga Saga 33
European Magazine 27, 28
Eunson, Karen 48-49
Evening with the Heretics, An 188

Fairley, Barker 124, 128
Fielding, Penny 2, 14-15, 16, 17, 26
Findlay, William 41
Finlay, Ian Hamilton 144
Fladdabister 158
Foula 176

Gaelic 3, 5, 191, 204-205
Gairm 146
Galloway, Janice 226
Garioch, Robert 188
Gibbon, Lewis Grassic 94
Gilbert, Susan 34-35
Glasgow 204
Glass, Rodge 226-227
Graham, John 64, 98, 108, 146, 146, 150, 163, **169-175**, 178, 187, 207, 214, 227, 232
    Shadowed Valley 169-172, 174, 175, 222
    Strife in the Valley 172-175, 218
Graham, Laurence (Lollie) 2, 46, 47, 54, 72, 74, 79, 146, 154, **163-169**, 169, 187, 232, 239, 244
Graham, W.S. 188
Gray, Alisdair 226
Gray, Joseph 92, 107, 110

Greig, Peter 92
Grieve, Christopher Murray see MacDiarmid, Hugh
Grieve, Michael 119, 137
Grieve, Peggy 136
Grieve, Valda 119, 137
Grind o da Navir 223
Gruting 92
Gunn, Neil 1-2, 49, 169

Hadfield, Jen 215, 228-231, 232, 236-237, 240
Haggard, H. Rider 33
Hall, Simon W. 5-6, 32-33, 149
Halligarth, Unst 54
Hardy, Robina R. 56
Heaney, Seamus 114, 132
Hibbert, Samuel 3
'Hildina Ballad' 4, 11n
Hogarth, D.G. 119
'Hogmanay Sermon, A' (Tait) 195-196, 197
Horace 191
Horn, Da 158
Housman, A.E. 149, 150
Hunter, John 146
Huxley, Aldous 237

In Memoriam James Joyce (MacDiarmid) 114, 128, 132, 134, 136
Incomers 228-231
Inkster, James 92, **93-97**, 105, 107, 110, 157, 173, 189, 236, 246
Inkster, Willie 195
Iosa, Liam Mac'Ille 121
Irvine, Thomas 13, 15, **27-32**, 37, 41, 68
Islands of Scotland, The (MacDiarmid) 114, 120

Jabberwock 169
Jakobsen, Jakob 3-4, 129, 192, 200, 217-218
Jamieson, Christina 97
Jamieson's dictionary 118
Jamieson, Peter 142, 144, 146, 169, 183n, 187
Jamieson, Robert Alan 3, 155, 159, 161, 214, **216-227**, 228, 231, 236, 240, 246
Johnson, Laureen 154, 191, 192, 231-233, 236, 238, 240

Kaddal, Mohamed 120, 129
Kailyard 88-89
Keats, John 100
Kelman, James 8
Kent, Alan M. 5
Kerr, Roderick Watson 102
Kind of Poetry I Want, The (MacDiarmid) 114

Laing, R.D. 63
Lallans 146
Langholm 132, 192
Laurenson, Arthur 4-5
Leith Thule Club 42
Leonard, Tom 2, 41, 188
Lerwick 1, 13, 15, 18, 23, 36, 46, 52, 72, 142, 147, 159, 172, 187
Lerwick Central School 147
Leslie, Brydon 72
Levenwick 42
Lewis 204
Life and Letters 188
Lindsay, Maurice 144
Lines Review 146
Linklater, Eric 144
Literary Society of North Yell 27
Lochead, Liz 188
Low, George 4
Lucky Poet (MacDiarmid) 114, 126
Lumsden, Alison 7
'Lux in Tenebris' (Tait) 200, 202
Lyall, Scott 115

MacCaig, Norman 136, 188
McCarey, Peter 118
McClure, J. Derrick 194
McCulloch, Margery Palmer 144, 149, 204-205
MacDiarmid, Hugh 2, 3, 8, 13, 16, 51, 90, 92, 109, **113-141**, 144, 149, 151, 169, 183, 188-189, 190, 192, 195, 200-201, 204, 228, 244, 245, 247
   'Charles Doughty and the Need for Heroic Poetry' 131
   Complete Poems of Hugh MacDiarmid, The 114
   Drunk Man Looks at a Thistle, A 114, 127
   'English Ascendancy in British Literature' 130, 131
   In Memoriam James Joyce 114, 128, 132, 134, 136
   Islands of Scotland, The 114, 120
   Kind of Poetry I Want, The 114
   Lucky Poet 114, 126
   'On a Raised Beach' 114, 120-121, 123-126, 127, 128, 134, 151
   Red Scotland 114
   Scottish Eccentrics 114
   'Shetland Lyrics' 114, 115
   Stony Limits 113, 119, 121, 126, 128, 136
MacLean, Sorley 188, 204-205, 240
MacNeil, Kevin 113-114, 147, 240
MacQueen John 146, 188
McQuillan, Ruth 114, 137
Mack, Douglas 34-35

INDEX

Mainland, Jim 189, 211, 237-240
Makars, The 194
Mallarmé, Stéphane 149
Manson's Shetland Almanac and Directory 41, 52, 176
Manson, Thomas 92, 93
Marwick, Ernest 147, 150, 244
Marxism 79-80, 89, 97
Mavis Grind 203
Mencken, H.L. 200
Midbrake, Yell 27
Mitchison, Naomi 144, 183
Modern Scots Verse 188
Moffat, Alexander 127
Moffat, William 97
Moncrieff, Jim 236-237
Montrose 204
Morgan, Edwin 88, 120, 121, 135
Muir, Edwin 6, 64, 204
Muir, Willa 64
Mundair, Raman 242n

Nabokov, Vladimir 6, 34
Nash, Andrew 88-89
Nesting 46
New Shetlander 54, 107, 108, 111, 113, 137, **142-186**, 187, 188, 195-196, 207, 210, 212, 213, 216, 227, 231, 240, 241, 245, 246
Nicolson, John 97
Nicolson, Laurence James **51-54**
Nordern Lichts 2, 163, 245
Norn 2, 3-5, 217
North Idea 183
Norwick, Unst 4
Noss 19-21, 176

Ollason, T.P. 97
'On a Raised Beach' (MacDiarmid) 114, 120-121, 123-126, 127, 128, 134, 151
Orkney 1, 2, 5, 35-37, 149, 204
Orkney and Shetland Literary Association 42
Orkney and Zetland Chronicle 14
Orkneyinga Saga 5-6, 10n
Oxford Book of Scottish Verse, The 146, 188
Owen, Wilfred 102

Papa Stour 155-156
People's Friend 52
Peterson, George P.S. 155-156, 165, 173, 195, 240
Peterson, John 72, 92, **97-110**, 111, 113, 142, 246

265

PN Review 241
Poetry (Scotland) 188
Poet's Pub (Moffat) 127
Porteous, William 111n
Pound, Ezra 9, 99, 117, 149
Powell, Michael 176
Press Gang 48, 166, 172, 174
Private Pat see Peterson, John
Pugh, Sheenagh 189, 228

Raasay 204
Rasmie's Büddie (Burgess) 73-81, 165
Red Scotland (MacDiarmid) 114
Rendall, Robert 149
Rendboe, Laurits 2
Renwick, Jack 154-155, 162, 165, 166, 175
Riach, Alan 123, 124, 134
Riddell, Linda 24
Riding, Laura 133, 135
Rilke, Rainer Maria 121
Ritch, Paul 233-236, 240
Ritch, Paolo Dante see Ritch, Paul
Robertson, Bobby 184n
Robertson, James 225
Robertson, Laurna 190
Robertson, Martha (Pat) 147, 154, 207
Robertson, T.A. see Vagaland
Robertson, Tom 139n
Robertson, Walter John 142
Rock Bound (Saxby) 41, 58, 59-64
Royle, Trevor 101

Sandness 216, 218, 219, 224
Sandwick 187, 201
Sassoon, Siegfried 102
Saxby, Jane 97
Saxby, Jessie M.E. 41, 42, 48, **54-64**, 68, 86, 90, 149, 245
   Rock Bound 41, 58, 59-64
Schmidt, Michael 114, 245
Schuyler, James 117-118
Scotia Review 188
Scots Review 169
Scott, Alexander 144, 169, 188
Scott, L.G. 73, 84
Scott, Tom 146, 188, 194
Scott, Walter 2, 13, **32-37**, 62, 118, 172, 228, 244
Scottish Eccentrics (MacDiarmid) 114

INDEX

Scottish International 188
Scottish Renaissance 144, 182, 205, 246
Scottish Review 188
Scottish Society for the Propagation of Christian Knowledge (SSPCK) 173
Semblister 142
Shadowed Valley (John Graham) 169-172, 174, 175, 222
Shaw, George Bernard 13
Shetlander 142
Shetland Advertiser 14
Shetland Anthology, A 2, 163, 187, 245
Shetland Folk Society 147, 150
Shetland ForWirds 232, 237
Shetland Islands Council Education Committee 163
Shetland Labour Party 187
Shetland Life 158
'Shetland Lyrics' (MacDiarmid) 114, 115
Shetland Museum and Archives 146
Shetland News 41, 93
Shetland Poetical Circle 142, 144
Shetland Times 14, 41, 49-50, 56
Shetland Writings 142, 144
Shore Poets 210
Sisson, C.H. 102-103, 132-133, 135
Smith, Brian 2, 5, 32-33, 54, 72-73, 94
Smith, Ian Crichton 169, 204
Smith, Sydney Goodsir 169, 188
Snell, K.D.M. 7
Sodom, Whalsay 114
Sound, Lerwick 21-22
Soutar, William 128
Soviet Union 98, 106, 107, 112n
Spenser, Edmund 129-130
Stevens, Wallace 66
Stewart, George 41, **42-46**, 49, 51, 54, 63, 73, 110, 149, 192
Stony Limits (MacDiarmid) 113, 119, 121, 126, 128, 136
Stoorbra Hill, Walls 150
Strife in the Valley (John Graham) 172-175, 218
Sullom Voe 146, 162, 175, 222
Sutherland, Lollie 176
Sutherland, Stella **176-182**, 207, 240
Swan, Annie S. 56
Swinburne, Algernon Charles 120

Tait, E.S. Reid 98
Tait, William J. 64, 81, 90, 113, 137, 147, 151, 167, 182, **187-206**, 207, 217, 218, 228, 238-239, 244, 246
    'Day Atween Waddirs, A' 201-204

267

Day Between Weathers, A 188, 195, 196
'Hogmanay Sermon, A' 195-196, 197
'Lux in Tenebris' 200, 202
Villon: Le Testament and Other Translations 190
Tang (Burgess) 88-90, 227
Taylor, Grant 119
Temporary Marriage, A (Burgess) 86-88
Thatcher, Margaret 168
These Islands, We Sing 113-114, 147, 240
Thomson, David 149
Tingwall 172
Treasure of Don Andres, The (Burgess) 84-85
Treneer, Anne 128, 129
Tucker, Herbert F. 130

University of Edinburgh 72, 147, 165, 169, 187, 194, 216
University of Glasgow 72
Unst 4, 54, 56, 64, 154, 233
'Unst Lay' 4-5
Up Helly Aa 17, 72

Vagaland **146-156**, 157, 158, 159, 161, 163, 165-166, 167, 169, 172, 173, 175, 176, 178, 182, 183, 187, 190, 191, 192, 195, 205, 207-210, 215, 217, 218, 231, 232
Veng see Sutherland, Stella
Viking Path, The (Burgess) 81-84
Villon François 190-194
Villon: Le Testament and Other Translations (Tait) 190
Voice of Scotland, The 188, 190

Walls 147, 207-209, 213
Watson, Roderick 35, 187
Wawn, Andrew 13, 33, 36
Weisdale 169, 172
Welsh, Irvine 6-7, 8
Westerwick 147
Whalsay 16, 111, 114, 115, 118, 119, 133, 136, 142
Whitman, Walt 180
Whyte, Christopher 191
Wullver's Hool, Unst 56

Yeats, W.B. 98-101, 117, 195
Yell 13, 27, 187
Young, Douglas 144

Zetland Patriotic Society 27